Illinois in the War of 1812

Illinois
in the
War of 1812

GILLUM FERGUSON

University of Illinois Press
Urbana, Chicago, and Springfield

Library of Congress Cataloging-in-Publication Data
Ferguson, Gillum.
Illinois in the War of 1812 / Gillum Ferguson.
p.   cm.
Includes bibliographical references and index.
ISBN 978-0-252-03674-3 (hardcover : alk. paper)
1. Illinois—History—War of 1812.
2. Illinois—History—War of 1812—Campaigns.
3. United States—History—War of 1812—Campaigns.
4. United States—History—War of 1812—Participation, Indian.
5. Indians of North America—Wars—Illinois.
6. Indians of North America—Wars—1812–1815.
I. Title.
E359.5.I3F47   2012
973.5′2473—dc23   2011034716

FOR MY FATHER,
Richard Ferguson,
guide and companion
on many a ramble through
the history of our native state

CONTENTS

LIST OF ILLUSTRATIONS

Maps

Illustrations

ACKNOWLEDGMENTS

So important was the War of 1812 in laying the groundwork for the future State of Illinois that it is more than surprising that, with the exception of Frank Stevens's long article, published by the Illinois State Historical Society in 1904, there has never been an attempt to tell the story in a comprehensive way. Now as the bicentennial of the war approaches, enough people have apparently understood the need to fill this gap in the historiography of the state that I have had no shortage of encouragement and assistance in completing the project.

First mention must go to two priceless resources of the Illinois History world: Evelyn Taylor, editor of the *Journal of Illinois History*, and Dr. John Hoffmann, curator of the invaluable Illinois History and Lincoln Collections at the University of Illinois Library, the successor to Clarence Alvord's Illinois Historical Survey. Both Evelyn and John have generously helped me every step of the way. At the outset they confirmed the value of the project and helped me find the confidence needed to attempt it, and thereafter provided insight, advice, and technical assistance from beginning to end. Without their support, this book might well have waited another 200 years to be written.

The staff of the many institutions I have visited or corresponded with have been unfailingly helpful and courteous, but I should single out a few for special mention: John Reinhardt of the Illinois State Archives in Springfield has been a patient and knowledgeable guide to the materials contained in that collection, while Jenny Johnson, of the University of Illinois Map Library in Urbana, has shared not only her extensive knowledge of nineteenth-century American maps but her zest for historical detective work. Karen Deller was especially helpful in locating valuable materials in the Special Collections of Cullum-Davis Library, Bradley University, which would otherwise have been invisible to me. Molly Kodner of the Missouri History Museum on several occasions went well beyond what her position required her to do, in helping me profit from the museum's fine collection.

Many individuals have enriched the book with information or provided valuable logistical support. In this regard I should mention Chief Gordon J. Beck of the LeRoy Police Department, Gail Blankenau of Lincoln, Nebraska, Teran Buettel of Morning Sun, Iowa, Ken Cochran of the Jackson County Historical Society, Sarah Cooper of the Bureau County Historical Society, Robin Boone Crooks and Linda Hallmark of the Henderson County (Ky.) Historical and Genealogical Society, Claudia Dant of Mount Carmel, Illinois, Jim Dunn of rural Mitchellsville, Illinois, Alan Gehret of the Audubon Museum, Henderson, Kentucky, Lecta Hortin and Diane Waggoner of the Mary Fay Smith Genealogy Library, Carmi, Illinois, Gordon Howe of Robinson, Illinois, June Huff of the Hancock County Historical Society, Laura Jones of Fairview Heights, Illinois, John M. King of the Lawrence County Historical Society, Max Lude of the Frankfort Area Genealogical Society, Larry Mears of Rockbridge, Illinois, Rev. Ronald Nelson of McLeansboro, Illinois, John O'Dell of the Saline County Historical Society, Phil Petti of Naperville, Illinois, Alec Purdy of El Segundo, California, Ryan Ross of the Illinois History and Lincoln Collections, Willard Saunders of Washington, D.C., Mr. C. Mart Watson of Eldorado, Illinois, and a member of the Jersey County Historical Society who wished to remain anonymous, but who, I hope, knows who she is.

I am also grateful to the Illinois War of 1812 Bicentennial Commission for embracing and supporting the project at a crucial juncture. Chairman William Wilson and Historian Kevin Kaegy were kind enough to read extensive sections of the manuscript and their generous comments and suggestions have been taken to heart. John G. Victor of Chicago made a very careful reading of what is now chapter 4, and that chapter has profited from his thoughtful criticism. Thomas Schwartz, formerly Illinois State Historian, has given me helpful advice and kindly permitted me to test-drive the present chapter 6 by reading it at the 2009 Conference on Illinois History in Springfield. My father, Richard Ferguson of Hinsdale, Illinois, read very significant portions of the manuscript and commented with his customary perceptiveness. Finally, I am grateful to Dr. Willis Regier of the University of Illinois Press for his enthusiastic support and to Geof Garvey, an astute and observant editor whose expert assistance has made this a better, stronger book. Needless to say, any shortcomings of this work must be laid at my door.

Amidst all the tales of murders, cabin-burnings, raids, and atrocities, nine wonderful grandchildren kept me grounded in happy reality. My two sons, Thomas M. Ferguson of New York and Dr. John H. Ferguson of Denver, assisted me in ways too numerous to mention. My brothers, Stanley and Andrew, sisters-in-law Mary and Denise, and three stepchildren, Ben, Julie, and Philip, have been consistently encouraging, while my son-in-law, David Semyck, patiently helped my nineteenth-century mind to cope with the mysteries of twenty-first century technology. Finally, what my wife, Dr. Susan Ferguson, endured for two years while her husband refought the War of 1812 from behind a wall of books, maps, files, and photocopies can only be imagined. Amazingly, her support for the project never wavered.

Map 1. The Northwest Territory in 1812

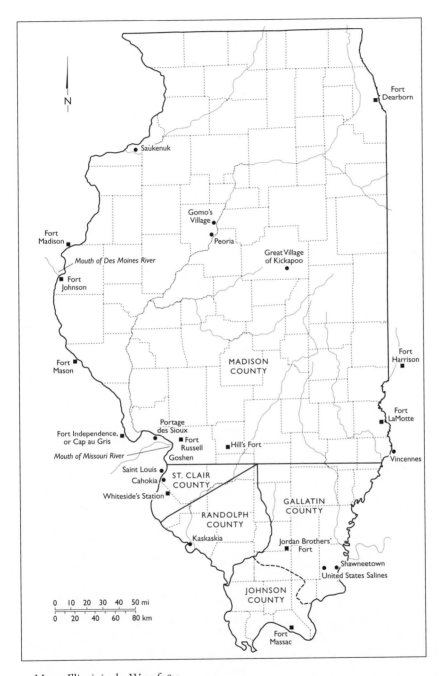

Map 2. Illinois in the War of 1812

Fort Dearborn

Saukenuk

Gomo's Village

Peoria

Great Village of Kickapoo

Fort Madison

Mouth of Des Moines River

Fort Johnson

Fort Mason

MADISON COUNTY

Fort Harrison

Fort LaMotte

Portage des Sioux

Fort Independence, or Cap au Gris

Fort Russell

Hill's Fort

Goshen

Mouth of Missouri River

Vincennes

Saint Louis

ST. CLAIR COUNTY

Cahokia

Whiteside's Station

GALLATIN COUNTY

RANDOLPH COUNTY

Kaskaskia

Jordan Brothers' Fort

Shawneetown

United States Salines

JOHNSON COUNTY

Fort Massac

N

0   10   20   30   40   50 mi

0   20   40   60   80 km

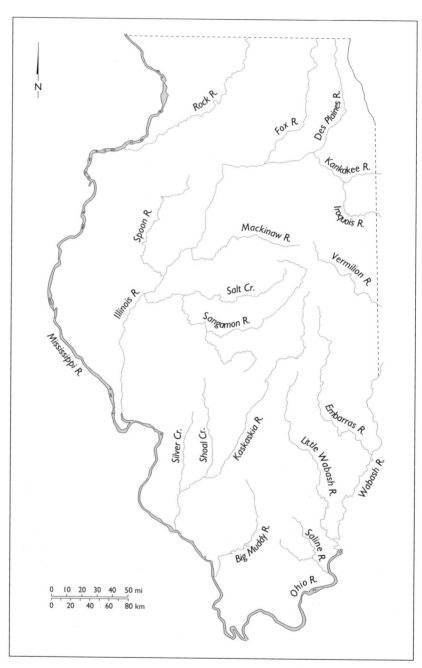

Map 3. Rivers of Illinois

ONE

Morning

For more than twenty years, between 1792 and 1815, much of the world was wracked by war as Great Britain fought for its life against the dynamic power of Revolutionary and Napoleonic France. Other European nations were drawn in, on both sides, and although the war was centered in Europe, few regions of the world were untouched by the fighting. Warfare eventually spread even to North America, drawing the United States into a largely unwanted war, against Britain and British-controlled Canada, that has been remembered as the War of 1812.

For twelve years the pacifist administrations of Thomas Jefferson and James Madison had done all they could to avoid war, as both Britain and France interfered with American trade, kidnapped American sailors on the high seas, tampered with Indian tribes in U.S. territory, and in general treated the new country as a second-class sovereignty. The Americans had responded with ineffective diplomatic protests and the self-defeating policy of an embargo on their own trade, until at last, goaded beyond endurance, the young nation proved to the world that there were some insults it would not swallow and a point beyond which it would not be pushed, by declaring war on Britain on June 18, 1812.[1]

For more than two and a half years, the United States fought with varying success against Britain and its Indian allies. The war was one that Britain also had not wanted, a sideshow to its life-and-death struggle with France, and one to which it could afford to devote only meager resources. To maintain its position in North America, Britain had to rely heavily on Indian allies who had their own grievances against the Americans. Although, on the more populous fronts of the northeast, British troops opposed American forces directly, in the sparsely populated territories of the Northwest the character of the war was very different.

One of the frontier regions touched by war was Illinois Territory. Only recently split off from Indiana Territory in 1809, the new territory ran from the junction of the Ohio and Mississippi Rivers north to the U.S. border with Canada, embracing the current states of Illinois and Wisconsin, together with a part of the Upper Peninsula of Michigan and Minnesota east of the Mississippi River. All those states, especially Illinois, would eventually owe their existence, at least in part, to the War of 1812.

Although in its extreme southern part, along the main rivers, and in the northwest corner Illinois was rich in timber—black walnut, ash, bur oak, and sugar maple in the bottom lands and, in the uplands, post oak, white oak, hickory, and cherry—the dominant feature of the future state as a whole was its characteristic tall-grass prairie. Beginning in the south, and extending to what is now the Wisconsin border, stretched a series of prairies, growing ever wider and more extensive the farther north they lay. Separating them were lines of timber along the streams and rivers, as well as intermittent groves, "like islands in the ocean," ranging from four or five trees to woods, or "timbers," covering hundreds of acres. The largest prairie of all was the Grand Prairie, which ran without significant interruption from Chicago for more than 300 miles southwest to the northeastern corner of what is now Jackson County.[2]

The first reaction of a traveler seeing the prairie for the first time was wonder at its beauty. Easterner Timothy Flint thought the prairie "a most glorious spectacle" and compared it to "an immense flower garden."[3] In spring, when the grass was short, it was adorned with delicate flowers such as the violet and wild strawberry, but, as the coarse prairie grasses grew to a height of six to ten feet, the spring flowers disappeared and were succeeded by others that grew with the grasses, until soon millions of flowers produced a riot of color and fragrance, which in its turn gave way to the darker colors and lesser variety of autumn. As a traveler proceeded farther into the prairie, the pleasure he took in its first appearance was apt to give way to awe and unease at its vast extent and loneliness. Indians were almost the only human inhabitants. Springs were few in the high prairies and the lack of timber for firewood and building had thus far made white settlers reluctant to venture onto it. Over the prairies quiet reigned, broken here and there by the booming of prairie chickens in the tall grass or the persistent cry of the dickcissel. On rare occasions the sky might be darkened by huge flocks of passenger pigeons flying overhead, millions of them migrating together from one roost to another, the noise of their beating wings like thunder and their dung falling like snow.[4]

Two hundred years later the prairie has all but disappeared, along with many of the animals that once thrived upon it. The hordes of buffalo were already nearly gone, the great herds having been destroyed, according to the Indians, by severe winters fifty or sixty years earlier, but a few stragglers remained, for a buffalo was reportedly killed in Edwards County as late as 1816. Still, travelers on the prairie frequently encountered their horned skulls and bones, and in some places acres of ground were covered with bones, showing that a large herd had once perished there. The tracks the buffalo had made, moving in single file from the prairies to the rivers and salt licks, were still followed by Indians and other travelers, the first roadways of the territory. Still present, but following the buffalo on the path to extermination was the elk. Large herds once thronged the Illinois River region, but they too were decimated by heavy snows in the 1760s. In the early 1800s there was still a brisk trade in elk hides along the upper Illinois River, but within a few years overhunting with firearms and dogs would cause that trade to disappear. Still plentiful were the herds of white-tailed deer, which were a principal source of meat and hides, but they too were beginning a long decline to extinction. (The deer that are now so abundant in the state all descend from a different herd successfully reintroduced beginning in the 1930s).[5]

During the day black bears slumbered in the timbers along the rivers, emerging at dusk to hunt for food. They themselves were hunted for meat and hides by red and white alike, and their numbers were declining. Mountain lions, "panthers" to the pioneers, were never common, and they always avoided the open country, but they lurked in the forests and around the riverbanks in southern Illinois. As late as about 1860, a panther killed and devoured a little girl who had strayed too near the woods in Jackson County. Throughout the territory, true wolves, *canis lupus*, could be heard howling around the cabins at night, and farmers would bring their animals into the farmyard to protect them from the circling packs. Often, however, the wolves would drive the dogs under the house and kill a sheep or a young pig before they could be chased away.[6]

In all the Illinois Territory's vast expanse of more than 110,000 square miles, the takers of the 1810 census counted only 12,282 inhabitants, excluding Indians, most of them clustered along the rivers that now form the southern rim of the state of Illinois. Except for the tiny remnants of the Kaskaskia and Piankashaw tribes, the oldest residents of Illinois were the French. They had lived along the Mississippi since the days of Louis XIV, in the old villages of Cahokia and Kaskaskia, but defeat in the French and Indian War, twenty years of British rule, and the chaos that followed the transfer to American authority drove many Illinois Frenchmen to migrate to the west bank of the Mississippi, where the new city of Saint Louis, founded by Pierre LaClede and Auguste Chouteau in 1760, became the most enduring achievement of their migration.[7]

By 1812, what remained of the Illinois French population was concentrated in three principal villages along the Mississippi River, a tiny outpost on the Illinois River at Peoria, and some small settlements along the Wabash in the shadow of Vincennes, Indiana. At a greater distance, but still within the boundaries of the territory, were two small French communities in what is now Wisconsin. Most important of the Illinois settlements was Kaskaskia, on the river of the same name just three miles north of where it then flowed into the Mississippi. By the end of the eighteenth century the village was falling into ruin, but when Illinois Territory was formed in 1809 Kaskaskia was named the capital. As capital, the village became the resort of ambitious English speakers coming from the east, and its French character became somewhat diluted. An acerbic visitor to the capital observed a few years later that "The inhabitants are all generals, colonels, majors, land speculators or adventurers, with now and then a robber and a cutthroat."[8] Although selection as territorial capital and later as the first state capital prolonged the importance of the village for a time, Kaskaskia had already lost its former position as the metropolis of the upper Mississippi. The 1810 census reported the population of the village as only 622, although two years later a visitor estimated the population as being between 800 and 1,000.[9] By contrast, in 1810 its younger rival, Saint Louis, had already reached a population of 5667.[10]

French culture also survived in the small neighboring village of Prairie du Rocher, and, farther north, in Cahokia, which dated from 1699 and so has a well-founded claim to be the oldest town in Illinois. By 1812 English was on the way to becoming the majority language in the village, but the French were

still strong in Cahokia and would retain some political importance until the
Saint Clair county courthouse was moved to Belleville in 1814. Cahokia would
then lapse into obscurity, but even today it retains a few tangible reminders of
its French past.[11]

The new English-speaking residents distrusted the French and doubted
their loyalty to a country they had never asked to be part of. Moreover, the
French were conservative in retaining their customs. They cherished the Catholic religion, uncommon among the American newcomers, and continued their
own traditional amusements, such as community dancing. They still wore their
traditional garments, such as the *capot*, a white-blanket coat equipped with a
cape to pull over the head in cold weather. The blanket coat was adopted by
many of the Americans, but the distinctive and invariable mark of a French
man or woman was a blue kerchief covering the head. All the French villages
along the Mississippi were bordered by common fields, in which each of the
habitants was assigned a long, narrow strip to farm and also by a commons for
grazing the villagers' cattle. The English-speaking incomers had no very high
opinion of the French work ethic, which sought to maintain a large space for the
enjoyment of life. Especially suspicious was the traditional cordiality between
the Frenchmen and the Indians, with whom they frequently intermarried, and
it cannot have helped that the Indians themselves looked back at the days of
French rule as a kind of Golden Age.[12]

Some of the English-speaking immigrants came originally from northeastern states such as Pennsylvania, often by way of frontier Ohio, but the
majority came from or through Virginia, Kentucky, or Tennessee. For them
the Indians were the hereditary enemy, and the settlers' inborn hatred of them
was further aggravated by the frontier war that raged in Illinois, as elsewhere in
the Northwest, until the battle of Fallen Timbers and the Treaty of Greenville
imposed a temporary peace in 1795. The first predominately English-speaking
settlement was made along the Mississippi, in what became known as the
American Bottom, "extending" said an early observer, "along the eastern bank
of the [Mississippi] river ... to the Piasa hills, four miles above the mouth of
the Missouri. It is several miles in width, and has a soil of astonishing fertility,
consisting of comparatively recent depositions from the river. It has all the
disadvantages usually attending tracts of recent river alluvion, the most valuable parts of it being liable to be swept away by the current of the Mississippi,
and its surface descending from the brink of the river to the stagnant hills and
lagoons, at the outskirts of the valley. But the inexhaustible fertility of its soil

makes amends for the insalubrity of the air, and the inconveniences of a flat and marshy situation; and this valley is undoubtedly destined to become one of the most populous parts of America."[13] The first home of the English-speaking settlers was the New Design community, in the present Monroe County.[14] New Design suffered severely in the Indian war of the late 1780s and early 1790s, and after 1799 it came to be overshadowed by the Goshen Settlement, farther north along the Mississippi. The Goshen settlement was a decentralized farming community embracing much of present Madison County, or at least the part southwest of a line drawn between the modern communities of Bethalto and Saint Jacob.[15]

These settlements sprouted a few small branches along waterways such as the Kaskaskia River and Shoal Creek, where a handful of fearless pioneers had ventured into the present Bond and Clinton counties and now maintained themselves with difficulty along the streams and rivers that formed the main avenue of transportation. For the most part, however, American settlement extended no more than twenty miles from the Mississippi River. Beyond that frontier lay the vast and empty prairie, where a shortage of wood for fires and building, along with the chilling unfamiliarity of the wide-open spaces, had, for the time being, retarded settlement. East of the American Bottom lay 150 miles of wilderness to cross before a traveler would once again encounter even the rudiments of civilization.

Beside the Ohio River, at the eastern edge of the territory, was Shawnee-town. This new city, the port of entry for travelers approaching Illinois from the east, was built on the site of a village of the Shawnee Indians, who in the 1740s had lived there briefly before moving on, having perhaps realized that the combination of low ground and frequent high waters made the location unsuitable for habitation. The Shawnee left behind them only two small burial mounds and the persistent, though unfounded, local legend that southern Illinois was once the domain of the Shawnee.[16] The new city was surveyed by order of Congress, a rare distinction, but even William Rector, the surveyor who laid out the city in lots, recognized that the location had been poorly chosen and tried to have the new city moved inland. His pleas were to no avail; and Shawneetown would remain subject to flooding for more than a century. Only after the great flood of 1937 would a majority of the citizens, finally heeding both Rector's warnings and the example of the Shawnee Indians, move the city to higher ground. At the time, however, Shawneetown was booming. Barges and keelboats tied up at the docks, taking on loads of salt and furs, after unloading merchandise and passengers bound by land for Kaskaskia or the other western settlements along the Mississippi. Shawneetown was one of the few places in the territory where there were retail shops and also, because of the nearness of the United States Salines (on which more later), one of the few places where there was plenty of money to spend in them. Despite the presence of money and commerce, however, inability to get title to land had discouraged building. Most of the houses were mere log cabins, with now and then a frame structure interspersed among them. It was just as well that more elaborate buildings had not been raised: during the wet spring of 1813 water stood twelve to fourteen feet deep in the streets of Shawneetown and some cabins simply floated away downriver. Outside flood season, the town was noted for a rough-and-tumble atmosphere created by the ubiquitous boatmen: "a rough set of men, much given to drinking whiskey, fighting, and gouging, that is they fight up and down, trying to put out each others eyes with their fingers and thumbs, and sometimes biting off each others noses or ears." There was no church in Shawneetown.[17]

A few miles to the west of Shawneetown, near the present village of Equality, lay the source of much of Shawneetown's prosperity, the United States Salines, the site of the most important industry in the new territory. There, bubbling from two large springs, came saltwater in sufficient quantities to permit commercial production of salt. In those days before refrigeration, salt was no mere table seasoning, but a vital commodity that enabled the pioneer to cure meat and vegetables for preservation. So important were the Salines that when the public lands were at last put on sale in 1814 the government retained ownership of a tract of more than 150 square miles around the salt springs, although it leased the actual operation to a series of entrepreneurs. Along with hard currency and the blessing of salt, the Salines also spilled onto the free soil of Illinois the stain of slavery. Although by the terms of the Northwest Ordinance of 1787 the lands north of the Ohio were declared to be free territory, in practice the government winked at a form of slavery practiced at the Salines. The severe shortage of labor in the territory led the lessees to import slaves from across the Ohio River to labor at salt making under "voluntary" short-term indentures, under which their masters in Kentucky and Tennessee would reap the monetary reward of their labors.[18]

Farther north of Shawneetown a string of tiny settlements clung to the west bank of the Wabash River. In the small settlements on the Illinois bank, French, white Americans, and free blacks appear to have lived together on

reasonably friendly terms. The Wabash settlements looked for trade and protection to nearby Vincennes, the metropolis of Indiana Territory, rather than
to distant Kaskaskia, and when war came the governor of Illinois Territory,
Ninian Edwards, admitted the impossibility of coordinating the defense of the
Wabash from a capital from which it was separated by 160 miles of prairie.[19]
Connecting the eastern and western settlements by land were three or four
"roads," although the term may give a misleading impression when the track
referred to was one "made by one man on horseback following in the track of
another, every rider making the way a little easier to find, until you came to
some slush, or swampy place, where all trace was lost, and you got through as
others had done, by guessing at the direction, often riding at hazard for miles
until you stumbled on the track again."[20] Travel across the prairies by land
was further complicated in the summer months by vast swarms of flies that
tormented travelers and were sometimes known to kill their horses. To protect
them from flies, the poor beasts were frequently covered with blankets as they
labored in the summer heat.[21]

By 1812, there was a fairly well established route that ran from Vincennes to
Kaskaskia and Saint Louis, along which were scattered a few isolated inns and
blockhouses, with the recent additional luxury of a ferry across the Kaskaskia
River. There was a trace, but no formal road, between Kaskaskia and Shawneetown, and Congress would not even order such a road to be constructed
until 1816. The need for a road between the capital and the port of entry, the
two largest towns in the territory and the location of the two land offices,
was critical, and without waiting for congressional action horseback travelers
established such a route on their own. Their route went by way of the Salines,
through the northern part of the present Saline and Williamson counties and
the southern part of Perry County. At least as early as April 1813, and perhaps
earlier, mail was carried over it once per week, on a schedule that called for
the carrier to leave Shawneetown at 2:00 P.M. Sunday and to arrive in the
territorial capital on Wednesday afternoon. Kaskaskia was also connected by
mail routes to Vincennes, Fort Massac, and Cahokia.[22] Despite the schedules,
the mail was irregular, being frequently interrupted by bad weather, flooding,
Indian attacks, and the negligence of contractors. Governor Benjamin Howard
of Missouri considered himself fortunate if within two months he received
an answer to a letter he had sent to the Atlantic states, because on occasion a
letter from the government in Washington might take as long as six months
to reach him at Saint Louis.[23]

In the absence of good roads, the main arteries of transportation were the rivers, but even those posed difficulties. Boats were moved by a combination of sail, oar, and pole. Movement downriver posed little problem except the ever-present risk of becoming grounded on a sand bar. Going upriver, however, often required backbreaking labor. Timothy Flint recalled the difficulty of moving against the current on the Mississippi:

No employment can be imagined more laborious, and few more dangerous, than this of propelling a boat against the current of such a river.... At one time you come to a place in the current, so swift that no force of oars and poles can urge the boat through it. You then have to apply, what is commonly known as a "cordelle," which is a long rope fastened at one end to the boat, thrown ashore, and seized by a sufficient number of hands to drag or track the boat up the stream. But, owing to the character of the river, and the numberless impediments in it and on its banks, this "cordelle" is continually entangling among the snags and sawyers, between the boat and the shore, and has often to be thrown over small trees, and carried around larger ones.... Sometimes you are impeded by vast masses of trees, that have lodged against sawyers. At other times you find a considerable margin of the shore, including a surface of acres, that has fallen into the river, with all its trees upon it. Just on the edge of these trees, the current is so heavy as to be almost impassable. It is beside the question, to think of forcing the boat up against the main current any where, except with an uncommon number of hands.[24]

Beyond what has already been described, the only significant settlements in the Illinois Territory were at Chicago, (where a small garrison at Fort Dearborn guarded the important portage route between southern Lake Michigan and the tributaries of the Illinois River) and at the tiny French villages of Peoria, Prairie du Chien, and Green Bay ("La Baye"), the last two being in what is now Wisconsin. To protect the settlements scattered in the vast frontier, the federal government had done almost nothing. At the outbreak of war, the only regular military force within the boundaries of Illinois Territory consisted of fifty-four soldiers at Fort Dearborn (Chicago) and, 365 miles away on the Ohio River, another thirty-six soldiers at Fort Massac (at the present Metropolis).[25] Fort Dearborn was in the heart of Indian country, but Fort Massac lay far behind the line of settlements. That fort had originally been erected by the French, to block British penetration of the Ohio River Valley, and in 1794 it had been revived and rebuilt by order of General Anthony Wayne, to serve as a frontier military and customs post at a time when an Indian war raged north of the Ohio and the territory west of the Mississippi was still held by Spain. The Louisiana Purchase of 1803 sharply diminished the importance of Fort Massac, but during the coming war it still had a role to play as a supply depot and training center. The fort itself was a square enclosed by pickets, with a bastion at each corner, overlooking a wide view of the Ohio, from which it was separated by an esplanade and a row of Lombardy poplars. Despite its beautiful setting, Fort Massac was a lonely post, for the garrison had no neighbors except a few settlers who supplied the fort with fresh vegetables and meat.[26]

Although a few additional troops were stationed not far from the territory's borders, at Vincennes, Indiana, and near Saint Louis at Fort Bellefontaine, the military headquarters for the region, the shortage of troops in the neighboring territories was not much less severe than in Illinois.[27] For defense, Illinois Territory would have to look primarily to its own militia. The entire territory was divided into militia districts, and every white man between the ages of eighteen and forty-five was by law a member of the company drawn from his district. Every militiaman was required by law to provide himself with a rifle or musket, a bayonet, ammunition, and a knapsack. Despite that requirement, good guns were surprisingly rare in the territory; the governor estimated that not more than one man in ten owned a rifle, and because few firearms were brought into the territory, they could be acquired only at exorbitant prices.[28] Although officers' commissions were awarded by the governor, it was the practice for the men to choose officers for themselves, and only rarely were their choices overruled. In peacetime the duties of the militia were light; except during winter, each company was required to meet for muster once every two months, with battalion musters in April and regimental musters in October. In war, however, service in the militia could be crippling. Nearly every man called from his farm into active military service was the sole support of himself and his family, and extended service in the field could severely disrupt his ability to meet the unforgiving rhythm of the growing season. The hardship was especially acute because payment for active service might come many months later, if it came at all.[29]

The commander-in-chief of the militia was the territorial governor, and throughout the entire existence of Illinois Territory that governor was Ninian Edwards. The position was not an elected one; the territorial governor was appointed by the president for a three-year term and answered not to his citizens but to the secretary of war in Washington. Edwards owed his appointment to a lucky accident. When Illinois Territory was created out of Indiana in 1809, President James Madison's choice for governor fell on a member of the Kentucky Court of Appeals, who soon reconsidered his original acceptance and in his place recommended Edwards, the chief justice of the same court. Edwards was a lawyer and a judge, without significant administrative or military experience, and with no previous connection to the territory he was to govern, but he was also a friend of the Madison administration and the appointment was regarded as an unimportant one. In due course the recommendation was accepted.

The new governor did not arrive in Kaskaskia until June 11, 1809, so the Illinois Territory was organized by its territorial secretary, Nathaniel Pope. In the governor's absence the territorial secretary was by law the acting governor, and Pope lost no time before organizing the first territorial government, reaffirming some of the arrangements inherited from Indiana, such as the two established counties of Saint Clair and Randolph, and appointing the first slate of territorial and county officers. Although, like Edwards, Pope was a Kentuckian who owed his appointment to politics, he was a very able man. He was also the new governor's cousin. For the next seven years the two men would work comfortably together, and whenever Edwards was absent from the territory, as he was for almost the entire second half of 1813, he was able to leave the government in Pope's capable hands.[30]

Born into a wealthy Maryland family, Edwards had been tutored by his lifelong friend, William Wirt, afterwards attorney general, and he later studied at Dickinson College. To a good education Edwards joined a sound legal mind and a certain political acumen. He moved to Kentucky in 1795 and a year later, not yet having reached the age of twenty-one, he was elected to the Kentucky legislature. After a brief bout of youthful dissipation, Edwards entered the practice of law at Russellville in 1798 and four years later even received a major's commission in the Kentucky militia, although the duties of that office were no doubt largely ceremonial. Such was Major Edwards's legal ability, however, that the next year he was made a judge of the general court. He climbed rapidly through the judicial ranks, becoming chief justice of Kentucky's highest court in 1808. His political loyalty to the party of Jefferson and Madison, and the support of Henry Clay, helped him secure appointment as governor of Illinois, but why he wanted the position is a question to which no satisfactory answer has ever been given. To go to Kaskaskia, Edwards interrupted, and as it turned out abandoned, a successful career in a more important state, to live among backwoodsmen in a territory where he had never been and where he

would never quite fit in. Although in Illinois his political career was successful enough, and although both Edwards County and the city of Edwardsville
would be given his name, the citizens he served seem never to have fully accepted the well-educated and elegantly dressed Edwards as one of themselves.
As territorial governor, Edwards held office by appointment, and it was the
legislature that elected him to the U.S. Senate. In the Senate he fought with real
passion for cheap land and the small farmer, but whenever he offered himself
to the people for election, the results were less than impressive: he was only
narrowly elected the state's third governor in 1826, and in 1832 he was defeated
for election to the House of Representatives, with a very poor showing for
so prominent a man. It can at least be hoped that some of those who so long
disliked and distrusted Edwards, as an aristocrat and an opportunist, might
later have relented a bit after his death from cholera, contracted while nursing
the sick in Belleville during the epidemic of 1833.[31]

Figure 1. Ninian
Edwards. Artist
unknown. Courtesy
of the Abraham
Lincoln Presidential
Library and Museum,
Springfield, Illinois.

The economy of Illinois Territory was primitive. Aside from the manufacture of salt and the fur trade, almost the only industry in the territory was farming and, with few exceptions, farming was the occupation of all citizens. Crops included corn, wheat, flax, cotton, sorghum, and tobacco, all grown on a very small scale, primarily for personal use.[32] Several factors retarded the development of large farms. One was the absence of a market. Money was scarce in the new territory and the uncertainty, difficulty, and expense of transportation hindered the development of remote markets. Another obstacle was an acute shortage of farm labor; with so much land open for the taking, few men wanted to work for another when they could just as easily set up for themselves.[33] Finally, there was the difficulty of gaining title to real estate. Out of a population of more than 12,000, it was estimated that there were no more than 200 to 300 freeholders.[34] Those lucky few held title under ancient grants, from France, England, or Virginia, but most of the newcomers remained squatters; the federal government would not put a portion of the public lands on sale until 1814. Like the citizens of Shawneetown, farmers who made improvements ran the risk that they might lose the fruit of their labors to speculators who could outbid them when the lands eventually went on sale. Although there was a common expectation that the government might grant preemption rights, a sort of right of first refusal, to the settlers who had occupied and improved the land—and indeed that hope would eventually prove to be justified—not until the Preemption Act of February 5, 1813, were the people of Illinois given some level of assurance that their farms would not be bought from under them.[35]

Where all but a few wealthy merchants were limited to the income that they could produce on their own small farms with their own two hands, there was little surplus, and so few artisans or professional men took up residence. There was no newspaper in the territory until 1814, although the *Louisiana Gazette* (renamed the *Missouri Gazette* in July 1812) was printed in Saint Louis and circulated in the western part of the territory. What few schools existed were taught by itinerant schoolmasters, paid by private subscription, and as late as 1816 there was no school in Kaskaskia, the capital. Mercifully few lawyers made their home in Illinois, and federal judges were almost invariably appointed from outside the territory.[36]

At the same time, the lack of an economic surplus created a refreshing degree of community and social equality among the pioneers. Manufacture or retail sale of clothing was unknown; what the settlers wore, they made at home themselves. In Illinois the usual garment worn by male Americans was the blue linsey hunting shirt, large enough to wrap twice around the body and held in place by an often brightly colored belt. Governor John Reynolds later praised the comfort afforded by this "excellent garment." Women also dressed in homemade linsey, colored and woven to taste. Men wore pantaloons made of deerskin or linsey. Boots were unknown, and in summer children and many grown men went barefoot. Only adult women wore shoes in summer. Winter wear included moccasins of deerskin and white blanket coats. Most of the American settlers lived in log cabins, which their neighbors would gather and raise for them, often in a single day. A "house-raising," like a wedding or a muster, became a festive social occasion for the whole community. The furniture inside the cabin was usually made at home, from the materials at hand. Food was plain, usually featuring corn bread, broiled meat, often game, and the universal solvent of whiskey.[37]

The life of a pioneer was simple and therefore hard. Mortality on the Illinois frontier was high, although not necessarily higher than in other frontier communities. The settlers who had located in the river bottoms were often racked by recurrent fevers and malaria, which they called "the ague." The ague was usually not fatal, but it was debilitating and increased the sufferer's susceptibility to more serious diseases. Visitors traveling in the territory often commented on the sallow and unhealthy appearance of the people. Death in childbirth was common, but partly offset by a high birthrate. Nevertheless, adversity had made the settlers hardy in spirit and there was no challenge they feared to take on. Poverty, hunger, illness, and death they took in stride, for these were the daily incidents of pioneer life. John Reynolds, who had been one of them, remembered that "No people delighted in the free and full enjoyment of a free government more than they did. This passion for freedom . . . gave them a personal independence, and confidence in themselves that . . . made them believe they were adequate and competent to any emergency, and [they] frequently commenced enterprises above their power to accomplish."[38]

By 1812 a race of sturdy farmers had gathered in the wooded fringes around the best agricultural land in the world, looking out over the empty prairies with both longing and trepidation. Illinois was on the verge of explosive growth that would bring civilization and prosperity, but first the public lands had to be put on sale and the Indians removed. Both those things would be soon accomplished, the one despite the coming war and the other, in part, because of it. That the future was bright was clear to all who had eyes to see.

Even at remote Fort Dearborn, a lonely young army doctor named Isaac Van Voorhis, musing by the shore of Lake Michigan, wrote to a friend at his faraway home in New York: "In my solitary walks I contemplate what a great and powerful republic will yet arise in this new world. Here, I say, will be the seat of millions yet unborn; here the asylum of oppressed thousands yet to come. How composedly would I die could I be resuscitated at that bright era of American greatness."[39]

TWO

Evening

From this vision of Illinois's future, the Indians were excluded. Their number is hard to estimate, because contemporary estimates vary significantly and, in any case, usually account only for the number of warriors in a tribal group. Nevertheless, it may be fair to estimate that the number of Indians in the territory probably did not far exceed the number of white and black Americans, whom the census of 1810 numbered at 12,282. Just as the whites were not distributed evenly throughout the territory, so neither were the Indians. Except for the remnants of the Kaskaskia and Piankashaw, in southwestern Illinois and along the Wabash, respectively, few tribes had permanent villages south of a line drawn across the state through the present Springfield and Decatur, although either war or hunting might carry parties of Indians deep into the southern part of the territory.[1]

Except the Kaskaskia, all the tribes were relative newcomers to the future state of Illinois. None of them had been established there for longer than two or three generations. The Kaskaskia, however, had been, within the limits of historical memory, the original owners of the soil. They were a remnant of the Illinois confederacy of five related tribes, together often called the Illini, which had at one time ruled a vast territory that stretched from the Ohio River to the Wisconsin River and from the Wabash into the present states of Iowa and Missouri. How many souls the confederacy numbered at its height is unknown, but when the first French explorers arrived the number was probably between 10,000 and 20,000.[2]

Beginning about 1656, the Illinois came under a relentless series of shockingly savage attacks from the Iroquois to the east and the Sioux to the northwest. The attacks recurred over a span of fifty years. Constant warfare fatally weakened and demoralized the Illini, and their numbers plummeted. Seeing an opportunity, neighboring tribes, such as the Sauk, the Fox, the Kickapoo, and the Potawatomi, began seizing lands that the Illini were no longer strong enough to defend. By the dawn of the nineteenth century, the confederacy was a pitiful shadow of its former self. A small band of Peoria still survived in southeastern Missouri, but in Illinois Territory the total population of the Illini had been reduced to a few families, much addicted to drink and unable to stray too far from Kaskaskia, for fear of other Indians. Although a few individuals still identified themselves as Cahokia, Tamaroa, or Michigamea, the U.S. government recognized the Kaskaskia tribe as the representative of all the Illini Indians remaining east of the Mississippi. The tribe still had a technical claim to much of the present state of Illinois, and in 1803 the government bought that claim from the Kaskaskia in exchange for an annuity of $1000, two small reservations in what are now Randolph and Jackson counties, and the government's commitment to afford the Kaskaskia "a protection as effectual against the other Indian tribes and against all other persons whatever as is enjoyed by [American] citizens."[3]

At the opposite side of southern Illinois, but otherwise somewhat similarly situated, were the Piankashaw. This tribe was one of the six bands that made up the larger nation of the Miami, a group closely related in language and culture to the Illini. Even before the first French explorers encountered them, the Piankashaw had split off from the others and developed a separate identity, settling along the lower banks of the Wabash. Their hunting grounds extended into southern Illinois, as far as the watershed between the Saline and Embarras Rivers, but, like their distant cousins the Kaskaskia, the Piankashaw eventually found themselves claiming more land than they could possibly use or defend. Their numbers cannot be estimated with anything like precision. In 1797 a traveler estimated that the Piankashaw had been reduced to 120 men, but by 1802 Governor William Henry Harrison estimated their fighting strength at only twenty-five to thirty warriors. Like the Kaskaskia, the Piankashaw had been corrupted by proximity to the whites and drunken Piankashaw warriors were a common sight on the streets of Vincennes. In 1804 and 1805 the tribe entered into treaties with Governor Harrison that surrendered most of its lands along the Wabash, retaining in Illinois only a reservation of 1280 acres, or two square miles. That reservation was never formally surveyed, so its precise location is uncertain, but the Piankashaw considered their reservation to lie between the Little Wabash and Embarras Rivers, near the present village of Albion. Some tribesmen soon became convinced that they had been cheated, and before the battle of Tippecanoe nearly half the tribe had joined the Shawnee Prophet. To remove them from such dangerous influences, and to keep them out of the way of the coming war, Harrison encouraged the chiefs to move their people farther west. By the summer of 1812, many of the Piankashaw had settled alongside the Kickapoo in the Illinois River valley.[4]

Although the governor's purpose in recommending the move had been to keep the Piankashaw friendly, or at least neutral, in the coming conflict, their new location in fact encouraged the opposite result. Their new neighbors, the Kickapoo, were one of the most intractable tribes in Illinois Territory. According to John Reynolds, "This nation was the most bitter enemy the whites ever had. It may in truth be said of this tribe, that they were the 'first in a battle, and the last at a treaty with the Americans.'" Harrison considered the Kickapoo "a strong and warlike Nation" and their warriors "better than those of any other tribe" in Illinois and Indiana territories. All together the Kickapoo could field about 400 warriors, which suggests a total population below 2000. Although the Kickapoo were therefore one of the smaller tribes, they were made dangerous by their proximity to the American settlements.[5]

The Kickapoo were relative newcomers to Illinois. Not until about 1765, after the Illini confederacy had collapsed under the repeated attacks of the Kickapoo and other tribes, were the Kickapoo able to establish a homeland in east central Illinois, which they proudly claimed by right of conquest. The tribe then divided into two geographical groupings. The Vermilion Band lived in villages along the Vermilion River, in Vermilion County and across the present border in Indiana. In 1809 this band agreed to cede their lands to the United States in exchange for a small annuity, but, although they accepted the annuity, they proved to be in no hurry to move. The other group, the Kickapoo of the Prairie, lived chiefly on the Sangamon River and its tributaries, roughly speaking in the region between the present Bloomington and Lincoln, in what are now Logan, McLean, and DeWitt counties. The Prairie Kickapoo had several villages, but their principal town was the fortified Grand Village, northeast of the present city of Le Roy. Because this band had never had a treaty relationship with the United States, they received no annuities and so had nothing to lose by continually stealing horses from the settlements or, when the mood struck them, making murderous attacks on the hapless Kaskaskia.[6]

Bordering the Kickapoo on the north was the large and powerful tribe of the Potawatomi. In earlier times the Potawatomi had formed a confederation with the Ottawa and Chippewa that was sometimes known as "The Three Fires." Attacks from the Iroquois put the confederacy on the move, and by 1700 the Potawatomi had found their way into southern Michigan. As the power of the Illini waned, the Potawatomi joined with the Kickapoo, Sauk, and Fox in driving them first from northeastern Illinois and then from the Illinois River valley.[7]

By 1810, the territory of the Potawatomi extended from Green Bay down the western shore of Lake Michigan, and to the east through northern Indiana as far as Detroit. Potawatomi lands also extended southwest from Chicago down the Illinois River to Peoria Lake and southeast to villages on the Kankakee and upper Wabash Rivers. In 1815 their total population was estimated at 4800, including 1200 warriors. In Illinois, the tribe had villages along many of the waterways in the northeast. At the portage between the Chicago River and the Des Plaines was the village of chief Mittitass. There were small villages along the Fox River, and a few miles east of present-day Morris, near the mouth of Aux Sable (Sandy) Creek, was a large mixed village of Potawatomi, Chippewa, and Ottawa, presided over by the Little Chief, and, after his death in 1811 or 1812, by a chief named Pepper. From this village perhaps 200 warriors could be led into battle by their war chief, Black Bird (also known as Le Tourneau), an Ottawa. At the head of Peoria Lake, where Chillicothe now stands, was the village of Gomo (also known as Nasima). This village housed at various times from 50 to 150 warriors, but Gomo generally favored a policy of peace with the Americans. Across the lake on the southern side was the village of Shequenebec. This chief was a mystic, ruled by visions sent by the Great Spirit, and as time went on those visions became increasingly anti-American. About fifteen miles below Peoria, on the Mackinaw River in present Tazewell County, was a mixed village of Kickapoo, Potawatomi, Ottawa, and Chippewa, containing 60 warriors "all desperate fellows and great plunderers," under a chief named Le Bouree or Sulky. To the southeast there were Potawatomi villages along the Kankakee River. The most notable of them was a village of 50 warriors led by the notorious war chief Main Poc (Main Poque, Main Poche, Marpock). In 1812 he would move his village to the present Kendall County, along the Fox River. Indeed, all these villages were mobile, and during the winter, when game in the vicinity of the village became scarce, the tribesmen would remove to winter quarters, lower down the Illinois River or as far afield as Missouri and Iowa.[8]

None of these chiefs had power to command, even in his own village. The authority of a Potawatomi chief was weak and the chief's power derived mainly from example and persuasion. A few chiefs had wider influence. Among the chiefs of northeastern Illinois, Gomo was recognized as first among equals, while along the Saint Joseph River in southwestern Michigan, Topinebee claimed a sort of primacy among all the chiefs of the Potawatomi. Eclipsing both of them, however, was Main Poc, the most famous Indian in Illinois, whose influence extended beyond his own nation. To the Americans, he was "a monster who was distinguished by a girdle, sewed full of human scalps, which he wore round his waist, and strings of bear's claws and the bills of owls and hawks, round his ankles—as the trophies of his prowess in arms, and as a terror to his enemies."[9] To the Indians, however, he was their most illustrious warrior and *wabeno*, or holy man. Born without a thumb or fingers on his left hand, Main Poc proclaimed that the defect was a special mark placed on him by the Great Spirit to distinguish him from other men. He was a master orator, who would also from time to time retire alone to the woods to commune with the Great Spirit for four or five days, before reemerging to announce the divine plans for his nation. Those who opposed Main Poc often made their own sudden and mysterious journeys to the next world; trader Thomas Forsyth, who knew him well, believed that the chief had obtained a supply of arsenic.[10]

To his spiritual gifts, Main Poc added the laurels of a successful warrior. During the first decade of the century he led a series of bloody raids on the Osage tribe of Missouri. In November 1805, for instance, Main Poc and his warriors attacked an Osage village while the men were absent hunting. The raiders succeeded in killing thirty-four women and children and carried about sixty others back to slavery in Illinois. The Great Spirit had given Main Poc the power, he said, to see flying bullets and to avoid them, but when he was severely wounded in a raid in 1810, the chief modestly explained to his followers that he had seen the bullet heading toward one of his many wives and had intentionally stepped into its path to shield her. Above all, Main Poc hated the Americans, and all their efforts to appease him ended in failure, although he was practical enough to accept their bounty whenever it was offered. William Wells, the Indian agent at Fort Wayne, even went so far as to escort the chief to Washington, where he met President Thomas Jefferson. Jefferson tried to persuade Main Poc to cease his raids on the Osage, who were American allies, but the chief defied the great man to his face, telling him that just as the United States wanted the tribes to remain neutral in its own wars with foreign enemies, so the Americans should keep their noses out of quarrels between Indian tribes. He then retired to his room to drink whiskey and to loudly threaten any of the hotel staff who came near him. Drunkenness, in fact, was Main Poc's crippling vice.[11]

Along the Mississippi River two closely related tribes hesitated between the Americans and the British, and offered the prospect of a valuable alliance to both sides. The Sauk (Sac, Sakies) and Fox (Renards, Mesquakie)[12] spoke nearly indistinguishable Algonquian dialects. For generations the tribes had lived on terms of mutual friendship, often side by side, but they nevertheless always maintained distinct identities and sometimes followed different, or even opposing, policies. According to legend, the tribes had at one time lived around Montreal, but under pressure first from the Iroquois and then from the Sioux, they made a slow migration westward that led them into southern Wisconsin, and then toward Illinois. They moved into the vacuum caused by the collapse of the Illini, to which the Fox, especially, had contributed, and about 1764 the Sauk established their principal village, later sometimes called Saukenuk,[13] near the mouth of Rock River, on the present site of the city of Rock Island. The Fox began to settle near them, and by 1805 both tribes had abandoned their old homes in Wisconsin. The Sauk had outlying villages near the mouth of the Des Moines River and near the present site of Oquawka in Henderson County. The Fox tended to settle on the west side of the Mississippi, with large villages just above the mouth of the Rock River and near their lead mines at the present site of Dubuque. That same year, Zebulon Pike estimated the number of the Sauk at 2850, including 700 warriors, and the Fox at 1750, including 400 warriors.[14]

By the outbreak of the War of 1812, the Sauk village on the Rock River may have been the largest town, red or white, in Illinois. Certainly it could support a large population. Fish were abundant in the waters of the Rock and Mississippi Rivers, and the horses of the Sauk grazed on the extensive blue grass that surrounded the village. In the fields west of the village, women cultivated corn, beans, squash, and melons, while nuts, berries, and other fruit grew abundantly on nearby Rock Island. Every September the tribal council picked a date to move across the Mississippi into their winter hunting grounds in Iowa and Missouri. The tribe would not return to Saukenuk until spring, when they would open their buried caches of dried corn and vegetables, plant their fields, and begin another cycle in their existence.[15]

A dark cloud hung over the Sauk and Fox. In 1804, Quashquame, a civil chief in one of the Sauk bands, and four other chiefs or prominent warriors, one of them a Fox, arrived in Saint Louis to surrender a tribesman who had murdered an American. By the time the five Indians left Saint Louis they had signed a treaty with William Henry Harrison that purported to cede to the United States all the Sauk and Fox lands between the Illinois and Wisconsin Rivers, as well as a large slice of land west of the Mississippi. Included in the tract were Saukenuk, most of the Sauk hunting grounds, and other lands to which the Sauk had no shadow of a claim. Whether the five bewildered Indians were bribed, or drunk, or even understood anything of the paper to which they put their marks is disputed, but clearly they had no authority to sell tribal lands. The consideration for the sale, an annuity of $600 to the Sauk tribe and $400 annually to the Fox, in exchange for lands that had provided the tribes as much as $60,000 every year from the fur trade, also brands the treaty as a fraud and as a deep stain on the generally honorable memory of William Henry Harrison.[16]

The tribes angrily rejected the treaty, and relations with the United States became severely strained. In the spring of 1806 the inhabitants of Saukenuk came close to blows with a visiting detachment of American troops, and when in 1808 the army began building a fort, originally called Fort Bellevue but later renamed Fort Madison, along the Mississippi River in the hunting grounds of the Sauk,[17] warriors led by a prominent war chief named Black Hawk[18] devised a ruse to capture the fort and massacre the garrison. The plot was foiled, but the depth of the resentment felt by the Sauk can hardly be overstated. Although the two sides avoided an open breach for a few more years, one faction of the tribe, of which Black Hawk became the guiding spirit, saw no solution to the problem of the treaty but war. Others, however, were comforted by a provision of the treaty that permitted the tribe to remain on the ceded lands as long as they remained the property of the United States, a right that would exist—as they could not have fully understood—only until the government could survey the Sauk homeland and sell it in parcels to white settlers.[19]

Farther up the Rock River from Saukenuk was the country of the Winnebago. These Indians called themselves Ho-Chunk, but to the French and the first American settlers they were known as "Puants." They spoke a language dissimilar to that of neighboring tribes, and one tradition held that they came from beyond the Missouri River. The Winnebago were primarily a Wisconsin tribe, with villages along the Wisconsin River and the upper Rock River, but they had a cluster of villages around what is now Prophetstown, Whiteside County, and also hunted over an area that included the Illinois county that now bears their name.[20]

Like the Sauk and Fox, and the Prairie Kickapoo, the Winnebago had no treaty with the United States. Indeed, having had little contact with white culture, they had been neither tamed nor corrupted by it. American agent Thomas Forsyth, who narrowly escaped death at the hands of the Puants, called them "a fierce, brave nation." Governor Ninian Edwards considered the Winnebago "the most ferocious Indians in the world." To British trader and officer Thomas Anderson "They were the most filthy, most obstinate, and the bravest people of any Indian tribe I have met with." In 1814 British Indian agent Robert Dickson, who depended heavily on the Winnebago, explained his haste to depart from winter quarters: "I shall move from this [place] as soon as I can one way or [an]other as the Puants are beginning to draw round me & one had as well be in hell as with them." The fighting strength of the Winnebago was estimated at only 400 to 500 warriors, but their fierce courage and hostility to the United States made them formidable. Moreover, although their villages in Whiteside County were surrounded by prairie and "fine open woodland," those farther upriver were protected from reprisals by the nature of the country. According to Forsyth, "it appears to me, to be impossible to subdue them in the spring, summer, or fall months, from the situation of their country, as it is one continued swamp, marsh, Lake or River, and almost all their traveling is done by water, and should they be attacked they can immediately embark in their canoe and go up or down a river, or into a swamp."[21]

Neighboring the Winnebago to the east were the Menominee. This small tribe lived along both sides of Green Bay, although by 1810 some Menominee could also be found in Illinois, living along the Fox River, in a village mingled with Potawatomi, Ottawa, and Chippewa. The Menominee had developed friendly relations with the British, whom they aided against the Americans in the Revolution. British traders remained welcome, and although the tribe and chief Tomah were hospitable enough when visited by Lieutenant Zebulon Pike in 1806, the 200 warriors could be expected to side with the British in the event of war.[22]

All these tribes were struggling to survive. The traditional economy of the tribes had begun to collapse soon after their first contact with European technology. Such trade goods as copper kettles, iron knives, flint and steel, firearms, powder, and ammunition may have begun as luxuries and exotic novelties, but they quickly became the necessities of everyday Indian life. Unable to produce such goods themselves, the tribes soon became dependent on purchases from white traders and on gifts from white patrons. The only commodity the tribesmen had to exchange was furs. The result was all too predictable. Large game such as elk and buffalo, never overabundant, began to disappear as the Indians' increased demand for these animals coincided with a greatly increased ability to kill them with weapons purchased from the white man. At once the tribes were deprived of both their principal trade commodity and their main source of protein. By the dawn of the eighteenth century, the records are full of references to hunger and even starvation among the Indians of the old Northwest. Tribal society became increasingly demoralized, with alcoholism rife and the old patterns of authority breaking down.[23]

As the means of subsistence dried up, the Indians turned to selling off their one valuable asset: their land. President Jefferson, for one, recognized exactly what was happening and the future Sage of Monticello advocated a policy of offering credit to leading tribesmen, "because we observe that when these debts get beyond what the individuals can pay, they become willing to lop them off by a cession of lands."[24] When the northwestern tribes surrendered most of Ohio to the United States at the Treaty of Greenville in 1795, a pause in the rate of acquisitions might have been expected, but it was not to be. On the contrary, the hunger of American settlers for land and the need of the tribes for cash met in the person of William Henry Harrison, governor of Indiana Territory.[25] Harrison was by birth a Virginia gentleman, son of a signer of the Declaration of Independence. During the Indian war that ended at the Battle of Fallen Timbers, Harrison had served as an aide to General Anthony Wayne, learning both strategy and tactics from the master. After the war, Harrison remained in the northwest, serving first as territorial secretary and then as delegate to Congress, before Jefferson appointed him the first governor of Indiana Territory in 1800. Harrison was not without a measure of sympathy for the plight of the Indians. He was solicitous of the safety of friendly Indians, always insisted that his troops show mercy to defeated enemies, and was disgusted by the persistent refusal of white juries to convict whites who had murdered Indians, whatever the evidence. Recognizing, however, the impossibility of the tribes' position and firmly believing that the Indians' day was over, Harrison was determined to ease them quickly into the sunset with maximum advantage to the government of which he was the official representative. Between 1802 and 1809, Harrison negotiated treaties that extinguished Indian claims to a third of Indiana, most of Illinois, and a large piece of northeastern Missouri.[26]

The accelerating disintegration of Indian society provoked a reaction in the person of the man known as the Shawnee Prophet, or, more commonly, simply as the Prophet.[27] Originally known as Lalawethika, "the Noisemaker," a derisive name given him by his fellow Shawnee in Ohio, the future prophet began life as a notorious drunkard and ne'er-do-well. In the spring of 1805, however, he recovered from a fit of unconsciousness to announce that he had communed with the Master of Life, who had called him to save his people. The former butt of tribal jokes took the new name of Tenskwatawa, "The Open Door," and began to preach a gospel of social and spiritual renewal. Accurately

Figure 2. William Henry Harrison. Artist: Rembrandt Peale. Courtesy of the Grouseland Foundation, Vincennes, Indiana.

tracing the Indians' decline to the demoralization brought on by contact with the alien culture of the whites, he preached rigid separation and a return to the old ways. The Prophet urged his followers to renounce the material culture of the whites: the white man's clothing and the animals, such as hogs and cattle, that the white man relied on for food were to be rejected, or at least avoided. Firearms were permitted for self-defense, but warriors were to hunt only with the traditional weapons of their ancestors. Americans were the spawn of evil, and physical contact with them was forbidden. While a warrior might greet an American from afar, he must under no circumstances shake his hand. Where Indian women had borne children to white men, those children must be sent to their fathers, so that the Indian race would not be diluted by children with divided loyalties. Above all, the Prophet's followers must renounce the curse of alcohol, with which the white man had poisoned and demoralized the Indians.[28]

Much of what the Prophet preached was benign, but the new religion had an ugly side as well, shown by the savage persecution of "witches" that disgraced some of the Prophet's followers, especially among the Delaware. Resistance grew among the traditional chiefs, who saw the Prophet as a threat to their authority. The movement also worried the American authorities. Governor Harrison openly mocked the Prophet and called for him to prove his connection to the Master of Life by performing a miracle: "if he really is a prophet, ask of him to cause the sun to stand still—the moon to alter its course—the rivers to cease to flow—or the dead to rise from their graves. If he does these things, you may then believe that he has been sent from God." In June 1806, the Prophet gave Harrison the miracle he had demanded.[29]

As the month began, the Prophet summoned his followers to assemble at his camp near Greenville, Ohio, where he would blot out the sun. On the morning of June 16, the Prophet remained in his lodge throughout the morning, as the sky began to fade into twilight and then into total darkness. At this moment the holy man emerged from his lodge to remind his terrified followers that he had predicted this event. He then began to intone the magical incantations that removed the blot from the sun and restored the light of day. Whether the Prophet had learned of the eclipse by direct communication with the Master of Life or by some more mundane expedient such as consulting an almanac has never been established. What is certain is that for a time scoffers were silenced and the Prophet's prestige rose to new heights.[30]

Inseparably intertwined with the religious revival represented by the Prophet was a political project of which the ruling spirit was his older brother

Tecumseh, one of the great men of American history.[31] Already known as a distinguished warrior who had fought against the armies of St. Clair and Wayne, Tecumseh emerged as the architect of a grand plan to unite the western tribes in defense of their heritage. Tecumseh argued that tribal lands were the common inheritance of all the Indians, and that no single tribe, and certainly no chief, could alienate them without the consent of the rest. He rejected past treaties that had ceded Indian lands and denounced the chiefs who had signed them, even threatening them with death. His red brothers, he taught, should cease warring among themselves. They should live in peace with the Americans so far as possible but must unite to defend themselves and their hunting grounds when necessary. With the vision to conceive grand schemes Tecumseh combined the energy needed to execute them. Even his chief opponent, William Henry Harrison, admired Tecumseh, whom he regarded as "one of those uncommon geniuses, which spring up occasionally to produce revolutions and overturn the established order of things. . . . No difficulties deter him. His activity and industry supply the want of letters. For four years he has been in constant motion. You see him on the banks of the Wabash and in a short time you hear of him on the shores of Lake Erie or Michigan, or on the banks of the Mississippi and wherever he goes he makes an impression favorable to his purposes."[32]

Both Tecumseh and the Prophet found their most willing converts farther to the west, outside the area overshadowed by American power and beyond the influence of the chiefs who had accommodated themselves to it. Illinois provided especially fertile ground. While some eastern tribes remained lukewarm and divided, the Potawatomi, Kickapoo, and Winnebago provided some of the most fervent converts to the movement. Among those who made the journey from Illinois to meet the Prophet was Main Poc himself. In 1807 the two holy men conferred at length and found much to agree on, although Main Poc soundly rejected the Prophet's prohibitions of alcohol consumption and intertribal warfare. The Great Spirit, Main Poc said, had told him that if he ever refrained from drinking liquor or going to war, he would become just a common man. Nevertheless, by the time he returned to Illinois, Main Poc had formed a working alliance with the Prophet.[33]

The following year the brothers moved their camp to the banks of the Tippecanoe River in western Indiana, where they founded Prophetstown, a village that they intended as the model for a new kind of Indian community. The new Prophetstown stood on what was still indisputably Indian land and game

Figure 3. Tecumseh. Sculptor: Tom Allen. Saline County Fish and Wildlife Area, Harrisburg, Illinois.

was abundant. The new town was more easily accessible to visitors from the west and also provided a more convenient starting point for Tecumseh's missionary journeys to the West and South. In late summer of 1810, for instance, Tecumseh left Prophetstown to visit the Indian villages in northern Illinois and southern Wisconsin. At Lake Peoria he found Gomo, the senior chief, polite but noncommittal, but his reception was warmer among the Ottawa and

Potawatomi of the upper Illinois and Fox Rivers. At a grove on the prairies of what is now southern DeKalb County, he gained the adherence of a warrior named Shabbona.[34] Shabbona was an Ottawa by birth, but he had married a Potawatomi woman and had already risen to prominence in that closely related tribe. He now joined Tecumseh's traveling party and soon became one of the chief's closest lieutenants. Together they traveled north to Wisconsin, reaching the Mississippi at Prairie du Chien, and then turned south to Rock Island, meeting with Winnebago, Menominee, Sauk, and Fox Indians.[35]

Visionary though he may have been, Tecumseh was also a realist. To oppose the overwhelming power of the United States, the Indians needed allies. Tecumseh had no illusions about the British, being well aware that during the Revolution they had enlisted the Indians to fight alongside them and then at the treaty of peace had abandoned their red allies without a second thought. Tecumseh himself had fought at Fallen Timbers, and with his own eyes he may have seen the British commander shut the gates of Fort Miami in the face of the fleeing tribesmen. Nevertheless, the British possessed power and modern weapons, and they had no designs on Indian land. Tecumseh had no choice but reluctantly to embrace his enemy's enemy as a friend. Neither, as it happened, had the British. In all of Canada there were only about 7000 British soldiers to defend the long border with the United States. The British were deeply ambivalent about using the Indians as allies and unleashing the horrors of an Indian war. In fact, at one point the British ambassador at Washington had even warned the Americans about the danger of an Indian uprising. Nevertheless, the British knew that in the event of war between the two powers there was no chance that the high-spirited tribesmen would remain quietly neutral, and that if they failed to embrace the Indians as friends they might possibly have to confront them as enemies.[36]

For the Indian tribes, the coming struggle would be one for their very existence. Darkness was falling on the Indians of the old Northwest, but Tecumseh and the Prophet offered them one more day in the sun.

THREE

Rumors of War

The slide toward war began on June 2, 1811, at a cabin about two miles northeast of the present village of Pocahontas. Most members of the Cox family were absent picking strawberries when three Potawatomi warriors rushed their cabin. Disappointed in their hope of a raid on the Osage, they had turned toward the settlements looking for plunder. In the cabin they found Elijah Cox, twenty years old, and his younger sister, Rebecca.[1]

The intruders held the young man screaming on the floor, first slicing off his scalp and then cutting the heart from his living body. They threatened his sister with the same fate if she did not turn over the hidden family savings. Terrified, but still defiant, Rebecca brought out only a small part of the money hidden in the house. Taking with them the money, a couple of guns, five horses, one scalp, and the captive girl, the Potawatomi set out for the Indian country, traveling day and night. Early the next day, they met two other warriors, traveling southbound. The three murderers bragged about their exploit, mimicking and mocking young Elijah's screams as he died. All five Indians enjoyed a hearty laugh before parting.

Major William Pruitt led a party of eight or ten militiamen in pursuit of the murderers.[2] The Indians had a long head start, but one account says that the rescuers were assisted by a trail of small strips Rebecca surreptitiously tore from her apron and dropped from her horse behind her. About fifty miles north of what is now Springfield, and not far from the Potawatomi village, Pruitt and his men caught up with the murderers. Then followed what Governor John Reynolds afterwards called a "kind of bashful fight."[3] The militiamen were reluctant to press their attack too closely, for fear that the Indians would kill their prisoner, but the brave Rebecca took matters into her own hands. She broke away and ran toward her rescuers, suffering tomahawk wounds to the back and head as she did so. Nevertheless she escaped to Pruitt's party, who turned their horses back toward the settlements, taking the rescued girl with them.[4] Rebecca recovered from her wounds and the next year married William Gregg.[5] The young couple moved to Kentucky, where the husband was reportedly afterwards killed by Indians. Rebecca's unfortunate brother was buried near the cabin, where in 1900 a monument was raised to mark the resting place of Illinois's first casualty of the war of 1812.[6]

An eighteen-year-old settler named Lindley had intended to join the pursuit but arrived too late. While returning home alone on foot he found himself face to face with the two warriors who had found the tale of young Elijah's death agonies so hilarious. Outnumbered as he was, and armed with only a single-shot musket, the young man ran for his life, until he was too exhausted to run farther. Then, taking his stand behind a fallen tree, Lindley waited until the first of the pursuing Indians came near, shot him dead, seized the Indian's gun, and with it shot and killed the second Indian as well.[7]

Before the month of June was over, there was one more fatal clash between red and white. In the evening of June 20, two men named Price and Ellis[8] were plowing a cornfield near Hunter's Spring, in what is now lower Alton.[9] They had built a small cabin in the vicinity, which was then a few miles beyond the line of settlements. According to most accounts, five Menominee warriors approached the two farmers. When the two men warily asked the Indians whether they came in peace, the leader of the Indians, who was a large and powerful man, put down his weapons and advanced toward the men with hand outstretched, calling "Bonjour, bonjour." Price, relieved, took his hand, but the Indian held him fast, while the others tomahawked him, or, in another version, shot him through the heart. Ellis also was wounded, but he managed to unhitch his plow horse and escape.[10] He succeeded in reaching the Wood River settlements, where he told his story before dying of his wounds a few weeks later. Captain Samuel Judy's company and Major John

Moredock's battalion of militia rode in pursuit but were unable to overtake the murderers.[11]

Another version of the story was current among the Indians. According to this version, one of the Indians, wanting for some reason to visit the cabin, was seized by two white men. Seeing this, his comrades ran to rescue him, killing one of the white men and wounding the other.[12] What really happened is unknowable, but it is unlikely that five Menominee warriors would have been found so far from home unless bent on mischief.

The Cox and Price murders brought the settlers to something approaching panic. Rumors of more killings, sometimes of whole families, swept the frontier, only to be exposed in time as unfounded.[13] Many settlers gave up their farms to head back to Kentucky, or planned to do so, and whole communities were reported to be deserted.[14] Settlers who had guns could be quick to use them. A certain Michael Squires, operating his ferry across the Mississippi River just west of the present city of Alton, opened fire on an approaching canoe carrying five Potawatomi Indians when they failed to heed his warnings to keep away. One of the Indians, a chief, was mortally wounded.[15]

Governor Edwards acted promptly. He gave immediate orders that the militia "erect a chain of block houses in advance of the settlements at about twenty miles from each other commencing on the bank of the Illinois river, and a sufficient force to be distributed among them, with orders to scout from one to another every day."[16] The organized efforts of the militia were supplemented by the initiative of individual settlers in building blockhouses to which their families and neighbors could flee when the alarm was sounded. By March 1813, twenty-two family forts could be counted in the sixty miles between the Mississippi and Kaskaskia Rivers.[17] The line of forts and blockhouses ran in a generally southerly direction parallel to the Mississippi and then turned east to protect the scattered settlements in the present Jackson, Williamson, and Saline Counties, before again turning north to guard the settlers who clung to the Illinois bank of the Wabash. The chain of blockhouses finally came to its eastern end at Fort LaMotte, near the present village of Palestine.[18]

Most important of the new forts was Fort Russell, built during the summer of 1812 by Colonel William Russell. He chose the location because it lay midway between the Mississippi and Kaskaskia Rivers, enabling troops stationed there to patrol along the banks of both.[19] Russell called the post Camp Edwards, as a compliment to the territorial governor, but it soon became known by the name of its builder. Fort Russell stood about two and one-half

Figure 4. Replica of frontier blockhouse, Saline Creek Pioneer Village
and Museum, Harrisburg, Illinois.

miles north of the present Edwardsville.[20] The stockade enclosed about half
an acre, with huts for the troops, and was armed with cannon recovered from
old Fort Chartres, the former stronghold of New France. Although the few
regular troops stationed there, commanded by Captain Thomas Ramsey, were
evacuated in June 1813 by order of General Howard, the fort remained important, as a base for Rangers riding out beyond the frontier and as the territory's
main depot for munitions and military stores. When Governor Edwards was
there, as he often was, Fort Russell became "the resort of the talent and fashion
of the country."[21]

Although his office made him commander-in-chief of the territorial militia, Edwards candidly admitted that he had no military experience and little
knowledge of Indians. Fortunately he was able to turn for support to a remarkable family who had plenty of both: the Whitesides. The acknowledged
head of the family was William Whiteside, a soldier of the Revolution who

had fought at King's Mountain. After the war he led his family west from
North Carolina, first to Kentucky, and then, in 1793, to Illinois. Along with his
many sons, daughters, and relations, William settled in what was then part of
Saint Clair County (now Monroe), where he established a fort and family seat
called Whiteside's Station on the road between Kaskaskia and Cahokia.[22] The
Indian War was still raging, and the area where the Whitesides settled was a
battleground. The family threw themselves into the struggle, and although they
had a reputation for shooting first and investigating afterwards, the Whiteside
family provided powerful support to the American cause.[23]

Whiteside was appointed to both civil and military offices under Indiana Territory, and after the creation of Illinois Territory, Edwards appointed
him colonel of the Saint Clair County militia, which then guarded the most
important frontier in the new territory. To Secretary of War William Eustis,
Edwards explained that the colonel "though not blessed with a good education,
possesses a strong discriminating mind, is highly distinguished as an Indian
fighter, and has all the influence that such characters never fail to command
on a frontier, in times of danger."[24] Colonel Whiteside organized the Saint
Clair County Regiment[25] and commanded it throughout the war, dying in
1815, with peace at last in sight.[26]

Several members of the Whiteside family served in the war, but two deserve
special mention. William Bolin Whiteside, the colonel's eldest son, had taken
part in many of his father's adventures and served under him as major in the
militia.[27] Edwards had a high opinion of the son, recommending to the War
Department that he be appointed captain of the first company of U.S. Rangers raised in the territory: "He has been raised on our northwestern frontiers,
with which he is well acquainted; and on several occasions of the greatest
danger and difficulty, he has manifested so much prudence, self-command
and intrepid bravery, that he has both acquired the confidence of his fellow-
citizens and become a terror to the savages. . . . .In times of danger, he is one of
the most active and useful men in the territory—his reputation and influence
enabling him to associate his fellow-citizens with him in the most hazardous
enterprises, in which he is always foremost to volunteer his own services."[28]

His cousin, Samuel Whiteside, was a somewhat younger and less experienced soldier, but by the end of his life he would perhaps see more of Indian
fighting than any other man in Illinois and would give his name to Whiteside
County. Throughout the war, Samuel Whiteside commanded companies, first
of militia and later of U.S. Rangers, and by 1819 he had risen to the rank of

brigadier general in the state militia. He represented Madison County in the first General Assembly (1818–20). Whiteside remained active as brigadier through the beginning of the Black Hawk War, but when the army he commanded was disbanded in late May 1832, he reenlisted as a private in a company of Illinois Mounted Volunteers.[29]

An incident of the Black Hawk War provides a suitable epitaph for Samuel Whiteside, and perhaps for the whole Whiteside clan. When the company of mounted volunteers in which Samuel was then serving took flight in the face of a much larger party of hostile Indians, the only man who declined to flee was the white-haired Samuel Whiteside. He dismounted, stood alone on the prairie, and with his single-shot rifle took careful aim at the chief leading the

Weinel & Schubert, West Main st., Belleville, Ills.

Figure 5. Samuel Whiteside, late in life. Photographer: Weinel & Schubert, Belleville, Illinois, 1863. Courtesy of Kevin Kaegy, Greenville, Illinois.

charge. Whiteside fired and brought him down. Evidently fearing a trap, the remaining warriors milled about in confusion, until Whiteside's shame-faced comrades rallied and returned to drive the Indians from the field. When asked why he had chosen to stand alone in the face of near-certain death, the old man answered simply: "I have never yet run from an Indian and I never will."[30]

Edwards instructed Colonel Whiteside to order his captains to stand ready to march on a moment's notice, to pursue any Indians who stole horses or murdered settlers. One company of volunteers, under William B. Whiteside, acting as captain, and Samuel Judy, acting as lieutenant, was to leave for the frontiers immediately, "with instructions to resist all invasions, repel all attacks and aggressions from the Indians, and afford protection to the settlers on the frontiers in the most effectual manner in their power." If too few volunteers came forward, the colonel was authorized to institute a draft.[31] Spies were sent into Indian country, to try to learn the sentiments of the tribes and the identities of the murderers.[32]

In all, three companies of militia were sent to the frontier to scout between the blockhouses the governor had ordered constructed.[33] The territory had no money to pay them, however, and few arms to give them. The few weapons brought to the territory sold at exorbitant prices. Edwards appealed to the War Department for arms from the U.S. arsenal at Newport, Kentucky, but most of the weapons he asked for were issued instead to Governors Harrison of Indiana and Howard of Missouri, a pattern that would persist throughout the coming war. Under such circumstances, Edwards felt compelled to discharge the militia companies as soon as he determined that their service was not absolutely necessary.[34]

A company commanded by Captain Samuel Whiteside had already caused a minor diplomatic incident. They were stationed in a blockhouse near the mouth of the Illinois River, in what is now Jersey County, with orders to stop and question anybody, red or white, either descending or ascending the Mississippi.[35] All went well until July 23, when two canoes full of Indians refused to put to. Whiteside fired a warning shot in front of them. The warning shot led to a firefight, in which, fortunately, nobody was hurt, a consequence of the distance that separated the combatants. Afterwards the Indians proved to be part of Quashquame's band of friendly Sauk returning home from a visit to Saint Louis. The chief complained to Governor Howard, who, in turn, complained to Edwards. The incident required the good offices of William Bolin Whiteside, who was his cousin's superior officer, to assure the governors that while "the buoys was rather too forward," the officer in charge was a deliberate man who in this particular instance had acted without considering the consequences.[36]

The warning-shot incident received the attention it did because to that point the Sauk had remained at least nominally friendly. The governors were trying to avoid an open breach with them, especially at a time when Edwards was beginning difficult negotiations with the Potawatomi of the Illinois River. A year earlier, in July 1810, a mixed band of ten Potawatomi, Kickapoo, and Ottawa Indians, fleeing the Missouri settlements with stolen horses, had doubled back and surprised a small pursuing party of Missouri militiamen. Four of the whites were killed, including their leader, Captain William Temple Cole. The leader of the Indian band was Nuscotnumeg ("The Mad Sturgeon"), a Potawatomi of the Illinois River, who had come under the influence of the Prophet. He and some of the other murderers were eventually traced to Illinois, where they were thought to have placed themselves under the protection of Main Poc and to be living among the Indians of the Illinois River. Governor Howard asked Edwards to extradite them to stand trial in Saint Louis.[37]

Because simply arresting the murderers was impossible, Edwards decided to approach Gomo, senior chief of the Illinois River Potawatomi. Gomo's village stood about twenty miles upriver from Peoria, at or near the present site of Chillicothe, Illinois. Although this village was one of the smaller ones along the river, and although the authority of a Potawatomi chief even among his own band was weak,[38] the neighboring chiefs looked to Gomo as first among equals and usually chose him as spokesman in their dealings with the Americans. The chief himself was friendly to the whites. When orphaned as boys, Gomo and his brother Senachwine had been adopted by a French trader at Peoria, a friend of their father, who raised them in the Catholic faith. After the Treaty of Greenville, Gomo had remained at peace with the United States and had even visited Philadelphia, where he met President George Washington. Nevertheless, Gomo was a born diplomat for whom the favored course between two points was rarely a straight line. His position was difficult. Because the Illinois River Potawatomi were the Indians nearest the settlements, they were apt to be blamed for any act of hostility. That some Potawatomi bands, and some leaders such as Main Poc, were indeed hostile to the United States further complicated his position. Nevertheless, Gomo was an able man and for a time he managed to balance the competing claims upon him.[39]

As his envoy to the Potawatomi, Governor Edwards selected Captain Samuel Levering of Kaskaskia.[40] Levering was about 33 years old and a native of Philadelphia. He had held the rank of captain for less than two months and had no extensive experience with Indians, but Edwards evidently saw in Levering personal qualities that made him a good choice for the assignment. On July 24, 1811, Levering set out from Kaskaskia in a boat provided by General William Clark, the Indian agent at Saint Louis. With him was a small party of thirteen men, including eight boatmen, a Potawatomi Indian, and a Frenchman named Fournier, who passed as an interpreter but was really a spy for the Americans. Among Levering's companions was Nelson Rector, whose name will appear frequently hereafter. At Portage des Sioux the envoys encountered Samuel Whiteside and his company returning to the settlements after the warning-shot incident. After turning up the Illinois River, Levering and his men stopped briefly at Prairie Marcot, in Calhoun County, apparently near the present Hardin, where Lieutenant John Campbell and a small detachment of regulars were building a blockhouse to serve as a base for scouting Indian movements. Levering reached Peoria on August 3, 1811.[41]

By an odd chance, the story of Levering's mission to Peoria has survived in great detail. After a less than satisfactory first meeting with Gomo at Peoria, the intrepid Levering traveled upriver to Gomo's village uninvited and unannounced, accompanied only by an interpreter, and entered the chief's lodge at midnight. Once awakened, Gomo good-naturedly offered hospitality to his unexpected guest. The next day's talks went better, and Gomo agreed to invite chiefs of outlying Potawatomi bands to attend a council at Peoria. Main Poc was at Detroit and some other chiefs were either absent from the area or had been influenced by British agents not to attend, so the conference that began on August 16 was lightly attended. Gomo and a chief from Aux Sable Creek known as the "Little Chief"[42] acted as spokesmen for the Potawatomi. The chiefs listened silently as Levering read a letter from Edwards, reminding the chiefs of their treaty obligation to deliver up Indian offenders to justice and demanding surrender of the warriors who had murdered Cox, Price, and the Cole party in Missouri.

After the captain had finished, Gomo rose to speak. Although he stressed his tribe's desire for peace and a quiet life, Gomo gave a spirited recital of Indian grievances. While the Indians had given up to the Americans many fugitives, who were invariably hanged, the Americans had never surrendered any white man who had murdered an Indian. In the eyes of the white man, an Indian was always wrong. If an Indian should kill a hog he was a bad man, but for their part the whites thought nothing of entering Indian land to hunt their deer or bears. Unlike the French and British, who had given the Indians presents out of friendship, the Americans always asked for something in return. If a tribe accepted presents from the Americans, they were afterwards told that they had given up a tract of land. The whites had crossed the waters to come to the land where the Great Spirit had placed the red men, but if an Indian entered an American village he was hunted like a dog. Many of the young men were restless for these reasons, and the chiefs could not control them. It was impossible for the chiefs to deliver the murderers, who were residing in distant villages. Gomo closed by repeating his hope that both sides could avoid the horrors of war.[43]

The next day Little Chief made many of the same points. He blamed the Shawnee Prophet for fanning the discontent that had led to the murders and repeated that the chiefs had had no knowledge of them. He ended, though, on a slightly less conciliatory note. "If the Americans should commence war with us, we would have to fight in our own defense. The chiefs are of opinion that it is best to remain at peace. I have finished, my friends. Perhaps you take us for little children. We whip our children, but men will defend themselves. For myself I am indifferent. It would be the same with me to raise or bury the tomahawk. I can but die at last."[44]

On August 9, Levering had sent two of his companions, Captain Edward Hebert and Joseph Trotier, along with Jacques Mette, a resident of Peoria, to carry the governor's message, and a gift of four pounds of tobacco, to the Kickapoo village on Sugar Creek in the present Logan County. Hebert met in council with two chiefs, Pemwatome (The Mink) and Shee-pee-men (The White Beaver), and forty-six warriors. The Kickapoo assured Hebert in general terms of their wish "to hold fast the whites by the hand," but their answers were otherwise as noncommittal as those of the Potawatomi.[45] Levering returned to Kaskaskia with nothing accomplished except the recovery of two stolen horses that Gomo had surrendered to him. Nevertheless, Levering had conducted himself with firmness and tact. His early death, within a month of his return from Peoria, deprived the Illinois Territory of talents that would have been valuable to it in the years ahead.[46]

The problem of the fugitives appeared insoluble by diplomatic means, especially when the Cox murderers were seen feasting at Gomo's village not long after Levering and his party had left the area.[47] Increasingly a show of force began to seem necessary. Governors Edwards, Howard, and Harrison enjoyed good relations at this time, and the first two tended to look to the more experienced Harrison for military leadership. Indiana Territory also had the benefit of a larger population and greater resources than the other two territories, and Harrison was in frequent contact with Tecumseh, whom the governors had come to regard as the source of the tribes' growing hostility.[48] At a conference at Vincennes in early August, Tecumseh told Harrison that he was heading south to visit the Creek, Choctaw, and Chickasaw tribes in what is now Alabama and Mississippi and that he would return the following spring by way of the Osage tribe on the Missouri River. Tecumseh acknowledged that he hoped to persuade those tribes to join his confederacy, but he assured the governor that his visit was for peaceful purposes and that the Americans should have no more objection to the tribes uniting than the Indians did to the union of states.[49]

After the conference, Tecumseh headed west across the Wabash River into Illinois. Some later accounts may indicate his route. Near the present Clay City, John McCawley, the first white settler in Clay County, heard that Tecumseh was camped not far from his cabin and paid him a visit, but the chief was sullen and refused to speak to him.[50] About a mile south of where Marion is now, Tecumseh and his escort of twelve picked warriors encountered a solitary traveler named John Phelps. Surrounded by painted warriors, Phelps believed himself a dead man, but Tecumseh chatted with him amiably and asked about the trail south before moving on.[51] Tecumseh's party crossed the Ohio River near the mouth of Hodge's Creek, in Pulaski County, and then he was gone, providing Harrison with his opportunity.[52]

Although Tecumseh had asked the governor to maintain the status quo in his absence, Harrison regarded the Prophet as a much less able man than his brother and, should force be necessary, a less formidable adversary. His armed effort to disperse the Indians gathered at Prophetstown led on November 6 to the famous and controversial battle of Tippecanoe. Both sides lost heavily, but the Indians' withdrawal from the fighting enabled Harrison to burn Prophetstown and gave the battle enough of the appearance of a victory to help Harrison into the White House nearly thirty years later.[53]

Only one soldier from Illinois is known to have marched in Harrison's army: Colonel Isaac White. White commanded the Third Regiment of Illinois territorial militia but found himself in Vincennes at a Masonic function when Harrison's army marched, and he joined it as a private soldier. He was killed at Tippecanoe.[54] White's death prompted an organizational change in the Illinois militia. The Third Regiment, which covered the eastern settlements along the Ohio, Saline, and Wabash Rivers, had lost its commander. Edwards now divided the regiment into two, promoting its two majors Hamlet Ferguson[55] and Philip Tramell,[56] to lieutenant colonel as commanders of the Third and Fourth Regiments, respectively. The Third Regiment would be based in the settlements along the Ohio, while the new Fourth Regiment would cover the Wabash settlements and the Salines.[57]

One Indian from the Illinois Territory gained lasting individual fame during the campaign. As one of Harrison's supply boats was cordelling up the Wabash River, a Potawatomi warrior leapt from the shore onto the deck, killed one of the boatmen, and escaped unharmed. From this exploit he took a new name, Waubansee, meaning either "Daybreak" or "Foggy Day," referring to the atmospheric conditions that had permitted him to approach the boat unobserved. Waubansee later took part in the Fort Dearborn massacre, although he is said to have helped save some of the survivors. In later years he became reconciled to the Americans and actually took the field alongside them during the Black Hawk War of 1832. Today, echoes of Waubansee's exploit can be heard in a host of Illinois place names.[58]

In fact, on the side of the Indians, many, perhaps even most, of the warriors who opposed Harrison were from Illinois. Gathered at the Prophet's village had been warriors of the Kickapoo, Winnebago, and Potawatomi tribes, and many of them were killed in the fight. When the Prophet's band was dispersed, the survivors returned to their villages in Illinois, spreading the gospel of resistance among their own tribes.[59]

For two or three months the battle seemed to bring quiet to the frontier. The Kickapoo seemed especially submissive.[60] Nevertheless, resentment over their losses burned in the hearts of the tribesmen, especially the Winnebago, and the desire to avenge the dead led directly to the outrages that followed.

A similar change took place in the sentiment of the frontiersmen. In the wake of the Cox and Price murders, a public meeting of the citizens of Saint Clair County, chaired by Colonel Whiteside, had adopted addresses to both the governor and President James Madison, expressing their alarm, but still calling only for defensive measures, such as asking that arms be procured for the militia and that forts be built on the Mississippi River and at Peoria.[61] After Tippecanoe, however, the frontiersmen came to believe that the time for petitions had passed and took matters into their own hands. In December, on a scout beyond the line of settlements, Major William Bolin Whiteside took prisoner a Kickapoo who told him that there was a Kickapoo village of seven lodges about thirty miles from the settlements and also a band of Potawatomi camped nearby. The Potawatomi were in fact those led by Shequenebec, a hostile band described by trader Thomas Forsyth as "composed of the very worst Indians in the country." They had spent the summer pillaging and threatening the French inhabitants of Peoria. Now they were moving downriver to winter at a place called the Grand Pass in present Greene County,[62] about sixty miles from the mouth of the river, and only thirty to forty miles above the settlements.[63]

Without waiting for orders, Major Whiteside summoned his captains to rendezvous on December 5. When the news reached his father, the colonel, the old man dashed off a note to the governor and set out the next morning for the place of assembly. The old Indian fighter hoped to restrain the men but doubted his ability to command them. The mood among the militiamen was ugly, as "the most is for killing all that is like an Indian" and they were already blaming the major for not killing his Kickapoo prisoner. Without authority, a mounted company of "eighty-six well mounted riflemen" set out in search of Indians. The governor sent an express messenger to recall them, but the volunteers had already ridden, and only the withdrawal of the Indians, who had also heard of the coming attack, prevented a clash.[64]

Another ominous development in December was the return of Tecumseh from his mission to the Creeks and Cherokees of the South. Traveling up the Mississippi River to Missouri Territory, he preached the gospel of pan-Indianism to the Shawnee and Delaware, and possibly to the Osage, before continuing on to visit the Sauk of Rock River and the Sioux of Minnesota. In Missouri he had little success, but the Sauk and Sioux were more receptive. On his return, Tecumseh crossed Illinois Territory, no doubt again visiting the Kickapoo, the Ottawa, and the Potawatomi, before returning to the Wabash about the end of January 1812. Some of the tribes had taken his words to heart, but they were not yet ready to stand together against the Americans.[65]

Edwards, for his part, was still determined to preserve the peace, if possible. He immediately sent envoys to the Potawatomi and Kickapoo. To the Kickapoo he sent Major William Bolin Whiteside and to the Potawatomi he sent Captain Edward Hebert. Hebert (often spelled Ebert) was a longtime resident of Cahokia who had accompanied Levering on his mission the previous summer.[66] The tribes were invited to send representatives to Kaskaskia, escorted by Whiteside and Hebert. The messengers were absent nearly two months, but on returning, they advised the governor that the chiefs had declined to visit him. Gomo had answered that he could do nothing until he had conferred with all the Indians with whom his own band was related by alliance or friendship, but he warned Edwards to be on guard against the Winnebago, who would certainly attack the frontier seeking revenge for their losses at Tippecanoe.[67]

Edwards distrusted Gomo, not unreasonably, but Gomo's warning about the Winnebago proved to be true. The Winnebago were burning to avenge their losses in the battle. On December 30, 1811, thirty Winnebago warriors attacked the houses of Americans at the lead mines near modern Dubuque. Two men were cut into small pieces and eaten, while two others were spared only after some Fox women assured the war party that they were Englishmen. The Winnebago proclaimed that they were going to war with the Americans because Harrison had slain many of their people.[68]

The Winnebago continued their hostility. On February 8, they fired on an express rider returning to Saint Louis from Fort Madison.[69] Because of its small garrison and its isolation, Fort Madison (at present Fort Madison, Iowa) was especially vulnerable. Its small garrison of forty-four effective men was not sufficient even to mount a proper guard. Winnebago warriors hovered near the fort, looking for an opportunity, and twice during March succeeded in killing soldiers of the garrison.[70] All but one or two of the remaining Americans fled from Prairie du Chien, and the Winnebago closed the Mississippi above Rock River, announcing they would stop all boats and would tomahawk or burn any Americans caught trying to pass.[71]

Kickapoo tribesmen committed an even more dramatic outrage, for the same reason. From the Kickapoo winter camp on the Sangamon River, a kinsman of Elk's Hoof, a warrior killed at Tippecanoe, led a party across the Mississippi to seek revenge. On February 9, they slaughtered nine members of the O'Neal family, all women and children, as well as a young neighbor, on the frontier about two miles north of the present Clarkson, Missouri. Spies followed the trail of the murderers across the Mississippi as far as the Illinois River.[72]

Colonel Daniel Bissell commanded the only force of U.S. regulars in the upper Mississippi valley.[73] From his headquarters at Fort Bellefontaine, just north of Saint Louis, he oversaw the garrisons at Fort Madison, Fort Osage (near present Sibley, Missouri, not far east of Kansas City), newly built Fort Mason,[74] and Fort Massac. Possibly because he had been implicated in the Burr conspiracy, Bissell was curiously passive, failing to consult with the governors about defense of the two territories, or even to visit the posts under his command without permission from the War Department.[75] Nevertheless, at Governor Howard's request, Bissell sent two officers and thirty men to build a blockhouse near the site of the O'Neal massacre.[76] Edwards, for his part, asked Bissell to reoccupy the blockhouse on the Mississippi, which had apparently been abandoned after the warning-shot incident.[77] Finally, when urged by Secretary of War Eustis to build and garrison a post at Peoria, Bissell had to protest that, after garrisoning the posts he already had, he had only twenty-nine men remaining at Bellefontaine.[78]

Fortunately, Congress had finally awoken from its long slumber and recognized that some steps must be taken to defend the western territories. In March, the governors received word that Congress had authorized the raising of six companies of U.S. Rangers to guard the northwest frontier. One company each was to be raised in Illinois, Missouri, and Indiana Territories, one in Kentucky, and two in Ohio.[79] The Rangers would serve as a federal force halfway between regulars and volunteers. Unlike the militia, they could be kept on duty or on call for an extended period, because they would be paid enough to prevent hardship. Those who enlisted were expected to provide their own clothing, weapons, provisions, horses, and fodder, for which they would be paid one dollar per day when in actual service (70¢ if serving on foot).[80] Each company was to consist of no more than sixty-eight enlisted men and four commissioned officers. The obvious choice as captain in Illinois was William Bolin Whiteside, whom President Madison appointed on the recommendation of Edwards and others.[81]

Until the Rangers could be recruited and put into service, the territories had to defend themselves. The eastern part of Illinois was remote from the seat of government at Kaskaskia, and settlers there took action on their own. Reacting to a rumor that 1500 hostile Indians were gathered 200 miles from Shawneetown, the citizens of that place sent out a corps of volunteers to hunt for them. Fortunately they seem not to have encountered any Indians.[82] To the westward, governors Edwards and Howard consulted frequently. Both governors brought militia companies into service. On March 3, Edwards ordered out three companies of militia from the Second (Saint Clair County) Regiment.[83] The companies were commanded by Captains Jacob Short, Samuel Judy, and John Scott.[84] They were called out for three months, but since the territory had no money and none of the militiamen who had been out on active service in 1811 had yet been paid, Edwards had to promise to pay these men himself if the government did not.[85] Edwards still insisted his troops remain on the defensive, however. When Major William B. Whiteside proposed to lead his militia battalion against Peoria, Edwards sternly forbade him to do so.[86]

Instead, Edwards once again offered the hand of friendship to the Indians of the Illinois River valley. In March he ordered Captain Edward Hebert to ascend the river a third time, to invite the chiefs to a council with the governor at Cahokia. Hebert also carried a message to the traders on the river, directing them to withdraw until relations with the Indians were resolved.[87] This diplomatic mission was more successful than its predecessors. In early April, canoes full of Indians, including women and children, began streaming downriver toward Cahokia. The chiefs had been promised safe conduct and flew American flags from the lead canoes. Major William Bolin Whiteside had gone ahead, warning settlers along the river not to molest them. Nevertheless, near the mouth of the Missouri, canoes escorted by Hebert were fired on from the Illinois bank. The chiefs were alarmed and for a while it looked as if the conference would not be held.[88]

Indian Agent William Clark reassured the Indians, and on April 16, 1812, Edwards's grand council opened at Cahokia.[89] Edwards and Clark represented the United States. The Potawatomi were represented by Gomo, Pepper (who had succeeded the deceased Little Chief as head of the band at Aux Sable Creek), Black Partridge,[90] White Hair, Esh-kee-bee, and seventeen other chiefs. Conspicuous by his absence, but much on the minds of those who did attend, was Main Poc. Pemwatome, the principal chief of the Kickapoo, was not present, but he had instead sent a representative, Blue Eyes. Among the eight other chiefs attending for the Kickapoo was Little Deer, a hostile chief who was loud in his professions of friendship. Three Ottawa chiefs attended, including Mittitasse, whose village was at the Chicago Portage and who represented Black Bird. Also present was The White Dog, a chief of the Chippewa.

Edwards opened with a formal speech. If, as he expected, war should break out between the United States and Great Britain, he asked only that the tribes remain neutral. Edwards reviewed past British betrayals of their Indian allies and predicted disaster if the Indians sided with the British again. He told the chiefs a great truth, later tragically confirmed by the outcome of the war: "My Children, the British pretend to be your friends, but their object is to get you to fight their battles; and they care not what becomes of you afterwards." He went on to rebut the points Gomo and the Little Chief had made at the conference with Levering. Although the chiefs had professed not to know where the Cole and Cox murderers were, they had in fact known that the murderers were of their tribe and had resided near Peoria ever since. Having told the chiefs a truth, and caught them in a lie, Edwards closed his speech with a lie of his own: "My Children, we do not want your land. We have more land already than we can use, and I shall neither propose to buy it, nor does your Great Father, or myself, wish to take a foot of it from you."[91]

The assembled chiefs announced that Gomo would speak for them all. Gomo responded with a flood of Indian eloquence, proclaiming the desire of the chiefs for peace and his own past good conduct, but offering no specific commitments. On the subject of the Cole and Cox murderers, he had only this to say:

> My Father, if there could be found among us one chief who had influence enough to deliver a murderer, I would be happy to see such a chief.
>
> My Father, you probably think I am a great chief. I am not! I cannot control my young men as I please. . . . I am a chief whilst my young men are growing, but when they become grown I am no more master of them. . . .
>
> My Father, I could very easily secure or kill the murderers you mention; but unless the whole of my chiefs and young men are consenting, I would be killed.
>
> My Father, concerning the murderers, we will consult all together, and we will then know what we will do.

Although Gomo expressed reluctance to join the British, he also reminded Edwards of the Americans' broken promises of material support. More ominously, although he denounced the Prophet, he echoed Tecumseh's doctrine that the Great Spirit had given the land to all the Indians, and that no chief could sell their land.

After two days, the council adjourned across the river to Saint Louis, for two more days of speeches and negotiations. It all ended amicably enough, with the chiefs promising to consider the words of their "Father" and Edwards providing food and clothing to the ragged and hungry Indians. The Indians went home well satisfied with the council.[92] Edwards, for his part, called out another company of mounted riflemen.[93]

Soon afterwards, Illinois Territory suffered its first act of Indian hostility since Tippecanoe.[94] At Chicago a tiny civilian community of Indian traders, farmers, and discharged soldiers had begun to grow around the walls of Fort Dearborn. One of the more outlying cabins, known as "Lee's place," stood about three miles from the fort along the south branch of the Chicago River, in the vicinity of the present Racine Avenue and 22nd Street.[95] On April 6, 1812, a Winnebago war party from Rock River entered the farmhouse. Inside were three men, Liberty White, a native of New Hampshire, Jean Baptiste Cardin, a French Canadian, John Kelso, a recently discharged soldier, and also a boy named Lee, son of the owner of the farm. At first the Indians seemed peaceable enough, but Kelso and the boy, not recognizing the Indians and not liking their looks, found an excuse to go outside and then ran for the fort. Their flight extended their lives until the following August. Behind them they heard cries and gunshots. The next day a column of soldiers and civilians went down to Lee's place, where they found White and Cardin dead. White had been shot and stabbed many times, his throat cut, and his face skinned from ear to ear. Captain Heald described the body as "the most horrible object I ever beheld in my life." Cardin, the Frenchman, perhaps in deference to his nationality, had merely been shot through the neck and scalped. The frightened settlers fortified the Indian Agency House, where the men formed themselves into a small company of militia.[96]

Five days later the violence shifted to the Wabash frontier.[97] This time the killers were thought to have been Potawatomi from the headwaters of the Iroquois River, including two of those who had killed the Cole party in Missouri the preceding year.[98] During the winter of 1811–12 the Isaac Hutson family had crossed the Wabash to what is now Crawford County. Hutson helped with the building of Fort LaMotte, while his family lived inside the partially completed fort. In the spring, however, Hutson disregarded warnings of danger and moved his family a few miles north, to open a farm in the vicinity of the present Hutsonville. On the evening of April 11, 1812, Hutson returned home from a nearby horse mill to find his cabin collapsed in flames. In the yard lay the body of Dixon, a young man who lived with the family, mutilated beyond recognition, his heart impaled on a branch stuck into the ground nearby. The next day the bones of Mrs. Hutson and her four children were found in the smoking ruins.[99] Mounted men from Fort LaMotte pursued the murderers, without success. Hutson himself is said to have joined the army at nearby Fort Harrison, seeking revenge, and to have been killed soon afterwards in an Indian ambush.[100] The unfortunate family is commemorated by the names of Hutson Creek and the village of Hutsonville, as well as by a memorial park near the scene of the massacre.[101]

Along the Embarras River, at a place called Mussel Shoals, a few miles southeast of the present Lawrenceville, lived William and Olive (Parker) Har-

riman and their five young children.[102] The Harrimans were natives of Mont-
pelier, Vermont. With them lived a young man named Seneca Amy. The sulky
disposition of the Indians in the neighborhood made the family uneasy, and
at last, undoubtedly influenced by the fate of the Hutsons, Harriman agreed
to move the family for safety to Vincennes, only a few miles away across the
Wabash. On the evening of April 22, as the family loaded their belongings into
a canoe, Harriman sent young Amy back to the cabin to fetch a gun they had
left behind. Approaching the cabin, the young man saw that it was surrounded
by Indians and saved himself by plunging into the brush unnoticed.[103] The
family was not so fortunate: the Indians descended upon them, shooting down
Harriman at the outset. Young Amy ran a half mile downriver to warn two
neighboring families. At one cabin the lady of the house was actually engaged
in giving birth, but the fugitives loaded her into a boat and proceeded by water
to Vincennes, which they reached in the middle of the night. The next day
Lieutenant Colonel James Miller[104] led a well-armed party to the spot. Harriman had been shot through the head, tomahawked, and his entrails torn out.
Nearby lay the bodies of his wife, two little girls, aged nine and seven, twin
boys of three years, and a baby, all of them shot, tomahawked, stabbed. All
had been scalped except the baby, held tight in its dead mother's arms. Miller
wanted to take the bodies to Vincennes for burial, but he was dissuaded by
his men, who argued that the sight would create panic in town. Accordingly,
he had the family decently buried where they had died. Rangers and militia
rode after the murderers, but a heavy rain the night before had washed away
the trail and the party had to return. In June a company of mounted volunteers
from Kentucky patrolled the areas along the Wabash where the families had
been murdered, hoping to deter the killers from returning.[105]

The effect these atrocities had on the eastern frontier of Illinois can well
be imagined. Settlers along the Wabash began leaving, and the Coffee Island
settlement, in what is now southern Wabash County,[106] was "intirely broken
up,"[107] most of its inhabitants fleeing to nearby Vincennes. The area from
which one "tolerable large" company of militia had been drawn was reduced to
two families. The settlers in what is now White County were dissuaded from
fleeing to safety only by the exertions of Captain William McHenry, a fearless
pioneer who had once killed a bear with a knife after his gun misfired.[108] Even
the Vincennes area faced depopulation. The exodus threatened the continua-
tion of work at the United States Salines, Illinois Territory's largest industry.
Unless military protection were provided, it was feared, the southern owners

of the slaves contracted to labor as "hands" at the salt works might conclude that the wages did not justify the danger to their investment and withdraw them to Kentucky or Tennessee. The free inhabitants along the Saline River were also considerably alarmed and only the expectation that the area would soon be protected by a company of Rangers kept them from flight.[109]

A small scouting party led by Captain McHenry found many signs of Indians between Coffee Island and McHenry's own settlement in the present White County. He sent a messenger to the Salines to ask for arms. From Shawneetown, Captain Craig wrote the governor that his company of militia was ready to march when ordered. Without waiting for orders, Colonel Philip Tramell of the Fourth Regiment sent Captain Willis Hargrave[110] with about twenty or thirty men to "range" along the Wabash.[111] This was awkward. Although as military commandant for the district Tramell had authority to call out the militia to meet an actual or threatened invasion,[112] it was not clear that he could send them out on a scout without an order from Edwards and Edwards himself had no authority from the War Department to call out the militia at federal expense. Nevertheless, in light of the emergency, Edwards approved what Tramell had done.[113]

In late April or the beginning of May, there may have been additional murders. On May 12, Edwards wrote to Secretary Eustis: "I am informed by a Colonel of militia [obviously Tramell] that considerable mischief was lately committed within between forty and sixty miles of the United States Saline. By a letter of the 3d inst., he states that two militia Captains in that quarter [presumably Hargrave and McHenry] had raised a party and pursued the murderers, but had not returned on the date of his letter."[114] No other reference to these killings has been found, and they cannot be identified with certainty.

In the western part of the territory, the measures taken in concert by Governors Edwards and Howard prevented Indian incursions for a time. The Missouri Rangers, under Captain Nathan Boone,[115] were stationed about 120 miles above Saint Louis, at or near Fort Mason. In Illinois, William Bolin Whiteside's company of 72 Rangers patrolled from the same point on the opposite bank of the Mississippi east to where the Sangamon River empties into the Illinois, about ten miles east of the present Rushville. East of the Illinois River, Edwards deployed volunteer mounted riflemen, who ranged from the mouth of the Sangamon east to the "heads" of the Kaskaskia River, apparently not far from the present Champaign. Sometimes these men would range as far east as the Wabash. Each volunteer company was divided into two units, one commanded by the captain and one by the lieutenant, which patrolled their long frontier from opposite ends, passing each other *en route*.[116]

The service demanded of the volunteers was arduous and caused significant disruption to the lives of the volunteers and their families during planting season. Edwards had no way of knowing whether the volunteers would even be paid. To lessen the hardship on them, Edwards devised the expedient of limiting and staggering their active service.[117] To lead the volunteers, he turned to two warhorses: Captain James B. Moore[118] and Captain Jacob Short.[119] Moore's first company was in service between April 15 and May 3,[120] followed by Short's company between May 3 and May 17.[121] Moore's company returned to the field May 17, staying out until May 31,[122] when it was replaced by Short and his men, who remained on duty until June 29.[123] During this longer tour of duty, Moore's company was also ordered back into the field between June 11 and June 25, to oppose an Indian force collecting on another part of the frontier.[124] In late June, after learning that Colonel William Russell had arrived at Vincennes to take over command of the Rangers and the defense of the frontier, the governor discharged his volunteers from service.[125]

To command the six new companies of Rangers, President Madison appointed Colonel William Russell of Kentucky, one of the country's most experienced Indian fighters.[126] Russell had trod his first warpath in 1774, as a companion of Daniel Boone, and over the next five years he had been constantly engaged in Indian warfare. During the Revolution, Russell commanded a company at the battle of King's Mountain. During the Indian wars of the 1790s, Russell served under Generals James Wilkinson, Charles Scott, and James Winchester and commanded a regiment of Kentucky volunteers under General Anthony Wayne. He returned to active service in 1808, when he was appointed colonel of the 7th U.S. Infantry. To long experience, Russell added a simple, unassuming manner that made him popular with the men he commanded. John Reynolds, who would serve under Russell in the Peoria campaign, later remembered him as "a plain old man, dressed in Kentucky jeans, or linsey, [who] seemed to need no aids, and had none, but was a good and efficient officer himself."[127]

Russell was at Newport, Kentucky, when he received the order appointing him to command. He issued orders for the company of Rangers raised in Kentucky to meet him at Red Banks (now Henderson, Kentucky), from which he led them to Vincennes, where they arrived about June 7. Russell's natural instinct was to launch an immediate punitive attack on the Indians along the Wabash, but when he arrived at his post, and saw the vast extent and weakness of the territories he was ordered to protect, he understood that his first arrangements must be defensive. He ordered that one of the companies of Rangers raised in Ohio, as well as any new recruits raised in Kentucky and Ohio, join him at Vincennes. Until they arrived, Russell deployed some Rangers to cover the weaker frontiers, while others were sent to scout the area beyond. Prophetstown had been rebuilt since Harrison had destroyed it, and Russell expected the Indians there to be joined by those known to be massing at Peoria. For this reason, he regarded Indiana as the most endangered of the territories, although he promised to lead a company of Rangers to Illinois as soon as he was able. He continued to hope for offensive operations when circumstances would permit.[128]

In Illinois, Edwards made one more effort to reach accord with the Indians of the Illinois River. In May, Thomas Forsyth, newly appointed as an Indian subagent, was sent back to Peoria. He reported that 600 Indian warriors had gathered there, and that hundreds more, many of them Winnebago, were gathering along the Wabash at Prophetstown. The tribes on the Illinois had been augmented by the addition of half a band of Miami, probably Piankashaw, who had formerly lived on the Illinois prairie, the other half having gone to join the Prophet. Forsyth estimated that with a call to outlying villages, 1200 warriors could be gathered at Peoria within ten days.[129]

About the beginning of 1812, the Kickapoo abandoned some of their villages in present-day Logan and McLean counties and formed a new village along the east side of the Illinois River, near the head of Peoria Lake.[130] Forsyth had been ordered to read them a "talk" prepared by Edwards requesting the tribe to remain neutral in the coming war. Edwards's message denounced the British and the Prophet and emphasized the certainty of American victory over both, as well as the awful consequences that would befall the tribe if it backed the loser. The "talk" concluded with a demand for surrender of the O'Neal murderers. Previously the governor had been reluctant to make a demand that he could not enforce, but more recently he had received indications that the chiefs were now willing to comply. He further reasoned that if the murderers were surrendered, it would drive a wedge between the Prophet and the Kickapoo, helping to ensure the neutrality of that small but warlike tribe.[131]

Before his recent trip to Saint Louis, Forsyth too had believed that the chiefs were inclined to surrender the murderers, but on his return to Peoria he found the Kickapoo "much changed." Pemwatome, their principal chief, replied to the governor's message with a recital of his tribe's own grievances. After a perfunctory assertion that the tribe had no intention to do wrong, the chief listed one occasion after another when whites had killed members of his tribe without punishment. "You ask us to do justice. You did not do us that justice you ought to have done." Pemwatome acknowledged the "bad affairs" that had resulted from the battle of Tippecanoe and the many Kickapoo who had died there. The chief urged the governor to forget the past, as he and the other chiefs were willing to do, although he admitted that not all the young men agreed. "Let the hatchet be buried deep; think with us it is better to have peace than war." The tribe wished only to feed its women and children, but could not do so, when young white men were continually coming and going through the tribe's hunting ground. Pemwatome closed with an assurance that "the Kickapoo will never do you any injury for the time to come." Having said this, the chief departed for Canada to visit his "British Father."

Forsyth also talked with Gomo. That chief continued to express his personal friendship for the Americans, but he said the time was not yet come to act on it. Nothing, he told Forsyth, could be accomplished without a general council of the Potawatomi tribe. He acknowledged that the tribe was almost out of powder and ammunition and had not been able to procure more. If the traders were withdrawn from them, he did not know how the Potawatomi could live. Gomo had heard, however, that British goods would soon be coming into the country through Mackinac. The one piece of good news Forsyth was able to report was that the hostile chief Main Poc was detained at Malden in Canada, unable to get back across the river into the United States, adding "God keep him there and that he may never return from that country."[132]

On June 18 the United States declared war on Great Britain.[133] There could be little doubt that the tribes would join the British. The government invited the Indians to a grand conference at Piqua in Ohio, but the Indians expressed little interest. Even Gomo declined to go, expressing fear that if the chiefs attended the conference, the Americans would give them gifts and then claim they had bought the Indians' land. The Indians of the Illinois River had met in council and Gomo admitted that the Potawatomi were merely awaiting a signal from the British to go to war.[134]

On June 26, representatives of nine tribes met at the Sauk village on Rock River to discuss what they should do. The Prophet had sent them red wampum as a call to war, along with a message inviting them to his village on the Wabash to prepare. The Americans never told the truth, he said, but instead cheated the Indians out of their lands and kept them in poverty. At least five of the tribes favored war, while the Sauk and Fox strongly favored peace with the Americans.[135] Between June 15 and July 11, a Frenchman, Antoine LeClair, traveled through what is now northern Illinois and southern Wisconsin as a spy for Forsyth. Wherever LeClair went, he found the Indians dancing the war dance and impatiently awaiting a signal from the British.[136]

Across Illinois Territory, relations between red and white were already changing. At Chicago, the members of the small American community remained confined to Fort Dearborn and the fortified agency house nearby.[137] At Peoria, French villagers who had long enjoyed cordial relations with the Indians now began finding great numbers of their cattle killed, and the carcasses sometimes left at their very doorsteps.[138] At the southern end of the territory, in what is now Pope County, a family named Crawford lived at the mouth of Grand Pierre Creek. There were few resident Indians, but the family lived on civil terms with passing Indian hunting parties. The day the Indians learned of war, they painted their faces, assumed a hostile attitude, and with great dignity walked past the cabin to the riverbank, where they commandeered the family's boat, loaded it with game, and then paddled off down the river, never to return.[139]

On the Little Wabash River, in the present Clay County, stood the isolated cabin of John McCawley.[140] McCawley was on friendly terms with his Indian neighbors. In June 1812, however, two Indians came to his cabin to tell him that he must leave his home. Tecumseh had ordered that any whites in the area be killed, and they advised that he leave immediately for Vincennes. McCawley set out the next morning. The trip was uneventful, and McCawley did not see a living soul until he came within sight of Vincennes. At that moment, however, he heard a whoop behind him and turned to see his Indian friends wave to him and then disappear into the forest.[141]

At Kaskaskia, Ninian Edwards planned to defend the territory. His three-year appointment as governor expired on June 21, 1812. As the day approached and then passed, nobody in the Madison administration bothered to tell him whether he would be, or had been, reappointed. Illinois Territory needed a leader, however, and for more than two months Edwards continued to act as governor without knowing whether he had any legal authority to do so. To meet any invasion by water, he sent Captain William Bolin Whiteside's Rangers up the Illinois river in an armed boat, while Edwards himself rode with his militia to the northern frontier.[142] On August 4 he wrote to Secretary

Eustis: "No troops of any kind have yet arrived in this Territory, and I think you may count on a bloody stroke upon us very soon; I have been extremely reluctant to send my family away, but, unless I hear shortly of more assistance than a few rangers, I shall bury my papers in the ground, send my family off, and stand my ground as long as possible."[143]

FOUR

Chicago

In the early morning hours of July 17, 1812, Lieutenant Porter Hanks,[1] American commander at Fort Mackinac, awoke to the startling sight of red-coated British soldiers mounting cannon on the ridge overlooking his fort. Outside the walls, hundreds of painted Indians shouted for blood. It was the first notice the lieutenant had received that his country was at war.[2]

Surrounding Hanks and his fifty-seven soldiers were about 220 British regulars and Canadian militia, commanded by Captain Charles Roberts.[3] During the night they had crossed by canoe from the British post at Saint Joseph Island, Ontario. They were supported by a force of several hundred Indians, including Sioux, Winnebago, and Menominee warriors led from the west by trader Robert Dickson, and local Chippewa and Ottawa warriors under the command of John Askin Jr., the Indian storekeeper at Saint Joseph.[4] The surprise was complete.

About midmorning, Roberts sent the Americans a flag of truce and a summons to surrender. Despite his small garrison, Hanks might have withstood an attack by Indians alone, but he knew that the British artillery on the heights would knock his wooden walls to splinters and that the inevitable sequel would be massacre at the hands of the Indians. Roberts offered honorable terms, which Hanks wisely accepted.[5] Askin believed that had a gun been fired, not a soul in the fort could have been saved.[6] The American garrison marched out with the honors of war, and the British flag was hoisted over Mackinac. Lieutenant Hanks returned on parole to Detroit, where he requested a court of inquiry into his conduct, but, unlucky to the last, he was killed by a British cannonball lobbed into the room where the inquiry was proceeding.[7]

The fall of Mackinac began a series of events that eventually led to disaster in Illinois. The immediate effect was felt 250 miles away at Detroit, where General William Hull commanded all U.S. forces in the Northwest. After making a feeble incursion into Canada, Hull dithered until the British were able to close the door to their stronghold at Malden. When news of the fall of Mackinac reached the general on July 28, Hull ceased all offensive operations.[8] "The whole northern hordes of Indians will be let loose upon us," he is said to have exclaimed. Hearing of the surrender of Mackinac, the Wyandot tribe, which had been neutral, joined the British, and the prestige of that tribe was expected to bring the other tribes over to the British as well.[9] On August 7 Hull ordered his disgusted army back across the straits to Detroit. Even worse, Hull was now opposed by a soldier of genius, Major General Isaac Brock, working in perfect harmony with Tecumseh. From his command in Lower Canada, Brock had taken Hull's measure, concluding from Hull's behavior that something must be wrong with either Hull or his army.[10] He hurried from the New York frontier to take command at Malden, and pressed his advantage. From the Canadian shore the British began to bombard Detroit, and on August 15 Brock's army crossed to the American side without opposition. Indians from Illinois crossed with it, among them Main Poc. The next day, terrified by Brock's warning that, if fighting began, he would not be able to control his Indian allies, Hull surrendered both his army and Detroit.[11]

In the wake of these British victories, both Governor Ninian Edwards of Illinois and Governor Benjamin Howard of Missouri expected an attack on their territories by the Potawatomi, Kickapoo, and Piankashaw Indians massing along the Illinois River near Peoria. They expected an attack by water, but the attack, when it came, moved in quite a different direction.[12]

Of the remaining American military posts in the Northwest, one of the most exposed was Fort Dearborn near the mouth of the Chicago River.[13] The fort itself was remarkably well calculated to hold out against Indians—lying in the bend of a deep river and nearly surrounded by it; built of very substantial materials, with two rows of high pickets and two Block houses which guarded every

Figure 6. Model of Fort Dearborn, 1803–1812. Courtesy of Chicago History Museum.

point including the communication between the Lake and Chicago River."[14] Another observer described Fort Dearborn as "the neatest and best wooden garrison in the country."[15] Near the fort were clustered some public buildings, such as the Agency House and the United States Factory, and the homes of a handful of civilians, most of them Indian traders and discharged soldiers.

Nevertheless, isolation made the fort vulnerable. Because the fort lay on the portage route between Lake Michigan and the Illinois River, Indians were constantly passing and repassing in large numbers. The nearest American military post was the small and exposed garrison at Fort Wayne, over 160 miles distant. Mail was brought once a month by express from Fort Wayne.[16] So remote was Chicago from the other Illinois settlements that Governor Edwards was not even sure that it lay in his territory.[17]

Perhaps because of its isolation, Fort Dearborn was not a happy post. Throughout its history, the officers were often at bitter odds with each other. Much of the antagonism centered on the sinister figure of Indian trader John Kinzie. Kinzie had been born in 1763 at Québec and grew up in British Detroit before running away from the family home. As an adult he settled in British-controlled northern Ohio, where he made his living as a silversmith and Indian trader, supplying the Indians who were fighting against the armies of Generals

Arthur St. Clair and Anthony Wayne. Kinzie settled at Chicago in the spring of 1804, the year after construction of Fort Dearborn.[18]

At Chicago Kinzie became popular with the local Indians, but he also engaged in a long-running and unseemly feud over the suttling business with the post commandant, Captain John Whistler, that bitterly divided the civil and military officers at Chicago. At last the War Department resolved the quarrel by scattering the officers of Fort Dearborn to other posts.[19] Whistler was succeeded as commandant at Fort Dearborn by Captain Nathan Heald, a native of New Hampshire who had previously commanded the garrisons at Fort Massac and Fort Wayne.[20] After a furlough, Heald brought with him to Chicago his bride Rebecca Wells Heald, niece of the famous Indian fighter Captain William Wells. During 1811 Heald received a new complement of officers: Lieutenant Linai T. Helm,[21] Ensign George Ronan,[22] and Surgeon's Mate Isaac Van Voorhis.[23]

This team did not work well together, or with their commanding officer. Helm had obtained a transfer from Detroit to Fort Dearborn in search of a lower cost of living. At Chicago he married Margaret McKillip, stepdaughter of John Kinzie, and thereafter fell under Kinzie's sway. Dr. Van Voorhis had a low opinion of Helm, writing that "In favour of Lieutenant Helm nothing earthly can be said; if there be anything striking in him it is ignorance."[24] Surviving accounts agree in depicting Ronan as courageous, but also as arrogant, insubordinate, and overbearing.[25] The few surviving letters of Dr. Van Voorhis reflect bitter unhappiness with the dissension prevailing at Fort Dearborn.[26]

As before, this dissension centered on Kinzie. In January 1812, Captain Heald gave Kinzie and his half-brother Thomas Forsyth an effective monopoly on the suttling business, by refusing to give "certificates of pay due" to any other trader. Because pay for the soldiers of the garrison was usually in arrears, such certificates were often the only currency available to them. Matthew Irwin, U.S. factor at the post and formerly Kinzie's ally,[27] attacked Kinzie and Heald in terms reminiscent of those he and Kinzie had previously used against Whistler, but his charges are lent some credibility by the fact that Van Voorhis agreed with them. According to Irwin, Kinzie used his monopoly to charge extortionate prices to the enlisted men, securing the acquiescence of the officers by providing them with goods at cost. Irwin frankly alleged that money had changed hands to secure Kinzie & Forsyth the concession as sutlers to the garrison, and hinted that some unnamed secret gave Kinzie power over Heald.[28]

These allegations were serious enough, but they paled next to another made against Kinzie. After the killings at Lee's place,[29] Irwin and Van Voorhis became convinced that Kinzie was plotting with Helm and Ronan to murder friendly Indians in hopes of starting an Indian war. Why Kinzie, who made his living from the Indian trade, would want to start a war is not easy to understand; Irwin believed that Kinzie hoped to shut down the U.S. Factory at Chicago in the hope of increasing trade by his own agents at Peoria, Rock River, and Milwaukee. It seems unlikely, however, that Kinzie intended things to go as far as a war that would have endangered his own family, and probably he was merely undermining Heald for some obscure reason of his own. Ronan's conduct was especially violent: He publicly threatened to shoot friendly Indians and Frenchmen. When six friendly Sauk Indians visited Chicago to profess their loyalty, the subalterns engaged two noncommissioned officers to kill them. Van Voorhis got wind of the plot and told Irwin, who squelched it by going to Heald. Although Heald was pursuing a determinedly pacific policy toward the Indians, Helm and Ronan worked to thwart him at every turn, even stirring up discontent among the enlisted men. At last, when Helm violated one of Heald's standing orders while Heald was in council with the Indians, the exasperated captain ordered Ronan to place Helm under arrest. Ronan flatly refused, forcing the captain to make the arrest himself. Helm afterwards apologized and was released.[30]

The quarrels roiling Fort Dearborn came to a head with the killing of John LaLime. LaLime was a Frenchman who had long been employed as government interpreter at Chicago. The few of LaLime's letters that survive appear to be the work of an intelligent and reasonably well educated man. Apparently, though, LaLime was regarded as aligned with the factor and the surgeon's mate, and all three were coming under increasing pressure. On one occasion Ronan threatened to shoot LaLime, while Helm swore that "he would take the scalp of the factor." Kinzie himself even went so far as to hand Van Voorhis a challenge from Helm.

On June 17, 1812, at about 6:00 o'clock in the evening, Kinzie killed John LaLime by stabbing him in the heart. The killing took place inside the walls of Fort Dearborn, and after stabbing the interpreter, Kinzie retired to his quarters in the fort with seeming nonchalance. Only after learning that Irwin and Van Voorhis had witnessed the killing did Kinzie give way to despair. Ronan advised the trader to flee, and Helm conducted him outside the fort. For the next several days, Kinzie was seen skulking in the woods near the fort, but Heald made no serious move to arrest him. Indeed, Helm, the fugitive's son-in-law, was frequently seen carrying food and wine into the woods.[31]

In Kinzie family lore, which has found its way into history, Kinzie killed LaLime in self-defense, only after LaLime, jealous of Kinzie's success as a trader, had stabbed and badly wounded him.[32] At this date, of course, it is impossible to judge the claim of self-defense, but the rest of the Kinzie family story is suspect. LaLime was not merely a rival trader, if he was even a trader at all, but a salaried employee of the government. Kinzie was never wounded, as his participation in subsequent events showed. In order to give his mythical wounds time to heal, the family story moves the killing back to 1810, two years before the actual date. Van Voorhis, however, described the killing as "a perfect assassination," brought on by LaLime's verbal defense of Irwin when Helm was abusing him behind his back. The few civilians at Chicago called for an inquest, but Helm brought a column of soldiers to take the body away.[33]

Irwin and Van Voorhis now believed their own lives to be in danger. Irwin noticed strange Indians hanging around the factory, but Heald refused his request for protection. Van Voorhis offered Irwin lodging in his own quarters. At this moment, however, Heald learned that Irwin had written to Secretary of War William Eustis, asking him to order Heald to fortify the factory and other public buildings outside the stockade, and that Eustis had in fact issued such an order. Heald became enraged and ordered Irwin from the fort. Heald had recently asked Irwin to accompany Ensign Ronan into the woods in search of Kinzie, but Irwin, distrusting Ronan and fearing an attempt on his own life, had refused. Heald assigned this refusal as his excuse for expelling Irwin from the fort.[34]

Irwin's position was now perilous, so on July 5 he handed over the keys to the factory to the surgeon's mate and set out for Mackinac in an open boat, giving as his reason the need to hire an interpreter to replace the murdered LaLime. Irwin arrived at the island on July 16, only to be taken prisoner with the garrison the following day. Leaving Chicago saved Irwin's life. Van Voorhis, who had repeatedly requested transfer from the dysfunctional post, remained behind and perished with the garrison. Kinzie sent his clerk, Billy Caldwell,[35] to Vincennes to plead his case with Governor Harrison and fled to Milwaukee, where he sought protection from the Indians. Captain Heald soon announced, however, that the civil authorities had been given enough time to arrest Kinzie and sent an Indian runner to bring him back to Chicago. Whether because Kinzie really did have some secret power over him or because LaLime's death had left him in desperate need of an interpreter, Heald ordered that nobody was to molest Kinzie.[36]

On August 15, 1812, the garrison of Fort Dearborn, accompanied by civilian men, women, and children of the settlement, marched out of the fort and into a massacre. What was once known as the "Fort Dearborn massacre" has been the subject of a large secondary literature.[37] Nevertheless actual documentation of the event is unsatisfactory. Of the defeated whites, Captain Heald,[38] Lieutenant Helm,[39] Private James Corbin,[40] Private James Van Horne,[41] John Kinzie,[42] and Corporal Walter K. Jordan[43] left written firsthand accounts of the massacre. At one remove are the accounts of eyewitnesses as later remembered and recorded by third parties, after a lapse of time ranging from a few months to many decades. The witnesses whose recollections have been preserved in this manner include Isabella Cooper,[44] Susan Millhouse Simmons,[45] Sergeant William Griffith,[46] and an unidentified wounded soldier.[47] On the Indian side, the only thing resembling an eyewitness narrative is the reminiscence of half-blood chief Alexander Robinson, as related in 1866 to Dr. Lyman Draper.[48] The Indian viewpoint is also to some extent reflected by a letter of Lieutenant Thomas Hamilton relating an oral account of the massacre brought to him at Fort Madison by an unnamed Indian chief,[49] by Black Hawk's recollection of what he had heard about the affair from other Indians,[50] and by oral traditions preserved by Potawatomi Chief Simon Pokagon, whose father took part in the massacre.[51]

Unfortunately, the various accounts of the evacuation and massacre cannot be reconciled in detail. In the wake of the disaster, the animosity and division that had flourished at Fort Dearborn spilled over into score settling and the few primary sources are so contradictory as to leave many details forever in dispute. Nevertheless, the outlines of the story can be discerned. On August 9 Captain Heald received an order from General Hull directing him to evacuate Fort Dearborn and lead his command to Detroit. Heald was ordered to destroy unneeded arms and ammunition and authorized to dispose of goods in the U.S. Factory by giving them to any friendly Indians who might be willing to escort the garrison to Fort Wayne.[52]

The Indians learned of the order for evacuation as soon as Heald did, possibly from Winnemeg, the friendly chief who carried Hull's order to Chicago.[53] A large and growing crowd of Indians gathered around the fort, hoping to share in the distribution of goods. Most of them were Potawatomi, some from villages near Chicago and others from villages as remote as Milwaukee, southwestern Michigan, and Aux Sable Creek, near the present Morris, Illinois. Others came from Main Poc's new village at the Great Rapids on the Fox River, in the present Kendall County.[54] According to Heald, the Indians behaved "with perfect propriety" until after the garrison had left the fort.[55]

Heald was a soldier under a direct order from his commanding general, and he prepared to obey. Nevertheless, he has been plausibly criticized for delaying his march for seven days, during which time the crowd of Indians around the fort continued to grow. The Indian courier who brought Heald the message advised the captain to set out the next morning. Kinzie gave him the same advice, and, in light of the outcome, this view has received assent from subsequent historians.[56] Heald chose to delay, however, telling Kinzie that he was expecting an escort from Fort Wayne. Detroit was over 230 miles distant, Fort Wayne over 160. Even had it been possible to set out immediately, the refugees would probably have been some weeks on their route, plenty of time for hostile Indians to mass and attack. Heald may reasonably have preferred to remain long enough to purchase goodwill by a generous distribution of presents, while negotiating for an escort from the somewhat friendlier Indians who lived in the neighborhood of the fort.

On August 13, the expected escort from Fort Wayne arrived, in the form of Captain William Wells and a single noncommissioned officer leading about thirty nominally friendly Miami Indians. Wells was the uncle of Heald's wife Rebecca. He was also one of the most famous frontiersmen of his time. As a boy, Wells had been kidnapped by Indians and raised by the Miami tribe as one of their own. He took happily to the Indian life, marrying a relative, perhaps a niece or daughter, of the famous chief Little Turtle, who became Wells's lifelong friend. When the northwestern tribes defeated the armies of Generals Josiah Harmar and Arthur St. Clair, Wells fought alongside them in war paint, and at St. Clair's defeat he was said to have killed nine American soldiers with his own hand.[57]

Eventually, however, Wells returned to his own people. His thorough knowledge of the Indians made Wells invaluable to the frontier army. He served Anthony Wayne as captain of scouts in the campaign against his Indian friends that ended in the decisive battle of Fallen Timbers, although wounds received in a skirmish a few days earlier prevented Wells from fighting in that battle. Many tales were told of his courage and sagacity. After the war, Wells was appointed Indian agent at Fort Wayne, where his renewed friendship with Little Turtle was useful, but whether more useful to his country or to Wells

Figure 7. Captain
William Wells. Artist
unknown. Courtesy
of Chicago History
Museum.

himself is an open question. His record at Fort Wayne was at best ambiguous. Governor Harrison respected Wells's energy and abilities but also deeply distrusted him, suspecting Wells both of enriching himself though his office and of favoring the interests of the Indians against those of the government. At last in March 1812, Wells was dismissed as Indian agent by Secretary of War Eustis, thereafter lingering at Fort Wayne as an interpreter.[58]

After a council with the Indians, Heald ordered the goods of the shuttered U.S. Factory distributed among the Indians gathering in the neighborhood, in exchange for their promise of an escort to Fort Wayne. Excluded from the distribution, however, were gunpowder, ammunition, and whiskey. The Indians later claimed that Heald had promised that they would receive powder and ammunition, but such a promise seems unlikely, for Hull's order required Heald to destroy "all arms and ammunition."[59] Heald also ordered destruction of all the whiskey and ammunition held for sale by the firm of Kinzie & Forsyth. The ammunition was dumped into a well inside the fort, and the whiskey was poured either into the well or the nearby river. This work was performed secretly at night, and when Indians who heard the heads of barrels being stove in inquired about the cause, they were told that the garrison was simply opening provisions for the march.[60] Destruction of the ammunition and whiskey had a bad effect on the Indians, who were desperately short of gunpowder, a necessity for hunting, as well as for warfare.[61] Their anger and disappointment undoubtedly contributed to what followed.[62] Heald, however, always believed that had he distributed the whiskey and gunpowder to the Indians not a single member of his command would have escaped the tomahawk.[63]

The perennial claim that the junior officers opposed evacuation originated in Juliette Kinzie's vivid but unreliable chapters on the massacre in her book *Wau-Bun*. Heald's report, however, mentions no opposition to the evacuation, and his widow expressly denied that any of the officers had opposed evacuation. The only opposition, she stated, came from Kinzie, who stood to lose financially should the post be abandoned.[64] Significantly, Thomas Forsyth wrote shortly after the massacre that "Mr. K[inzie] with others advised the Commandant not to evacuate the place but poor Capt Wells was too sanguine," which certainly implies that Wells, at least, was in favor.[65] Recalling what his mother had told him, Heald's son later said that "Wells thought there would be difficulty, yet thought they might effect their escape, & strongly advised the attempt, saying the longer they remained the more Indians there would be to intercept them when they should start, as they would have to do when starved out."[66]

Whether Hull's order left the officers any room for discussion is uncertain. Heald's own account implies that Hull's order to evacuate was peremptory, but later accounts have claimed that the decision whether to evacuate had been left to Heald's discretion. The assertion derives from the statement in *Wau-Bun* that Hull's order required the garrison to evacuate only "if practicable," and Mrs. Kinzie's assertion can be traced to her brother-in-law, Helm, who used similar language order in his memoir of the massacre.[67] That version was long bolstered by Hull's own contemporaneous statements that he would leave the decision whether to evacuate to Heald's discretion.[68]

Nevertheless, the language of what purports to be Hull's original written order, preserved among Heald's papers, supports Heald's version.[69] Possibly Hull did intend to leave the decision to Heald, but his hastily scrawled order, on which the lives of nearly one hundred people depended, failed to carry such an intention into effect, a failure characteristic of Hull's incompetence as a general. This is true, however, only if the order is genuine. Helm tells a bizarre story of Kinzie's forging an order, with Heald's acquiescence, requiring destruction of the arms and ammunition at the fort, to replace Hull's order that all public property be turned over to the Indians. The surviving order is not in Hull's handwriting, but neither is it in Kinzie's or Heald's, and it is difficult to imagine either that Hull would have ordered arms and ammunition to be given to the Indians or that Heald would have imagined that a forged order would have been of any possible use had Hull later called him on the carpet for violating Hull's actual order.[70]

The survival of the order to evacuate is significant. The fort itself was burned, the soldiers' belongings were looted, and Heald himself was stripped of his uniform, yet this crucial order survived the wreck. Before the garrison marched out, Heald's wife had sewn money into the captain's undergarments, and after the battle this money helped them to reach safety at Mackinac. Hull's order could only have survived in the same way, and the fact that Heald also had this order, which would exonerate him if the evacuation turned out badly, sewn into his undergarments strongly supports its authenticity and suggests that, far from being recklessly insistent on evacuation, as he has so often been portrayed, the captain foresaw the possibility of disaster and carried out his orders with misgivings.[71]

Certainly misgivings were warranted. The Indians who surrounded the fort counseled throughout the day before the evacuation, deciding what action to take. The older chiefs, among them Black Partridge[72] and Topinebee,[73] opposed attacking the whites. Some of them, especially those who lived nearer the fort, may have had no particular love for Americans in general, but over the years had come to know those at Chicago personally. The chiefs had no authority to command obedience, however, and the decision was up to the 500 mostly Potawatomi warriors assembled near the fort. Leader of the hostile party was Nuscotnumeg, a brave of mixed Potawatomi and Chippewa blood from the Kankakee River band, who had already taken up the tomahawk.[74] He had been one of the murderers of the Cole party in Missouri and had fought against Harrison's army at Tippecanoe. Arguing that "Now's the time—we have them within our grasp; we must kill [th]em all," Nuscotnumeg carried the young men with him. Any doubt was removed when about sunset a belt of red wampum arrived from Main Poc at Malden, with a message announcing the retreat of Hull's army and urging an attack on the fort. The word of so celebrated a war chief tipped the scales. The braves began singing their war song, and decided to attack the troops on the morrow. The belt of red wampum they sent on to the Illinois River.[75]

Although Black Partridge was a famous warrior, he had been at peace with the whites since the battle of Fallen Timbers, in which he had fought.[76] Now, having failed to prevent the attack, the chief went to warn Captain Heald of what was to come. According to one story, the chief returned to Heald a medal presented to him by General Anthony Wayne, which he had long worn in token of his friendship for the Americans.[77] The surplus ammunition had already been destroyed, however, and most of the provisions had been given to the Indians. There was now no alternative but to go through with the planned evacuation and hope for the best.

The evacuation began at nine o'clock on the morning of August 15, 1812. A procession of about ninety-three Americans, soldier and civilian, passed slowly through the gates of the fort to begin the long journey toward Detroit. At the head of the party rode half of Wells's Miamis, and behind them those of the regulars who were well enough to march. Their total strength was about 55, but the sick list was long, and not all the regulars were able to do full duty. Behind them came the wagons, drawn by horses and oxen, carrying the sick, the women and children, and the provisions required for the journey. Guarding the wagons were the twelve militiamen of the little civilian community. Behind them as rearguard rode the other half of the friendly Miami warriors.[78]

Heald placed the wagons under the general supervision of Van Voorhis and John Kinzie. Kinzie's presence requires comment. Early on the morning of the evacuation, Kinzie's friend Topinebee had come to Kinzie's house to warn him of the impending attack. At the chief's suggestion, Kinzie placed his family and servants in a boat that would proceed by water to the mouth of the Saint Joseph River, where they would rendezvous with Kinzie and the column. After helping his family aboard, Kinzie himself, in an uncharacteristically selfless act, decided to march with the troops.[79]

Also in the procession rode Captain William Wells. A well-known version, derived from *Wau-Bun*, places him at the head of the column, with face blackened in token of impending death. Heald's report, though, placed Wells with the rearguard and Kinzie agreed. It seems to be true that he was dressed as an Indian and had blackened his face, but he had probably not done so because he expected to die, since Thomas Forsyth says the captain was "too sanguine" about the success of the march. His niece, Rebecca Heald, believed that Wells painted his face to disguise his identity, a not unlikely supposition. Wells was hated by many Indians as a turncoat and as Indian agent at Fort Wayne he had been a leading opponent of Tecumseh and the Prophet.[80]

The evacuation must have begun in eerie silence. The Potawatomi had promised an escort, but as the troops left the fort the Indians were nowhere to be seen. In fact the warriors waited massed behind sand hills about two miles south of the fort. Leaving the gates, the column proceeded slowly south along what is now Michigan Avenue but was then the lakeshore. To their right, 100 to 200 yards distant, was a line of sandbanks that hid the country beyond them from view.[81] After a distance variously estimated at between a half mile and two miles, but usually at a mile and a half, Heald's command was forced to halt. The location is usually identified as the area around the present Eighteenth Street and Prairie Avenue, but a persuasive case has also been made for the vicinity of Roosevelt Road and Michigan Avenue.[82]

The usual account has Wells riding back from his position in front, circling his hat around his head, as a sign that the party was surrounded, and warning Heald that the Indians were about to attack. If Wells was really riding with the rearguard, this version may not be strictly correct, but one Indian account said that Wells rode up to Heald from his position in the rear. The Indians were concealed by a sandbank to the column's right, but they now became visible all along the bank. Heald, perhaps urged by Wells, gave his troops the order to charge.[83]

Some of the criticisms that have been leveled against Captain Heald are unjust, but his order to charge the sandbank is hard to defend. Later historians have reasonably wondered why Heald did not mass his troops behind the wagons, with the lake at their backs, to defend themselves and the civilians until the Indians' fury was spent.[84] Instead, the regulars charged, scattering the Indians before them, but those driven off merely joined their fellows on the flanks in falling in behind the troops and separating them from the wagons that carried the women and children. Fighting was hand-to-hand. Sergeant Otho Hayes died in single combat with an Indian, piercing him with his bayonet as the Indian felled Hayes with his tomahawk. Ensign Ronan went down fighting, by all accounts with a determined courage that did honor to West Point.[85] Heald and Helm were both wounded, Heald seriously, and Helm slightly in the foot. Within ten or fifteen minutes no more than ten to twenty regulars were left in fighting condition. The firing slackened, however, and Heald led his surviving men farther west to a little hillock on the open prairie, out of range of the Indians' weapons, but also out of sight of the wagons.[86]

At the wagons, a horrifying scene was enacted. The militia and a few regulars had been detailed to guard the sick, the women, and the children. They had just enough time to fire a single volley, before the Indians were upon them. Having no time to reload, the men fought using their weapons as clubs,

Figure 8. Fort Dearborn Massacre. Artist: Samuel Page.
Courtesy of Chicago History Museum.

until all were cut down.[87] Among the dead was Van Voorhis.[88] The women fought just as bravely as the men, and two were killed, one Mrs. Heald's black servant, Cicely,[89] who perished with her infant son, and the other the pregnant wife of Private Fielding Corbin, who fought until she was cut to pieces. The unborn child was cut from her body, scalped, and beheaded.[90] Worst of all, a young warrior named Benac climbed into the wagon containing the younger children, killing twelve, and earning the lasting contempt of his tribe.[91] Among the children in the wagon was nine-year-old Isabella Cooper. As she later recalled, a young Indian pulled her from the wagon by her hair and would have tomahawked her, but she fought so hard, biting and scratching, that he was only able to take her scalp. An old Indian woman who had often visited in her house then intervened to save the girl's life.[92]

When the first shot was fired, Wells's Miami friends fled the field,[93] but Wells himself stayed to fight. At first, Wells fought with the troops, but at some point he broke away and galloped back toward the wagons, in an apparent attempt to defend the women and children. There are several versions of his death, impossible to reconcile, but the most trustworthy is probably that of his niece, Rebecca Heald, who was near him when he died.[94] As she told the story, Wells rode up to her, badly wounded, with blood flowing from his nose and mouth. His horse was also wounded and fell, briefly pinning the captain beneath it. Managing to free himself, Wells told his niece he could last only a few minutes and urged her to be brave. Now too weak to stand, he continued to fight, felling two more Indians with shots from his rifle and pistol. As more Indians charged him, Wells reloaded and brought down one more warrior. Then he quickly bade his niece good-bye, signaled to the advancing Indians to shoot, and redeemed a stormy and sometimes ambiguous life with a heroic death.[95] His body was dismembered, and his heart cut out and eaten, in tribute to his courage. Wells County, Indiana, and Wells Street in Chicago honor the captain's memory.[96]

Perhaps the best-known incident of that bloody day is the rescue of Margaret Helm, Kinzie's stepdaughter and Lieutenant Helm's wife, by Black Partridge, which provided the theme of the monument that for many years stood near the presumed site of the massacre. As the story is told in *Wau Bun*, as the fighting raged round her, the young woman was seized by a young warrior who tried to tomahawk her. She was struggling for his knife, when a powerful older Indian intervened and dragged her to the lake. At the lake the Indian held her head under water, but in such a way that she was still able to breathe. Mrs. Helm ceased struggling when she recognized the Indian as Black Partridge and understood that he had chosen this way to save her life.[97]

At the hill on the distant prairie, all firing had ceased. Most of Heald's men had been killed or wounded, leaving only ten men unharmed and no more than twenty in a condition to fight against the more than 500 Potawatomi warriors who surrounded them.[98] During the lull, the Indians signaled to Heald that they wanted a parley, and the captain walked out onto the prairie alone.[99] He was met by Black Bird and an interpreter, a young man named Pierre (or Peresh) LeClerc, who was half French and half Potawatomi.[100] Black Bird was a war chief of Pepper's band of Potawatomi, whose village stood a few miles east of the present Morris, near where Aux Sable Creek empties into the Illinois River.[101] After Heald and Black Bird shook hands, Black Bird promised the captain that if the troops surrendered, the lives of the prisoners would be spared. Heald didn't fully trust the promise, but he saw no alternative. After a few moments' consideration, he handed over his sword and ordered his men to lay down their arms.[102]

Now prisoners, the soldiers were marched by their captors back toward the beach, where a shocking sight met their eyes. In Helm's words: "When we arrived at the bank and looked down on the sand beach I was struck with

Figure 9. Fort Dearborn Massacre Monument, formerly at 18th and
Calumet Streets, Chicago. Sculptor: Carl Rohl-Smith. Courtesy of
Chicago History Museum.

horror at the sight of men, women, and children lying naked with principally
all their heads off."[103] Helm broke into tears at what he thought was the body
of his wife lying with her head separated from her body. He was mistaken;
Black Partridge had saved her life, and the body Helm saw must have been
that of Mrs. Corbin. Every male civilian but Kinzie and a badly wounded
Thomas Burns had been killed, as well as two women and twelve children.
Of the fifty-five soldiers, twenty-six had died in the battle, including Ronan

and Van Voorhis.[104] As usual, the Indian loss is impossible to determine, but it was certainly much lower than that of the Americans.[105]

Despite Black Bird's promise to Heald, worse was to come for many of the survivors, especially the wounded. Most of the prisoners were divided among the warriors present. Prisoners taken in good condition had value as slaves, with the prospect of a reward to be gained from eventual ransom. The wounded, especially those likely to die before they could be ransomed, had no such value and would merely impose a burden. About an hour after the surrender, an enraged Indian woman killed the wounded Burns with a pitchfork. As many as seven soldiers, some wounded and some not, were killed soon after the surrender, either by the tomahawk or by less merciful means.[106]

The day after the battle, the triumphant Indians burned the fort.[107] Through the help of Chandonnai, a friendly Indian, Heald and his wife, both severely wounded, were first taken to the mouth of the Saint Joseph River and then, accompanied by Sergeant Griffith, permitted to "escape." Alexander Robinson took them by canoe to Mackinac, where Captain Roberts, a brother Freemason, received them kindly and released them on parole. The Healds went next to Detroit, where British colonel Henry Procter sent them on to Buffalo.[108] Helm was separated from his wife and taken to the Potawatomi village at the mouth of Aux Sable Creek, where the following month trader Thomas Forsyth, his father-in-law's half-brother, ransomed him and took him to safety in Saint Louis.[109]

Kinzie had marched among the militia who guarded the wagons. Although he afterwards claimed to have carried a musket, it is unlikely that he fired it, for while every other white man at the wagons was butchered, Kinzie came through the battle without a scratch. According to his own account, he surrendered his weapon to a friendly warrior who saved his life.[110] Kinzie was then returned to his cabin across the river from the fort and reunited with his family. Over the next few days, Black Partridge, Waubansee, and other friendly Indians remained at the Kinzie home to protect the family. At one point they were in great danger, when some black-painted warriors from the Wabash appeared at the house. These warriors had arrived too late for the battle, and because of the distance they lived from Chicago, they did not know Kinzie. They were in an ugly mood and would have killed the family without hesitation, but the friendly chiefs succeeded in buying them off and sending them on their way. According to a later story, not mentioned by Kinzie himself, it was only the chance arrival of his half-blood clerk Billy Caldwell that saved the family from massacre on this occasion. After a period of time, the Kinzies were permitted to travel to Detroit.[111]

The lot of the enlisted men and civilians was much harder. After being divided among the victors, the whites were taken on forced marches to their captors' home villages, often far away. Those who could not keep up the pace were killed.[112] Many, though not all, were subjected to abuse and deprivation, women and children not excepted. Susan Simmons had lost her husband and young son in the massacre. Afterwards she and her infant daughter fell prisoner to a band from the Green Bay area. On the return march, they came to a village where the prisoners were forced to run the gantlet. Mrs. Simmons carried her baby, wrapped in a blanket and clutched to her breast, as with head bowed she ran between two lines of Indians raining blows upon her with fists, sticks, and clubs. Mother and daughter survived the ordeal, the daughter living until 1900, the last survivor of the massacre.[113] Less fortunate were the family of John Needs, a private soldier. Needs himself died in captivity in January 1813 and, to keep his child from crying from hunger, the Indians tied it to a tree and left it to die from starvation or to be eaten by wolves. The unhappy mother herself died soon afterwards, worn out by the cumulative effects of cold, hunger, and misery, or, according to another account, of exposure from being tied outdoors to a tree on a freezing January night.[114]

Thomas Forsyth, regarded by the Indians and by some Americans as a British trader, but secretly an agent of the U.S. government, visited the Potawatomi village on the Aux Sable in April 1813. He found several captives from the garrison of Fort Dearborn held there, and from them he learned of the cruel conditions under which some of the prisoners had perished.[115] On his return to Saint Louis, Forsyth tried to interest the authorities there in ransoming the prisoners: "I dont know but it might be done from this place [Saint Louis] if Goods and Whisky could be collected for that purpose; I myself made the offer to go up on my return from that place (River aux Sable) if the necessary articles were given me to purchase them from the Indians but as no person appeared to interest themselves for the poor prisoners and I not having the means myself, those poor creatures are doomed to remain in slavery and god Knows if one of them will be able to live over another winter."[116]

Those of the prisoners who did survive captivity had their British enemies to thank. The British had had no advance warning of the attack at Chicago. Always ambivalent about the alliance with the Indians, General Isaac Brock had instructed his officers to use "all prudent and proper means" to protect both

British and American settlers from "the depredations and lawless violence of the Indians." After the surrender of Detroit, but before he knew Fort Dearborn had fallen, Brock gave instructions to seek the surrender of the fort for the express purpose of saving the lives of its garrison.[117] Although from first report the British believed all the Americans except Kinzie and the Healds to have been killed, they soon learned the truth. By early October American judge Augustus Woodward was able to provide Colonel Procter, now commanding British forces at Detroit, with a reasonably accurate list of those still prisoners. Procter promised Woodward to do whatever he could to secure the speedy release of the prisoners and ordered the Indian Department to instruct the chiefs to have the prisoners brought to him at Detroit.[118] Unfortunately, most of the prisoners were held by tribes who were far from Detroit and with whom the British had little influence. The prisoners continued in harsh captivity, and additional lives were lost.

The prisoners' fortunes improved in late winter when Robert Dickson arrived on the scene. After taking part in the capture of Mackinac, Dickson had gone to Lower Canada where Sir George Prevost had accepted Dickson's plan for gaining the alliance of the western Indians and sent him west with commissions as agent and superintendent. Dickson's instructions required him to restrain allied Indians from "acts of cruelty and inhumanity," an order very much in accord with Dickson's own inclinations. On March 16, 1813, Dickson was able to report from Saint Joseph River on Lake Michigan that from the garrison of Fort Dearborn seventeen soldiers, four women, and some children remained in the hands of the Indians, adding "I have taken the necessary steps for their redemption and have fullest confidence I shall succeed in getting the whole."[119]

Dickson's primary mission, however, was to raise an Indian army for the defense of Canada, and he had to hurry on to visit all the tribes west of Lake Michigan. To carry out the redemption, Dickson selected Louis Buisson[120] and François DuPin, also known as "Le Moyne."[121] These men were "British" traders from Peoria, who had wintered at Chicago in the abandoned house of John Kinzie. They were equipped with trade goods from Mackinac and were instructed to send to Mackinac or Malden such of the prisoners as they were able to ransom. By the summer of 1813 they were able to ransom at least the nine captive soldiers later released at Plattsburg, New York.[122] They also succeeded in effecting the release of two women prisoners, one of them Mrs. Lee, whom DuPin subsequently married.[123] Still mysterious is the case of little

Peter Bell, purchased from the Indians by a trader and brought to Mackinac in July 1813 on the orders of Robert Dickson. He was described as a boy of five or six years, "whose Father and mother were killed at Chicagoe." Nobody else named Bell is known to have been involved in the massacre, however, and possibly Peter was instead the small boy kidnapped from the Huffman family, near Charlestown, Indiana, in March 1813. Who exactly young Peter was, and what became of him afterwards, remains a mystery.[124]

With the collapse of the American position on the western Great Lakes, the Indians saw their opportunity. September 4 and 5 brought Indian attacks on the three nearest inland posts: Forts Harrison, Madison, and Wayne. Nearly simultaneous attacks by different tribes on three such widely separated forts cannot have been mere coincidence; it is tempting to imagine the hand of Tecumseh behind them.[125]

Fort Harrison, near the present Terre Haute, was a small post commanded by Captain Zachary Taylor. Sickness had reduced the garrison to only ten or fifteen fully effective men.[126] On the night of September 4–5 the fort was attacked by Winnebago and Miami warriors. They actually succeeded in burning one of the blockhouses, but Taylor, displaying the courage and resourcefulness that would eventually carry him to the White House, filled the gap in the walls with an improvised breastwork and managed to hold the fort until relieved on September 13 by a force Colonel Russell led from Vincennes.[127]

Fort Madison stood on the site of the present Iowa city of the same name.[128] The fort was poorly situated for defense, almost surrounded by ravines that offered cover to attackers, and overlooked by a ridge from which almost any part of the parade ground was vulnerable. In command was Lieutenant Thomas Hamilton, one of the officers the War Department had previously removed from Fort Dearborn in an attempt to quell the dissension at that post.[129] On the morning of September 5, while the battle was raging in faraway Indiana, Winnebago Indians began an attack on the fort that kept the garrison pinned down for three days. The Indians burnt most of the outbuildings around the fort, destroyed the hayfields, and shot the cattle. They tried to burn the fort itself with flaming arrows, but Hamilton and his men managed to keep the roofs damp. By September 9, the Indians had run out of ammunition and departed, but Hamilton, disgusted with the location of the fort, wrote that unless measures were taken by November 15 to render the lives of his men more secure, he would evacuate the garrison on his own authority.[130]

The tribes around Fort Wayne had long appeared friendly, but on the evening of September 4, Indians warned Captain James Rhea[131] that Mackinac, Detroit, and Chicago had fallen, and that Fort Wayne would be next. The fort was well prepared to resist, but Captain Rhea doubted that he could hold out, and when the attack began the next day, he sought refuge in the bottle. The defense was led with great gallantry by Lieutenant Philip Ostrander[132] and Ensign Daniel Curtis,[133] who confined their captain to quarters, "drunk as a fool," and relieved him of command. The fort was kept under fire for five days, and the besiegers even made cannon out of hollow logs, wrapped round with steel bands, but the logs exploded when the Indians touched off the powder.[134]

While the siege continued, two armies raced toward the fort. One was a relief column commanded by General William Henry Harrison. The other was a force of 200 British regulars and 1,000 Indians, including Main Poc, under the command of Major Adam Muir, which Procter had dispatched less to help the Indians than to restrain them from massacring the garrison if the fort should fall.[135] Harrison reached Fort Wayne first. Learning of Harrison's approach, the Indians ceased firing on September 10, and two days later they were seen running from the field, just before the arrival of Harrison's advance guard.[136] Because Harrison's army was much superior in numbers, Muir's British force returned to Malden.[137]

The attack in Illinois territory was slower getting underway, possibly because some of the chiefs, such as Gomo and Pemwatome, had been dragged into war against their wishes. At the beginning of September, the Illinois River Indians received tobacco from Main Poc, along with his message that Detroit had fallen, and on September 7 Gomo and Shequenebec[138] set out to attack the settlements. Shequenebec was heard to say that "the Great Spirit will deliver him a fort." Even Black Partridge, who had done what he could to prevent the massacre at Chicago, joined in the raid. The ranks of the raiders were increased by the addition of Kickapoo and Piankashaw warriors, as well as Potawatomi from Fox River, Aux Sable Creek, and even Milwaukee, until at last 400 warriors set off in canoes down the Illinois River. From Peoria, Thomas Forsyth, who was being watched by the Indians, still managed to smuggle a warning to Howard, adding "It is impossible to tell what place this party will attack, as they don't know themselves until they get off."[139]

Illinois Territory was thinly defended. Governor Edwards's repeated warnings that the territory was the most exposed on the frontier and needed federal troops had in fact, caused him to be regarded as an alarmist.[140] What little outside assistance had been sent to the territory had been withdrawn or diverted. In August, Colonel William Russell had been sent to Illinois and had established Fort Russell, but by the end of the month General Harrison had ordered him back to Vincennes. Behind him in Illinois, Colonel Russell left only a handful of regulars, commanded by Lieutenants Ramsey and Todd, who refused to obey the governor's orders unless directed to do so by Russell.[141] In response to Edwards's request, Governor Isaac Shelby had ordered a regiment of Kentucky militia under Colonel Philip Barbour to rendezvous at Red Banks (now Henderson, Kentucky), preparatory to marching to Kaskaskia. Without Shelby's knowledge, and to his great disgust, acting governor John Gibson of Indiana contacted Barbour directly and succeeded in diverting the regiment to Vincennes.[142]

Fortunately Edwards had the willing cooperation of Governor Howard of Missouri. An invasion down the Illinois River would threaten both territories, and in fact, advance elements of the Indian force reached the frontier around Portage des Sioux, Missouri Territory, where they wounded a man and woman, stole some horses, killed a cow and carried off the beef. Edwards had already called three of his four regiments of militia into service and had them ranging the frontiers.[143] Now Howard came to his aid, sending armed boats under Captains Risdon H. Price[144] and Musick (first name uncertain)[145] up the Illinois River. The boat encountered a fleet of canoes that fled back upriver with Price's boat in pursuit. Followed closely, the Indians abandoned eight of their canoes, including the one carrying the stolen beef, escaping when low water prevented Price's boat from going farther.[146] In an effort to intercept the fleeing warriors, Howard ordered 200 Missouri militiamen under Major Henry Dodge[147] to cross the river into Illinois "high up," presumably into the present Pike or Adams county, but the Indians had already escaped up the Illinois River and Dodge and his men returned to Missouri without having accomplished anything.[148]

To avoid the American gunboats, the main invasion force had left the river not far below Peoria and proceeded by land. Gomo and his warriors later claimed that they could have killed a number of ranging militiamen, who passed by Indians lying hidden in the bushes and tall grass, but they had held their fire for fear of alarming the country. Approaching the mouth of the Illinois River, probably in what is now Calhoun County, the war party stopped to decide what to do next. One party, led by Shequenebec and Eshkeebee, boasted that they would cross the Illinois River, hunt up Captain Whiteside of the Illinois Rangers, and bring home his head. Another, led by Black Partridge, resolved to go out the mouth of the river, cross the Mississippi, and attack the district of Saint Charles. The next morning, however, some young warriors out hunting ran into a party of Missouri Rangers who had crossed into Illinois on a scout. One of the Indians was killed and one wounded, and the others fled back to tell the main body that they had been discovered. Having lost the advantage of surprise, the war party fled back upriver, traveling day and night till they arrived at Peoria, almost worn down by hard traveling. They had accomplished nothing except the theft of a few horses.[149]

Nevertheless, smaller war parties continued to threaten the Illinois frontier. On September 9, the inhabitants of Fort Allison (the present Russellville, Illinois) on the Wabash appealed for aid from Governor Gibson of Indiana, and on September 21 hostile Indians, probably returning from the siege of Fort Harrison, burnt down empty Fort LaMotte (at the present Palestine, Illinois), whose defenders had abandoned it.[150] One of the most exposed forts on the frontier was Hill's Fort, near Shoal Creek, not far south of the present Greenville.[151] On October 2, one day after Edwards had reinforced the fort, a war party attacked. Moments earlier, a soldier named Lindley had gone outside the fort to feed his horses, leaving the gate open. The Indians rushed the gate, but the defenders managed to close it in their faces. Lindley, left outside the walls with the Indians, saved himself by clinging to the belly of an ox in a herd left grazing outside. The attackers tried to tear down the pickets and punched a hole through the wall of a blockhouse, through which they wounded one or two men. They then disappeared with eight stolen horses, but blood found on the ground outside the fort suggested that the Indians had also suffered in the fight.[152]

October also brought the Pond Settlement massacre. John Pond and his family had settled a clearing in what is now Indian Creek Township in the southwestern corner of White County. Returning home one night from assisting in a cabin-raising, Pond found his wife dead in the cabin, and his two young sons lying outside, one dead and one left for dead. All had been scalped. The next day Pond, with two neighbors named Pearce and Trousdale, went up the Wabash in search of the murderers, three Piankashaw Indians whom three days later they surprised in the bottoms along Coffee Creek. Two Indians were killed, but the third escaped up the creek where his tracks were lost. Pond and his friends returned home with the scalps of the family recovered.[153]

Neither Whiteside's company of U.S. Rangers nor the Illinois volunteers had been paid a cent for their services, but Edwards kept his exhausted troops in motion, almost constantly in the woods, patrolling from blockhouse to blockhouse.[154] The energy the Indians had gained from their victory at Chicago dissipated with the failure of their offensive. They would not have long to wait for a response.

FIVE

Peoria

As the Indians' offensive of August and September 1812 stalled and re-
ceded, Governor Ninian Edwards began to prepare a counterstroke.
The natural target was Peoria, where hostile Indians—Kickapoo,
Potawatomi, and Piankashaw—were gathered in large numbers, and from
which they had just launched their abortive raid on the settlements. Lack-
ing assistance from outside the territory, Edwards would have to rely on the
territory's own resources, which were very slender. The governor estimated
that there were no more than 2000 adult white males scattered between the
Mississippi and the Wabash, while more than 1000 Indian warriors could
assemble at Peoria within a matter of days. None of the militiamen who had
defended the territory during the spring and summer had been paid, and to
obtain volunteers, Edwards was forced to pledge his own resources to guarantee payment.[1]

Nevertheless, Edwards was able to muster a force of more than 300 men.
His senior officers included many of the most able men in the territory, beginning with Nathaniel Pope, the territorial secretary. Benjamin Stephenson acted
as brigade major, and three of the gallant, but ill-fated, Rector brothers, William,
Elias, and Nelson, served on the governor's staff.[2] Edwards divided his force

into two small regiments, one commanded by Benjamin Stephenson as colonel and the other by one of the Rectors. John Moredock served as a major.[3]

Stephenson was a close ally of Governor Edwards, who had invited him from Kentucky to serve as sheriff of Randolph County. His service in the war would eventually help Stephenson secure election as territorial delegate to the Thirteenth and Fourteenth Congresses and as a member of the convention that drafted Illinois's first state constitution in 1818. Stephenson County perpetuates his memory.[4]

The three Rector brothers who served on the campaign as part of the governor's staff were among nine brothers and four sisters who had been born in Fauquier County, Virginia, and migrated to Kaskaskia about 1806. All or most of the brothers were surveyors, and between them they laid out the section lines over much of southern Illinois, Missouri, and Arkansas. All nine brothers stood at least six feet tall and weighed at least 200 pounds. All of them laughed at danger. John Reynolds, who knew them, described the brothers' passionate and impulsive natures, calling them "the most fearless and undaunted people I ever knew."[5]

William was the head of the family.[6] In 1811 he was appointed brigadier general of the territorial militia. Ninian Edwards recommended Rector for the post, saying that "to a modest gentlemanly and unassuming deportment . . . he unites an integrity universally acknowledged—a sound discriminating mind & a dauntless intrepidity." In October 1813 William would resign as brigadier after moving to Saint Louis to accept appointment as principal deputy surveyor for Missouri Territory.[7] Elias served the territory as adjutant general and later as clerk of the chancery court of Randolph County until October 1813, when he, too, would resign and follow his older brother to Saint Louis.[8] Nelson held no official position at the time, but he was always ready for any dangerous enterprise. As a surveyor he was accustomed to working beyond the settlements in Indian country, where it was often difficult to get a crew to follow him. A year earlier Nelson had accompanied Captain Samuel Levering on his mission to the Potawatomi, and he now served on the governor's staff as a volunteer.[9]

Major John Moredock was the only man in the territory whose renown as an Indian fighter equaled, and perhaps eclipsed, that of the Whiteside family. He was famous for his unrelenting hatred of the Indians. The traditional explanation for his passion was that as a boy, hiding in the rocks, Moredock had watched a band of Indians butcher his mother and family, after their boat touched land at what is now Grand Tower, Illinois.[10] Although this story has been shown to be fiction, the reality was bad enough. On separate occasions Moredock's father, mother, and two stepfathers were killed by Indians. Even after he had tracked and killed those he believed to be the murderers of his mother, Moredock vowed never to pass up a chance to kill an Indian.[11]

His obsessive thirst for Indian blood contrasted strangely with Moredock's manner among the whites. Although not well educated, he was credited with a vigorous intellect. A handsome man, Moredock spoke French and played the violin well and was at the same time an expert horseman and marksman. His varied talents and affability made him popular among his neighbors in what is now Monroe County, leading them to send him as their representative to the first territorial legislatures of both Indiana and Illinois. He was in fact mentioned for governor when Illinois attained statehood, but he declined to seek the honor. In his later years, he fell prey to dissipation, especially gambling, but at his death in 1830 Moredock was sincerely mourned. Moredock Lake, near his home in Monroe County, preserves his memory, but the legislature thought better of proposals to name the new counties of Cass and Saline in Moredock's honor.[12]

The company of Rangers that Congress had authorized for Illinois Territory formed part of Edwards's force and was commanded by Captain William Bolin Whiteside. Riding alongside the Rangers were at least five companies of territorial militia, commanded by Captains James B. Moore, Jacob Short, Samuel Whiteside,[13] Willis Hargrave,[14] and Nathaniel Journey.[15] The army was led by a company of "spies," or scouts, commanded by Captain Samuel Judy.[16] Two future Illinois governors rode as privates in the ranks.

To protect the settlements in his absence, Edwards detailed the company of Captain Absolem Cox of Randolph County, strengthened by additional troops detached from other militia companies.[17] Also in service between October 14 and November 5 was a company commanded by Captain Dudley Williams, not mentioned in any account of the expedition and so probably left behind on the same service as Cox's.[18]

Shortly before the army was to set out, Edwards received a message from Major General Samuel Hopkins, commanding Kentucky volunteers at Vincennes, telling him that Hopkins was about to march, while neglecting to mention the intended destination. The message also offered Edwards aid, but with the end of the campaigning season fast approaching, Edwards had to march quickly, if he was to march at all.[19] Any doubt was resolved when

Colonel William Russell arrived from Vincennes with parts of two companies
of regulars, totaling about 50 men. Russell told the governor that Hopkins was
planning to lead a force of 2,000 mounted men across the prairies against the
Indian towns near Peoria. The news opened the prospect of a two-pronged
campaign that could sweep the Illinois River valley clear of hostile Indians.
Pleased to have the assistance of such a renowned Indian fighter, Edwards
offered Russell the position of second in command and incorporated his men
into the little army, bringing the total to 360 privates plus officers.[20]

Edwards's men were traveling light, without baggage wagons, and few, if
any, pack horses, so each man would be dependent on what food and ammunition he could carry with him. Hopkins's men were carrying only ten days'
provisions and so could be expected to reach Peoria in short supply. Accordingly, Edwards ordered two boats—one armed and fortified, and the other
carrying tools and provisions—to ascend the Illinois River to meet the two
armies when they converged at Peoria.[21]

Edwards and his army set out from Fort Russell on October 18, 1812. The
governor's later report to the War Department gave only the most meager indication of his route, and Russell's laconic correspondence is less helpful still.[22]
The army had ridden across largely unexplored prairies, with few established
landmarks, perhaps making it difficult for either man to describe clearly the
route the army had taken. Fortunately, their official reports are supplemented,
and occasionally contradicted, by the memoir of John Reynolds, later governor
of Illinois and still later a historian, who rode as a young private in Captain
Judy's company of spies.[23]

Leaving Fort Russell, the army traveled up the west side of Cahokia Creek,
following the creek almost to its source, and presumably passing somewhere
between the present cities of Litchfield and Gillespie. Edwards and his troops
thus became the first white men known to have set foot in Macoupin County.
They crossed Macoupin Creek not far from the present Carlinville and continued north, crossing the Sangamon River somewhere east of where Springfield
now lies. The army continued into the present Logan County, passing to the
east of Elkhart Hill, then, as now, an unmistakable landmark.[24]

Crossing Logan County, Edwards and Russell came upon two deserted
villages of the Kickapoo tribe, on what was then called the Saline Fork of the
Sangamon River, but is now known as Salt Creek. There the soldiers found
samples of native artwork, depicting Indians scalping whites, and burned both
villages to the ground.[25]

Fearing that the flames would alert the Indians, Edwards and Russell led their troops on a forced march that lasted until midnight. Their route across the present Tazewell County has been conjectured to have passed through the eastern tier of townships before turning northwest to enter Washington Township somewhere near the middle of its southern boundary.[26] Four or five miles from the Indian village, the exhausted army at last made camp. No fires were allowed, and the soldiers, sulky and sullen, slept in their clothes, clutching their weapons. Their horses were kept saddled near at hand. While most of the army took a short sleep, interrupted once by the accidental firing of a soldier's gun, four volunteers set out to reconnoiter the town. One of those volunteers was Thomas Carlin, later governor of Illinois.[27] The scouts reached the village and returned safely to report to the governor that the army was so far undiscovered.

The village the little army was about to attack was a large one, recently established at the head of Peoria Lake, inhabited by Kickapoo and "Miami" Indians probably led by Pemwatome.[28] Pemwatome was a hostile chief, albeit a reluctant one. The Indians Edwards called Miami were Piankashaw.[29] The village sat at the base of the river bluff, probably near or along Richland Creek, separated from the Illinois River by three miles of bottomland that was so wet and swampy as to be all but impassable.[30] In 1954, a monument to the village was erected in Partridge Township, Woodford County. Although the monument's inscription wrongly identifies the location as "Black Partridge's Village," it does probably stand at, or reasonably near, the site of the Kickapoo village Edwards and Russell attacked early in the battle.[31]

At dawn the army moved out, with Captain Judy's company of spies in the lead. Before reaching the village, however, Judy's men surprised two mounted Indians, who immediately tried to surrender. According to Reynolds, who rode as a private in the company, the soldiers called on the captain to spare the Indians, but saying that he did not leave home to take prisoners, Judy raised his rifle and fired. As the bullet entered his body, the first Indian raised his rifle and fired a shot of his own. Most of the soldiers had taken cover behind their horses, but the Indian's bullet struck Tolliver Wright in the groin, dealing him a wound that afterwards proved to be mortal.[32] Many guns snapped at the surviving Indian, but all misfired. Only then did the second Indian's cries reveal her to be a woman, and her life was spared.

This ugly story apparently embarrassed the authors of the 1879 *History of Jackson County*. Without citing any authority except Judy's known good character, they claimed that Reynolds's memory was in error, that Judy's company took both Indians prisoner, and that it was only later that the man was shot by other soldiers, while he was attempting to escape. Many years after the event, however, Nehemiah Matson questioned the aged Samuel Whiteside about the incident and, while declining to repeat what Whiteside had told him, Matson plainly implied that Whiteside had essentially confirmed Reynolds's account.[33]

The advantage of surprise had been lost. As the army advanced toward the village, Reynolds could see Indians moving in the trees across a muddy creek. The troops expected an attack, but the Indians held their fire, and the army reached the top of the bluff without a fight. Edwards had planned to attack directly down the hill, but his guides accidentally led him to the bottomlands about three quarters of a mile below the village. By now, "considerable numbers of Indians" were seen running from the village, and at first Edwards thought they were forming for battle. The governor led the center of his army directly for them, ordering his right wing to turn their flank and his left to cut off the Indians' escape to the river. Almost immediately, though, Edwards saw that the Indians were running toward the river, in a direction perpendicular to his own line of march.[34]

As Edwards ordered his men to charge, the fleeing Indians scattered into the broad swamp that lay between the town and the Illinois River. It was impossible to hold the men back, and they rode their horses straight into a swamp choked with cattails and brush. Many of the horses went down; as Reynolds sailed over his own horse's head into the mire he saw the governor near him floundering in a mud hole, horse and rider finally emerging black with mud. The swamp saved the Indians. Abandoning their horses, and led by Captain Samuel Whiteside, the troops followed on foot, up to the waist in mud and water. Some of the fugitives were killed, both in the swamp and at the river, but most of the Indians escaped up the river or crossed to Gomo's village on the opposite bank. The fight was sharp; Moore's company was in the thick of it, and three bullets pierced the captain's clothing. At one point the fleeing Indians rallied and drove back their pursuers, but Edwards sent reinforcements who scattered them again. Caught up in the chase, three eager Rangers swam the river and returned safely with captured canoes and the bodies of some Indians who had been killed in them.[35]

In the meantime, other soldiers had proceeded three miles downriver to destroy a Potawatomi village on the riverbank, perhaps near the mouth of what is now Partridge Creek. Presumably the residents had already fled, for there is no contemporary mention of any fighting. Reynolds did not mention this village, while Edwards said only that it was the village of Shequenebec and that it was burned.[36] Tradition, though, identifies the Potawatomi village Edwards's men destroyed as the village of Black Partridge, and Matson gives a rather too highly colored portrait of the devastation that the chief encountered when he returned to his village after the attack.[37]

What happened at the village or villages when the troops entered is disputed.

The *Missouri Gazette* praised the soldiers' "clemency" in sparing "hundreds" of women and children found squatting in the tall grass.[38] Matson gives a different picture. Although he wrote years after the fact, and relied on oral sources, his source in this instance was the aged Samuel Whiteside, who had taken part in the battle and whose entire life acquits him of any suspicion of undue partiality to the Indians: "The rangers pushed forward in great haste, shooting down squaws and papooses, as they fled panic-stricken from their homes. But little resistance was made by the Indians, who fled up the river, leaving behind them their ponies, camp equipage, and everything valuable. Some of the Indians, being badly wounded, were unable to make their escape; these, together with a number of small children, were butchered in cold blood."[39]

There were some saving instances of humanity. Hearing firing in a distant part of the swamp, Abraham Pruitt, a soldier of Madison County, found a six-year-old Indian girl, abandoned by her family, mired in the swamp. Two of Pruitt's fellow soldiers were using the child for target practice, but had so far been unable to hit her. Pruitt denounced the two as cowards, extricated the girl, and set her on his horse behind him. He brought the girl home and raised her in his own household, until at the age of sixteen she died and was buried in the same pioneer graveyard that holds the victims of the Wood River Massacre. According to Reynolds, some other children found in the ruined village were spared, and an Indian brave, too badly wounded to flee, was fed and protected by the soldiers, although a straggler murdered him after the army had moved on.[40]

Edwards and Russell had dealt the Indians a sharp blow. A large flourishing town of the Kickapoo and a smaller one of the Potawatomi had been burnt to the ground, but more important, an immense quantity of plunder had been seized and destroyed: over 1,000 bushels of corn, a "prodigious quantity" of beans, dried meat, pumpkins, furs, tallow, and peltry. A hungry winter loomed for the tribes. In addition, the army seized eighty horses, some of them recently stolen from Saint Clair County, 200 brass kettles, silver ornaments, guns, flint, and bags of gunpowder, and the army destroyed whatever it could not carry away. Also found in the village were six white scalps, believed to have been taken from women and children of the O'Neal family in Missouri.[41] From the number of bodies recovered, Edwards initially estimated that between twenty and thirty Indians had been killed, although later information he received from the Indians themselves led him to revise the estimate, including those dead of wounds, first to between forty and fifty-two, and eventually to eighty among the Kickapoo alone. Four prisoners were taken. Four of the attackers had been wounded, two seriously: Tolliver Wright, who later died, and John Teeter, a private in Samuel Whiteside's company, who, it was feared, would permanently lose the use of an arm.[42]

Edwards and Russell had to decide what to do next. There was no sign of Hopkins and his Kentuckians, and no certainty that they would ever arrive. Captain Craig's boats of troops and supplies were proceeding up the Illinois River, but Edwards and Russell decided not to wait. They knew that if they tarried too long, the tribes might rally and in a few days could outnumber their little force by three to one. Accordingly, the next day Edwards sent a detachment to the village of Peoria to leave a message telling the boats to return. The detachment found a small village of Miami, probably Piankashaw, which had recently been built within a half-mile of Peoria. This they burnt, before rejoining the main army. It was perhaps during this delay that Edwards's men saw a solitary Indian walking down the bluff toward them. About two hundred yards from the troops he fired his gun, laughed loud and scornfully, and then slowly walked away. Men sent in pursuit could not find him. Later legend has identified this Indian with Black Partridge himself.[43]

The victorious army then returned to Fort Russell "with all convenient speed," in Reynolds's phrase. The first day of the march home was miserable. The army rode along the top of the bluffs in a torrential rain, dreading a counterattack every step of the way. By the time the officers called a halt after dark, many of the exhausted men simply lay down to sleep in the trampled mud, without food, fire, or drinking water. The next day was better: the rain stopped, fires were lit, guns were fired and reloaded, and the army got underway on time and in good order. No Indians appeared on the way back. On October 31, after a tour of thirteen days, Edwards's little army arrived back at Fort Russell, where it was greeted by the boom of the fort's antique cannon.[44] On November 10 Edwards discharged his troops with thanks and praise and afterwards reported to Secretary of War William Eustis that "The conduct of both the men and officers under my command was highly honorable to themselves and useful to our country."[45]

The raid had been a modest success.[46] Edwards and Russell deserve credit for having taken an Indian village by surprise, a feat rarely, if ever, to be repeated during the war. Their destruction of Indian supplies threatened the Kickapoo, always living near subsistence level, with starvation. The demonstration to the Indians of the Americans' long arm may have had some cautionary effect, although after the raid the Potawatomi moved their villages farther up the Illinois and the Kickapoo for a time joined the Sauk on the distant Rock River. These were places the whites could not reach, but which could still serve as bases for small war parties raiding the settlements.[47] It has been claimed, notably by Matson, that the brutality of the raid alienated Black Partridge and other chiefs and caused them to throw in their lot with the British, but this is quite incorrect.[48] The Kickapoo had long been hostile, as the white scalps found in their village attested, and Black Partridge, Gomo, Shequenebec, and other ostensibly friendly Potawatomi chiefs had been the leaders of the unsuccessful raid down the Illinois River the month before Edwards's troops had marched.

By the time Edwards and Russell had been on the trail for two days, the army they were marching to meet was streaming back toward Vincennes, an army no more. The fiasco had begun with high hopes. When Governor Isaac Shelby of Kentucky had called on his citizens to ride to the aid of Illinois and Indiana territories, so many had come forward that Shelby had to send hundreds of disappointed volunteers back to their homes.[49] For days the governor posted himself at Louisville, dispatching volunteers in companies and detachments across the Ohio River, toward the assembly point at Vincennes. Shelby called these mounted volunteers "the flower of Kentucky," including "the most respectable citizens that perhaps ever were embodied from this or any other State." To command them, the governor appointed Major General Samuel Hopkins, a member of the state senate of Kentucky.[50]

The appointment was a plausible one. As a staff officer for Washington during the Revolution, Hopkins had been one of the band of heroes who endured the winter at Valley Forge and crossed the Delaware to surprise the Hessians at Trenton. Later he commanded troops at the battles of Brandywine and Germantown, where he was severely wounded. After the war, Hopkins made his living as a surveyor and lawyer. In 1797 he settled on the Ohio River at Red Banks, now Henderson, Kentucky, where he entered politics, serving as a judge and state legislator throughout the opening years of the century.[51]

Figure 10. General
Samuel Hopkins.
Artist: Bert Mullins,
1940. Courtesy of
Henderson County
Historical and
Genealogical Society,
Henderson, Kentucky.

General William Henry Harrison, who knew Hopkins, appointed him to the
command of all U.S. forces in Indiana and Illinois Territories, although his
authority to make such an appointment for Illinois was at best unclear.[52]

Hopkins's campaign went badly from the beginning. The volunteers had
been ordered to leave home carrying thirty days' provisions. Many of them
depleted their food supplies on their journey to Vincennes, and those who
arrived early consumed the rest while waiting for those who arrived late. No
provision had been made at Vincennes to feed the 2000 hungry volunteers
and their horses. The contractors engaged by Acting Governor John Gibson
failed in their duty and Hopkins had to send to Kentucky for 100 barrels of
flour. To secure enough food for his army, the general had to pledge his own
funds in payment. There were not enough grist mills at Vincennes to grind
corn and wheat for so many men, so the general commandeered all the mills
in the vicinity, posting guards to prevent nonmilitary grinding until his army
was fully provided for.[53]

The army had been ordered to assemble at Vincennes on September 24, but
it lingered there for ten days while the general wrestled with issues of supply.

Sickness was common, and within days more than 100 men were confined to the hospital. Some died. Further delay was also caused by organizing the army into battalions and regiments. The men of each company elected their own officers, as was customary, but instead of appointing the field officers himself, Hopkins permitted the captains to choose them. Hopkins had once been a soldier, but he was now a politician, and he chose this method as being more congenial to the feelings of volunteers.[54] At the same time, Hopkins ordered Colonel Russell, the most experienced Indian fighter in the army, and a regular officer on whom he could have relied, to Illinois. These decisions were to cost the general dearly.

By October 6, the army was camped on Bussaron Creek, about ten miles north of Vincennes.[55] There Hopkins's army came into contact with the "Busro" community of Shakers. The Shakers were, and are, a religious sect practicing communal living, common ownership of property, and strict separation of the sexes. "Hands to work and hearts to God" was the Shakers' rule of life, and the nearly twenty communities they formed in the eastern United States were organized around prosperous farms and productive workshops. They were a practical people, who enriched American life with such inventions as the clothespin, the flat broom, and the circular saw. Their spare and elegant furniture remains among the most prized of American antiques.[56]

The Busro, or West Union, community had been organized just three years before, as the westernmost community of Shakers in America. Some of the believers had in fact come there from General Hopkins's own hometown of Red Banks. Despite struggles with malaria, the community had begun to prosper. The Shakers had built dwelling houses, barns, and mills, and planted fields and orchards on more than 1,300 acres. The outbreak of war posed a challenge for the community. Although Tecumseh is said to have promised not to harm them, the real danger came from the Shakers' own countrymen. Frontier militiamen resented the Shakers' pacifist creed. On the march to Tippecanoe, Harrison's army had handled the Shakers roughly, but the Busro community nevertheless tended the wounded as the bloodied army passed by on its return from battle. In August and September 1812 the Indiana militia camped at the community, turning its dwelling houses into barracks. While marching to the relief of Fort Harrison, Russell's troops had requisitioned the community's horses, despite the colonel's humane efforts to limit the damage. By the middle of September, the Shakers had had enough. Leaving behind five or six young men to look after the property as best they could, the remaining

300 believers set out by land and water for temporary refuge in the Shaker communities of Kentucky and Ohio.[57]

Hopkins's Kentuckians exceeded in destructiveness all that had come before. The Shakers' fields of corn, wheat, potatoes, and buckwheat were destroyed, and foraging horses destroyed more than 7,000 small trees in the apple nursery. The volunteers plundered houses, barns, and beehives, slaughtered poultry and 150 hogs, and cooked the edible portions of their booty at campfires made from the Shakers' planks and fence rails. Hopkins was appalled at the destruction visited on inoffensive American citizens by American soldiers, but he was unable to stop the looting by his troops.[58]

After four days, the Kentuckians continued their slow march toward Fort Harrison, which they reached on October 10. Here forage for the horses was plentiful, and Hopkins obtained a valuable recruit in the person of Captain Zachary Taylor, the fort's commanding officer, who agreed to accompany Hopkins as an aide. These factors should have heartened the army but did not. The mood of the soldiers had been sour since Bussaron Creek and worsened as sickness and desertions increased. Among the sick was the general himself, who throughout the campaign was weakened by severe dysentery, to the point where he could barely sit upright on his horse. His collapsed appearance and slurred speech, as well as his habitual profanity, led many in the army to conclude, perhaps wrongly, that their general was intoxicated, further undermining morale. By October 12, more than 200 men had simply walked away from the army, and many more deserted the next day.[59]

On October 14, before his army could melt away, Hopkins led it west across the Wabash. By the time the army crossed, it was late in the day, and the troops rode only three miles west before making camp. Here Hopkins for the first time shared his plan of campaign with his senior officers. It was vague enough. He intended to strike out across the Illinois prairies for Peoria, attacking the Kickapoo towns on his route and "breaking up these or as many as our resources would permit." He hoped vaguely that at Peoria he would meet with a force led by Colonel Russell, and that their combined forces would then continue up the Illinois River as far as circumstances might dictate, before heading back to the Wabash, "chastising" any of the tribes they happened to meet along that river. To accomplish all this, each man had been issued ten days rations, which he had to carry himself. No baggage wagons accompanied the army, and the only artillery it is known to have carried was a single six-pounder. Despite the obvious impracticality of the plan, Hopkins's officers expressed support, and early the next morning the general led his army out into the vast tall-grass prairies of Illinois.[60]

The first day's march west or northwest across the present Edgar County was uneventful, and the army estimated that it had covered thirty miles.[61] On the second day, October 16, the army turned north along an Indian trail, finding some cartridge boxes that appeared to have been taken from a supply convoy that had been surprised and cut to pieces on the way to Fort Harrison the month before.[62] This discovery gave the troops confidence that they were on the right course. The third day (October 17), the Kentuckians found two more cartridge boxes and a canteen, as they pressed on northward. The guides assured the general that the Kickapoo towns were near. The army continued onward the next day (October 18), the day Edwards and Russell were just setting out from Fort Russell, but some rumblings of discontent were again beginning to be heard in the ranks. About sunset, Hopkins called a halt, the first of the day, at "a fine piece of grass in the prairie," where he planned to let the horses rest and graze. He intended to resume the march at 10:00 p.m., hoping to surprise the Indians at daybreak, but he was accosted by Major Jechonias Singleton.[63] According to Hopkins, the major began to berate him in a rude and peremptory manner, telling him that if the general did not order the march resumed immediately, the major and his battalion would break off from the army and return home. As Singleton later told the story, however, his intention was merely to hold together an army that was about to disintegrate. This was a moment of truth, but instead of asserting his authority, Hopkins, weakened by illness, meekly acquiesced. The army marched till midnight, when it at last made camp beside an Indian council house and cabin, which were surrounded by two small fields of corn. From all appearances the buildings had been recently vacated and in the council house the soldiers found a white scalp and floor mats made from flags. The army spent the night tormented by thirst.[64]

In the morning light the guides discovered trails leading in three directions. One showed the tracks of a cart. The army was eager to march; the general sent the guides on ahead to follow the tracks. From the summit of a hill, the guides saw what they thought was smoke rising from behind a grove of trees six or eight miles distant. The general and his army concluded that the smoke must come from an Indian village and hurried toward it "in high spirits and good order." These high spirits fell immediately when the soldiers reached the grove and found no village. They had marched six to eight miles out of their way for nothing, and it was obvious to all that the guides were lost. The army changed to a southwesterly course, and that night (October 19) camped by water in a small grove of trees, only about ten miles from the council house where they had camped the night before.

The Kentuckians had been camped no more than an hour when they saw a raging fire racing toward the grove, driven by a high wind. The Indians had fired the prairie, or so the soldiers believed. The danger was great, and the army saved itself only by setting a backfire to protect their camp. Local historians have identified the grove where the army camped as the Big Grove, which once covered the north side of Urbana, but that identification cannot be correct.[65] The Big Grove covered ten square miles, but Hopkins called the grove where his army camped "thin," while an aide described it as being no more than twelve acres, barely large enough to feed the army's campfires for the night.[66] Indeed, as might be expected of an army that had wandered lost in a trackless prairie, the actual route taken by Hopkins and his men can only be a matter of conjecture, unless a clue is provided by two iron cannonballs discovered in 1869 by workmen cutting a railroad route ten miles west of Danville.[67]

The troops spent a sleepless and discouraged night. Rations were now running low, and the horses were very weary. On the morning of October 20, Hopkins assembled his senior officers and presented to them the arguments both for pushing on and for turning back. He asked his officers to test the sentiments of the army, and to report back to him, promising that if even 500 men would agree to continue on, he would lead them against the Indian towns. In less than an hour the officers reported that the campaign was over; the army was almost unanimous for returning home. Believing that the general, who had exhausted his own supply of flour, was merely posturing about continuing on, the officers hadn't bothered to relay his call for volunteers to the troops.[68] The general had no choice but to acquiesce, asking only that he be allowed to lead the army the first day of the retreat and pledging that he would lead it no more than six miles out of its direct route. Hopkins still believed the Indian towns to be nearby and hoped to pick up signs that would change his soldiers' minds.

The army assembled on parade in the prairie outside the grove. For the last time, the general placed himself at the head and ordered his troops to follow him. Instead of following, however, the troops moved off in quite a different direction. Hopkins sent Major Lee and Captain Taylor to plead with the officers in the lead to turn the columns, but they reported that it could not be done. It is by no means clear, in fact, that the senior officers even tried to stem the tide; according to one observer, their only concern was "to please the boys before the next election."[69] The retreat became a rout that not even the exhausted state of the horses could slow; with the old general trailing along in the rear, the former army, now a mob, hurried back to Fort Harrison and Vincennes to be mustered out.[70]

The campaign had been a disaster. The "flower of Kentucky" had accomplished nothing, their only "victory" being against the gentle and unoffending Shakers. The Indians were emboldened: the Miami, from whom General Harrison had been seeking hostages, broke off negotiations when they learned of the retreat of the Kentuckians. Harrison, in fact, expected that the most likely result of the campaign would be another Indian move against Fort Wayne. Throughout Kentucky the disgraceful performance of the volunteers was thought to be a blemish on the military reputation of the Commonwealth. Charges and countercharges would fly among the general, the officers, and the enlisted men.[71]

Hopkins felt the disappointment keenly. Determined to accomplish something before winter brought the campaigning season to an end, the general raised another army, of Rangers and infantry, that in a freezing November proceeded up the Wabash, where it burned the Prophet's rebuilt town and a nearby Kickapoo village, both deserted. A detached column of his army was surprised by Indians with the loss of eighteen men; Hopkins hurried to give battle but his attack was prevented by a blinding snowstorm. By the time the storm subsided, the Indians had slipped away. The men were poorly prepared for freezing weather, and Hopkins led his army back to Fort Harrison with little accomplished but partial retrieval of the commander's—and Kentucky's—honor. On December 18, 1812, Hopkins resigned his command and returned home.[72] Charges were brought against the general, but after hearing evidence, a court of inquiry found that none of the charges was justified and absolved Hopkins of all blame for the failure of the expedition. His good name restored, Hopkins was elected to Congress and served a single term. The old general died on September 16, 1819, and was buried in the family cemetery near Henderson, Kentucky. He is remembered today as the "Father of Henderson," and both Hopkinsville and Hopkins County, Kentucky, bear his name.[73]

Unaware that the two armies were returning homeward, the one in triumph and the other in disgrace, the two boats Edwards had sent out with provisions proceeded up the Illinois River to meet them. Manning the boats was a company of roughneck militiamen commanded by Captain Thomas E. Craig of Shawneetown.[74] Craig was a prominent man in the new city and seemed to enjoy the governor's confidence. Earlier in the year, Edwards had appointed

Craig both a captain of militia and a justice of the peace and had also designated him to receive arms and military stores shipped to the territory from the federal depot at Newport, Kentucky.[75] Nevertheless, other than leaving a message for Craig at Peoria, Edwards had done nothing to recall the detachment.

Exactly when Craig and his men left on their voyage upriver cannot be determined. Ordinarily the trip between Peoria and the settlements took about a week, and the fact that Craig's boats, by his own account, did not arrive until November 5 indicates that, absent a strong headwind, they could not have left at the same time as the land troops. The most likely explanation is that the company had to wait for supplies, perhaps the "military stores" brought from Shawneetown to Fort Russell under the protection of a militia company commanded by Lieutenant Colonel (acting Captain) Philip Tramell.[76] Eventually, though, Craig's boats did set sail up the Mississippi River and onto the Illinois, as far as Peoria. On the way, Craig passed two large canoes full of Frenchmen, who were fleeing Peoria for fear of the Indians. When he arrived at the village, Craig found it deserted, and saw no sign of either of the armies he had been ordered to meet and supply.[77] He decided to wait.

The village of Peoria was a relic of a bygone era. The French settlement on Lake Peoria had had a flickering existence since the days of Tonti, but in the 1790s the inhabitants had moved from the original site, a mile and a half upriver, to what they called La Ville de Maillet, or the New Village, at the foot of the lake. The villagers were nearly all French: *voyageurs*, hunters, and Indian traders, who also depended on small farming in the fields behind the village. They lived on friendly terms with the Indians, with whom they intermarried, and whose villages were all around them. Narrow unpaved streets separated houses built of vertical logs in the French colonial style. In the village were fenced gardens, and outside were the common fields on which the settlers grew their crops and grazed their livestock. The population has been estimated as having been as high as between two and three hundred, but this number may be too large for a village that consisted of little more than thirty households.[78]

Captain Craig had been dealt a very bad hand, but he now proceeded to make a bad situation worse.[79] Finding nobody at home, Craig permitted his men to ransack the unguarded cottages and storehouses and to carry whatever they wanted back to the boats. The soldiers dined well, after helping themselves to the villagers' hogs and poultry, but at night they slept on their boats, moored across the river from the village.

Late that night, Craig's sentinels spied a canoe with six Frenchmen ascending the river. Craig ordered the men brought to him, and found them to be employees of the trading firm of Kinzie & Forsyth. They told him that Thomas Forsyth had returned upriver from Saint Louis, and hearing that U.S. troops had arrived at Peoria had sent the men ahead to reconnoiter. Suspicious, Craig released four of the men, but retained two as hostages. The next day Forsyth himself arrived, bringing with him the French villagers Craig had passed in his voyage upriver, but whom Forsyth had persuaded to return home.

Besides being a resident of Peoria, Forsyth was employed by the War Department as an Indian agent.[80] From his post at Peoria, deep in Indian country, he had provided valuable information to the territorial authorities. His official position was a closely guarded secret, and whether Craig knew of it was later disputed. Certainly Craig was acquainted with Forsyth, to whom he had delivered a message from Edwards while Forsyth was visiting Saint Louis. Craig later claimed that he had been glad to see Forsyth, and that at first their relations had been friendly. The remaining villagers, all Frenchmen, Craig held in deep suspicion, regarding them as indistinguishable from the Indians. This opinion was common among the frontiersmen of southern Illinois, many of whom regarded "the seditious village of Peoria [as] the great nursery of hostile Indians and traitorous British Indian Traders."[81]

Discovering that their homes had been plundered by the soldiers, the villagers demanded return of their property. Forsyth, who may have been the only English speaker among them, acted as spokesman. Here the accounts begin to diverge. Craig later claimed that he had merely taken the property on board for safekeeping and that when requested he had freely returned it all, except that belonging to two men he believed to be in Canada with the British.[82] Forsyth, on the other hand, claimed that the soldiers returned only a small portion of their booty, grudgingly and a little at a time, while stalling and using various evasions to avoid doing so.

Relations were already badly strained when one night a windstorm broke the cable of the armed boat, forcing it aground just below Peoria. Not having seen any Indians, Craig decided to deal with the problem in the morning. Just before daybreak, however, the captain believed he heard gunfire directed at his boats from shore. None of his men was hit, and he could not see the culprits in the dark, but Craig immediately blamed the Frenchmen. He armed his troops and sent them ashore to arrest the villagers.

What had happened is impossible to determine. Craig later claimed that he had followed tracks from the place where the shots had been fired directly to the village, where he found empty guns that he believed to have been fired. According to Forsyth, on the other hand, one of Craig's officers, Ensign Harrison Wilson, admitted to him privately that after the firing he had seen a party of Indians fleeing across the prairie, one of them on horseback.[83] Forsyth and the villagers adamantly denied firing on Craig's boats; the longer they denied the charge, the angrier the captain became. Shouting and cursing, he showered them with profane abuse. At last he ordered the villagers arrested. Among those arrested were Forsyth, Antoine LeClair, who had recently returned from a dangerous and confidential mission for the government, and all the other men in the village, as well as the "squaws" and children. In all, more than forty villagers were taken on board the boats under guard.

The prisoners were roughly handled by Craig and his men, although the accounts of the two sides differ. The town was looted once again and, according to Forsyth, Craig's men even stole food from the kettle where Forsyth had been cooking his breakfast. Some of the villagers' cattle were shot by the soldiers, but the rest of the livestock, over 200 head of cattle and many hogs and chickens, were simply left to roam untended. Before leaving, Craig and his men burned part of the town, including houses and barns full of grain. Craig reported that he had destroyed half the village, adding that Forsyth "and the rest of the dam'd rascals may think themselves well off they were not scalped."[84]

The soldiers sailed downriver with their prisoners until they reached Savage's Ferry, about a mile above the mouth of Wood River.[85] There the prisoners were held for four days, enduring a good deal of verbal abuse from Craig and his men. Craig hurried to Fort Russell, but finding Edwards absent, he sent the governor a rather plaintive letter, reporting that he had brought down prisoners and asking what to do.[86] His answer came in the form of a visit from Colonel Whiteside, relaying the governor's order to set the prisoners free. Left cold and hungry on the bank of the Mississippi, the prisoners made their way to Saint Louis. The old French village of Peoria was finished.

Both Craig and Forsyth stated that Craig arrested all the villagers, while Reynolds wrote that Craig arrested "all he could capture."[87] Historian Nehemiah Matson, however, preserves a story that Craig arrested all the men, but left some of the women and children behind when he sailed from Peoria. The story may be apocryphal, but in this instance Matson's account deserves attention, since he identified as his sources René LaCroix and Hypolite Pilette, who described how they and their mothers had been left behind at Peoria when their fathers were carried away by Craig and his men.[88]

As Craig's boats disappeared downriver, leaving much of the village in flames, the women and children, left without food or shelter in a cold November wind, wept helplessly. Their men had been carried away, perhaps forever, and they did not know what was to become of them. At this moment, a lone Indian was seen walking toward them along the lakeshore. On his shoulder was a rifle, in his belt were a tomahawk and scalping knife, and his face was painted for war. It was Gomo. He had watched from hiding until the soldiers left. Now he conducted the women and children to his village, where his people sheltered and fed them, before giving them canoes to go downriver to join their husbands and fathers.[89]

Craig's expedition had done much damage to the American cause. Not only had he destroyed the only listening post the United States had been able to maintain in Indian country, he had undone whatever advantage had been gained from Edwards's and Russell's raid on the Indian towns. Their destruction of Indian food supplies had threatened the tribesmen with starvation, but now the Indians were able to live comfortably on the cattle Craig had forced his prisoners to leave behind untended.[90] American citizens had been driven from their homes, and the litigation they brought to assert their rights would not conclude until 1867.[91] Nevertheless, Governor Edwards, perhaps conscious that he had left Craig badly in the lurch, continued to appoint him to important offices: judge of common pleas, colonel of militia, and county judge of Gallatin County.[92] After Craig's death in 1816, Edwards wrote that although he had not authorized and could not approve what Craig had done at Peoria, in "justice to his memory" it was his own "firm belief that he was influenced by honorable motives."[93]

Others have been less forgiving. To Thomas Forsyth, Craig and his men were "banditti" and the captain "the worst of the whole crew."[94] The opinion of the *Missouri Gazette* was that Captain Craig "did more injury to his Country in that expedition, than he can repair, if he lives an hundred years."[95] To John Reynolds, the destruction of Peoria was "useless" and "a wanton act of cruelty," while historian Frank Stevens denounced Craig's conduct as "assinine and criminal."[96] The last word, however, should go to Hypolite Pilette, who as an eleven-year-old boy had been turned out of bed on a cold November morning to see his home put to the torch by the soldiers from Shawneetown. Telling the story many years later, his voice rose and his eyes flashed with anger as he said: "I hate Yankees."[97]

SIX

Dickson and Forsyth

A fter the war had ended, two former enemies met in Saint Louis. During a cordial evening, Robert Dickson and Thomas Forsyth talked over their exploits during the war, and Dickson entertained Forsyth with an account of how close Dickson had once come to capturing him. He might also have added that he himself had come close to violent death at the hands of Potawatomi Indians possibly under Forsyth's influence.[1] The two men had a lot to talk about.

Robert Dickson was one of the most colorful figures on the frontier.[2] As a young man he had migrated from Scotland to Canada, where for many years he made his living as a fur trader along and west of the Mississippi. The Indians idolized Dickson. He was a large man of commanding appearance, with a ruddy complexion and blazing red hair, for which the Indians gave him the name "The Red Head." For nearly twenty years Dickson lived in the Indian country, principally among the Sioux, and his influence with that tribe was confirmed by his marriage to the sister of a chief named Red Thunder. The marriage was more than one of convenience. The couple had four children and lived together faithfully till parted by death.[3]

Although he remained a British subject, Dickson got on well with the American authorities. In 1802, Governor William Henry Harrison even appointed him a justice of the peace for Saint Clair County, which was then part of Indiana Territory and extended as far north as Lake Superior.[4] Dickson was always happy to perform small services for his American hosts. On his search for the source of the Mississippi, the explorer Zebulon Montgomery Pike found Dickson to be "a gentleman of general commercial knowledge, and possessing much geographical information of the western country, of open, frank, manners."[5] Dickson was generous in sharing information with Pike. Frederick Bates, secretary of Missouri Territory, regarded Dickson as "a man of honor" and one "on whose friendly aid I have the utmost reliance." Bates even gave him a license to trade on the upper Missouri, despite his being a subject of a foreign power.[6] Indeed, so friendly were Dickson's relations with American authorities that it was reported that he had even made the journey to Washington in hope of securing an appointment as U.S. Indian agent.[7]

The appointment, had it been made, would have been disastrous. However accommodating he may have been in peacetime, Dickson's loyalty to king and country never wavered. A correspondent who professed to know him well wrote to Secretary Bates that Dickson had "done what has perhaps advantaged the U. States . . . [b]ut believe me not from any love he bears our Country. . . . He is a Br. Subject in heart & sentiment [and] possesses not the smallest wish for the happiness of the American people."[8] Nevertheless, Dickson remained liked and respected by Americans on the frontier to such an extent that, when he sided with his own country during the ensuing war, the *Missouri Gazette* branded him a "Traitor."[9]

In fact, the government had done much to alienate Dickson and other British traders from the United States. Despite the undoubted right Jay's Treaty gave British subjects to trade with the Indians of the old Northwest, a proclamation in 1805 prohibited subjects of foreign powers from entering the country west of the Mississippi to trade with the Indians.[10] Had it been enforceable, the edict would have severely restricted Dickson's access to the Sioux, who were his wife's relations and his own best trading partners. As time went on, successive congressional enactments tightened the screws on foreign commerce. By the end of the decade, Dickson was required to smuggle his trade goods into the country, by secret and sometimes roundabout routes, in defiance of American law.[11]

Thomas Forsyth was born at Detroit in 1771, when the city was still subject to King George III.[12] In dangerous times, Forsyth's ambiguous citizenship enabled him to live safely among the Indians by posing as an Englishman, but some Americans on the frontier distrusted him as a British subject.[13] In fact, however, Forsyth had no love for the British, who during the Revolution had imprisoned his father for befriending American prisoners and for denouncing the use of Indians against the colonists.[14]

Forsyth entered the Indian trade as a young man and often wintered in the wilderness, where he became conversant with Indian languages, especially Potawatomi and Chippewa. In partnership with his half-brother, John Kinzie, Forsyth opened a trading post at Chicago, under the name Kinzie & Forsyth, but by 1809 he moved his part of the operation to Peoria, then one of the most important trading points in the Mississippi Valley. He was on friendly terms with Indians of the Potawatomi tribe, especially Gomo, and he even claimed some influence with Main Poc, the bitter enemy of the Americans.[15]

Governor Reynolds has left a pleasing portrait of Forsyth, saying that "benevolence and kindness of heart were his predominant traits of character."[16] These qualities were the source of much of his standing with the Indians. Black Hawk, who regarded Forsyth as a friend, said of him, "He was a man who always told us the truth, and knew everything that was going on."[17] There was a darker side to Forsyth, however, as shown by his and Kinzie's long enslavement of Jeffrey Nash, a free black man whom the Supreme Court of Louisiana finally freed from what it found to have been unlawful bondage.[18]

The outbreak of war brought Dickson and Forsyth into the service of their respective countries, and thus into conflict with each other. From his home in Peoria, the crossroads of many important Indian trails, Forsyth was in a position to monitor Indian activity throughout much of the Old Northwest.[19] By 1811 he had begun sending reports of Indian activity downriver to American authorities, while seeking an official appointment as subagent to the Indians of the Illinois River.[20] Forsyth was well suited to the post, as Governor Ninian Edwards acknowledged in writing to the secretary of war that Forsyth "is a very intelligent, gentlemanly man, has a perfect knowledge of the Indians, and would make a first rate agent." Nevertheless, although he asserted that he wanted the position not for "lucre" but "to serve my country," Forsyth drove a hard bargain with the authorities. A dispute over the salary Forsyth would receive stalled the appointment through the winter, until at last in a meeting at Kaskaskia Forsyth abruptly broke off negotiations and announced that he would return to Detroit to conduct his own personal business. Edwards yielded, and Forsyth was sent back to Peoria with instructions.[21]

When Robert Dickson reached the upper Mississippi to trade with the Indians in the fall of 1811, he found American agents trying to influence the Indians in favor of the United States. They were urging the chiefs to travel to Washington, where their "Great Father" the President would tell them something "of the utmost importance." Although Dickson was a private citizen, he was also the only man on hand with the means and the inclination to bolster the tribes' loyalty to their competing "Great Father," the king. Dickson made a generous distribution of the trade goods he had just smuggled into the country with much difficulty. His motives were humanitarian, as well as political. The Indians were starving. Their summer crop had failed from drought, and the drought had also driven large game animals north in search of food. Moreover, the interruption of supplies from British traders had also left the tribesmen short of the powder and ammunition they needed to hunt. Dickson's generosity bore fruit. When he returned east in the spring, he was accompanied by a large band of Indian warriors ready to fight the Americans whenever war broke out.[22]

Dickson was already in communication with Major General Isaac Brock, lieutenant governor of Upper Canada. Leading his band of Sioux, Menominee, and Winnebago up the Wisconsin River, across U.S. territory, Dickson was met at the Wisconsin Portage by two Indians carrying a smuggled message from Brock. The Indians had been detained by suspicious authorities at Chicago, but they had wrapped the message in their moccasins and buried them in the ground until they were free to go.[23] In cryptic language, Brock asked Dickson how many of his "friends" he could bring to Canada, whether they would support the British cause, and what would be needed in order to supply them. Dickson replied immediately that the "unparalleled scarcity of provisions" had limited his "friends" to about 250 to 300 of different languages, but that he and they would reach the British fort on Saint Joseph Island, in Lake Huron, about the middle of July 1812.[24] At Green Bay, Dickson halted briefly to dispatch 30 Indian warriors to join General Brock immediately at Malden. They served in Brock's forces throughout the campaign that ended in the capture of Detroit.[25]

The rest of his Indians Dickson led to Saint Joseph, where Captain Charles Roberts commanded a small company of British regulars. As soon as war broke out, Roberts and Dickson led their combined force across the straits to Macki-

nac Island, to surprise its sleepy American garrison in the early morning. The
fort surrendered without firing a shot. Dickson's Indians played a crucial role. In
a pattern that was to become familiar, the Indians brought little of actual military
value to an assault on a fortified place, but the fear of what they *might* do should
the fort fall after a battle was a powerful argument in favor of surrendering to
the British before the Indians' blood was up and their white handlers lost control
of them. As it was, the Indians were disappointed at losing the opportunity
for a massacre. Dickson sternly forbade his warriors to kill soldiers who had
surrendered but gave them some captured cattle to slaughter instead.[26]

Feeding the Indian warriors Dickson had brought to the island became
an immediate issue, as was keeping them occupied. As quickly as they could,
Dickson and Roberts dispatched their Indian allies to join Brock, who was
closing in on the American stronghold of Detroit. Detroit fell before they arrived, but knowledge that the Indians were "swarming down" on him after the
fall of Mackinac contributed to General William Hull's decision to surrender.[27]

Dickson now sent messengers to the western tribes, inviting them to a
conference. Years later, Black Hawk told of traveling from Rock River to meet
Dickson at Green Bay. There he found a large assemblage of Potawatomi,
Kickapoo, Ottawa, and Winnebago tribesmen. Dickson received Black Hawk
courteously, offering him arms and ammunition, and asking him to lead an
army of Indian warriors to join the British at Detroit. Black Hawk would
have preferred to attack the settlements along the Mississippi, but Dickson
told him that he would not send brave men to murder women and children.
Instead would send them where there were soldiers to fight. If the Indians
defeated them, the Mississippi River country would be theirs.[28]

Black Hawk considered this the answer of a brave, but he was still not
wholly satisfied. Earlier in the summer Black Hawk had gone to Peoria to seek
the counsel of his friend Forsyth about which side to join, but had found him
absent. He now asked Dickson about Forsyth, and Dickson shook his head.
He said that he had tried to persuade Forsyth to join the British, and had even
offered him money, but Forsyth had refused. Now, though, Dickson said, he
had laid a trap for Forsyth, having sent a party of Indians to capture him and
bring him to Dickson alive. Black Hawk started for Detroit the next morning
with five hundred Indians, who joined the British in defeating the Americans
on the River Raisin in January 1813.[29]

Dickson had done well. On his own initiative, without holding any official
position, he had secured an alliance with the Indians of the upper Missis-

sippi Valley, and had contributed to the American collapse in the upper Great
Lakes. He now set off eastward toward Montreal and Quebec, to lay before
Sir George Prevost, the supreme British commander in Canada, a proposal
for enlisting the western Indians in support of the British. He also hoped to
obtain compensation for the large sums he had expended in supplying the
Indians during the preceding year.

Meanwhile Forsyth had been sent back to Peoria in May. What he reported
was alarming. Increasing numbers of hostile Indians were massing along the
Illinois River.[30] Forsyth recruited two agents to travel among the Indians and
provide him with information about what they were thinking and doing. One
was the half-British, half-Mohawk Billy Caldwell, who reported to Forsyth
from the Wabash.[31] In addition, Forsyth's fellow villager, Antoine LeClair, who
as a Frenchman could travel with relative safety, was sent to make a wide circuit
through what is now northern Illinois and Wisconsin.[32] Dislike of Governor
Edwards initially made LeClair reluctant to go, but Forsyth overcame his
reluctance by offering to pay him two dollars a day and to replace his horse if
the Indians stole it, which in fact they did. Everywhere LeClair went, he found
the Indians preparing for war, especially the Menominee and the Winnebago.
"The Red Head," as they called Dickson, had renewed their past loyalty to their
British Father. When the British gave the signal, the Indians would strike in
different places, but the first blow would fall on Chicago.[33]

In fact, Forsyth's own position was perilous. He repeatedly urged the governors to whom he reported to keep his appointment a secret. Nevertheless,
word that Forsyth was writing frequently to Saint Louis had leaked out, forcing
him to deny to the Indians that he was an American or that he had friends
at Saint Louis. He urgently requested that Edwards not mention his name,
LeClair's, or Caldwell's to anyone, "for I can assure you," he wrote, "the country
is full of disaffected persons to our government."[34] The whole community at
Peoria was in danger. The Kickapoo had begun killing cattle belonging to the
French settlers. Many of the cattle they killed were simply left for the wolves,
often at the very doorsteps of the settlers, who were told they were lucky the
Indians didn't kill them too. When war did break out, the Kickapoo wished
to attack the villagers at Peoria, and only the protection of Gomo and his
Potawatomi saved the Frenchmen from being killed or driven away.[35]

The capture of Mackinac and the Fort Dearborn massacre dealt a severe
blow to Forsyth's business interests. At Mackinac the British seized a cargo
of furs belonging to Kinzie & Forsyth, while at Chicago the firm's stock of

whiskey and ammunition was destroyed in preparation for the evacuation.[36] The massacre occurred as Forsyth was on his way to Chicago, and he arrived there the day afterward, while the ruins of the fort were still smoldering. The danger was extreme, and not until August 24 was Forsyth able to return to Peoria, where he found himself hardly safer than he had been at Chicago. Having learned of the Indians' plans to attack other forts along the frontier, he prepared letters to send downriver to warn the authorities, but he was forced to destroy them when he heard that a party of Indians was coming to search his house for gunpowder. All the whites at Peoria were closely watched by the Indians. Forsyth went to Gomo's village to ask permission to go to Saint Louis for supplies, but Gomo saw through the ruse. He told Forsyth that the whites could not leave now but would be permitted to do so later.[37]

In fact, after many months of evasions, Gomo was now prepared to take sides. With Black Partridge and Shequenebec, he was preparing to lead a force of 300 to 400 warriors downriver to attack the settlements in Illinois and Missouri. It was essential that Forsyth warn his superiors. He managed to smuggle letters to Howard and Edwards, who deployed troops in a way that blocked the Indians' route and forced them to return home without having done more than to steal a few horses.[38]

After the failure of the raid, the restrictions on the whites were eased. Forsyth had been able to ransom the captive Lieutenant Linai Helm, captured at Fort Dearborn and held prisoner at the Potawatomi village at the mouth of Aux Sable Creek.[39] In late September, Forsyth was permitted to accompany Helm to Saint Louis.[40] In the boat, Forsyth brought with him his most valuable personal effects. Whether Forsyth intended to leave Peoria for good is unclear, but, in a meeting at Fort Russell, Edwards told Forsyth that his services had been valuable and urged him to return to Peoria to stay as long as he was able.[41]

Forsyth started back up the Illinois River. Before he reached Peoria, though, he met two large canoes full of men, women, and children, fleeing the settlement. They told Forsyth that Indians, presumably Kickapoo and Piankashaw, had looted their houses of clothing, arms, and ammunition. Forsyth prevailed on them to return, but it ended badly. At Peoria Forsyth and the villagers encountered two boatloads of militiamen under Captain Thomas Craig, who burned much of the village, arrested Forsyth and other villagers, and carried them down the river as prisoners.[42] After the destruction of Peoria, Forsyth had to remain at Saint Louis, where he was instructed to obtain information by whatever means he could.[43]

The beginning of the year 1813 found Forsyth and Dickson in very different circumstances: Forsyth stranded at Saint Louis, and Dickson proceeding in triumph to Montreal and Quebec. When Forsyth sought compensation for his losses, and for those of his fellow villagers at Peoria, he found Governor Edwards coldly unsympathetic.[44] By contrast, when Dickson reached Quebec in January, he was reimbursed for all the expenses he had incurred the preceding year, and appointed first agent and later deputy superintendent to the western Indians, with wide powers to draw on public stores for supplies and presents to the Indians. He was instructed to promise the Indians that the British would fight to drive the Americans behind the treaty line of 1795, which would restore to them almost all of Illinois and Indiana and much of Ohio. He was to resolve intertribal feuds, persuade the Indians to ally with the British, and lead them in the spring to defend Canada, while restraining them from "acts of cruelty and inhumanity." [45] That Dickson largely succeeded in his mission, traveling nearly alone through more than 1,500 miles of wilderness inhabited only by angry Indian tribes, was a remarkable feat.[46]

His journey cannot be traced in detail. Dickson was at Montreal on January 18, at Detroit between February 15 and March 4, at the mouth of the Saint Joseph River on March 16, at Chicago on March 22, and on the Rock River on April 13. For most of this time Dickson was entirely out of communication with his superiors, who had no idea of his whereabouts and little idea when he would reappear.[47]

At Chicago, Dickson viewed the ruins of Fort Dearborn and called a council of tribes. As Gomo later told Forsyth, Dickson told the Indians that he was two months out of Quebec and could not stay long, as he was in a great hurry to get to the Mississippi. He showed the tribesmen a long belt of wampum from their Great Father, the king, intended for the Sioux, so they would take up the war club beside him. Dickson's work was not to be the work of a day, as he would next visit the Potawatomi of Milwaukee, the Winnebago on Rock River, and the Sioux at Prairie du Chien. His orders were to send to Detroit all the Indians who would go. He told the tribesmen that 1500 Ottawa and Chippewa had already gone to Detroit, where the British were strong and would soon defeat Harrison's army. The Great Father would supply all his Indian children's needs. Dickson himself would descend the Mississippi River with the Sioux. Those warriors who could not go to Detroit should descend the Illinois River to meet him and hundreds of Sioux, and "they would all go to a country where they could get plenty to eat and drink & plenty of clothing." Dickson assured the warriors that their Great Father was now standing upright with his war club in his hand, and that he would never bury it until all his white and red children were satisfied.[48]

At Rock Island, Dickson brought the Sauk red wampum and a barrel of gunpowder, asking the tribe to send warriors with him to Prairie du Chien. The Sauk expressed fear that if they joined the British the Americans would come up the Mississippi to attack them. Dickson assured them that the Americans were too busy trying to recover Detroit, in order to cut off supplies to the tribe and starve them out. Nevertheless the Sauk questioned the ability of the British to support them effectively and decided to wait and see, although they kept the gift of powder.[49]

Dickson's mission was not only military and diplomatic, but humanitarian as well. The British were always ambivalent about their reliance on Indian allies, and Sir George Prevost had instructed Dickson to do all he could to restrain their cruelty. Such instructions accorded well with Dickson's own inclinations. Even before he reached Chicago, Dickson had learned of the survivors of the massacre and set in motion the process that would eventually bring them to freedom. Throughout his service Dickson strove to alleviate the sufferings of prisoners among the Indians. After the war, former American prisoners Dickson had rescued wrote to thank him, sometimes enclosing gifts of money.[50]

To the American West, however, Dickson represented the face of the enemy. Even before war was declared, while the Scotsman was still a private citizen, and continuing throughout the war, both newspapers and official correspondence were full of talk about "the celebrated Dickson," his whereabouts, and his intentions.[51] American agents such as Thomas Forsyth were expected to relay to their superiors any rumor they might hear about him. There was pervasive fear that Dickson would lead an Indian army down the Mississippi or the Illinois River to lay waste Saint Louis, Kaskaskia, and the other weakly defended settlements in Missouri and Illinois. Dickson himself was not above encouraging this belief, both to keep the Americans on the defensive and to encourage his Indian allies.[52]

In fact, however, there was never any real danger of such an attack. Dickson's first responsibility was the defense of Canada. Early in his journey Dickson received messengers warning of the danger Harrison's army posed to the British position around Detroit and Malden. Accordingly, Dickson sent Indians from the Wabash valley and the southern edge of Lake Michigan directly to Detroit, while he himself hurried on.[53]

Dickson's recruiting was greatly assisted by the high prestige the British had gained from the surrender of Mackinac and Detroit, and the capture of an American army at the River Raisin in January.[54] The tribes loved to back a winner. The Potawatomi, Kickapoo, and Winnebago tribes flocked to the British, as did the Menominee, a tribe Forsyth sarcastically called "Dickson's bodyguard."[55] Despite their resentment at the treaty of 1804, which had stripped them of their lands in Illinois, the Sauk were still divided. Some, such as Black Hawk, took the field with the British, while others remained aloof for the time being. Their close allies the Fox also hesitated to take the field against the Americans, whom they saw as potential allies in their own war with the Winnebago.[56] Dickson also had reason to be disappointed with the response of the Sioux, the largest and most warlike of the western nations. Although the tribal groups nearer the Mississippi mostly favored the British, the larger groups of Sioux along the upper Missouri, possibly influenced by Spanish-American trader Manuel Lisa,[57] remained neutral, or even favored the Americans.[58]

On June 10, 1813, Dickson emerged from the wilderness at Mackinac Island. With him was a force of more than 600 Indians, in addition to the 800 he had already sent directly to Detroit. He had also recruited, largely from the ranks of the western fur traders, a number of capable lieutenants. The task of feeding Dickson's red army was enormous. Dickson remained at the island for two weeks, grappling with issues of supply, while the tribesmen ate voraciously and occasionally helped themselves to civilian livestock. The islanders were much relieved when Dickson finally led the Indians away to join General Henry Procter at Malden.[59] Dickson took with him most of the fighting Indians of Illinois, Wisconsin, and the upper Mississippi valley, giving the Illinois and Missouri territories a much quieter summer than they had feared, and leaving the British position west of Lake Michigan largely undefended.[60]

Thomas Forsyth had spent the past winter more comfortably at Saint Louis. The expulsion of the villagers from Peoria had left the American authorities blind and deaf to what was happening beyond their own lines. In January, Forsyth sent two Frenchmen, Auguste LaRoche and Louis Chevalier, up the Illinois River. Their destination was Milwaukee, but the Indians rightly suspected them of being spies and detained them through the winter at the mouth of Bureau Creek. The Kickapoo wanted to kill them, but the Potawatomi were still friendly with the French, if not with the Americans, and spared their lives. When spring came, they permitted the two Frenchmen to return to

Saint Louis, where they reported what they had heard about the movements of Robert Dickson and the hostile chief Main Poc.[61]

With Edwards's concurrence, Forsyth volunteered to go back upriver himself.[62] With a boat and crew, Forsyth left Saint Louis on April 13, 1813. He carried with him a boatload of trade goods, of the sort he had been accustomed to sell the Indians, but only enough gunpowder for his own use. The trip upriver was uneventful, and Forsyth did not encounter any Indians until he had traveled forty-five miles above Peoria. On April 27, he arrived at Sandy Creek, now Aux Sable Creek, about five miles east of the present Morris, where Gomo, Black Partridge, and other Potawatomi had moved their villages. Gomo greeted Forsyth cordially, telling him that the roads by both land and water would always be open to his friends, and in fact urging Forsyth to encourage his French friends to return to Peoria, where, Gomo promised, they would now enjoy the same rights as the Indians, and both peoples would live together as one family.[63]

Forsyth was especially interested in news about Dickson, and Gomo gave him a minutely detailed account of Dickson's visit to Chicago the month before. As he was perhaps meant to do, Gomo repeated Dickson's threats to attack the American settlements on the Mississippi in the spring. Gomo's information that Dickson was sending on to Detroit all the Indians who would go was corroborated by Main Poc himself, who sent for Forsyth the morning he was to leave Aux Sable Creek, and told him that he himself was on the way to Detroit with a large band of warriors, who would "fight the Americans completely." Once they had defeated Harrison's army in northern Ohio, they would turn west, destroying Fort Wayne and Vincennes, and driving the Americans—those "troublers of the Earth"—over the Ohio River.[64]

Main Poc's hopes were destined to be disappointed. By the time Dickson's army of western Indians reached Detroit, the campaigning season was far advanced, and the first siege of Fort Meigs was over. Procter believed his forces inadequate for another invasion of Ohio, but the Indians clamored for action. At first the western Indians Dickson had brought with him surprised the British with their tractability, but as they mingled with the other Indians they soon became as ungovernable as the rest. At last, solely to quiet his Indian allies, whom he could barely feed and whom forced inactivity made dangerous, Procter led his combined force back into Ohio for a second unsuccessful siege of Fort Meigs, followed by an equally unsuccessful assault on nearby Fort Stephenson. In that assault the British lost heavily, while the Indians, who had insisted on the attack, contented themselves with firing at the fort from a safe distance. Among the laggards was Main Poc, whom Dickson later charged with having held his warriors back.[65]

After these failures, the western Indians began to drift away. Black Hawk and his Sauk were dismayed at the lack of success; the Sioux, it is said, were lured home by a rumor that their western cousins along the Missouri River were planning to attack their families.[66] Dickson had taken part in both the sieges, but after the desertion of most of his Indians, he returned briefly to Lower Canada.

During the last half of 1813, Thomas Forsyth all but disappears from the historical record. The only thing known of his activities is that he and Antoine LeClair took part in General Benjamin Howard's march to Peoria to establish an American military post there.[67] Forsyth's knowledge of the Potawatomi language and his familiarity with the Indians of the Illinois River made it natural for him to accompany the expedition, but, as it turned out, Howard's men never saw an Indian. They did, however, make firewood of Forsyth's few remaining buildings at Peoria, the third severe financial blow the war had dealt the Indian agent.[68] Return of American authority to Peoria did not, however, lead Forsyth to reestablish his residence at that place. Despite repeated trips upriver to meet with the Indians, Forsyth continued to reside at Saint Louis for the rest of his life.

The winter of 1813–14 found Robert Dickson in far less comfortable quarters. Destruction of the British fleet on Lake Erie, and Harrison's destruction of Procter's army at the battle of the Thames on October 5, cut the supply line to Mackinac. Although allied Indians continued to come there seeking food and presents, the commanding officer could barely feed his own garrison.[69]

After making arrangements for supplies to be sent to Mackinac by an overland route, Dickson left York (now Toronto) on October 2, only pausing at Mackinac before continuing on with six boatloads of provisions and a small detachment of militia through Green Bay. At frozen Lake Winnebago Dickson built a camp on Garlic Island, where he and his command would spend a cold and hungry winter.[70] The camp was close enough to Green Bay for him to draw provisions, but far enough away to prevent his men from looting it.[71] At the village Dickson posted two of his lieutenants, John Lawe[72] and Louis Grignon,[73] and over the winter the unlucky villagers found themselves compelled to supply both the garrison at Mackinac and the Indians who swarmed around Dickson's camp at Garlic Island.[74] Hungry Indians flocked to the camp, usually with their families. Although Dickson and his men were themselves often on the edge of starvation, both his natural humanity and strategic considerations compelled him to feed the Indians as well as he was able. Dickson's letters to his lieutenants refer repeatedly to the difficulty of finding food for the Indians: "I have very little provision, but trust to a kind Providence" (November 14, 1813). "I am most heartily tired of this distributing of Goods and wish for the Spring. I hear nothing but the cry of hunger from all Quarters" (December 25). "I have very little flour, obliged to keep Indians from starving, no fish. . . . flour . . . what I have is hardly eatable, being quite black" (January 13, 1814). "We are absolutely without provisions" (January 31). "Hunger is staring us in the face, but Providence will not abandon us" (March 9). "I am heartily tired and sick of this place. There is no situation more miserable than to see objects around you dying with hunger, and unable to give them but little assistance. I have done what I could for them, and will in consequence starve myself" (March 15).[75] The letters show him constantly busy, feeding, cajoling, and sometimes threatening the Indians. He fully trusted only the Menominee and the Winnebago, and his confidential letters contain harsh words about many of the allied tribes, but never did he lose sight of the need to hold them to the British alliance.[76]

His only failure was with the Potawatomi. After the disaster at the Thames, a portion of that tribe had joined several eastern tribes in signing an armistice with the Americans, under which they agreed to surrender prisoners, give hostages, and return home peacefully. Even Main Poc had signed the agreement, although observers noted that he did so with an ill grace and only in order to receive rations for his hungry warriors.[77] The Illinois River Potawatomi were not parties to the armistice, but the fort General Howard built at Peoria in October 1813 duly impressed them, and after an unsuccessful attack on the fort Black Partridge and Gomo also sued for peace.[78]

Nevertheless, Potawatomi tribesmen continued to visit Dickson's camp. By February 1814, Dickson became convinced that the Potawatomi, whom he called "Villains to both sides" and "Our worst enemies" were spying for the Americans and plotting to assassinate him. He took extra precautions to guard his camp and even made a written list of thirty-four reasons to distrust the tribe. He swore to "punish those rascals," and his letters contain oblique references to a plan, involving sending a party of Winnebago to Peoria, that would "frighten [the Potawatomi] out of their wits."[79]

Thomas Forsyth may have been his target. In March 1814 Forsyth visited Gomo, who had returned to his village near the present Chillicothe. Gomo had little firsthand information about Dickson's plans, but he sent his American friend farther upriver to visit the Grand Quet, a Potawatomi chief who had been with Dickson at Lake Winnebago during the winter. The Grand Quet told Forsyth that Dickson had offered him half a houseful of goods if he would capture Forsyth and deliver him to Dickson. The chief claimed to have answered that Dickson was a brave man; he should go to Saint Louis and capture Forsyth himself.[80]

The danger was greater than Forsyth knew. He later learned from Gomo that, shortly after Forsyth had left the Illinois River country to return to Saint Louis, six Winnebago warriors arrived with orders to kidnap him and take him to Dickson. Finding Forsyth gone, the Indians had had to content themselves with stealing horses from the garrison at Fort Clark.[81] The Winnebago had gone away much disappointed, because they had pledged to bring Dickson either Forsyth or his scalp.[82]

The contest for the loyalty of the Illinois River Potawatomi was now essentially over. The theater of war shifted away from the Illinois River valley, and Dickson became preoccupied with other tribes, on other fronts. For the duration of the war, however, Forsyth continued to visit the Potawatomi frequently, always inquiring about Dickson's activities and obtaining from his friend Gomo much detailed information, some of it true. At Governor Edwards's urging, Forsyth tried repeatedly to bring Gomo, Black Partridge, and their warriors into the field on the side of the United States, but Gomo was a master of the art of evasion, and the Illinois River Potawatomi clung tenaciously to a friendly neutrality. They were willing to continue refusing Dickson's invitations to visit him, to provide Forsyth with information, and even to hunt and supply game to the garrison at Fort Clark, but for them the fighting was over. Whenever Forsyth pressed Gomo for action against the British, the chief would change the subject to the tribe's grievances.[83]

Those grievances were genuine. That the Potawatomi did not return to the British alliance is a tribute both to Forsyth's deft management and to the coercive power of the fort that had been built in their midst. When Gomo and Black Partridge had submitted, the tribe had surrendered hostages, who were held at Saint Louis in conditions of squalor. Forsyth pleaded with Missouri's governor, William Clark, to provide them with adequate clothing. As other hostages were released, these Potawatomi continued to be held. At every meeting with Forsyth, Gomo would raise the matter of the hostages and Forsyth would report the chief's requests to his own political masters. Edwards replied sarcastically that he would release one hostage for every enemy the Potawatomi killed in battle.[84]

Equally damaging was that the American government provided neither presents nor provisions to the tribe. Forsyth complained that every pipe of tobacco or slice of bread he shared with his Indian friends had to come from his own pocket. Because the Indian economy depended on supplies from the whites, the Illinois River Potawatomi were left naked and hungry. Forsyth wrote that he had never seen Indians suffer from want like the Potawatomi of the Illinois River.[85]

Nevertheless, the tribe remained at peace, even when a company of Rangers mistakenly massacred a group of friendly Potawatomi out hunting to supply meat to the garrison at Fort Clark. The prospect of a breach with this war-like tribe was alarming: Edwards at first instructed Forsyth to "gloss it over if possible" and cynically advised him to place the blame on the slaughtered Indians. Gomo, however, responded with moderation and Forsyth succeeded in appeasing the surviving kinsmen by "covering the dead," that is, by offering presents in atonement.[86]

When the ice broke in the spring of 1814, Dickson drew off many western Indians to defend Mackinac Island from the American attack that had become inevitable after Perry's victory on Lake Erie gave the United States control of the Great Lakes. Although Dickson detached a portion of his Indian force to assist British colonel William McKay in the recapture of Prairie du Chien, he himself stayed at Mackinac with the remainder to help repel the American attack that eventually came on August 4.[87] Afterwards, Dickson served as a volunteer in the daring surprise and capture of the American ships *Tigress* and *Scorpion* that broke the American blockade of the island.[88]

Despite his services, Dickson's career as Indian superintendent came to a bitter end. In November 1814 he traveled with a shipment of Indian presents to Prairie du Chien, where he was shocked by the condition of the Indians who flocked to the fort seeking food. Many of them had been reduced nearly to skeletons, unable to walk from hunger. Provisions at the fort were low, and Dickson quarreled with Captain Andrew Bulger, the fort's commander, over Dickson's right to feed the Indians from military stores. Colonel Robert McDouall at Mackinac supported Bulger, and in April Dickson was ordered to Mackinac, where McDouall arrested him and dismissed him from the service. Although the war was now over, an angry Dickson traveled to Montreal and London seeking vindication; the authorities seem to have sided with him, for Dickson was raised to the rank of lieutenant colonel and awarded a pension for his services.[89]

The war had destroyed Dickson's livelihood as a fur trader, and he spent the next few years traveling throughout the northwest, partly as agent for Lord Selkirk, who was attempting to found a colony in the Canadian West, but also engaged in other activities that are not fully understood.[90] Certainly the American authorities regarded him with suspicion; Forsyth, now Indian agent for the Sauk, kept his superiors informed of Dickson's movements.[91] In 1818 American authorities even arrested Dickson for suspicious behavior with the Indians. He was taken to Saint Louis, but was quietly released.[92] While moving his family to the East, Dickson stopped at the British post on Drummond Island, now part of Michigan, where he died suddenly on June 20, 1823.[93]

Forsyth also came into conflict with the authorities. The War Department regarded his continuous residence in Saint Louis as an abandonment of his post and superseded him as Indian agent at Peoria.[94] Although Edwards had sometimes quarreled with Forsyth, and on one occasion had even inquired whether he had the right to fire him, he nevertheless respected Forsyth's ability and recommended him as agent to the Sauk at Rock Island. In 1818, Forsyth was appointed Indian agent for Missouri, a position he held until 1830, when he was again dismissed for reasons never made clear, but possibly for his continued insistence on residing at Saint Louis.[95] His dismissal was a mistake. It was the opinion of some, including Forsyth himself, that had he been left in place, the Black Hawk War of 1832 might have been avoided.[96] Thomas Forsyth died at his farm near Saint Louis on October 19, 1833.[97]

Neither Dickson nor Forsyth had much success in mobilizing the tribes as an offensive force.[98] At the same time, however, the anarchic nature of Indian society, the geographic position of the tribes between the warring nations, and the inescapable fact that the Indians had far more to lose than the whites, made tribal neutrality impossible. The greatest contribution that either agent could make lay in diverting the restless energies of the Indian warriors away from his own countrymen. In the end, the hopes of the Indians were betrayed, as they must inevitably have been, and both Dickson and Forsyth lie open to the charge that they manipulated the Indians in a cause that was not their own. True that may be, but nevertheless both men seem to have had for their Indian wards a genuine concern, to which the Indians themselves responded. Forsyth long retained the friendship of so shrewd an operator as Gomo, and even Black Hawk, no friend of the whites, always spoke of Forsyth with respect.

At his last council with his Indian allies after peace was proclaimed, Dickson told them that the treaty rendered it necessary for him to retire to the North, but "that it caused the deepest gloom in his mind to be compelled to leave his much-loved children, and that he could never recover from this sorrow." By some Indians, at least, his feelings were returned. At a council in 1822, the Sioux chief LaFeuille reminded the Americans that "for . . . Col. Robert Dickson, with whom they were so long on terms of intimacy, they cherished feelings such as words could never express."[99]

SEVEN

Edwards

Ninian Edwards's commission as governor expired June 21, 1812. As the day approached and passed, no word came from the Madison administration. The president finally made a recess appointment on July 7, but the mails were so slow that as late as September 2 Edwards still had not received his commission. This did not deter him from calling the First, Second, and Fourth Regiments of territorial militia into active service for the campaign that culminated in his march to Lake Peoria.[1] Edwards also was undeterred by a dispute with Governor William Henry Harrison over military precedence. The Madison administration had left the lines of authority in the territories unclear, but over time it became clear that Harrison was favored. Both Colonel Russell at Vincennes and Colonel Bissell at Saint Louis were made subject to his orders. Finally, on October 7, Secretary of War William Eustis brusquely informed Edwards that Harrison would provide for the defense of Illinois territory.[2] Harrison, however, never made any real provision for the territory, leaving Illinois to defend itself out of its own meager resources.

Fortunately, winter brought a lull in the fighting. After Edwards's and Russell's expedition, the tribes moved their villages farther from the American settlements, leaving their old haunts around Peoria Lake nearly deserted. Many of the Potawatomi moved up the Illinois River to swell the size of Pepper's Village on Aux Sable Creek, three to four miles east of the present Morris. It was there that Thomas Forsyth found Gomo and Black Partridge the following year.[3] At the mouth of Bureau Creek, the Kickapoo and Potawatomi combined to build a more formidable defense. At the top of a hill, they erected five blockhouses, surrounded by a wooden breastwork, with portholes for firing from both the blockhouses and the breastwork. The fort was protected on one side by a large marsh and by the river on the other.[4] Many of the Kickapoo who had lived along the Illinois River, however, united in a village of about 200 warriors on the Iroquois River, about five miles south of its mouth on the Kankakee River.[5] Those Piankashaw who had been living with the Kickapoo near Peoria withdrew after the raid to the lower Rock River, where they lived alongside the Sauk.[6] Before long, however, the Piankashaw moved across the Mississippi, where they tried to find a new home on the Missouri River.[7]

By the end of 1812, all the tribes remaining in the Illinois Territory were at war with the United States, except the tame Kaskaskia, and the Sauk and Fox. The Sauk were divided among themselves. At least half the Sauk, led by chiefs Quashquame and The Blue Chief ("Le Bleu"), favored maintaining the peace, while another faction, led by Black Hawk, moved their lodges away from the others, having already taken up arms in support of the British.[8] Understanding the need to conciliate the Sauk and Fox, Edwards recommended that the government support them in their ongoing war with the Winnebago, a suggestion the secretary of war did not even acknowledge.[9] Instead, beginning with Samuel Whiteside's warning shot in the summer of 1811, the Americans did much to annoy the tribes. An attempt by American speculators to take over the prized lead mines of the Fox near modern Dubuque enraged the tribe, and only the intervention of Indian agent Nicholas Boilvin prevented a violent confrontation.[10]

When violence did occur, it was the fault of the Americans. Captain Nathan Boone of the Missouri Rangers, a conscientious officer, was already concerned about his inability to distinguish friendly Sauk Indians from hostile Winnebago.[11] The Sauk were warned to stay a certain distance from American territory, but in January a young Sauk hunter strayed over the line. Some of Boone's men patrolling in Illinois, across from Fort Mason, captured the young man and brought him back to the Missouri side, where they shot him out of hand and then took his scalp. According to an Indian account that surely refers to this incident, the hunter's friends followed the soldiers' tracks across the river to the neighborhood of the fort, where they found the body: "He had been most cruelly murdered! His face was shot to pieces—his body stabbed in several places—and his head *scalped*! His arms were tied behind him!"[12]

The slaughtered Indian had been friendly and, even more disastrously, was the brother of Chief Quashquame. Two other chiefs, the Blue Chief and Two Hearts, came to the fort to demand reparation. Across the council-fire from them was Maurice Blondeau.[13] Blondeau was a former fur trader, half French and half Indian, who had previously served the British but had been appointed American subagent under William Clark the preceding August. The chiefs warned him that the murder undermined their own efforts to restrain their young men. Blondeau was also indignant at the murder, and at his own lack of authority to make gifts to the dead man's relatives in order to "cover the dead." The Sauk were insistent, but it was not until April that Blondeau was finally able to give them the gifts that put the matter to rest.[14] Throughout these months, moreover, the Sauk were under great pressure from other tribes. Both the Prophet and Main Poc sent them wampum and messages urging them to war. The Potawatomi, the Kickapoo, and even the Sioux all warned the Sauk and Fox that if they did not join the other tribes, they would be treated as enemies. For the time being, however, most of the tribe listened to Blondeau and remained at peace with the Americans.[15]

Some American leaders took advantage of the winter lull to leave the area. Colonel William Russell and Governor Benjamin Howard both returned to their homes in Kentucky. Howard, in fact, did not even communicate with his territory for more than two months and did not return to Saint Louis until March 31, 1813. Even William Henry Harrison, now a major general and deeply engaged in trying to recover Detroit, resigned his commission as governor of Indiana Territory.[16] Only Ninian Edwards, it seemed, remained at his post, building forts, drilling the volunteers, and riding on horseback to supervise his northern frontier.

The governor was also making plans for the day when fighting would resume. None of the volunteers he had requested from Kentucky had ever reached Illinois. The only federal troops available for defense were William Bolin Whiteside's company of Rangers, which had been raised in the territory, and, at Fort Russell, a company of regulars commanded by Captain Thomas Ramsey.[17] In November, however, elements of the 24th Infantry Regiment began arriving at Fort Massac on the Ohio River. The 24th was a regiment newly recruited in Tennessee. Although the headquarters of its colonel, William P. Anderson, was in Nashville, the War Department had scattered the regiment throughout the west, from Saint Louis to Mississippi and Louisiana. Now Fort Massac, easily accessible from Nashville by way of the Cumberland River, was transferred to Anderson's command as a point for assembling, training, and outfitting the scattered units of the regiment.[18]

Fort Massac had been severely damaged in the earthquakes of a year before and was falling to ruin. Because it was being considered for abandonment, no significant repairs had been made. The fort was manned by a small garrison under a lieutenant detached from Colonel Daniel Bissell's command at Saint Louis, but, when the post was assigned to him, Anderson sent Captain Joseph Philips, an artillery officer with an understrength company, to take command there. When the new recruits began arriving at the fort in December, however, they found that an inept War Department had neglected to provide either clothing or shelter for them. Even the officers had trouble finding lodging, and the enlisted men, many of them nearly naked, suffered severely. Many recruits had arrived from the South unprepared for the cold and exposure to which they were subjected. Nevertheless, by March about 550 soldiers, many of them on the sick list, were stationed at Fort Massac. Although the governor must have eyed it longingly, the regiment contributed nothing to the defense of the territory in which it trained. In March, except for two companies sent to Saint Louis, the 24th was ordered to Cleveland, and late in April it marched away to join William Henry Harrison's army.[19] Captain Philips was left behind to command the fort, which he regarded as "intirely out of order for defense or comfortable quarters." He embarked, however, on a program of reconstruction that he predicted would "afford perfect security and comfortable quarters for our complete company."[20]

In January 1813, the inept William Eustis was replaced as secretary of war by the more capable, but somewhat sinister, John Armstrong Jr. The new secretary received proposals for offensive action from Colonel Russell, Governor Howard, the congressional delegates from Illinois and Missouri Territories, and Colonel (and Congressman) Richard Mentor Johnson of Kentucky, but he disapproved them all.[21]

Edwards's plan of defense was more modest than the others presented to the secretary. He recommended that garrisons be established at Peoria and at the mouths of the Rock and Wisconsin Rivers, and that armed boats patrol the rivers. The territory lacked the resources to take such action on its own, until Governor Willie Blount of Tennessee offered Edwards the services of two regiments of volunteers, provided Edwards would agree to supply them after they reached Illinois. The governor arranged for provisions to meet these reinforcements at Prince's Ferry on the Ohio on January 25 and promised to support them on their march to Fort Russell and thence up the Illinois River to build a fort 100 miles from the river mouth. Like the Kentucky volunteers that had been promised before them, however, the Tennesseans never arrived and the plan came to nothing.[22] Finally, in February, Congress at last authorized ten more companies of U.S. Rangers, including three to be raised in Illinois. Edwards was quick to nominate Captains Jacob Short, James B. Moore, and Samuel Whiteside to command them, but the new companies would not be ready to take the field until August.[23]

Meanwhile, in January the left wing of General Harrison's army, led by General James Winchester, was defeated and captured at the battle of French-town, or the River Raisin.[24] Winchester's men were tough Kentuckians, but he had led them too far in advance of the main army and Winchester was forced to surrender to a mixed force of British and Indians, led by Colonel Henry Procter. Among the Indians of Illinois who fought that day were Main Poc, Black Partridge, and Black Hawk. Procter promised protection, but after the surrender he hurried back to Detroit, leaving the American wounded in the hands of the Indians, who massacred many of them. The battle had been a close call, however, and Gomo, at least, believed that the Kentuckians would have prevailed had they held out just a little longer. All the same, the immediate result was another huge rise in the prestige of the British, and a corresponding fall in that of the Americans.[25]

Indian warriors who had taken part in the battle spread throughout the Midwest, bearing news of the British victory. Some of them passed through Illinois. In early February, 1813, a party of returning Indians was spotted cross-ing the Big Muddy River, apparently carrying the news toward Missouri. Ed-wards sent a detachment of militia after them, but the Indians could not be overtaken.[26] At the same time, a separate party of ten Creek Indians, led by two chiefs known as the Little Warrior and the Tuskegee Warrior, eluded Rangers along the Wabash while traveling toward their home in Alabama. These Indians had been inspired by Tecumseh during his visit to the southern tribes in 1811, and when war broke out had gone to Detroit to join the British. After fighting in the battle on the Raisin, they began the homeward journey down the Wabash and across southern Illinois. One account says that a British officer, finding these warriors too volatile to control, had given them presents and sent them home.[27]

On February 9 the Creeks reached the Ohio River where the Cache River then emptied into it, at what is now Mound City. Living there were two American families, the Thomas Clark family, consisting of a married couple, and the Phillips family, consisting of the pregnant Mrs. Phillips, her two grown children, possibly another child, and a man named Kennedy or Canaday. Visiting the Clarks was a neighbor named Shaver, who had come to buy whiskey. At first the Creeks appeared friendly and the Clarks gave them dinner, but after dining the Creeks attacked and murdered both families. Shaver was wounded, but ran for his life and escaped, eventually reaching a neighboring settlement. Armed men followed the Indians across the Ohio River into Kentucky, but lost the trail in a snowstorm. Captain Philips, commanding at Fort Massac, led a detachment of soldiers down the river to bury the dead. Kennedy, the Clarks, and Mrs. Phillips were all found dead at the cabins, and the bodies of young William Phillips and his sister were found in the river sometime afterwards. The unborn baby of Mrs. Phillips had been torn from her womb and impaled on a peg; the hogs were eating the mother's intestines.[28]

The Cache Massacre set off a chain of events that led directly to the Creek war in what is now Alabama.[29] Its more immediate effect, however, was to rekindle the war in Illinois. On February 17 Edwards called out a detachment of Johnson County militia commanded by Sergeant James N. Fox, presumably to guard the vulnerable frontier along the Ohio. They may have been the soldiers who for a time were stationed at Conyers's Fort in the present Pulaski County.[30] The governor also called out part of the Third Regiment of militia, composed of settlers who lived along the Ohio River. They were ordered to pursue the hostile Creeks. On February 27 the regiment was mustered into service at Fort Massac and immediately set out south across the Ohio River under the command of Lieutenant Colonel Hamlet Ferguson.[31] Included in Ferguson's command were the companies of Captains John Prichard and Owen Evans and a company of spies. During a forced march that killed several horses, including the colonel's, the regiment crossed western Kentucky and Tennessee at least as far as the headwaters of the Yazoo River and the country of the Chickasaw Indians. On March 4 Captain Prichard received a crippling bullet wound in the foot, but whether the wound was the result of hostile action or an accident is not recorded. Presumably the regiment failed to overtake the enemy, for it returned to Illinois to be mustered out on March 17.[32]

Over the next few weeks, Edwards put into the field several companies of militia, some mounted, some on foot. In early March he rode to the northern frontier himself, where he saw to it that the forts lying between the Illinois and Kaskaskia Rivers were put in readiness. Under the governor's watchful eye, mounted troops were kept in constant motion between them. Edwards's strategy was effective in protecting the more compact settlements along the Mississippi, but less so the small and scattered settlements along the distant Wabash.[33] Recognizing this, the Indians struck at the eastern end of the long line of stockades and blockhouses. On the night of February 17 Indians boldly stole five horses from the garrison at Fort Allison (now Russellville), and killed a sixth.[34] Five days later there was a more serious attack at nearby Fort LaMotte (now Palestine, Illinois). After being burned by Indians the preceding September, the fort had been rebuilt and by February it was occupied by a detachment of soldiers. On February 22, two men looking for timber about six miles away saw signs of Indians and hurried back to the fort. A squad of about ten men sent out to investigate divided into two groups, one in front and the other acting as a reserve. The area was flooded and at least one account says that the soldiers traveled in canoes. Near where the first two men had turned back, the advance party fell into an ambush. Three men, Isaac Price, Lathrop (or Lotshaw), and Daniel Eaton, were killed and two others, Job Eaton and John Waldrop, were wounded. Rather than come to their aid, the reserve unit fled back to the stockade. The wounded men who escaped estimated that twelve to fifteen Indians had been engaged, and that the soldiers had killed two of them.[35]

The skirmish was followed by four more killings along the Wabash. Heavy rains had brought widespread flooding, through which Indian raiders traveled more easily than could the militia. On February 28 a man was killed at a sugar camp near the Grand Rapids, about twenty to thirty miles below Vincennes,[36] and at about the same time another man was killed on Bon Pas Creek near where it empties into the Wabash at the present Grayville. Along the Embarras River, not far from where the Harriman family had been murdered, a blockhouse had been erected. On March 3, two soldiers went outside, contrary to orders, and were killed and scalped about a mile away.[37]

A few years earlier, Andrew Moore and his family had become the first and only settlers in what is now Jefferson County, giving their name to Moore's

Prairie Township. About the end of February 1813, Moore and his young son failed to return home after a visit to the mill at the Jordan brothers' settlement, near what is now Thompsonville, in Franklin County. The two were missing for about a week, until on March 7 a search party found the skull of the boy and part of the father's. The remains were surrounded by broken tomahawk handles and a vast quantity of blood, indicating that the Moores had died only after a fierce struggle.[38] Out of this event grew a legend that has found its way into all subsequent histories of Jefferson County. According to this story, father and son simply vanished on their return trip, and not until several years later was the father's skull found hanging on a tree not far from the home and recognized by a missing tooth. Supposedly no sign of the son was ever found.[39] As told, the story is fiction. The remains of both father and son were found within a week of their disappearance.

Even less support can be found for the legendary "Battle of the Long Ridge." According to an oral tradition preserved by a local historian, in February 1813 several companies of territorial militia met at what was called the Mustering Oak in what is now the old village cemetery at Equality. Captains Leonard White, Willis Hargrave, and William McHenry then led them in a night attack that destroyed a nearby camp of presumably hostile Shawnee Indians. The battle supposedly raged along the northwest side of a low ridge near the eastern edge of Saline County, in SE ¼ Section 14, T9S, R7E. Unfortunately for local pride, the letters and newspapers of the time make no mention of such a battle, nor is there any mention of a substantial band of Shawnee, hostile or otherwise, living or gathering in Illinois Territory at the time. The Shawnee were primarily an Ohio tribe, and the nearest band of Shawnee, settled in southeastern Missouri near Cape Girardeau, far from being hostile, actually served alongside U.S. troops in the war.[40]

Travel in the eastern part of the territory was dangerous. The governor assigned a detachment of militia to guard the mail between Kaskaskia and the Salines, but even so the carrier was sometimes harassed. The direct route was constantly watched by Indians, and travelers along it did well to travel in large groups, well armed.[41] During the second week of April, François Young and Rev. David McLean, a Baptist minister, traveling together on the post road between Saint Louis and Vincennes, reached the Kaskaskia River at Hill's Ferry, near the present city of Carlyle. The three families who lived there had moved back to the settlements, leaving the ferryboat tied to the west bank. The two men and their horses crossed the river, but before they had gone half a mile, a Kickapoo war party fired on them, killing Young instantly. McLean's horse was also brought down, but the minister threw his saddlebags into the brush and ran for the woods. The Indians followed him, but one by one they turned back, until only a single pursuer remained. McLean took various evasive actions to elude him, even stopping at one point to throw a bag of coins at the Indian. The warrior was relentless, however, and fired a shot that wounded McLean. Not until McLean dived into the icy water of the river did the Indian give up the chase. Eventually McLean succeeded in reaching the settlements, severely wounded. A company of volunteers led by Captain Samuel White-side rode out to bury Young's body, and also recovered McLean's saddle bags untouched. When much later it was rumored that Young had sewn $5,000 into his clothing, digging in search of his grave became a favorite pastime of the citizens of Carlyle.[42]

Perhaps a week after Young and McLean were ambushed, a young farmer named Joseph Boultinghouse (or Boltenhouse) was killed while herding live-stock south of the present Albion, Illinois. When his dog came home alone, friends and family went looking for him. They found his body, shot, scalped, and thrown into his campfire. His head hung from a nearby pole. The prairie in Edwards County on which the young man met his death was afterwards known by his name.[43]

There was a sequel to this story. Three years after the war, the dead boy's father, Captain Daniel Boultinghouse,[44] was hunting with several men from his old company. At a place about seven miles east of the present Fairfield, just south of where the railroad bridge would later cross the Little Wabash River, they came upon the camp of an Indian hunting party, consisting of four men and three women. With them the captain recognized the horse of his dead son. While his companions quietly posted themselves between the Indians and their rifles, the captain questioned the Indian leader about the horse. The Indian said that the horse was his, because he had taken it from a white man during the war, and he even went so far as to mimic the terrified boy's pleas for his life. This was unwise. The four Indian men were shot down immediately, one of them while struggling with the dead boy's dog. As for the three frightened women, because it was peacetime, the killings were unlawful, and so the men agreed that they could leave no witnesses. When the captain rode back to the settlement leading his son's lost filly, it excited comment, but nobody cared to inquire too closely, and the story did not come out until after the captain's death some years later.[45]

On March 22, the Boultinghouse killing was followed by the massacre of an entire family. John Lively was a tough frontiersman who had served in the militia under Captains William Alexander and William Boon.[46] In 1810 or 1811, Lively settled his family near a spring on the west bank of Crooked Creek, in what is now Washington County, a little over a mile southeast of the present Covington. After war broke out, Lively refused to leave, boasting that with his rifle and his dogs he could whip twenty Indians. By March 1813, however, with the death toll mounting, even Lively became apprehensive. The attack on Young and McLean, little more than ten miles away, cannot have escaped his notice. At last, Lively yielded to his wife's entreaties and the family began preparing to leave. About two hours before sunset, as Lively's wife and two daughters milked the cows, Lively sent his young son and a hired man out to gather in the family's horses. He himself kept watch, sitting on a stump with a loaded rifle across his knees. The hired man and boy had not gone far before they heard shots and cries at the farmyard. Turning back, they saw the clearing already swarming with Indians and set off on foot for the settlements. They traveled through the night, stopping to rest at a place afterwards called Lively's Grove. Finally reaching Nat Hill's Fort, they raised the alarm.[47]

A party rode out to bury the dead. Lively had been shot, but his body was neither scalped nor mutilated. The bodies of his wife and daughters had been cut to pieces. The headless body of a small son was found a few miles from the cabin. In the woods near Covington, a monument erected in 1936 marks the spot where the Lively cabin once stood and five rough fieldstones mark the graves of the murdered family.

The family had been killed by a Kickapoo war party led by Little Deer, a chief who at the conference in Cahokia the year before had professed his peaceable disposition. His war party camped overnight at the Lively farm, and then moved east, pursued by part of a company of mounted riflemen led by Captain Boon.[48] Boon's company patrolled the frontier between the Mary River and the Big Muddy and included a number of Indian scouts. Some accounts say that Boon and his men caught up with the war party and killed some of them, but others say that the Indians had too great a head start. According to the recollections of Boon's son, however, the pursuers succeeded in following the trail to a place just east of the present Springfield. There they unexpectedly came upon an encampment of hundreds of Indians. The pursuit changed immediately to flight. Boon and his men rode for three days and nights without food, but apparently the Indians had not seen them, and they returned safely to the settlements.[49]

The massacre of the Lively family was followed closely by other attacks, probably committed by the Potawatomi rather than by the Kickapoo. The first occurred just outside the Jordan brothers' fort near the present Thompson-ville.[50] On April 2, 1813, three men, James Jordan, William Barbrey (or Barber, Barberry, or Barbara),[51] and a man named Walker, were gathering firewood outside the fort when Indians opened fire on them from the brush. Barbrey was killed and Jordan wounded, but Jordan and Walker succeeded in escaping back into the fort.[52] A few days later, and a few miles farther east, an Indian war party chased a man into a blockhouse halfway between Jordan brothers' fort and the United States Salines.[53]

On a dark night in early April, eight or nine men sat shelling corn in a cabin between the present Carmi and Grayville, in what is now White County. Suddenly eight or ten rifles were thrust through the chinks in the cabin walls, firing at once. Hezekiah Davis fell dead, a man named Seabolt was mortally wounded, and Richard Davis was shot in the thigh. Another man, not named, was also badly wounded. The rest were saved by the quick action of James B. Davis, who sprang to the fireplace and stamped out the light of the fire, plunging the cabin into darkness. The Indians soon disappeared into the darkness, taking with them only an old blind horse. The survivors rode to safety at the stockade at New Haven,[54] but the wounded Seabolt died a few days later. The war party had been led by Gomo, a reluctant warrior who as a chief still had to do his part. After the attack, Gomo and his warriors turned homeward. In a display of bravado, along their trail the Indians marked trees with their tomahawks, as a taunt to Colonel Tramell's pursuing militia, who were unable to overtake them on the flooded prairies. Edwards later lamented that had it not been for the high waters, he would have had either Gomo or his scalp.[55]

Although still without a word of instructions or authorization from the government, throughout March Governor Edwards kept eight companies of militia in constant motion on the frontier.[56] Along the Mississippi his efforts remained successful, although occasionally a war party would slip through, as happened in mid-April when a party of Indians tomahawked and scalped a twelve-year-old boy outside his house southeast of Kaskaskia. He was expected to survive.[57] The main concern in Kaskaskia and Saint Louis was that an army of British and Indians, perhaps armed with artillery, might descend the river to attack them. Even Saint Louis was building fortifications. Both newspapers and official correspondence were full of reports about the whereabouts and activities of Robert Dickson, who was known to be gathering the

Indians together and was expected to lead the invading army. Anxiety was heightened by news that Main Poc had returned to Illinois and that the British were unloading gunpowder at Chicago. In Saint Louis, it was said, women and children would start from their sleep, imagining that Dickson and his Indians were "thundering at their doors."[58]

Of course, as the event proved, there was no real danger of an attack in force along the Mississippi. As he had been ordered to do, Dickson was sending all the Indians he could collect to Detroit, to join the fight against Harrison in northern Ohio. Acutely aware that they had weakened their right flank, the British for their part feared an American attack on Chicago, or even Mackinac, by way of the Illinois River. The preceding year, Main Poc had indeed returned to Illinois, where he relocated his village to the lower Fox River, with the evident intention of blocking the route to Chicago. Now, hearing a rumor that an American army was advancing up the Illinois River, he gathered a strong war party to meet it. At the same time, the inhabitants of Prairie du Chien, technically citizens of the United States, but French in heritage and British in sympathy, appealed to the Sioux chief La Feuille to defend them against the American attack they expected to come up the Mississippi River.[59]

The actual danger was to the isolated American cabins and settlements scattered between the Kaskaskia and Wabash Rivers. Although Edwards was unable to prevent attacks there, whenever a war party would strike, Edwards would dispatch mounted men northward to try to intercept the Indians as they returned toward their village. The local militia would also set out in pursuit. The companies of William Boon, William McHenry, and Willis Hargrave were especially active in this way. Usually their efforts were in vain, as when Boon and about thirty men of his company pursued a war party down the Little Wabash but finally had to break off the chase, having entirely exhausted their provisions after twelve days in the wilderness.[60]

There were occasional partial successes. In mid-April the governor ordered William Bolin Whiteside's company of U.S. Rangers to rendezvous with the militia companies of Samuel Whiteside and William Boon on Shoal Creek for a tour ranging on the east side of the Kaskaskia River. Boon's company failed to arrive in time, so about 100 men under the command of William Bolin Whiteside as senior captain, made their way to the river. Intense rains had so swollen the Kaskaskia that the riders could not cross, so they traveled up the west side of the river, over 100 miles into Indian country. Near the source of the Sangamon River, possibly somewhere around the present Ellsworth in

McLean County, the Rangers crossed the trail left by a small party of Indians. Whiteside dispatched twenty-five men under his cousin Samuel to follow them. Samuel's detachment quickly overtook them, but before the soldiers could fire, the Indians fled. Whiteside chased them for ten miles before turning back. The Rangers did succeed, however, in killing and scalping one of the warriors and recapturing all the Indians' plunder: guns, stolen horses, and a scalp with flaxen hair.[61]

Along the postal route between Shawneetown and Kaskaskia stood the house of Robert Cox. Cox lived on Beaucoup Creek, probably in the southern part of what is now Perry County, about five or six miles south and east of the present Pinckneyville. Cox's house was one of the loneliest post offices in the territory, there being only one other family within twenty miles of it. The house must have seemed an easy target to the war party who attacked it at dawn on April 19, 1813, but they found to their surprise that Edwards had stationed a detachment of volunteers there. One of the Indians was shot, but he regained his feet and saved himself by diving into the creek.[62] During the following week there were more attacks along the Wabash. Reportedly six men were killed and three or four wounded just above Vincennes, but the details are unknown.[63]

Two other incidents recorded by tradition may possibly date to this period. One began with a boy named Maurice Hyde, "playing Indians" outside his house in Gallatin County, who was kidnapped by two of the genuine article. A party rode in pursuit, killed one of the Indians, took his scalp, and ran the other into the river. Young Maurice was restored to his family.[64] The other was said to have occurred where Charles Humphreys kept a ferry over the Big Muddy, just above the present Blairsville, in the northwest corner of what is now Williamson County. One night three Kickapoo Indians attacked the house, but Humphreys was able to beat them off with the help of a friendly Indian, the two men firing their guns through cracks in the walls, while Humphreys's wife reloaded.[65]

Edwards understood that only another punishing blow against the Indians could deter their sporadic attacks on the eastern settlements. At the beginning of May he began to plan a spring offensive. The destruction of Peoria had made intelligence about enemy movements difficult to obtain, so the governor commissioned certain French traders to act as spies in Indian country. He even went so far as to offer a reward of $40 for capture of a prisoner whom he could question. In some of the agents he sent beyond the frontiers Edwards had only minimal trust, but he did rely heavily on Thomas Forsyth. In April he sent Forsyth up the Illinois River to gather intelligence that would help him attack the Indian villages, cut off their war parties, and destroy their corn. As already discussed, Forsyth succeeded in traveling as far as Aux Sable Creek, where he questioned both Gomo and Main Poc before returning. He was back in Saint Louis by May 6, and Edwards launched his offensive a few days later.[66]

Setting out from the beleaguered eastern settlements, three companies marched north along the Big Muddy, Saline, and Little Wabash Rivers. Their role was to flush out Indian war parties, which often used those routes, in hopes that they would be intercepted by a larger force under Major Benjamin Stephenson moving northeast from Fort Russell. With Stephenson were three companies commanded by Captains William Boon, James B. Moore, and Jacob Short.[67] A fourth company, also part of Stephenson's command, was to proceed up the Illinois River in an armed boat under the command of Captain Nicholas Jarrot.[68] Two other companies were to range as usual between the Illinois and Kaskaskia Rivers.[69] Presumably one of the two ranging companies was the one commanded by Captain William Jones, which was in service between May 9 and June 9, while the other may have been that commanded by Lieutenant Daniel G. Moore.[70]

All the companies ascending from the eastern part of the territory saw plentiful signs of Indians. The detachment that went up the Saline River, under Colonel Tramell, pursued a party of Indians from the United States Salines all the way to the Illinois River, where the soldiers' horses became too tired to proceed any further, forcing a reluctant Tramell to turn back. Jarrot's armed boat went as far as Peoria, which he found deserted. Although Jarrot heard shooting on either side of the river, the only Indian he saw was one who escaped by canoe into the flooded bottoms.[71]

Because Edwards blamed the Kickapoo, especially Little Deer, for much of the carnage on the frontier, the principal objective he gave Stephenson was to destroy the Grand Village of the Kickapoo in what is now McLean County. For years this village had been the tribe's principal residence; it has been plausibly, but not conclusively, identified with the spot known to archaeologists as the Warren Bane site, occupied today by a park, about five miles northeast of the village of LeRoy. Leaving Fort Russell on May 8, Stephenson led his men up the watershed between the Illinois and Sangamon Rivers on their left and the Kaskaskia River on their right. It was a difficult march; heavy rains had turned much of the prairie into a mire, into which the horses sank up to their knees.

The men remained orderly and in good spirits, however, and on the seventh day of their march they crossed the Sangamon to attack the Kickapoo town.[72]

Stephenson's men approached with caution to ensure surprise, but when they reached the town they found it empty. The town at one time was encircled by a stockade and bastions; the major's report does not mention a stockade, but it does say that in the town were "some very large houses built in the first style of Indian architecture and a considerable number of smaller ones." Nearby was a smaller Indian camp "containing fourteen lodges of considerable size." Both town and camp appeared to Stephenson to have been abandoned only a few days before he arrived. The soldiers burnt both. Having found no enemy to fight, Stephenson divided his force, so that each company could return by a different route in hopes of intercepting returning war parties. The major himself returned with Short's company. On the return trip they crossed a river that Stephenson called the Mink, but that was more probably the south fork of Salt Creek. Between that creek and the Sangamon the battalion found an Indian village that had been recently built and hastily abandoned. Other Indian signs were discovered on the return route, but only Moore's men sighted an enemy, six Indians whom they could not overtake.[73]

The results of the governor's spring offensive had been less than he had hoped but were still by no means negligible. The Americans had shown once again that they could march at will far into Indian country, forcing the tribesmen to flee for their lives. For a time, attacks on the settlements ceased and the territory had a quiet summer ahead.[74]

This was to be Edwards's last campaign as a military leader. Since the previous fall he had heard not a word from the Department of War. Although he had repeatedly asked for instructions, he had received none. His requests for more troops had also seemingly fallen on deaf ears. Although the governor wrote regularly to inform the successive secretaries of war of his actions, he had never received a word either approving or disapproving the course he had taken.[75] Now, characteristically, Secretary Armstrong left it to Governor Howard to inform Edwards that he had been relieved of command. Needing a commander for the new force of U.S. Rangers Congress had created, the government appointed Howard a brigadier general with authority over Missouri, Illinois, and Indiana Territories. As if to make the insult to Edwards more acute, Howard was told that if he decided to decline the appointment, he should give the commission to Indian agent William Clark. Howard, though, accepted the commission and Clark succeeded him as governor of Missouri Territory.[76]

Edwards was deeply hurt. Although he never said so, he might have re-flected that the previous winter and spring, while Howard had been warming himself at the fireside in distant Kentucky, Edwards had been riding through freezing rain along his northern frontier. He had not left his post for a single day. Nevertheless, he promptly turned over his military command to Howard. The enlistments of the militia companies Edwards had called out were expiring, and he had already determined not to renew them without instructions from the secretary of war. Now he ordered Colonel William Whiteside to discharge any militiamen still in the field. The three newly commissioned captains of Rangers—Moore, Short, and Samuel Whiteside—he directed to report to Howard and receive his orders. The civil administration of the territory was turned over to the territorial secretary, Nathaniel Pope, and then the governor rode home to Kentucky, to visit a family he had not seen in more than nine months.[77]

Edwards had a long political career: chief justice of Kentucky, nine years as territorial governor, U.S. senator, U.S. minister to Mexico, third governor of the State of Illinois. Despite those distinguished titles, however, his record in office rarely rose above the uninspiring and occasionally descended to the ridiculous. Edwards sometimes acted foolishly, and some of the political dif-ficulties in which he later found himself resulted from his own bad judgment. Moreover, his not infrequent displays of vanity, pomposity, and cynicism can make it hard to feel much warmth for him as a man. All that may be true, but for two years of grave public danger Edwards was true to the best that was in him. Despite all the obstacles placed in his path, he strove, with unceasing courage and energy, to do his full duty toward the territory that had been en-trusted to his care. For that, Ninian Edwards will always deserve the gratitude of the people of Illinois.[78]

EIGHT

Howard

The new commander in Illinois and Missouri Territories was Brigadier General Benjamin Howard, a native Kentuckian, then about fifty-three years of age. Although no professional soldier, in his youth Howard had fought Indians in his state's border warfare and he is said to have commanded volunteers attached to Anthony Wayne's army. After peace was restored, Howard entered a career in his native Lexington as a lawyer and, briefly, as a judge. In 1800 he was elected to the Kentucky legislature and in 1807 to the United States House of Representatives. Howard served in the Tenth and Eleventh Congresses, but in 1810 he resigned from Congress to accept appointment as governor of Louisiana (soon renamed Missouri) Territory, a post in which he succeeded the ill-fated Meriwether Lewis. During the early stages of the war he showed energy and initiative.

In December 1812, however, Howard placed government of the territory in the hands of the secretary, Frederick Bates, and returned to pass the winter at his home in Kentucky. Although Howard continued to correspond with Washington, nobody at Saint Louis heard from him during the three months following his departure. Quite possibly Howard was distracted by the illness of his wife Mary, but, believing that she was out of danger, he at last set out for

Saint Louis. He was still on the road when she died at Lexington on March 21, 1813. Ten days later Howard arrived at Saint Louis, after an absence of four months. Soon after his return the mail brought him a commission as a brigadier general and instructions to confer the office of governor on the Indian agent, General William Clark.[1] Shortly thereafter, Colonel Daniel Bissell, who had commanded the district for four years, was ordered to rejoin his regiment at Buffalo, New York. The transfer was for the best; Howard had a low opinion of Bissell and as governor had tried to have him transferred to another post. Now Bissell departed for the East, leaving Lieutenant Colonel Robert Carter Nicholas of the First Infantry to succeed him at Saint Louis.[2]

When Ninian Edwards turned over military command of Illinois to Howard on June 16, the territory was enjoying a respite from the bloodshed of the previous winter and spring. By the middle of June, not a single company of militia was in the field, a welcome relief to the citizen soldiers. Service in the field for the better part of a year and a half had reduced many militiamen to real distress. Despite many promises, none of them had yet been paid.[3] Edwards's spring offensive may have contributed to the lull, but even more important had been the success of British agent Robert Dickson in stripping the northwest of its fighting warriors for service under General Henry Procter at Detroit.[4] In neighboring Indiana the enemy vanished as well. During June, three separate American military expeditions, commanded respectively by Colonel Richard Mentor Johnson,[5] Colonel Joseph Bartholomew,[6] and Colonel William Russell[7] scouted hundreds of miles throughout that entire territory without ever finding the enemy.

In fact, by this time American authorities had begun to recognize that the likelihood of a major invasion of Illinois or Missouri was very small.[8] When Colonel Johnson returned from his wet and exhausting scout through northern Indiana, he found that the War Department had ordered his regiment to Kaskaskia to defend the settlements along the Mississippi. This news was unwelcome to the colonel. Although Johnson was a patriot, he was also a politician, and he knew that the real fight, and the real glory, would be in Ohio and Ontario. Johnson protested the order, coming very close to the edge of insubordination, but General William Henry Harrison was inflexible in insisting that Johnson obey orders with which Harrison himself disagreed. The colonel complied, but did so in slow motion, announcing that his regiment would go from Fort Wayne to Kaskaskia by way of Kentucky, where it could replace its horses and obtain new recruits. His gamble paid off: While Johnson's regiment was slow-walking toward Kentucky, new orders came from the War Department canceling the march to Kaskaskia and attaching the regiment to Harrison's army.[9] Johnson and his men afterwards rode to glory at the battle of the Thames, where their charge routed the British and where, badly wounded amidst a storm of arrows and bullets, the colonel himself was said to have killed the great Tecumseh.[10]

Along the Mississippi, the war resumed in July. On July 4, 1813, a party of eleven Rangers, patrolling the west bank near the recently evacuated Fort Mason, a few miles south of the present Hannibal, Missouri, met an equal number of Winnebago warriors in a desperate fight within a confined space of not more than twenty-four square feet. One Ranger was killed and three wounded, two of them mortally, while the Indians left two dead on the field. The next day Indians again attacked the surviving Rangers near their camp, forcing the outnumbered Rangers to withdraw.[11] Five days later, about 150 Missouri Rangers, returning to the scene of the July 4 fight, saw three canoes, carrying between twenty and thirty Indians. Believing that they were of a party that had recently attacked Fort Madison, now descending the river to attack the settlements, the Rangers opened fire, driving the canoes to an island along the Illinois shore, possibly what is now called Saverton Island. Both sides kept up a heavy fire until an Indian raised a flag of blue cloth. The Rangers ceased firing, but when the Indian fired a gun at them, firing was immediately resumed and was continued until the surviving Indians disappeared. It was thought that only two or three escaped.[12]

By contrast, the Illinois River had been quiet, and in May Captain Nicholas Jarrot's armed boat had found the village of Peoria deserted. Nevertheless, by July the Potawatomi had begun returning to Peoria Lake, where abundant fish enabled them to support their families. From Peoria, the Illinois River would also provide their war parties with an easy route toward the settlements. On July 8, Howard sent another armed boat up the Illinois River to reconnoiter. The boat was commanded by Lieutenant John Campbell, an officer for whom Howard had a high regard and in whose career he had taken an interest. In 1811 Campbell had led a small detachment that built a short-lived blockhouse at Prairie Marcot, in what is now Calhoun County, and in 1812 he had been assigned to build and command Fort Mason on the Mississippi. Howard considered Lieutenant Campbell a "useful" officer deserving of promotion, and one well suited to command a frontier post.[13]

Campbell had thirty-nine regulars under his direct command and he was operating in conjunction with a detachment of Rangers Howard sent by land toward the Sangamon River, in hopes of intercepting any Indians Campbell might scare away from the Illinois. At dawn on July 15, about eighty miles up the river, Campbell's boat came under heavy fire from the riverbank only forty feet away. The regulars returned fire, and the fight continued for "a considerable time" until the Indians withdrew. Two warriors were seen killed on the shore, and Campbell believed that others must have been hit among the bushes and tall grass. Campbell ordered his boat to proceed farther upriver in search of their canoes, but, not finding them, he dropped back down to where his boat had first been attacked. The Indians were waiting. They renewed the attack with increased fury, but after a firefight of half an hour, during which the troops claimed that several warriors fell, the Indians broke off the fight. Campbell now dropped his boat lower down the river, to permit his men to go ashore, but as they did so a sentinel warned that a canoe was approaching from upriver. Campbell's men returned to their gunboat and set out to meet the canoe, but the Indians fled to the bank, where they abandoned their canoe and gear to the soldiers. Now fifteen more canoes appeared from upriver, and Campbell sailed to meet them. The Indians began "a warm fire," but Campbell's boat was armed with a swivel gun that, along with volleys of musketry, soon dispersed them. Three soldiers on the gunboat were wounded. The detachment of Rangers cooperating with Campbell on land found a fresh trail leading from the river, pursued the Indians, and briefly overtook them, but the ground was unfavorable to the Rangers and the Indians escaped without further casualties on either side.[14]

The four companies of U.S. Rangers allotted to Illinois were now active. To the original company commanded by William Bolin Whiteside had been added new companies commanded by Captains Samuel Whiteside, Jacob Short, and James B. Moore, all officers who had been recommended by Edwards. The Rangers were usually stationed at or near the frontier but would range widely over the area beyond the settlements. In 1813 William B. Whiteside's company was based at a fort opposite the mouth of the Missouri River, from which it could guard the water route to the settlements as well as patrol beyond the frontier. John Reynolds, future governor and historian, served in this company. In later years, Reynolds's sobriquet "The Old Ranger" became an important part of his folksy political persona as a rough-hewn frontiersman, an image that might not otherwise have come naturally to a man who, unusually for that time and place, was a college graduate, a lawyer, and, by his own admission, a good Latin scholar. Many years later "The Old Ranger" recalled his first scout: "[O]ur company made a tour up the east side of Shoal Creek from Hill's Fort by the present site of Greenville, Bond County, and camped one night at Jones' cabins, north of Greenville. This was the first night I stood guard, and I considered it a lonesome, tedious affair. We marched high up Shoal and Silver Creeks, and crossed Cahokia Creek near the town of Edwardsville. This was ranging, and it was severe labor. But after a person is at home a few days he is anxious for another tour." Samuel Whiteside's company was accustomed to camp along Silver Creek, north of the settlements, while Captain Short made a large camp on Crooked Creek, on the site of the cabin where the Lively family had been massacred, not far from the present Covington.[15]

Short's company was camped at the Lively cabin on July 17, when six Rangers detached on patrol found and followed a fresh trail. Seven Indians had stolen fourteen horses on the frontier of Randolph County and were leading them back toward the Wabash. By hard riding, the Rangers caught up with the Indians about sunset. A sharp fight took place on the darkening prairie, in which the sergeant commanding the detachment was wounded, and the Rangers believed that two of the Indians had been killed. Both sides fought bravely, but the Indians held their ground and the Rangers were hard pressed. Unwilling to retreat, the Rangers sent an express back to Captain Short asking for reinforcements. The captain and thirty of his men were in the saddle immediately and rode all night before finally overtaking the war party on either the 18th or the morning of the 19th, near a fork in the Little Wabash River. The Indians must have thought themselves safe, for one of them shot a turkey for their meal. The sound of the gunshot alerted Short and his men that their quarry was near. Rather than run, the Indians prepared for battle, assuming they could hold off the Rangers as they had done before. Short and his men succeeded in surrounding them, however, and seeing that they were doomed, the warriors began to sing their death song. They died courageously, shouting defiance at the whites. According to one account, all were killed, but according to another four died and one escaped. One Ranger, William O'Neal, was killed in the fight, while others were slightly wounded. The stolen horses were recaptured, but many of the Rangers' own horses died from the rigors of the pursuit.[16]

Exactly where Short's battle took place is uncertain. Reynolds, writing long after the event, said that Short and his men pursued the Indians to "a fork of the Little Wabash, seventy or eighty miles from Lively's cabins," which, if read literally, would place the fight in the southeastern part of Shelby County. By contrast, the contemporary account in the *Missouri Gazette* states that the pursuit lasted forty miles, which perhaps suggests a location in either eastern Marion or southern Fayette County. It is interesting to note that there is a later tradition of an otherwise unknown battle in 1813 that might possibly refer to this event. According to that story, Samuel Whiteside and twenty rangers set out from Saint Clair County in pursuit of Indians who had killed a family near Kaskaskia. The rangers overtook the war party in what is now Marion County, Salem Township (T2N, R2E). The Indians took cover in the timber along South Creek, in section 25. Five Indians and one of Whiteside's men were killed, and the fight continued until nightfall, after which the surviving Indians fled.[17] No contemporary record has been found of such a battle with Whiteside in command, but if allowance is made for the vagaries of oral tradition, the description of the fight itself sounds very much like the accounts of Short's battle.

In January, Howard had written to the secretary of war with an ambitious plan for a spring campaign requiring 4,000 mounted troops. Half would march from Louisville up the Wabash via Prophetstown, while the other half would march from Saint Louis up the Illinois and Fox Rivers, joining the other corps on the Illinois River. The united army would then march overland to Rock River, where it would build a fort, before continuing on to the Wisconsin River and Prairie du Chien. The War Department rejected the plan, perhaps recalling how difficult Edwards and Hopkins had found it to unite their forces at the same place, but more probably deterred by the enormous expense such a campaign would cause to a parsimonious government.[18] Now in command in the northwest, Howard advanced a more modest proposal to move against the Potawatomi villages on Peoria Lake, and also to seize Prairie du Chien by water and to fortify it. Although his plan was approved by the War Department, approval came too late in the season to permit a movement against Prairie du Chien. Howard feared that the river would close up before he could obtain sufficient supplies to establish and maintain a garrison so far from Saint Louis. He may also have been influenced by the false rumor that Robert Dickson had arrived at Prairie du Chien with a force of Canadians and Indians, armed with artillery, and was daily expecting the arrival of British regulars. The objective of Howard's expedition would be limited to Peoria alone.[19]

Howard began to assemble an army. He was bitterly disappointed that he would not have the services of Johnson's regiment of mounted Kentuckians, on which he had been counting.[20] He would, however, have the understrength First Infantry Regiment, which was stationed just above Saint Louis at Fort Bellefontaine and Portage des Sioux, as well as two companies of the 24th that had been left behind at Bellefontaine. Captain Thomas Ramsey's small company at Fort Russell had already been withdrawn from that post and consolidated with the main body. The only regular troops now remaining in Illinois Territory were a handful at Fort Massac. Sickness had laid low much of that garrison, for whom the government had not troubled itself to provide a doctor.[21]

Howard also had authority to call on the territorial governors for their militia. On July 24 Howard wrote to Nathaniel Pope, acting governor of Illinois Territory in the absence of Governor Edwards, asking him to raise a company of five officers, eight noncommissioned officers, and 100 privates, to rendezvous at Savage's Ferry on the Mississippi on August 15. Pope assigned Captain Samuel Judy to raise the company, but Judy had to report to the acting governor that the people were "backward" about turning out and that the company could not be raised without a draft. The government's relaxed attitude toward paying the militia was bearing bitter fruit. Howard's response has not been found, but presumably there was a draft, for Judy led a company in the expedition.[22]

Provoked by continuing attacks in Missouri that he believed to have come from Illinois, Howard sent a detachment under Captain Robert Desha of the 24th Infantry up the Illinois River in an armed boat to hunt for Indians descending by water,[23] and also sent Major Nathan Boone with sixteen picked Rangers to scout the land route Howard planned to take. On August 12 or 13, Boone's detachment crossed the Mississippi in boats to what is now Calhoun County, Illinois.[24] Riding north for the first two days, Boone's men saw no sign of Indians, but as they lay camped on the night of August 15, a sentinel discovered Indians moving quietly through the woods to surround the camp. Not knowing from which direction the attack would come. Boone ordered his men away from the campfires and placed them behind trees around the camp. One of the sentinels, a man named White, came face to face with an Indian; both raised their guns to shoot, but the Indian's shot took off both White's thumbs. With that, the enemy rushed the camp from one side, and Boone's men took cover behind trees on the other. The Indians presented an easy target as they approached the campfires, but many of the Rangers' guns had become wet and would not fire. Boone ordered his men to fall back slowly, from tree to tree, and the major himself stepped backward into a sinkhole, falling to the ground. At that moment, the Indians fired a volley that, but for his fall, would have killed Boone. The Indians fired a few more guns from the campsite but didn't press their attack, having apparently been distracted by the opportunity to steal the Rangers' horses. At daylight Boone and his men rounded up about half their horses and made their way back to their starting point, the little fort across the Mississippi from Cap au Gris. Besides the unfortunate White, only one man had been wounded, and he but slightly in the shoulder.[25]

Howard's expedition set out on September 10 from Portage des Sioux, which under Howard had become the principal assembly point for troops in Missouri.[26] Howard planned to combine two forces. West of the Mississippi were about 400 men, including the Missouri Rangers and three companies of mounted militia, all under the command of Colonel Alexander McNair, later the first governor of the State of Missouri.[27] Majors Nathan Boone and William Christy[28] commanded battalions. On the east bank, Illinois troops had been ordered to gather at "Piasa," opposite Portage des Sioux. Possibly these troops were camped at the mouth of Piasa Creek, between the present Alton and Elsah, but more probably they assembled at the blockhouse near the present Grafton and the ancient Indian rock painting known as the Piasa Bird.[29] The Illinois troops were commanded by Colonel Benjamin Stephenson, with John Moredock and William Bolin Whiteside serving under him as majors. Included in the Illinois contingent were companies of Rangers and mounted militia, under captains Samuel Whiteside and Samuel Judy and Lieutenant Nathaniel Journey, as well as others whose names were not specifically recorded.[30] In addition, about 100 U.S. Rangers from Indiana Territory, commanded by Captain Pierre André,[31] also formed part of Howard's land force.[32] Ascending the Illinois River in armed boats would be 200 regulars of the First Infantry under Lieutenant Colonel Nicholas.[33]

Trying to protect the settlements behind him by covering as wide a front as possible, Howard ordered the land troops to march north along both sides of the Mississippi before uniting, while Nicholas and the regulars would sweep the Illinois River clear as they proceeded to Peoria to build a fort. With the aid of a large pirogue, Stephenson's force crossed the Illinois River not far from its mouth. They then marched north up the peninsula which is now Calhoun County, descended to the Salt Prairie, and halted to allow McNair's regiment on the west bank to catch up.[34] While Stephenson's men waited, scouts saw two Indian trails leading toward the Illinois River. Rangers rode in pursuit, but the Indians taunted them by stealing two or three of their horses. There was a skirmish in which a good deal of powder and ammunition were

Figure 11. Benjamin
Howard. Artist
unknown. Courtesy
of State Historical
Society of Missouri,
Columbia, Missouri.

expended but nobody was hurt, ending in the Rangers chasing the Indians across the Illinois River.[35]

Howard and McNair had been delayed because on September 14, just north of Cap au Gris, they had met a large band of friendly Sauk Indians descending the west bank of the Mississippi toward Saint Louis. After the affair at Fort Mason had been settled, subagent Maurice Blondeau had continued working to keep most of the tribe neutral. In May 1813, he had escorted Quashquame and a band of seventy or eighty warriors and their families to Saint Louis, seeking the protection of the government. The chief had met with Howard and offered his warriors to fight for the Americans. Quashquame explained that in the midst of a great war it would be impossible for him to keep his young men neutral and that he preferred that they fight for the Americans. Only a month earlier Howard had created a diplomatic incident by refusing a similar offer made by the Osage,[36] and he also declined to accept the services of the Sauk.

The present band of Sauk, however, was proceeding downriver by invitation. Recognizing how difficult it was for frontier troops to distinguish between friendly and hostile tribesmen, Ninian Edwards had frequently recommended removing the friendly Sauk behind American lines.[37] Understanding the need to draw the Sauk outside British influence, Governor Clark had sent Indian agents Maurice Blondeau and Nicholas Boilvin[38] to bring the Sauk to meet him, in the hope of persuading them to resettle on the Missouri River. Blondeau brought down the warriors and young men by land, while Boilvin brought the women, children, and old men by water. Presumably Howard met with Blondeau's band, for on September 15 he urged their chief, Black Tobacco, to wait with his people on an island near Cap au Gris until Boilvin arrived to conduct them to a council with Governor Clark at Portage des Sioux. What Howard did not want was for hundreds of Indians, even nominally friendly ones, to show up at Saint Louis while the army was absent. Black Tobacco reluctantly agreed, after Howard made arrangements for the military contractor to feed the Indians while they waited.[39]

Howard continued his march up the west bank to the vicinity of Ramsey Creek, where on September 16 the army crossed the river under the eyes of its general. To ferry men, arms, horses, baggage, and provisions to the opposite bank, the regiment had only two small pontoon boats, formed of boards laid across canoes. To have carried the whole regiment across in this fashion might have consumed days, so upwards of 300 men swam their horses across the Mississippi River. Before taking to the water, the Rangers removed every item of clothing but their hats, leaving their baggage to follow them on the pontoon boat. Years later, one of them recalled the scene:

> [T]his all answered very well, until the lads gained the Illinois side where on assending from the river they found themselves on low ground sorrounded by towering timber, the whole earth covered with a weed called *nettles*, four or five feet high, and standing thick as hemp, in addition to this there were clouds of *misquittos* which almost covered their dripping bodies. The nettles stung the horses, they snorted, reared and dashed about, tore the mens lower extremities through the tormenting briars, while the winged insects almost covered them,—the scene was ludicrous in the extreme, and no relief for some hours, until the platform came with the clothes. Now imagine 300 men all mounted, with nothing on but *hats*, contending with these tormentors, their horses so restive they were ungovernable, and you have the scene before you.[40]

Apparently the Illinois troops had gone a little ahead, but by September 19 Howard had his entire mounted force united on the Illinois side of the river at a place Howard called Tower Hill. Despite their adventure crossing the river, the troops from Missouri were healthy, but Howard found the Illinois contingent "sickly" and sent some of them home.[41]

Howard led his now-united army up the Mississippi River bottom to a place he called "Christy's Creek."[42] On the way, they passed another large encampment of Sauk. The Sauk professed to be friendly, but Howard and his army distrusted them. Their numbers were about equal to Howard's, and the two parties spent an uneasy night camped side by side. The next day, Howard urged the Indians to descend the Mississippi to meet with Governor Clark, who would resettle them along the Missouri.[43] The army then struck out east across the prairie for the Illinois River, which they reached at a point near the mouth of Spoon River.[44]

Howard had planned his route in such a way as to keep the Indians guessing about his intentions. The band of hostile Sauk still residing on Rock River, fearing that their village was the army's target, convened a council to decide what to do. In the absence of Black Hawk, their most determined war leader, and many of their bravest warriors, the tribal council decided to abandon their village and flee beyond the Mississippi River. At this moment, a young man named Keokuk,[45] who was not eligible to address the council because he had never killed an enemy in battle, asked, and was granted, permission to speak. Keokuk urged the council not to abandon the graves of their fathers merely because they had heard of the approach of an enemy, and offered himself as their leader. Moved by his eloquence, the council acclaimed Keokuk a war chief, launching him on a notable career as, ironically, eventual leader of the peace party among the Sauk and as Black Hawk's main rival. The new chief marshaled the warriors and sent out scouts to track enemy progress. A clash was avoided when Howard's army turned east toward Peoria, but Keokuk's conduct won the acclaim of his tribe.[46]

On the route, Howard and his army saw many signs that Indians had retired before them. The army continued along the bank and on the evening of September 28 halted a few miles from the site of Peoria. There Howard sent a messenger upriver to Lieutenant Colonel Nicholas, who came himself to report to the general.[47]

After an uneventful trip, Nicholas had arrived at Peoria about September 23, to find the old French village deserted and forlorn. Many of the houses had been burnt by Craig, and most of the remainder by the Kickapoo. A few outbuildings belonging to Thomas Forsyth were still standing, but Nicholas and his men knocked them down for firewood, while the good lumber was used for the fort Nicholas and his men immediately began to build.[48] The first buildings they began were the blockhouses, which were unfinished, but far enough along to be serviceable, when the Indians attacked on September 27.

As Howard's army approached, the Indians had withdrawn farther to the north. According to one later story, though, when he learned that the soldiers had come to build a fort in Indian country, Black Partridge armed himself with rifle and tomahawk and rode on horseback through the Indian camp, calling for warriors to join him. Although many chiefs and warriors, including Gomo, Shabbona, Waubansee, and Main Poc, were with the British in Canada, enough warriors remained for Black Partridge to lead a war party against the Americans.[49] At nightfall the Indians tried to approach Nicholas's camp by stealth. Sentries discovered them, however, before they had approached within 150 yards of the soldiers' position, and firing began on both sides. Three soldiers, including George Davenport, the future father of Rock Island, were outside the lines near the riverbank when the shooting began. With the Indians whooping and firing behind them, the soldiers ran for the armed boats, but the boats had pushed off from the bank when the firing began. Fortunately for Davenport and his companions, one of the boats ran aground. The three soldiers hurried to push it off and jump aboard. The Indians fired on the boats, whose guns returned fire from the river, although a ball fired by a too-hastily-aimed cannon tore the side off one of the boats. Nicholas also opened fire with blasts of grapeshot from the partially completed blockhouses, and the attackers slipped away. One soldier had been wounded and the Indians left blood on the ground.[50]

When Howard arrived below Peoria the next day, Nicholas sent a boat to transport the sick to his own camp. The rest of the army enjoyed a leisurely ride along the river, reaching Peoria in the evening. When the men first caught sight of the lake, the army halted involuntarily, charmed by the beauty of the scene. Howard and his mounted men spent one night camped beside the regulars at Peoria, but the night was a sleepless one. The men were turned out by one false alarm after another. Guns were fired at phantoms, and a young soldier from Kentucky was mistakenly shot and killed by a sentinel.[51]

The next day Howard's army drew out provisions, left its sick men at Peoria, and rode upriver after the Indians. At the head of the lake, they found Gomo's village deserted and, after digging up the buried supplies of corn, burned it to the ground. Howard and his men camped two nights among the ashes of Gomo's village, as if challenging the Indians to attack. Those two nights were the worst in the whole expedition for alarms and uproar, but no Indians were seen. On the third day, after burning a couple of smaller villages, Howard led his men back to Peoria, where the U.S. Rangers and volunteers crossed the river to camp on the southeast side. The horses swam across and boats ferried over men and baggage. The regulars remained on the north side, amidst the ruins of Peoria, where they continued work on the fort.[52]

Howard had divided his force and encamped his mounted men south of the river because that was where the timber was. Rangers and volunteers laid aside their rifles and took up saws and axes, brought up from Saint Louis in the armed boats. The logs they cut were dragged on sledges to the lakeshore, where the regulars rafted them across to the other side. Building a fort at Peoria had long been a dream of American authorities, and with a volley of cannon fire on September 23, Nicholas had christened the post Fort Clark, in honor of George Rogers Clark, the hero who had won the Illinois country for the United States. The fort stood alongside the river, near what is now the intersection of Liberty and Water streets. According to one who arrived at Peoria in 1831, when vestiges of the fort were still visible, the fort consisted of a square formed by two rows of palisades with earth between them, surrounded by a ditch protected by bastions. One corner of the enclosure pointed toward the river.[53] Howard described the fort as "completely commanding the river" and "unquestionably one of the strongest I have seen in the Western Country."[54]

Meanwhile, Howard sent out two detachments on separate scouts. One party, under Major Christy, went up the Illinois River in two boats. The other, under Major Boone, rode overland north from Peoria.[55] Christy and his men traveled upriver, intending to reach the mouth of the Fox River, but at Starved Rock they halted about nine miles short of their goal. Unwilling to risk his boats in the rapids that began at that point and extended as far as the Fox, Christy turned back without having seen any Indians.[56] The Indians, though, had seen him. Their scouts had been watching Christy's boats all the way up the river, and when on the return trip Christy put in at the mouth of Bureau Creek, the Indians knew immediately. Nine miles up the creek, at the present site of Tiskilwa, was a village of the Potawatomi.[57] Its women and children had been moved to a place of safety, a ridge called "The Backbone," a mile or two northwest of the present city of Princeton, while the men massed below to defend them. According to one story, Christy sent a detachment under Lieutenant David Robinson up the creek in search of Indians. After marching a few miles, Robinson realized that his men were in grave danger in the heavy timber. He turned back, not far, it is said, from where hundreds of Indian warriors lay waiting for him. The stream along which the lieutenant narrowly escaped disaster was for some years known as "Robinson's River," before the name gave way to the present one of Bureau Creek.[58]

Meanwhile Boone led about one hundred men to look for Indians in the direction of Rock River. Along the Spoon River he found several camps or villages that appeared to have been recently deserted, but Boone and his men saw no Indians before returning to Peoria. Howard had been considering a return by way of the mouth of Rock River, and part of Boone's mission had been to scout out a route for the army, but before his detachment returned, a change in the weather had made such an idea impractical. October proved unexpectedly cold, and many of Howard's men were not prepared for the frigid temperatures. On October 15, Howard's mounted men began their journey home.[59]

Six days later, the army arrived back at Fort Russell in good spirits. The Indiana Rangers under Captain André had been sent directly back to Vincennes, with an intermediate stop at "the old Kickapoos Towns," presumably the town Stephenson's troops had burned in May. One part of André's mission was to scout a route between Peoria and Vincennes, perhaps an echo of Hopkins's disastrous march the previous fall. He was also to keep an eye open for a Kickapoo war party that was harassing the eastern frontier of Illinois Territory from their village on the Iroquois River.[60] Howard was sufficiently concerned about the safety of André and his men that he delayed making his report to Secretary of War Armstrong until after he learned that they had returned safely to Vincennes.[61]

That the Kickapoo were still dangerous was proven by another attack near the Embarras River blockhouse. The blockhouse was manned by a detachment of Rangers from the Indiana company of Captain Frederick Shoults.[62] In the afternoon of October 16, a war party estimated at between fifteen and twenty Indians opened fire on two Rangers who had gone outside the blockhouse to shoot ducks along the river. One soldier was wounded in several places, and the other was killed. Five balls stuck the latter's body, and another seven pierced his hat. A party of U.S. Rangers started after the Indians, but it does not appear that they overtook them.[63]

Trouble along the Wabash was complemented by a serious setback along the Mississippi. Fort Madison, on the present site of Fort Madison, Iowa, was the most vulnerable American military post remaining in the Northwest, not only because it was isolated but because the terrain around it gave every advantage to attackers. Almost from the time it was built, the fort had come under continual assault, to the point where members of the tiny garrison feared to venture outside the walls. In July hostile Indians had actually succeeded in seizing an outlying blockhouse and killing four soldiers who defended it. At last, carrying out his threat of the year before to evacuate the fort on his own authority, Lieutenant Hamilton and his men slipped out of the fort on a dark night and crept silently to the riverbank on hands and knees. The entire command had embarked in boats before the besieging Indians saw the empty fort go up in flames. The American military presence on the upper Mississippi was at an end.[64]

This setback was offset by the removal of many of the Sauk to the remote Missouri River. At Portage des Sioux at the end of September, Indian agent William Clark persuaded 1,500 Sauk Indians to move west of the Mississippi to what is now Moniteau County, Missouri. These Sauk pledged to keep the peace with the United States and with the Osage, their ancient enemies and new neighbors. In return, Clark agreed to provide a factory (government trading post) and a blacksmith to supply the tribe's needs. The Sauk left immediately, conducted to their new home by Maurice Blondeau. At the time, the arrangement seemed successful. A large part of the Sauk nation had been placed beyond the dangerous influence of British agents, and any Sauk warriors found on their old hunting ground could now be presumed to be enemies.[65]

In its position along the Illinois River, Fort Clark was a success. After the failure of Black Partridge's attack, the Potawatomi made no further direct assault, and the fort had the intended effect of overawing them. More important, however, was the success of American arms to the east. On September 12, 1813, the American victory on Lake Erie gave the United States control of the lake, making the British position at Detroit and even Malden untenable. Recognizing the inevitable, British General Henry Procter withdrew his army and his Indian allies into Ontario, as William Henry Harrison launched his long-planned offensive. At the battle of the Thames (Moraviantown), Procter's army was destroyed. The British regulars ran like rabbits, but many of the Indians stood firm and died fighting. Among them was the irreplaceable Tecumseh, whose dream of an Indian confederacy died with him.[66]

With the collapse of the British position in lower Ontario, some of the tribes that had been allied with them sent envoys to Harrison's army seeking peace. Harrison was initially reluctant to grant peace to the Potawatomi, whom he considered "our most cruel and inveterate enemies," but upon reflection saw the benefit of a more conciliatory policy. On October 14, the general entered into an armistice with the Potawatomi and seven other tribes. The terms of the agreement required that the tribes give hostages and permitted them to return to their usual hunting grounds, there to remain unmolested "provided they behave themselves peaceably." Among the chiefs who signed the armistice agreement were Topinebee and Main Poc. Main Poc's followers, however, drew out their rations in silence, and Harrison had no faith in that chief's sincerity.[67]

The bands of Potawatomi who lived along the Illinois River were not parties to the agreement. Nevertheless, after the defeat of the British at the Thames, warriors who had fought alongside them began drifting back to their villages, bringing tidings of gloom. One of them was Gomo. The disaster of the Thames, coupled with the new fort planted in their midst, convinced realistic chiefs such as Black Partridge, Shabbona, Gomo, and his brother Senachwine that they had to reach an accommodation with the Americans. In December, with an escort provided by Captain Simon Owens, the commander at Fort Clark, Black Partridge led a Potawatomi delegation to visit Governor Clark at Saint Louis. Clark met them in council on January 2, 1814. Black Partridge explained that he had come as the representative of Gomo and the other chiefs, who were detained in their own country by the need to care for their women and children. He acknowledged the tribe's past hostility, but promised that they now understood their errors and asked for peace.

Clark received the Indians coolly. He scoffed at their promises of good conduct, reminding them that he had previously heard the same promises from them before they went on to murder helpless women and children. What would happen to the tribe now was up to the military authorities in the district. Black Partridge and his companions were described as "perfectly chopfallen" at this speech. Clark advised them to fly a white flag from their canoes as they returned homeward, and predicted that if the tribesmen remained peaceful in their hunting grounds, the Americans would not molest him. Clark hinted that giving hostages would help, and as the conference broke up, eight warriors offered themselves as hostages. Clark accepted six of them, and turned them over to Colonel Nicholas at Fort Bellefontaine. Black Partridge and the others returned to the Illinois River to inform their nation that for them the war was over.[68]

The year 1813 had ended well for the American Northwest, with Detroit redeemed and British power humbled. It had also ended well for the Illinois Territory, with the Potawatomi at peace, most of the Sauk safely resettled west of the Mississippi River, and a strong new fortress guarding the Illinois River valley. There was little hint of the disasters to come.

NINE

Clark

Although the Eighth Military District, containing the states of Ohio and Kentucky, and the territories of Michigan, Indiana, Illinois, and Missouri, was under the overall command of Major General William Henry Harrison, the War Department had also created a position for Brigadier General Benjamin Howard at Saint Louis.[1] Because the administration had failed to make the lines of authority clear, however, Howard regarded his command as independent. He habitually bypassed Harrison in communicating with the secretary of war even receiving some encouragement from the Department, but at last on December 31, 1813, Secretary Armstrong ordered Howard to report in person to Harrison at Cincinnati and receive his orders.[2]

Harrison needed a new commander at Detroit and, regarding the threat to the western territories as exaggerated, saw no need for a brigadier general at Saint Louis.[3] Proceeding cautiously, Harrison asked Armstrong himself to give the order reassigning Howard. To replace Howard in command at Saint Louis, Harrison suggested William Clark, whom he knew from the days when they had both served under "Mad Anthony" Wayne, and he assured the secretary that "To the Military Talents of Governor Clark and his intimate acquaintance with the Indians our affairs in that quarters can be safely confided."[4]

William Clark was then forty-three years of age. Son of a prominent
Virginia family, and the much younger brother of George Rogers Clark, the
conqueror of Kaskaskia and Vincennes, he had followed his elder brother into
the army. William was already experienced in Indian warfare when he commanded a column of riflemen at the battle of Fallen Timbers (1794), and the
next year he was present when the Treaty of Greenville brought the Indian war
to a close. After the treaty, Clark resigned from the army and for several years
occupied himself with his private affairs until Meriwether Lewis suggested
him as joint commander of the Corps of Discovery that President Jefferson
was sending to explore newly purchased Louisiana. Lewis and Clark's two-
year journey of geographic, scientific, and anthropological exploration first
brought the flag of the United States to the Pacific coast and confirmed one
of the great friendships of American history.[5]

On their return in 1806, Lewis and Clark were hailed as heroes and rewarded with appointments in the West they had done so much to open up.
Lewis was appointed governor of Louisiana (later Missouri) Territory, while
Clark served alongside him at Saint Louis as U.S. agent to the western Indians
and as brigadier general of the territorial militia. Clark thrived in the role of
Indian agent. He was a natural diplomat and no public man in America had
a greater knowledge of the western tribes, who soon grew to trust the "red-
haired Chief." Clark's attitude toward the Indians was not unlike Harrison's: He
sympathized with their plight and usually treated them as fairly and humanely
as official duty permitted, but he also believed that the Indians' day was over
and that they must now give way to a more numerous and powerful nation,
just as they themselves had displaced weaker tribes before them.[6]

Lewis, on the other hand, proved temperamentally unsuited to the role
of governor. Conflict with both superiors and subordinates alike led to growing depression of mind that finally ended in his tragic death at an inn on the
Natchez Trace. After his death, the open position as governor might have
been Clark's for the asking, but he declined to seek the appointment. Clark
may have felt that he was not ready for the post, but he was also reluctant to
seek the appointment from Secretary William Eustis, "a green pompous new
englandr" whom Clark held partly responsible for contributing to the despair
that had led to his friend's death. Instead, the position went to Congressman
Benjamin Howard of Kentucky, while Clark continued to serve as Indian agent.
Clark and the new governor worked well together, but in 1813, when Howard
resigned his office to accept a commission as brigadier general, (and after Eu-

Figure 12. William
Clark, about 1810.
Attributed to John
Wesley Jarvis.
Courtesy of Missouri
History Museum,
Saint Louis.

stis had been replaced by John Armstrong), Clark at last became governor of
Missouri Territory. He would remain as governor until the territory became
a state seven years later.

The reassignment of General Howard had a bad effect on public opinion
in Saint Louis.[7] There was no other senior federal military officer along the
Mississippi, so command of the Rangers and the few other regular troops in
Illinois, Missouri, and Indiana (except Fort Wayne) was transferred to Colonel
William Russell at Vincennes. Complicating his task was that the enlistments
of the Rangers who had protected the frontiers were expiring. Indeed, before
leaving Saint Louis, Howard discharged several companies of Rangers, leaving
in service only three companies raised in Missouri and a half-company raised
in Illinois. At the same time, the government marched the understrength First
Regiment to Pittsburgh for recruiting, leaving behind only thirty regulars,
part of an artillery company, to guard the two territories. Governor Clark
and the delegates to Congress from Missouri and Illinois territories, Edward
Hempstead and Shadrach Bond, all repeatedly protested to Secretary of War
Armstrong, but Armstrong doubted that the western Indians would renew
the war and refused even to give an answer.[8] Although on February 24, 1814,

Congress enacted a law extending the service of the Rangers for another year, "The Secretary of War," Bond reported in frustration, "seems determined not to give us any protection on our frontiers, notwithstanding the laws that has been passed to continue the rangers in service."[9]

While Armstrong dithered, a team of surveyors led by Nelson Rector was in the northern part of Gallatin County, Illinois Territory, engaged in mapping the system of townships, ranges, and sections that would permit the federal lands to be put on sale later that year. Rector had served with credit as a volunteer aide on Governor Edwards's expedition to Peoria in October 1812, but since that time he had been busy surveying the public lands. Surveying was an occupation as hazardous as soldiering; surveying parties worked well beyond the line of settlements and usually without a military escort. Moreover, they did so in the face of hostility from Indians who had come to understand that these harmless-seeming men with their chains and transits were somehow preparing the way for the rush of settlement that would destroy their way of life. Interference with surveying parties was not uncommon; indeed, only nine years earlier another surveyor named Rector had been killed by Indians not far away in the northern part of what is now Saline County.[10]

On March 1, having left his surveying party in order to go to the Salines, Rector was riding alone on the Goshen Road where it ran along the North Fork of the Saline River. Rector had no thought of danger until Indians concealed behind a high bank suddenly opened fire. One ball passed through his left shoulder, another struck his arm, fracturing the bone above the elbow, and a third passed through the shoulder of his horse. The horse's knees buckled, but he quickly recovered and Rector applied his spurs to break through a circle of warriors who had emerged to finish him off. Another ball skimmed Rector's scalp, knocking off his hat and cutting three holes in the kerchief he wore tied over his head. More Indians lay concealed just ahead, but Rector avoided them by turning his horse from the road. They fired after him in vain. Badly wounded and half-fainting, with one arm dangling useless at his side, Rector clung to his horse, part of the distance holding the bridle in his teeth. In this condition he managed to ride twelve miles to safety at a small fort located about three miles from the Salines. His wounds were serious, but Nelson Rector was no ordinary man, and he gradually recovered his strength. His brother William wrote of him: "I say that there are but few men, who under similar circumstances would have escaped the Tomhawk & scalping knife."[11]

Captain Leonard White,[12] with a detachment of militia from the Salines set out immediately in pursuit of the attackers, and Colonel Philip Tramell followed the next day with another force, but the Indians could not be over-taken. The soldiers saw many signs of Indians, but had to content themselves with bringing in Rector's team of surveyors, who were unaware of the danger, and one or two of the most exposed families. Rector's impression was that his attackers were Kickapoo, but Thomas Forsyth, who had good sources among the Potawatomi, believed that the leader of the ambush was the celebrated Potawatomi warrior Nuscotnumeg.[13] This pursuit was Colonel Tramell's last expedition; he resigned his commission on March 12, 1814, and Major Willis Hargrave was promoted to command the 4th regiment in his stead.[14]

After the ambush, Governor Edwards went to the Salines himself, and from there he wrote a letter to Harrison, the commanding general in the district, that somehow found its way into the newspapers. Edwards informed the general that the "The Indians have realized my expectations, by recom-mencing hostilities in this territory." Edwards described information he had received that indicated to him that Robert Dickson had penetrated deep into American territory and planned an attack on Illinois and Missouri territories. "And I am sure that I need not say to you, that a larger body of Indians can with more facility attack Saint Louis and Cahokia, than any other point on the American frontier." The governor went on to state that the danger and the defenseless condition of the frontier threatened to depopulate the territories, adding that "the settlements are so insulated and detached, so equally exposed, and the points of attack so numerous, that it would be impracticable to raise any force from the local militia by draft—and if raised it would be useless, unless it were mounted, which I have no power to order."[15]

Edwards probably wrote to Harrison because he himself had no influence with Secretary Armstrong, who seemingly held the governor in low regard. After the transfer of General Howard, congressional delegate Shadrach Bond lobbied the secretary to allow Edwards to command at least the forces in his own territory, but Armstrong would not hear of it. Bond had to report to Edwards that the secretary had treated all the governor's recommendations in such a manner that Bond would in future take them directly to President Madison.[16] Edwards was not alone, however, in his assessment of the danger. From his home in Kentucky, where he had stopped on his leisurely journey to Detroit, General Howard also advised Armstrong that Saint Louis was still important, and that he would like to return there. Governor Clark also wrote to inform the secretary that Dickson was on the Mississippi gathering a large Indian force, intended for a destination Clark admitted he did not know, but believed to be Missouri Territory. And Edwards had forwarded on to the War Department a report, now missing, from agent Thomas Forsyth that was apparently sufficiently alarming to get Armstrong's attention.[17]

By then, however, Armstrong had already been aroused from his torpor. On April 6 he wrote Howard to tell him that President Madison had ordered that Howard resume his command at Saint Louis and that he "keep the whole or part of the Rangers in Service."[18] Colonel Russell would be authorized to call discharged Rangers immediately back into service.[19] Armstrong carried out the president's orders but dragged his feet in doing so. Moreover, by communicating directly with Howard, while merely sending a copy of the order to Harrison, Armstrong had disregarded the chain of command in a way that perpetuated the uncertainty about whether Harrison was or was not Howard's superior officer. Harrison was furious, and considered resigning his command.[20] Not content with this, Armstrong dawdled in informing the western governors that Howard was being returned to command in their territories. Although mail from Washington might easily take as long as a month to reach Saint Louis or Kaskaskia, the secretary did not write to inform Edwards until April 21 and not until April 30 did he write to inform Clark.[21]

As it turned out, by the time the letter reached Saint Louis, Governor Clark had already gone. In the absence of any show of interest from Washington, Clark on his own authority took action to prevent the territories from being overrun. His original plan had been to send three armed boats, manned by 150 volunteers, to scour the Mississippi River as far north as Prairie du Chien, bombarding anything that looked hostile. Sometime during April, however, Clark decided on the bolder stroke of an expedition to seize and fortify Prairie du Chien. Clark knew that the previous year Armstrong had authorized Howard to do exactly that, and he also knew Howard's views on the subject from many discussions the two men had had.[22] Indeed, to station a garrison at the mouth of the Wisconsin River had been the dream of every senior American official in the Northwest since the time of the Louisiana Purchase.[23]

The arrival at Saint Louis of Major Zachary Taylor, leading a detachment of sixty-one regulars of the Seventh U.S. Infantry, apparently convinced Clark that Prairie du Chien was within his reach. Colonel Russell, himself sick at Vincennes, had sent Taylor's detachment to assist in the defense of the frontier.

From Taylor, Clark learned that Howard had been ordered back to the Mississippi, but neither man had any idea when the general would arrive. Clark still feared invasion, and he and Taylor conferred on the best means to thwart it. The major deferred to the governor, and Clark decided to use Taylor's men to seize and hold Prairie du Chien. At that critical moment, however, Taylor was called back to Vincennes by an illness in his family. Taylor was the only officer in the detachment so he entrusted command of his men to Lieutenant Joseph Perkins[24] of the 24th Infantry Regiment, who by mere chance had recently arrived in Saint Louis on a recruiting detail assigned him by his commanding officer, Colonel William Anderson in Nashville. Taylor directed Perkins to lead the detachment upriver and to receive orders from Governor Clark, an act that infuriated Anderson, who sought to have Taylor disciplined for countermanding his orders to an officer of his regiment.[25]

On May 1 Lieutenant Perkins set out with his unexpected command plus about 140 Missouri militiamen who had answered the governor's call for sixty-day volunteers. They traveled in armed boats, the most formidable of which was named the *Governor Clark*. After leaving a letter for Howard, explaining his decision and requesting reinforcement, the governor himself followed on May 5, overtaking the armed boats somewhere up the river. High water and strong headwinds made travel slow, but the journey was otherwise uneventful until the boats reached the mouth of the Rock River. There some of the Sauk made a hostile display, so the Americans fired upon them and seized some of their canoes. The Sauk immediately sued for peace, which the governor granted, on condition that they fight against the enemies of the United States, especially the Winnebago. The expedition reached Prairie du Chien on June 2, 1814.[26]

Prairie du Chien stood three miles north of the Wisconsin River, on a sort of island along the east bank of the Mississippi, separated from the mainland by a shallow slough that was dry in summer. Living in the village proper were between thirty and forty families, with perhaps 100 families in all in the general area. The houses were built primarily of logs, standing vertically, in the French manner, with white-washed interiors. Living there were mostly French Canadian men married to Indian women of different nations, there being not more than a dozen non-Indian women in the settlement. Partly because of family relationships, the *habitants* enjoyed generally good relations with the Indians, about 6,000 of whom visited the settlement every year to trade pelts for the corn and wheat the villagers grew. Although Prairie du Chien was located in what was then part of Illinois Territory, and the inhabitants were technically

American citizens, the sympathies of the villagers lay almost wholly with the British. In the preceding few years, anybody who favored the United States had fled or been driven from the village.[27]

In the spring of 1814, the village was in a state of agitation. American Indian Agent Nicholas Boilvin had sent to Prairie du Chien two secret messengers, Bibeau[28] and Demouchelle, carrying letters that warned the inhabitants in threatening terms to put up no resistance when the Americans came. Boilvin's letters were intercepted when the men were captured by Sauk Indians friendly to the British. The Kickapoo wanted to kill them, but the Sauk sent the messengers as prisoners to Robert Dickson. Dickson treated them kindly, allowing them reasonable liberty of movement around his winter quarters on Lake Winnebago.[29] When the ice broke in the spring, Dickson proceeded down the Wisconsin River to Prairie du Chien with several boatloads of supplies and ammunition. The panicked inhabitants implored Dickson to defend them, but there was little he could do, beyond organizing the Frenchmen into a militia company, under one of his own lieutenants, Captain Francis Dease,[30] and posting a guard of Indians downriver to give warning of approaching danger. Dickson professed to believe that there was little danger of an American attack in the spring, hoping that U.S. troops along the Mississippi would be sent south to quell the uprising of the Creeks. Indeed, Dickson lamented that with 500 or 600 men he himself could have captured Saint Louis. His orders were otherwise, however. After the American victory on Lake Erie, it was obvious to all that the next step would be an attack on Mackinac, and Dickson was ordered to lead a force of Indians to the defense of that critically important British post. He remained on the Mississippi only long enough to gather 300 Winnebago, Sioux, and Menominee warriors and on May 8 led them away toward Mackinac, leaving many of the inhabitants grumbling behind him.[31]

Clark's force reached Prairie du Chien on June 2 and landed without resistance. The Indians Dickson had posted downriver had fled when Clark's armed boats fired on them. At Prairie du Chien itself Captain Dease tried to rally the Fox and the Sioux to oppose the landing, but they refused, so Dease and his militiamen fled without firing a shot. Most of the other villagers also fled, but they soon returned to their homes. Lieutenant Perkins took possession of the Mackinac Company's warehouse as a barracks and on June 6 regulars and volunteers together began to build a fort. As the location, the governor had selected a small Indian mound behind the village, where the Villa Louis now stands. Blockhouses were erected at two diagonal corners of the fort, and in one of them Perkins mounted a six-pound gun and in the other a three-pounder. The new post was named Fort Shelby, in honor of the fighting governor of Kentucky.[32]

Sometime after the landing there occurred an incident that caused great harm to the American cause. Later in June Tête de Chien, a chief of the Winnebago, arrived at Mackinac telling a shocking story. He told Colonel Robert McDouall, the British commander, that upon arriving at Prairie du Chien the Americans had captured eight Winnebago prisoners. Feigning kindness, the Americans had offered them food, but while the Indians were eating, the troops had opened fire on them, killing all but one, who escaped. Shortly afterwards, Tête de Chien continued, Governor Clark had invited four Indians to meet with him. He promised friendship, but instead shut them inside a house and had them shot through gaps between the logs. Among the dead, he said, were Tête de Chien's own brother, and the wife of the Sioux chief La Feuille. Hearing the story of these atrocities, angry warriors flocked to the British cause. The story spread throughout the Indian country, and even at the faraway front along Lake Erie British General Drummond ordered that his Indian allies be told of the massacre at Prairie du Chien in order to increase their ardor for battle.[33]

Exactly what happened is impossible to determine. Certainly the story is contradicted by Clark's known character. Although he could sometimes be stern with Indians who did not behave as he thought they ought to, the treacherous murder of unarmed prisoners would be contrary to everything that is known about William Clark. Unfortunately the governor's one surviving reference to the incident is brief and distressingly offhand: "Twenty Winnebago men taken prisoner at Prairie de Chien made their escape in the dark night, from a Strong Guard under a heavy fire, several of them wounded & dead."[34]

How the Americans came to be holding twenty Winnebago prisoners is not recorded. While at Prairie du Chien, Clark did spend much time in council with visiting Indians. In this he had the assistance of Nicholas Boilvin, who had accompanied him. For the most part, these talks went well. Clark's impression was that the influence of the British among the Sauk and Fox was on the wane. At least part of the Sioux also appeared to be friendly, although Clark predicted that the Winnebago, the Menominee, and part of the Kickapoo would continue to make war. Despite Clark's hopes for the Sauk, a warrior of that tribe, who had supposedly been bribed by Robert Dickson, traveled to Prairie du Chien from the Rock River intending to assassinate the governor. When admitted to the council, however, the warrior saw armed Americans standing all around, and, with no possibility of escape, postponed the attempt. At one point he rose to harangue the governor on some matter or other, but when Clark shifted his sword to a handier position on his lap the Indian sat down in confusion.[35]

On June 7, the day after construction of Fort Shelby had begun, Clark and a small party departed down the river for Saint Louis in an armed boat. The journey was uneventful, and Clark arrived back in Saint Louis one week later. Behind him at Prairie du Chien the governor left the two largest armed boats, and, to support Perkins and his sixty-one regulars, two companies of volunteers under Captains John Sullivan[36] and Frederick Yeizer.[37] At Saint Louis and elsewhere, Clark's return was greeted with jubilation. A banquet was held in the governor's honor at Missouri Hall. The *Missouri Gazette* praised "this well conducted expedition—more important to these Territories, than any hitherto undertaken." Clark even received the high honor of a letter of congratulations from his distinguished older brother. The euphoria lasted into July, when boasts were heard at Saint Louis that the garrison at Prairie du Chien was "anxious for a visit from Dickson and his red troops."[38] Later, when those "red troops" had indeed paid Perkins and his men a visit, Clark's expedition came to be recognized as the strategic overextension it had been. Clark, however, continued to defend the gamble he had taken, pointing out that had Fort Shelby held out a little longer and had the American attack on Mackinac been conducted promptly and successfully, the war in the Northwest would have been effectively over. The British would have had no remaining foothold in the region, and without the supplies and material support they provided, Indian resistance would have collapsed.[39]

Howard reached Saint Louis on May 8, 1814, three days after Clark had left for Prairie du Chien. Howard found "the frontier of Illinois almost without protection." At Bellefontaine, military headquarters for the Illinois and Missouri territories, Howard found only seven or eight invalid soldiers, without an officer, whom the departed First Regiment had left behind to guard an almost equal number of Potawatomi hostages.[40] Except for the stronghold Clark was hoping to build at Prairie du Chien, the northernmost point of American control on the Mississippi was little Fort Independence, usually referred to as Fort Cap au Gris, so called from the striking sandstone bluff on the opposite bank of the Mississippi, in what is now the southern part of Calhoun County.[41] In Illinois, Fort Massac on the Ohio River had been ordered evacuated, and the only remaining regular troops in Illinois Territory were those at Fort Clark (Peoria). Its garrison of two subalterns and fifty-one enlisted men was about half what Howard thought necessary to ensure the safety of that isolated post.[42]

Fort Clark required attention. During its first winter, that important post had been under the command of Major Simon Owens of the First Infantry, a chronic drunkard who was frequently too inebriated to perform his duties, even when an Indian attack was imminently expected. On another occasion, Owens had summoned Gomo to the fort for a conference, but when the chief arrived the major was too intoxicated to rise from his bed. Eventually the major was removed from command, convicted by court martial of "conduct unbecoming an officer and a gentleman," and dismissed from the service.[43] Although built to dominate the Illinois River, the fort was so undermanned that its garrison could scarcely control the area immediately outside their own walls. The detachment Major Taylor had led to Saint Louis had been intended for the relief of Fort Clark, but instead Clark had taken them to Prairie du Chien. It was probably just as well. The garrison was sickly from living in what Thomas Forsyth described as "miserable huts," and Forsyth predicted that however many troops were sent, they would all become ill unless better quarters were provided.[44]

Although the local Potawatomi chiefs, such as Gomo and Black Partridge, had made peace with the United States, and even supplied the garrison with game, hostile Indians still lurked nearby. Many or most of them were probably Kickapoo, who had moved to the Rock and Iroquois Rivers, but frequently returned to their old neighborhood to steal horses. In the early spring of 1814, a company of U.S. Rangers commanded by Captain David Musick,[45] one of three remaining in the Missouri Territory, had been ordered to Fort Clark to relieve the regulars. In April the company ascended the Illinois River from its base at Fort Cap au Gris in an armed boat, but, once at Peoria, they were kept within the walls. Because fuel was a constant problem at Fort Clark, however, in late April two Rangers, Thomas Hooper and William Musick, were given permission to gather coal at some deserted houses outside the fort. They were set upon by Indians, who killed and scalped Hooper. Musick escaped back to the fort. At about the same time, Daniel Murray crossed the river alone to hunt ducks. He believed that his French descent would protect him, but his confidence proved to be unwarranted. Murray too was shot and scalped. One of these killings took place within sight of the fort, and the sentries fired upon the Indians who were taking the victim's scalp.[46] The Rangers themselves were on edge. Not long after Hooper and Murray were killed, a Ranger shot and killed an elderly Kickapoo man near the fort.[47]

Although Clark had set out up the Mississippi without consulting Howard, the general fully supported the decision and was eager to accommodate Clark's plea for reinforcements. Howard urgently requested that the secretary of war order four full companies of regulars to Saint Louis, to strengthen the garrisons at Peoria and Prairie du Chien, but his request was denied. Although the previous summer Armstrong had authorized building a fort at Prairie du Chien, now that the expedition was underway, he changed his mind, not, as might be expected, because it was too dangerous, but because it was too expensive. Armstrong took no steps, however, to recall the expedition.[48] Instead, he simply denied Howard's request for reinforcements, suggesting that the general should be able to raise an ample number of volunteers.[49] Howard had already begun raising troops for Illinois. Immediately after returning to Saint Louis he had called for volunteers to defend that territory. Within six days, three companies of U.S. Rangers, selected from among twice the number of volunteers needed, were enrolled in Illinois for one year. The first company marched to the frontier on May 14, the other two the next day.[50]

At the same time, Howard began to bring whatever regular troops he could find to Saint Louis. The small company of 34 regulars that had been stationed at Fort Massac, under Captain Joseph Philips, was destined for Fort Clark, where the enlistments of the existing garrison were expiring. Philips, a capable officer who would later serve as first chief justice of the Illinois Supreme Court, had chafed at inactivity while commanding Fort Massac. He had even requested transfer to the recruiting service, but instead he was given command at Fort Clark, a sensitive assignment more suitable to his talents.[51] From Fort Knox, at Vincennes, Howard withdrew all troops except twenty men left behind to guard public property. Interpreting the War Department's silence about the Prairie du Chien venture as acquiescence, Howard was gathering the reinforcements needed to maintain Fort Shelby. The troops from Vincennes, along with two companies of Rangers, would be the force sent to relieve it.[52]

The early summer of 1814 was the high-water mark of American fortunes in the war along the Mississippi. While there continued to be serious Indian raids across the river in Missouri,[53] depredations in Illinois Territory were confined to the Wabash settlements. On April 15, 1814, a party of Indians boldly broke open the stables at Fort LaMotte and stole six horses, on which they made their escape. The next morning nine men, provisioned for ten days, set out in pursuit. They caught up with the Indians, "but not feeling able to give them a fight, returned without doing any thing."[54] On April 19, two Rangers from Captain Frederick Shoults's company were killed outside Fort Harrison. On orders from Colonel Russell, Captain Pierre André filled the vacancies in his company of Rangers and on May 4 set out from Vincennes on a long scout up the Wabash, as far as the mouth of the Vermilion River, but after ten days he returned without finding any Indians.[55]

The principal danger along the Mississippi, however, was complacency. Settlers who had clustered together in forts and blockhouses began returning to their houses and farms, where something like normal life resumed. This was true in Madison County, where a small settlement of scattered cabins had grown up between the forks of Wood River. Among the settlers were three brothers, George, Abel, and William Moore, and their sister, Rachael Reagan, whose families lived close to one another on neighboring farms. On George's farm stood a blockhouse where the families had formerly taken shelter in times of danger, but in the tranquil atmosphere of this summer it stood all but empty.[56] On Sunday, July 10, 1814, Rachael Reagan and her two young children spent the day visiting the house of her brother, Abel Moore. At about four o'clock in the afternoon, Mrs. Reagan decided to return home on foot, taking her own children with her as well as four children of her brothers Abel and William. They never reached the Reagan farm. As darkness came on, William Moore and his wife became anxious because their children had not returned and went in search of them, by different routes. Along the dark path to the Reagan house husband and wife each came upon the stripped and scalped body of Rachael Reagan. The families hurried to the blockhouse, where they huddled through the night, fearing an attack at any moment. At dawn, they returned to the scene, where they found the scalped bodies of Mrs. Reagan and the six children strewn along the path. All were dead except little Timothy Reagan, who was still clinging to the body of his mother, but he soon followed her in death.[57]

Mrs. Reagan and the children had fallen victim to a party of ten Kickapoo warriors from Rock River. At Peoria, Gomo had previously advised Thomas Forsyth that such a war party had been seen on the Spoon River, and Forsyth assumed that they were "hovering about to get a scalp."[58] In fact, the war party was heading south toward Wood River. After the massacre, they set out for their own country, but close behind them rode Captain Samuel Whiteside and a company of Rangers, following a well-marked trail of broken bushes, trampled grass, and occasional bloodstains, doubtless from the seven dripping scalps. Indeed, the Rangers suspected that the Indians might purposely have exaggerated their trail, to give the appearance of greater numbers. The weather was hot and the pursuit was arduous, but the Rangers caught up with the fugitives at a stream identified by some as Indian Creek in Cass County and by others as a branch of the Sangamon, near the present city of Virden.[59]

When they spotted the pursuing Rangers, the Indians scattered into the thick brush around the stream. The Rangers separated to hunt for them. Among the Rangers were two brothers, James and Abraham Pruitt. Abraham was the humane soldier who had rescued a little Indian girl from the swamp during Edwards and Russell's attack on the Kickapoo town nearly two years before.[60] Now he and his brother were bent on vengeance. A shot from James's rifle wounded one of the fleeing Indians, and they chased him into the top of a fallen tree, where Abraham finished him. In the Indian's bag the brothers found the scalp of Mrs. Reagan. The other Indians escaped; Whiteside's exhausted men camped by the stream overnight and the next day turned their horses back toward Wood River. While they were gone, the women and children of the settlement buried the bodies of the victims in what is now called the Vaughn Cemetery. Because not enough men had remained behind to make coffins, the dead were buried in a single grave, lined with planks.[61]

TEN

Headwinds

At the British stronghold on Mackinac Island, the loss of Prairie du Chien was felt as a heavy blow. Construction of Fort Shelby threatened the route by which the British supplied their Indian allies on the Mississippi. Supplies could still be distributed at Green Bay, Chicago, and the mouth of the Saint Joseph River, but for western tribes such as the Sioux and the Sauk, the Wisconsin River route was essential.

Mackinac itself was in peril. After Perry's victory on Lake Erie, Mackinac was dependent on a longer and more difficult supply route overland through Ontario to Georgian Bay.[1] Even to supply his own soldiers with food proved a constant struggle for the British commandant at Mackinac, and the constant throng of hungry allied Indians, usually accompanied by their families, often forced him to choose between depriving his own troops and alienating the Indians.[2] The other danger threatening Mackinac was an American task force gathering under the command of Colonel George Croghan to retake the island.

News of the capture of Prairie du Chien reached Mackinac on June 21. The Indians clamored for action. Although he already had barely enough troops to resist the expected American attack on Mackinac, Lieutenant Colonel Robert McDouall,[3] assembled a force to march on Prairie du Chien. Two British traders, Thomas Anderson[4] and Joseph Rolette[5] enlisted sixty-three volunteers, mostly employees of the fur companies, into two companies, which they commanded as captains. McDouall also detailed fourteen militiamen of the Michigan Fencibles and Sergeant James Keating of the Royal Artillery,[6] who was in charge of a three-pound gun. To accompany them, Robert Dickson detached a portion of his Indian force, mostly Sioux and Winnebago, with two of his lieutenants, Duncan Graham and Michel Brisbois[7] of the Indian Department.[8]

To command the attacking force, McDouall selected Major William McKay.[9] McKay was then about forty-two years of age, born probably in New York to a Loyalist family that moved to Canada after the Revolution. He had followed the fur trade for most of his adult life, but when war broke out in 1812 he joined the British cause. In the early spring of 1814, he was appointed captain of the Michigan Fencibles, a provincial corps recruited from among the rugged *voyageurs* of Mackinac. McKay was brevetted major in April, and for the duration of the expedition McDouall gave him the temporary local rank of lieutenant colonel. The Indians greeted the selection of McKay with joy, confirming McDouall's opinion that "he is certainly well qualified for the task he has undertaken, being determined yet conciliatory, well acquainted with the language & mode of managing the Indians, & familiar with the place to be attacked." Augustin Grignon, who served under McKay on the expedition, later recalled: "He was a man of intelligence, activity and enterprise, and well fitted to command the contemplated expedition against Prairie du Chien."[10]

With his motley force, McKay set out for Prairie du Chien on June 28. At Green Bay, McKay added about thirty volunteers, many of them old men unfit for service, under Captain Pierre Grignon.[11] After tarrying there a few days, McKay led his men up the Fox River to the Portage and then down the Wisconsin River. Along the way Winnebago, Menominee, and Chippewa warriors flocked to join him. By the time he neared Prairie du Chien, McKay was leading a force that he later estimated to be 650 men, of whom all but 120 were Indians.[12]

At Fort Shelby were Lieutenant Joseph Perkins and sixty-five American soldiers, supported from the river by the *Governor Clark*, a gunboat with a crew of forty, armed with a six-pounder and ten howitzers. The crew's enlistments were to expire the next day, however, and it is likely that their fighting spirit was at low ebb. Captain John Sullivan had already sailed the other gunboat back to Saint Louis when his crew's enlistments expired. Much of Perkins's food and ammunition was still aboard the *Governor Clark*. [13]

Although McKay had sent word of his coming to the Indian tribes, for the Americans the surprise was complete. Indeed, so great was their sense of security that when McKay's force reached Prairie du Chien, the American officers were about to take a Sunday pleasure ride in the country. McKay immediately sent Captain Anderson with a flag of truce and a note summoning the Americans to surrender. In an unmistakable allusion to his Indians allies, McKay suggested that if the Americans chose not to surrender, they should send out any women and children to be placed under his protection. A laconic note from Lieutenant Perkins announced his intention to defend the fort to the last man, and the siege was underway.[14]

McKay directed his initial assault against the *Governor Clark*. From the eastern side of the river, Sergeant Keating began an artillery duel with the gunboat. In three or four hours, Keating fired eighty-six rounds at the gunboat, moving his three-pounder so frequently and skillfully that Captain Frederick Yeizer thought that he was under attack by two or three guns. The *Governor Clark's* larger and more numerous guns fired repeatedly without effect, but enough of Keating's shots struck the gunboat to severely damage it and to badly wound two officers and three privates. Fearing that his boat was within half an hour of sinking, Yeizer cut his cable and slipped off downriver. From the fort came cries not to abandon them, and according to one account, Perkins even ordered a shot fired across the gunboat's bow. Still the men in the fort assumed that the gunboat would return, and two days passed before they understood that Yeizer and his crew had left them to their fate.[15]

Meanwhile, McKay kept the fort under fire from all sides, although he afterwards claimed that the Indians had been "perfectly useless," merely firing at the fort from a safe distance. Even more annoying to McKay was that the Winnebago occupied themselves principally in shooting livestock at the surrounding farms. Captain Francis Dease and perhaps some of his militia joined in the attack on the fort, but most local militiamen remained at home to protect their families from their rampaging allies. Fort Shelby resisted stoutly for two days. Five soldiers were wounded, for whom neither a physician nor hospital stores were available. The well inside the fort ran out of water, and when the thirsty troops tried to deepen it, the sides collapsed. The ammunition and powder for Fort Shelby's artillery were also nearly exhausted, and when Perkins saw the British and Indians advancing trenches and breastworks near to his walls, he called a council of officers[16] and raised a white flag.[17]

Perkins was unaware that the British were also nearly out of ammunition for their gun and had been retrieving balls fired from the fort. McKay was in fact heating his last six rounds before firing them, in hopes of setting the fort on fire. At the last moment, an American officer, militia captain George Kennerly, came outside the fort with a white flag. By the terms of surrender, McKay was to protect the Americans from the Indians and to send them downriver on parole. It was evening, and McKay feared that if the Americans surrendered immediately, he would not be able to control his Winnebago allies, who had been enraged by the rumor that Clark had murdered their fellow tribesmen. McKay took immediate possession of the Americans' artillery but allowed them to remain inside the fort with their small arms. Outside the fort, McKay posted a guard of Sioux and Chippewa to keep the Winnebago at a distance. The next morning, the bullet-shredded American flag was hauled down, but so ungovernable were the Winnebago that until he succeeded in sending them away, McKay had to guard his prisoners inside the fort. On July 30, McKay paroled all the American troops, except two he claimed as British deserters and two Canadians he claimed as British subjects. The rest he placed in boats and sent downriver, escorted by Lieutenant Brisbois and a small guard of British soldiers. At the Rock River, Brisbois had to council with the Sauk before they would let the Americans pass, but on August 6 Perkins and his men reached Saint Louis safely.[18]

The British commander has received much praise from historians for his humanity.[19] How far that praise is really deserved may be doubted. After capturing Fort Shelby, McKay was daily expecting a counterattack from an American relief force. Three days before he was finally able to dispatch the Americans toward Saint Louis, McKay wrote to his superior officer at Mackinac: "My intention was to have kept the prisoners here till I got certain information from below, and if the enemy came here and fired a single shot, to have sacrificed them to the Indians." As it turned out, the American counterattack never came, so whether McKay would actually have carried out such a barbaric violation of the terms of the surrender can never be known. Nevertheless, that he voiced such a threat at all casts a shadow across the memory of William McKay.[20]

The relief force never reached Prairie du Chien. On July 4 General Benjamin Howard had sent reinforcements consisting of forty-two regulars and sixty-six Rangers. The relief force traveled in five boats, three of them gunboats and the other two unarmed boats that belonged to the sutler and the supply contractor carrying provisions to Fort Shelby.[21] The expedition was

commanded by Lieutenant John Campbell, who had already provided valuable service in the war. (Because Campbell filled the administrative position
of brigade major, he was often referred to by the courtesy title of "major.") The
two gunboats manned by Rangers were commanded respectively by Lieutenant
Jonathan Riggs[22] and Lieutenant Stephen Rector,[23] the latter being one of the
nine Rector brothers, who have already been mentioned. Evidently no trouble
was expected, for the expedition included some women and children.[24]

The only potential obstacle was the concentration of Sauk Indians near
the mouth of the Rock River, where the present city of Rock Island stands.
After the British failures at Fort Meigs and Fort Stephenson, Black Hawk
and his warriors had become discontented and returned home to Rock River.
There they had been joined by dissatisfied tribesmen returning from the Missouri River. Their new home in Missouri had proven unsatisfactory, bordering
as it did the country of their hereditary enemies, the Osage. When spring
came, many of the Sauk exiles remembered the cornfields and berry patches
of their summer home on Rock River and, as they did every year, returned
to Saukenuk.[25]

Throughout the winter of 1813–14, from his ice-bound camp on Lake Winnebago, Robert Dickson had sought to bring the Sauk into the war against the
United States, and his hopes had been raised when the "peace" party had moved
west of the Mississippi. Many of the Rock River band visited him to receive
presents, and Dickson dispatched Lieutenant Duncan Graham and sixteen
men to winter with the Sauk on the Mississippi. By Christmas Day, Dickson
could record his belief that "the Saukes have all quitted the Americans." As
spring approached, however, he became less certain that that was the case and
resorted to threats. "I have told the Sauks and Renards [Fox] that they sleep
too long. If they do not get up, that I shall rouse them with the hatchet, and
that Britain suffers no neutrals." At the end of March he wrote: "The Renards
have been here lately, they with the Sauks are playing a double game, but I
have given them a severe lesson & chastisement will follow. More if they do
not act as they ought."[26]

Dickson's threats were ineffective, so long as American power seemed to be
in the ascendant. In May 1814, Gomo told Thomas Forsyth that the western
tribes were quarreling. The Sioux, the Iowa, the Winnebago, the Menominee,
and the Rock River Sauk all favored war, while the Ottawa, the Chippewa,
and the Potawatomi were for peace. For the time being, however, the Sauk
hesitated to start a war they expected to lose. When Clark's boats had passed

Rock River and seized Prairie du Chien, they had flocked to the governor with professions of peace and friendship.[27]

Campbell therefore had no reason to fear any special danger as his boats made their way up the Mississippi. He was unaware that even then envoys from the Osage, Oto, and Kansas tribes were at Saukenuk trying to stir the Sauk to war. Initially their appeals met with a cool reception. While approaching the mouth of Rock River, Campbell encountered various Indians who assured him that the Sauk and Fox were friendly and invited him to their village. Campbell proceeded another four miles but then halted "to hear what they had to say." The Americans were met by about 150 warriors, accompanied by women and children. Their spokesman was a chief, quite possibly Black Hawk, who asked Campbell whether he had brought the tribe any presents from their Father. Campbell did indeed carry presents, but he conditioned them on the Sauk agreeing to make war on the Winnebago. After some parlay, the chief asserted that he was willing to fight the Winnebago if the Americans would provide the means. He further assured Campbell that "the Mississippi was a broad and straight road and the people of the United States should meet with no obstructions in traveling it."[28]

Campbell concluded that the Indians were friendly, and rewarded his new friends with a liberal distribution of whiskey. It was later claimed that some of the warriors took Frenchmen among the crew by the hand, encouraging them to desert the Americans, and that Campbell ignored the Frenchmen's warnings that an attack was imminent. Campbell was ill and had lost his wife not long before setting out, so it is possible that he was not at his best, but Black Hawk later denied that the Indians had dissembled, arguing reasonably that, had they been bent on mischief, they could easily have attacked during the council, when the soldiers were ashore and at their mercy.[29] Campbell and his men lay over at what he called Four Mile Camp, and on the morning of July 21 continued their journey toward Prairie du Chien.[30]

What Campbell did not know was that the previous night messengers from Prairie du Chien had arrived at Saukenuk. As soon as his gunner had driven away the *Governor Clark*, Lieutenant Colonel McKay had sent three Indians downriver in a canoe, carrying four kegs of powder, with orders to reach the Sauk before the crippled gunboat did. Learning that the British had surrounded Fort Shelby, Black Hawk recognized immediately that the balance of power had shifted. He summoned his warriors, and they set out together upstream with the hope "that some of their boats might get aground, or that

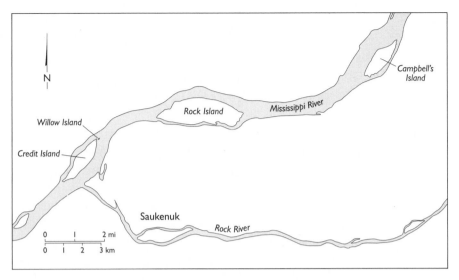

Map 4. Rock Island Area in 1814

the Great Spirit would put them in our power, if he wished them taken, and their people killed!" The envoys from the Missouri tribes went with Black Hawk to join in the fight.[31]

The Great Spirit may well have intervened, for suddenly everything began to go wrong for Campbell. The river's midsummer water level was low, leaving only a narrow passage for the gunboats.[32] Within three miles of setting out, Campbell's own boat, the *Governor Shelby*, ran aground. Riggs sent over a sergeant and ten men from his boat to assist Campbell. They shifted some of Campbell's cargo to Riggs's boat, but after the *Governor Shelby* floated off the bar, Riggs's men remained with Campbell. The wind now began to blow against the gunboats with hurricane force, causing Campbell's boat, the heaviest, to lag badly behind. Campbell ordered his boat closer to the Illinois shore, but it was a lee shore and the boat ran aground again, along the white northern beach of a small island covered with high grass, hazel, and willow bushes. That island has ever since been known as Campbell's Island. Campbell set out two sentinels while his men cooked their breakfast and probably worked to free the gunboat. Within half an hour, however, Indian gunfire erupted from the brush. Both sentinels and a third soldier fell dead at the first volley. Two more soldiers were killed and three wounded as the men struggled to push the boat free. The effort was hopeless. The *Governor Shelby* would remain stuck where it was until 1829, when scavengers stripped the timber from its hulk to provide flooring for their cabins.[33]

Campbell and his men now retreated inside the gunboat, which the major ordered his men to defend "to the last extremity." For two and a half hours they held out against what Campbell estimated to have been 200 to 400 warriors. The Indians could hear screams inside the boat as their bullets ripped through the hull, and the combat became so close that the attackers were able to fire through the oar portals at the soldiers trapped inside. Even the Sauk women joined in the assault, leaping aboard the stranded gunboat with hoes in hand, trying to break holes into the cabin. The wounded lay moaning in the bottom of the boat, tended by the surgeon's mate, Doctor Abraham Stewart,[34] until Stewart himself fell wounded with a ball in the chest.

Meanwhile, the other two gunboats had proceeded about three miles upriver before Riggs heard firing behind him and saw smoke rising from the island. He signaled to Rector, and the two lieutenants brought their boats about and proceeded back downriver to where Campbell's boat lay beached. In the violent windstorm they needed perhaps an hour to make their way back and even then they could not offer immediate assistance. Despite dropping anchor, Riggs's boat was also blown ashore and grounded about a hundred yards below Campbell. Rector was more fortunate. Many of his crew were Frenchmen from Cahokia who were experienced in handling boats, and they skillfully managed to keep Rector's gunboat afloat between the other two. For a time, the three gunboats beat back the enemy, but flaming arrows set Campbell's sail on fire and the fire could not be extinguished.[35]

As the fire raged on Campbell's boat, Stephen Rector came to the rescue. He cut away his anchor and with great difficulty succeeded in maneuvering his boat alongside Campbell's. To lighten his own boat and keep it from running aground also, Rector threw much of his cargo overboard, and some of his crew jumped into the water to push the boat toward shore, while trying to keep it between themselves and the Indians swarming on Campbell's deck. Somehow, everyone still living was saved from Campbell's burning boat. During the evacuation, Campbell was wounded twice,[36] and it was Lieutenant John Weaver[37] who took charge of bringing the wounded out of the burning boat. The extra weight nearly swamped Rector's boat and water ran in through the oar holes. Rector now threw overboard his remaining cargo, including all his provisions, as his crewmen, still in the water, dragged the heavy boat into the channel. With his anchor lost and his own dangerously overloaded boat buffeted by high winds, Rector could do nothing to assist Riggs and his crew. His men rowed night and day, without food, until they arrived in Saint Louis "worn down to skeletons by labor and fatigue."[38]

The third gunboat was left stranded alone. Riggs afterward complained that Campbell had left the scene without issuing him any orders, but a soldier who jumped off Campbell's boat and swam toward Riggs was shot and killed in the water. Riggs and his men tried to push off as well, but although they were able to shift the boat to a slightly more favorable position, they remained stranded. Once Campbell's boat had been abandoned, the Indians boarded it and put out the fire, but Riggs drove them from the deck with blasts from his swivel gun. The Sauk then turned their attention to Riggs. After one heavy exchange of fire, Riggs ordered his men to cease fire entirely. The Rangers held their fire for about ten minutes, until the Sauk, seeing no sign of life on the gunboat, rushed it and attempted to board. They were met with concentrated small arms fire and a blast of grapeshot from Riggs's howitzer. Only three warriors succeeded in reaching the boat, and the rest drew off leaving their dead behind. Eventually the Indians' fire slackened and the wind finally dropped. At last the Rangers succeeded in pushing off into the current, and, when they saw the boat escaping, the Indians opened a heavy fire that pursued the boat from shore until darkness fell.[39]

American losses had been heavy. Aboard Campbell's boat, ten enlisted men were killed and another ten wounded, while both Campbell and Doctor Stewart were severely wounded. Two women and a child who were traveling aboard Campbell's boat also were badly wounded, and the child and one of the women soon died. On board Rector's boat, one man was killed and four wounded, while Riggs lost three dead and four wounded. Both Campbell and Riggs believed that Indian casualties had been significant, but the Indians afterwards claimed that they had lost only two warriors and a woman. That figure seems suspiciously low, but Indians were prone to minimize the casualties they had actually suffered.[40]

Campbell's boat had carried most of the expedition's supplies and ammunition, and everything that had not been dumped into the river was captured by the Sauk, who looted the boat thoroughly. The Sauk returned to their village to dance over the scalps they had taken, but they were soon recalled to the riverbank. The two unarmed barges of the sutler and contractor had been in the lead and, abandoned by the gunboats, were still proceeding upstream toward Prairie du Chien. At this point, however, the barges met the gunboat

Governor Clark retreating downriver. After meeting the barges, Captain Yeizer decided to wait for Campbell's gunboats, but he also must have sensed that something was wrong, for he sent nine men downriver in a skiff to investigate. They saw Campbell's boat beached and burning, and Riggs's boat still battling the Indians. Night had fallen before the skiff made its way back to the *Governor Clark*, so Yeizer dropped anchor to wait for the morning. At 4:00 A.M. the gunboat set out downriver, shepherding the two unarmed boats past the stranded hulk of Campbell's gunboat. Indians opened fire from both banks and kept it up for fifteen miles, without doing any injury. The *Governor Clark* with the two barges reached Saint Louis safely, having suffered casualties of two officers and five privates wounded, one of them mortally.[41]

The battle of Campbell's Island was over. Stephen Rector and Jonathan Riggs were the heroes of the hour, although their fame proved fleeting. Colonel Russell recommended a regular army commission for Stephen Rector, but nothing came of it.[42] General Howard commended Campbell's "intrepid conduct . . . such as might be expected from his known character for bravery, combined with experience," but some others rendered an adverse judgment on Campbell's performance. He was given no other active command during the war but lingered at Saint Louis, trying to recover from his wounds. Campbell hoped to continue in the army, but despite recommendations from Clark and Russell, when peace came he was dropped from the service. He was, however, given an invalid's pension, for the wound to his wrist afterwards rendered his right arm useless.[43]

The battle opened an irremediable breach with the Sauk. The British flag now flew openly over the Rock River, and the Sauk became bitter enemies of the United States. So intense was their hostility that it was reported that the tribe put to death twelve of its women who had lived with American men.[44] Also contributing to the collapse of American prestige in the West was the failure of the half-hearted American assault on Mackinac. On August 4, 1814, Lieutenant Colonel George Croghan's force at last landed on the island, but it was routed by the British and Indian defenders and withdrew in confusion, leaving its second in command dead on the field. The Menominee and their chief Tomah particularly distinguished themselves in the battle.[45]

General Howard immediately began to plan a counterstroke. To deliver it, he selected Major Zachary Taylor. Throughout 1813 the hero of Fort Harrison had languished on recruiting duty in Illinois and Indiana, growing increasingly dissatisfied as junior officers of less merit were promoted above him. He even went so far as to tender his resignation to General Howard, but Howard declined to accept it.[46] Howard knew a fighter when he saw one, and he now gave Taylor a chance to return to action. The mission would be twofold. Instead of trying to recapture Prairie du Chien, which with Howard's meager resources was beyond American reach, Taylor was to lead an expedition against the Sauk. Howard ordered Taylor to ascend the Mississippi to the mouth of the Rock River and then, if possible, to row his gunboats the mile up the Rock to Saukenuk, which he was to bombard from the river. Then, but only if it could be done in perfect safety, Taylor was to destroy the Indians' cornfields. The watchword, however, was caution, "as it is well understood by the General that the Command is not competent to Contend with such a force as it is probable the enemy can collect at or near Rock River." Whether or not it proved possible to chastise the Sauk, Taylor was to conserve his forces and then to proceed back down the Mississippi to a point opposite the mouth of the Des Moines River. There he was ordered to build a fort that would prevent hostile river traffic from passing it on the way to Saint Louis. To Howard, building the fort was the principal object of Taylor's mission.[47]

Too few regular troops were available to Howard for even this limited mission. The regulars Perkins had surrendered at Prairie du Chien had been paroled and could not take up arms again until exchanged. Taylor afterwards recalled that Howard had available to him "not more than 120 efficient Regular Troops & 10 Companies of Rangers badly organized to defend the immence frontier of Indiana Illinois & Missouri."[48] Raising volunteers was to be Taylor's only chance of success.[49]

Nelson Rector was one of the first to step forward. At an Independence Day celebration at Cahokia three years earlier, Rector had proposed a toast to "The Militia of Illinois, may they not deserve to wear petticoats in place of pantaloons, may they not bleat like sheep, but roar like lions." Rector now proved once again his right to wear pantaloons. Although he had been severely wounded only five months earlier, by August he was busily engaged in raising a company of Illinois volunteers to sail with Taylor up the Mississippi.[50] Also commanding an Illinois company in Taylor's little fleet was that redoubtable Indian fighter, Samuel Whiteside. A company of Missouri Rangers was commanded by a grandson of Daniel Boone, Captain James Callaway, whose diary and letters to his wife have survived as a valuable source of information about the expedition.[51]

All told, Taylor's force amounted to 335 men, of whom forty were regulars and the rest Rangers and volunteers. Howard and Taylor carefully concealed the true object of the expedition, in hopes that their enemies would concentrate their forces around Prairie du Chien, leaving Saukenuk lightly defended. Taylor's force assembled opposite Cap au Gris and on August 22, 1814, headed north in eight fortified gunboats. At the same time, Howard sent another expedition under General Henry Dodge of the Missouri Militia up the Missouri River.[52]

At Prairie du Chien, the British were preparing to meet Taylor. Lieutenant Colonel McKay had returned to Canada, suffering from mumps and complaining of the oppressively warm southern climate of Wisconsin. To command at the fort, now renamed Fort McKay, he had left Captain Thomas G. Anderson, who proved himself an active and energetic officer. Anderson received early information that a party would be ascending the Mississippi. Frenchmen at Saint Louis had warned the Sauk to expect such an attack, and Sauk scouts had already seen gunboats collecting at Cap au Gris. At Rock River, this news came to the ears of a British officer, Lieutenant Duncan Graham.[53]

Graham was a native Scotsman who, until war broke out, had lived at Prairie du Chien and made his living in the fur trade.[54] His friend Robert Dickson had recruited him into the British Indian Department and Graham became one of Dickson's most trusted lieutenants. When Dickson detailed some of his Indians to assist McKay in the expedition against Prairie du Chien, Graham was ordered to lead them, and he was mentioned in dispatches for his part in the capture of Fort Shelby. After the Sauk defeated Campbell's force on the river, McKay had immediately sent them a present of ten kegs of powder. Graham, who had wintered on the Mississippi the preceding year and was already well known to the Sauk, was selected as their principal handler.[55]

Learning of Taylor's coming attack, Graham hurried back to Prairie du Chien to tell Anderson that the Sauk were requesting that the British send men and guns to help them. Anderson called a council of his officers, who agreed that, whatever the risk, they must help the Sauk or risk losing the support of all the Indians. Anderson was by no means sure of the Americans' destination, but he preferred, if it should be Prairie du Chien, to make a stand at Rock River. On August 27 he sent Graham back to Rock River in command of a detachment of thirty men, including Lieutenant Michel Brisbois and, crucially, Sergeant Keating. They took with them a three-pounder and two swivel guns. A few hours after Graham left, the Sioux chief La Feuille arrived at Prairie du Chien with fifty warriors and shortly afterwards forty Fox and about fifteen Winnebago arrived to volunteer. Anderson sent them downriver to join Graham.[56]

Taylor's 335 men were heading toward a collision with 1,200 Indian warriors, backed by thirty British soldiers and three pieces of artillery. The trip upriver was marred by an outbreak of measles aboard the boats but was otherwise uneventful until Taylor approached the mouth of Rock River. There at last he found Indians in "considerable numbers" running along both banks of the Mississippi and crossing the river in canoes behind him. Low water convinced Taylor that it would be impossible to force his gunboats up the Rock River to the Indian village as planned. Instead, he continued past the river mouth as far as Rock Island, hoping that the Indians would conclude that his destination was Prairie du Chien and divert warriors to that place. At Rock Island Taylor and his men saw large numbers of horses running free. Taylor suspected that the Indians had put them there as bait to draw small parties ashore, but in this he was probably mistaken. In fact, expecting an attack on the village, Graham had sent the women and children to the island as a place of safety.[57]

Taylor's lead boat flew a white flag from its bow. In light of the punitive nature of his mission, that fact has never been satisfactorily explained. Howard had previously instructed Taylor that if the Sauk sent a party to Taylor under a flag of truce, Taylor should take them prisoner. Taylor's subsequent report did not explicitly mention the white flag, but he did write that he hoped to "perhaps bring them to a Council, when I should have been able to have retaliated upon them for their repeated acts of treachery." Fortunately for the honor of the future president, he was given no opportunity to abuse the flag of truce. The wind shifted against him and became "a perfect hurricane." Taylor's boats were blown backward and tied up at Willow Island, located just upstream from Credit Island, now part of the city of Davenport, Iowa. Taylor knew that the anchors of some of his boats wouldn't hold in such a gale, and he was anxious that they not drift onto any of the several sandbars in that part of the river.[58]

The American boats tied up at about 4:00 P.M. on September 4.[59] Large parties of Indians could be seen on both banks, and canoes were crossing the river in both directions. Still, not a shot had been fired. High winds and beating rains continued all night. So severe was the weather that at last Taylor called in his sentinels and placed them in the bow of each boat. There the Americans spent an uncomfortable night, but while they slept Lieutenant Graham was ferrying his Indian allies and his artillery to the western (now Iowa) side of the Mississippi. Graham gave the Indians strict orders not to fire, but at first light some eager Sauk warriors fired on Whiteside's boat, on Taylor's extreme left. The volley mortally wounded a corporal who was standing watch on deck.

After the Indians shot the sentry, Taylor struck the white flag he had been flying and raised a red one. Despite return fire from Whiteside and his men, the Indians continued to hover about, and as the light grew stronger Taylor resolved to drive the Indians from the island. Leaving a guard on each boat, he formed his men to charge and they pushed through the willows that covered the island to the opposite shore. They met no resistance; the Indians who had fired on Whiteside's boat fled by wading through the shallow water to the eastern end of nearby Credit Island. As they reached that island, Whiteside sent cannon shot roaring after them, and at the same time Taylor ordered Rector's boat to drop down and anchor between the islands, being careful not to run aground. Rector's orders were to rake Credit Island with his artillery and to fire on any canoe he saw trying to pass between the islands.[60]

Rector stayed in this position for about an hour without seeing an Indian. Then he dropped about sixty yards farther down Credit Island to a spot where several empty canoes lay along the shore. Rector sent men ashore to destroy the canoes, but as they returned to the boat, the Americans received a surprise. From behind a hill on the Iowa shore Graham's artillery opened fire on Taylor's boats. Graham had moved his artillery during the night and around it had placed a contingent of Sioux warriors sworn to protect the British guns to the last man. Sergeant Keating directed the three-pounder, while Brisbois and Sergeant Colin Campbell of the Michigan Fencibles had charge of the swivels. The Americans were stunned. Until Graham's artillery opened up, they had had no idea that they were facing British soldiers as well as Indians. Now on shore they could see officers in red coats giving orders from horseback. The artillery fire was witheringly effective. Shots tore through the hulls of Taylor's boats, that of Missouri Lieutenant Thomas Hempstead being pierced by fifteen balls. Taylor ordered a six-pounder brought out, but immediately reflected that his boats would probably be sunk before a lucky shot could hit the concealed British artillery. He ordered his boats to drop farther downriver.[61]

Rector's men were returning to their boat when the artillery began firing. At that moment Indian warriors charged them from among the willows of Credit Island. Rector gave them three rounds of grapeshot and then formed his men on shore. Reynolds described the scene:

> In this sortie from his boat, Rector was elegantly dressed in military costume, with a towering feather in his cap, and a sword drawn, leading his men to the charge. In this exposed situation, with hundreds of guns fired at him, he moved on

undaunted as if he were in his mess room with his comrades. The Rector family never knew what fear was.

Rector and his men drove the Indians back into the willows, but the Indians were soon reinforced and they in turn drove the Americans back to the beach. Rector and his men reboarded the gunboat to follow the rest of Taylor's force, but their boat became stuck in the sand. Sauk warriors swarmed around it and only hard fighting kept them from breaking in. All the other boats had already moved downriver except Whiteside's. Whiteside saw Rector's danger and anchored nearby, his swivel gun blazing at the attacking Indians. Although the wind was still high and Whiteside's anchor began to drift, Rector and his crew took advantage of the covering fire to free their boat from the sand. The two boats now gained the main channel together and sailed after the others, with the Indians firing at them from the banks over the course of two miles. Taylor's men returned fire with small arms and occasionally with artillery, but they were three miles from Credit Island before they found a suitable place to tie up.[62]

Taylor had lost eleven men wounded, three of them mortally. Moreover, several of the boats had been riddled with cannon shot and would require repairs before men could safely embark in them once again. Some enemy boats had followed Taylor's force, but when Taylor halted and prepared for action, they beat a quick retreat back up the river. With this respite, Taylor called a council of his officers, asking them whether they thought that under the new conditions there was any possibility of destroying the village and the cornfield. The officers all thought their force far too small, so Taylor ordered his boats downriver to complete his second mission to erect a fort on the Mississippi.[63]

This was the battle of Credit Island, the only retreat under fire in the life of Zachary Taylor. His orders clearly dictated that he not endanger his force in a way that would prevent him from building a fort to guard the Mississippi, but Taylor himself seems to have regarded the retreat from Credit Island as a blot on his record. Eighteen years later he would meet Black Hawk again, with a different outcome. In the meantime, he might have taken some comfort from the opinion of Thomas Forsyth that had Taylor not shown that the United States could still threaten their homes and families, the Sauk would have struck next at Fort Clark.[64]

On the British side there was no doubt about the outcome of the battle. From Prairie du Chien Captain Anderson wrote his commanding officer that

without Graham's expedition to Rock River, the Sauk would have been murdered "in that inhuman and American-like manner" and the British would have
lost stature in the eyes of all the western tribes. Graham was promoted to the
rank of captain, but he himself gave generous credit to his artilleryman: "It
is to the skill and courage of Serg't. Keating, on whom everything depended,
that we owe our success and no praise of mine can bestow on him what he
deserves." Graham's superiors agreed. For his services at Prairie du Chien and
Rock River, Keating received a rare promotion from the enlisted ranks to the
rank of lieutenant.[65]

Having failed to punish the Sauk, Taylor dropped down the river about 100
miles to build a fort opposite the mouth of the Des Moines River, then about
a mile south of where the river now flows into the Mississippi. Taylor called
the new post Fort Johnson, in honor of Colonel Richard Mentor Johnson of
Kentucky. It stood at the summit of a tall bluff in what is now the southern
part of Warsaw, Illinois. From ninety feet above the river, the defenders had a
good view both up and down the Mississippi and over the mouth of the Des
Moines. Four blockhouses anchored the corners of a square stockade, with
walls twelve feet high, making the fort invulnerable to Indian attack, although
not to artillery. From the brush, Sauk warriors stalked the soldiers as they
worked to complete the fort, but there was no attack except on a single sentinel, shot and wounded from hiding by a companion of Black Hawk. Hidden
eyes kept constant watch on Fort Johnson, and any developments there were
quickly relayed to Captain Anderson at Prairie du Chien.[66]

Taylor sent most of his force back down the river to Saint Louis, but
he himself remained in command at Fort Johnson, which was garrisoned by
fifty men each from the companies of Captains Callaway and Whiteside. The
fort was far beyond American lines, however, and provisioning the garrison
was difficult. General Howard promised Taylor that he would send a relief
force with thirty-five days provisions, but Indians attacked the provision boat,
wounding five Rangers. The events are obscure, but apparently the relief force
turned back to Saint Louis, for Taylor told Callaway that he would evacuate
the post if it was not resupplied soon. Instead of supplies, what did finally
arrive at the fort was news that General Howard had died at Saint Louis on
Sunday, September 18, 1814. With the general's death, the western command
was thrown into chaos; Taylor seems to have realized that no relief would be
forthcoming in time and about October 20 he burned Fort Johnson and led
the garrison back to Cap au Gris.[67]

The cares and exertions of defending the territories with inadequate forces had at last destroyed General Howard's health, but he had carried out his duties to the last. Howard had never felt at home in Saint Louis and had not intended to seek reappointment as governor, much preferring his home in Kentucky, but when duty called, he answered, despite what proved to be his wife's last illness. When transferred to Detroit, he still pleaded to be allowed to return to the Mississippi, because he believed that it was there that he was needed. Benjamin Howard served his country faithfully, and he won the respect of such men as William Clark, Zachary Taylor, and William Russell. Howard County, Missouri, was named for him.[68]

Howard's death threw his headquarters at Saint Louis into confusion. When the news reached Vincennes, Colonel William Russell immediately assumed command in the three territories of Indiana, Illinois, and Missouri. He made arrangements to hurry to Saint Louis, turning over command at Vincennes to Captain Pierre André, but he was delayed by illness and did not arrive in Saint Louis until October 10. He had still not fully recovered his health.[69] The task that met Russell at Saint Louis was daunting. The Sauk had lost all fear of the United States and now raided the Missouri frontier with impunity.[70] Most of their raids were on isolated cabins or travelers, but shortly before Russell arrived, they had attacked a detachment of Rangers near Fort Independence (Cap au Gris), just above the mouth of the Illinois River, which, after Taylor evacuated Fort Johnson, was the northernmost point on the Mississippi under American control. That fort's exposed position made it a place of constant danger, and several Rangers were killed by Indians in the vicinity.[71]

In Illinois Territory, there was danger even behind the frontier. Sometime in July, not long after nearby Fort Massac had been abandoned, a company of militia led by Captain Jesse Echols[72] found the body of a man named John Humphreys along the bank of the Ohio River, probably in what is now either Massac or Pulaski County. Echols determined that Humphreys had been shot by a renegade band of Creek Indians who lived at the fork of the Saint Francis River, below New Madrid in southeastern Missouri.[73]

The next attack came soon afterwards, in what is now Bond County. Henry Cox was a tough and fearless frontiersman, who in 1811 had been part of the posse that rescued his niece Rebecca. Only with great difficulty had Cox been persuaded to move his family from their farm to the comparative safety of Hill's Fort, but Cox himself continued to visit his farm every day. On August 8, 1814, he and his young son rode to the farm as usual. Leaving his son with the horses,

Cox approached the cabin and as he entered was instantly shot and killed by Indians waiting inside. According to the story, the Indians signed to the boy that they only wanted the horses, but when the horses became unmanageable, the boy tried to escape and was shot dead by one of the warriors. The Indians left Cox's body at the door of the cabin, but hid the boy's, causing some to believe that he had been abducted. Only after the war did the Indians reveal where the boy's body had been hidden.[74]

All the outlying settlements were exposed. On the night of August 26, 1814, an Indian raiding party stole five horses in the little settlement outside the walls of Fort LaMotte. The next morning, Ensign David Gregg, commanding the fort, immediately led his Rangers in pursuit. They overtook the Indians that evening, but rather than fight, the Indians abandoned their booty and fled into dense thickets where they could not be followed. Gregg led the recovered horses back to the fort in triumph.[75]

Less than a week later, a more sensational attack, with a far bloodier outcome, took place at Hill's Fort. This little fort near Shoal Creek was garrisoned by a detachment of Captain Jacob Short's company of Rangers, commanded by Ensign John Journey.[76] On the morning of September 9, 1814, Journey led eleven mounted Rangers out of the fort on a scout. There was little sense of danger; according to one account the gates of the stockade stood open, and women were going about the morning milking. The Rangers had ridden no more than half a mile before they were ambushed by a band of Winnebago warriors lying in wait in the brush. Journey and three of his men were killed at the first fire, while others were wounded. The survivors scattered for cover, making their way back to the safety of the fort as best they could.[77]

One of the Rangers who had ridden with Journey was Tom Higgins. Unhorsed but only slightly wounded, Higgins was about to return to the fort when a wounded Ranger named William Burgess called out to Higgins not to leave him. Higgins sent Burgess to crawl back to the fort by the most direct route while Higgins took another route to draw off the Indians. Surrounded by three warriors, and armed only with a single-shot rifle, Higgins engaged in a desperate fight to the death. The details vary between the various accounts, but in all of them Higgins succeeded in shooting one Indian and clubbing another to death with the butt of his rifle. Then, wounded by four balls, bleeding from innumerable stab wounds, and with one ear severed by a blow from a tomahawk, Higgins was at the last moment saved from certain death by rescuers from the fort. The men, it is said, had hung back, watching the combat from the walls, until a woman, Lydia Pursley, shamed them into action by seizing a horse and rifle and starting out to rescue Higgins herself.[78]

Higgins was able to "dine out on" the story the rest of his life and told it to James Hall and John Reynolds, both of whom repeated his account in print. Higgins moved to Fayette County, where he farmed and also served for a time as assistant doorkeeper of the legislature in Vandalia. He died in 1829, and a granite monument now marks his grave beside Highway 51, on the grounds of the state correctional facility north of Vandalia. Occasional doubts have been raised, however, about the story of his combat with three Indian warriors. Higgins was universally admitted to have been a brave man, but he was neither the first nor the last old soldier to tell "tremendous yarns" in which he figured as the hero. Indeed, one researcher who carefully interviewed both Higgins and another witness to that bloody day outside Hill's Fort concluded that "about nine-tenths" of Higgins's story was "all bosh."[79]

The dead Rangers were buried where they fell, about a half mile west of the fort.[80] They were not the last casualties in the region. In the fall of the same year, Jesse Bayles and his wife were ambushed on a Sunday evening in the Sugar Creek bottom, not far above the present village of Aviston, in what is now Clinton County.[81] They had been hunting hogs running free near their cabin, when gunfire from the brush mortally wounded Mrs. Bayles. According to one version, she was carried back to the house of her father on Silver Creek, where she died, but according to another, the couple rode for their lives until the badly wounded Mrs. Bayles could ride no farther. Bayles left her sitting beside a tree, with his rifle across her knees, while he hurried to the settlement for help. When he returned, she was dead.[82]

Main Poc was again causing trouble. That implacable enemy of the Americans had indeed signed the armistice with Harrison, but he still hoped to restore Tecumseh's shattered coalition. He established a village in northwestern Indiana, at a place on the Yellow River, near the headwaters of the Kankakee, where he could more easily be supplied by the British. For the present, however, the chief had to content himself with small-scale raids near Fort Harrison.[83] On November 6, Captain André, the acting commander at Vincennes, assembled a force of 200 Rangers and mounted volunteers to strike a blow at Main Poc and the hostile Indians gathering near the Saint Joseph River. Learning on the way, however, that his small force was marching toward a much larger concentration of Indians than he had believed, André halted his march at Fort Harrison.[84]

In light of the growing carnage, Governor Ninian Edwards called for volunteers. On September 8, Captain Daniel Boultinghouse put a large company of mounted volunteers into service along the Wabash and on September 24, seventy Madison County men organized themselves into a company under John G. Lofton as captain.[85] In October, when Samuel Judy called for 113 volunteers, 153 men came forward, a contrast to the tepid response of a year earlier. Their services were not long needed. After arriving at Saint Louis, Colonel Russell discharged the militia companies, believing that Rangers would be sufficient to protect the frontier until spring.[86]

Public anger was growing. On Christmas Eve, the territorial legislature responded by establishing a bounty for any Indian warrior killed and for any Indian woman or child taken prisoner.[87] For the time being, however, the hostile tribes were largely immune to retaliation. The Sauk had recently proven that to chastise them was beyond the territory's power. Many of the Kickapoo had settled near them, but others remained on the Saint Joseph River alongside Nuscotnumeg's hostile band of Potawatomi near the junction of the Kankakee and Iroquois rivers. The Winnebago, blamed for killing the Rangers near Hill's Fort, were secure in their faraway villages within the swamps and bogs of Rock River.[88] Instead, the real danger was to the friendly Indians nearer the settlements, especially the remnant tribe of the Kaskaskia. Throughout the war that tribe had stood by the United States, and Kaskaskia warriors had served alongside American soldiers, which did not prevent some of the Kaskaskia volunteers being "roughly handled" by foolish whites in Illinois.[89] By treaty, the government was required to protect the Kaskaskia, but Edwards could find no way to ensure their safety except requiring them to remain at home. Once they were prohibited from hunting, the condition of the Kaskaskia became truly deplorable. For two years the government had unaccountably failed to pay the tribe its annuity under the treaty. Naked and starving, they were enabled to live only by the private generosity of Colonel Pierre Menard of Kaskaskia and by some support Edwards gave them from the limited public funds at his disposal. Edwards angrily protested the government's "impolitic and unjust" treatment of the Kaskaskia, but Secretary John Armstrong Jr. responded by transferring superintendence of the tribe from Edwards to Howard. Writing to delegate Benjamin Stephenson, Edwards bitterly reminded him that the Salines, which the Kaskaskia had ceded to the United States, each year provided the government with rents of $50,000, while for two years the government had neglected to pay the tribe its pitiful annuity of $600 in merchandise and $400 in cash. Only after James Monroe replaced Armstrong as secretary of war in September 1814 did the governor receive belated authorization from the new secretary to feed and clothe the tribe at the expense of the Department of War.[90]

Although more distant branches of the tribe remained hostile, the Potawatomi of the Illinois River clung stubbornly to the pledges of peace Gomo and Black Partridge had made early in the year. The destruction of French Peoria and the war's disruption of trade had reduced them to shocking poverty, but the chiefs nevertheless resisted the blandishments of British agents such as Robert Dickson, who offered to supply them with ammunition and merchandise. The tribe's patience was now to be sorely tested. The Potawatomi got on well with Captain Joseph Philips, now commanding at Fort Clark, and undertook to supply the isolated garrison with deer and other game, a trading relationship beneficial to both sides. Philips was aware of the danger to friendly Indians, however, so he and agent Thomas Forsyth urged the Potawatomi to hunt only above the Illinois River, lest they fall in with armed whites uninterested in making distinctions.[91]

What Philips and Forsyth feared soon came to pass. On November 10, a detachment of seventy Rangers under Captain James B. Moore set out from Fort Russell to escort a drove of cattle to Fort Clark as winter provisions for the garrison. William Boon accompanied Moore as his adjutant. The journey across the prairies was uneventful until November 15 or 16, when the Rangers had passed Sugar Creek "a few miles beyond the old Kickapoo town." Apparently they were somewhere in the northern part of what is now Logan County, when the front of the column saw Indians ahead. The Rangers in the lead rode toward the Indians, with Moore and Boon close behind, shouting orders not to fire. Before them was a warrior named Matatah, the leader of a party of about ten Indians, including some women and children, who were out hunting meat for the garrison at Fort Clark. Near Matatah stood a woman, but the rest of the Indians were about 200 to 300 yards off the column's flank. As a private named William Hewitt dismounted and approached Matatah, the woman began to run. Boon led some men after her, but Matatah remained where he was, clapping his hands on his breast and saying "Potawatomi" and "Gomo." He then threw his gun on the ground. Hewitt picked it up, and turned back toward his horse, but other Rangers rushed from behind Moore and shot the Indian. The wounded Indian sprang at Hewitt, tore the gun from his hands, and fired, mortally wounding Hewitt, before he himself collapsed and died.

The fleeing woman was soon overtaken, but Boon had to intervene physically to prevent his men from killing her.

Riding at the rear of the column was Major John Moredock. A few moments earlier he had ridden off toward a copse of trees, in the hope of bagging a deer. Seeing Indians, Moredock waved his hat over his head as a signal to other Rangers to follow him. The Indians ran, but the Rangers overtook and surrounded them. After a small scuffle, the Indians were disarmed and made prisoner. As Moredock and his men began to herd them back to the main column, they learned that Hewitt had been shot. At this moment, they later claimed, the prisoners broke away to escape. Moredock and his men shot them down. When the firing ceased, five Indians lay dead: three men, a boy of about thirteen or fourteen years, and a woman. The Rangers took two prisoners, a woman and a three-year-old boy. The rest escaped, among them Gomo's brother, who was slightly wounded.[92]

Once order was restored, Moore took stock of the situation. The captured Indian woman told the credulous Rangers that they were surrounded by a large number of hostile Kickapoo. Moore called a council of his officers, who decided to return to Fort Russell immediately. During a disastrous night march across the prairies, the soldiers were drenched with rain, Hewitt died of his wounds, and nineteen cattle became separated from the herd. At daylight Moore's men stopped to look for the lost cattle, but after an hour decided that it was unsafe to tarry any longer. They had seen fires on the prairie the night before and in the morning found the grass burnt in many places.[93]

On December 3, Colonel Russell returned to Saint Louis after leading a long march through eastern and central Missouri that was intended to relieve pressure on the exposed settlements on the Missouri River.[94] He cannot have been pleased at what Moore and his Rangers had done, but his most immediate concern was with the survival of Fort Clark. Russell feared that if the garrison ran out of food, Captain Philips would be forced to evacuate the post. Russell immediately dispatched a boat loaded with provisions up the Illinois River, and although the old soldier was in poor health and had just returned from an exhausting march, he decided to escort the cattle himself. He left for Peoria with the contractor's herd and three companies of Rangers on December 17.[95]

A touching story, supposedly told by Gomo himself, relates how that chief received the news that five of his people had been murdered. After spending the night lamenting the death of his friends, at daylight Gomo blackened his face and went to Fort Clark to see Captain Philips, a man he liked and respected.

They met at the gate, and when Gomo told Philips what had happened, he could see the change in the captain's face. At first Philips could not believe him, but when Gomo convinced him that the massacre had indeed occurred, the angry soldier exclaimed that the cowards who had murdered the Indians should be punished. There must indeed be revenge, Gomo admitted, so a war party would soon leave for the Wabash, but he assured the captain that there would be no trouble at the fort, as he did not hold Philips or any of his men responsible for what had happened. The next day Gomo and his hunters killed several deer and left them at the gate of the fort as a sign of continuing friendship.[96]

ELEVEN

Peace?

O n December 24, 1814, American and British commissioners signed a treaty of peace at Ghent.[1] Initially, the British had insisted on creation of a permanent and semi-independent Indian buffer state north of the line drawn by the Treaty of Greenville, within which the United States would be forever barred from demanding further cessions of land. The proposal was in fact no more than British officers in the field had led the Indians to expect. The American commissioners absolutely refused to consider such a proposal, and the British, weary of war after twenty years fighting against the power of Napoleonic France, yielded. Instead, they were able to obtain only a face-saving provision, Article IX of the treaty, which guaranteed their Indian allies "all the possessions, rights and privileges they may have enjoyed, or been entitled to in 1811," provided they ceased hostilities against the United States.[2]

By its terms, the treaty did not take effect until ratified by both governments, but throughout the northwestern frontier there was already a lull in the fighting. Black Hawk later said that upon returning to Rock River from Fort Johnson, he had intended to fight no more unless provoked.[3] The claim was disingenuous; Indian war parties rarely traveled in the depth of winter and the frontiers could usually expect to be left in peace till the end of February.[4]

When winter eventually eased its grip, Sauk war parties would once again set out toward the settlements.

The icy rivers and the lack of roads across the snow-covered prairies also prevented any offensive operations by the Americans. By January 7, Colonel William Russell was back in Saint Louis after his winter march to relieve Fort Clark. On his return, he was notified that he would be continued in command at Saint Louis, an order very much in accord with Russell's wishes. He was now the senior colonel in the regular army, and despite much good service and the intercession of the Kentucky congressional delegation, he was never to obtain further promotion. Russell believed that he had enemies in Washington, but possibly service in what the War Department regarded as a military backwater also told against him. Whatever the reason, he was pleased to be left in place at Saint Louis, which was, he noted bitterly, the only district in the country where he would not have to serve under a less experienced officer.[5]

The colonel had already begun planning a spring offensive. When the weather permitted resumption of campaigning, Russell hoped to establish a forward supply depot at the site of Fort Johnson and from there to proceed upriver, burning the Indians' corn and retaking Prairie du Chien. For this effort he would need 400 to 500 troops to man the gunboats and 2500 mounted men to follow them on land. He requested that heavy artillery be sent to him but predicted that governors Ninian Edwards and William Clark would be able to raise the necessary volunteers in their territories. Russell was by nature an aggressive officer, but he also regarded Saint Louis as indefensible and believed that without an American offensive the British would find it easy to lead an Indian force against it.[6]

Although Robert Dickson still nursed the dream of a joint British and Indian assault on Saint Louis,[7] Russell's fear of a large-scale invasion was groundless. The only place from which such an attack could have been launched was the remote, weak, and deeply dysfunctional garrison of Fort McKay, at Prairie du Chien. At the end of November 1814, Captain Andrew Bulger, a regular officer of the Royal Newfoundland Regiment, had arrived at Prairie du Chien to take command on the Mississippi. Bulger found the fort in a deplorable state. The barracks were a mere shell, unfit for human habitation, the guardhouse was open, the blockhouses were unfinished, the gate was inoperable, and the well sunk by the Americans was inadequate to supply the garrison with water. Within the walls was neither magazine nor storehouse. Although he had been informed that food was plentiful in the country, Bulger found that it lacked the resources to support even twenty men. The inhabitants were "miserably poor," having been ruined by the depredations of "rascally" Indians to the point where they had almost nothing left. In a village which had once boasted 400 head of cattle, there were now no more than 10. Joseph Rolette, now the supply contractor, had proven unable to fulfill his contract. Bulger regarded the place as indefensible and recommended that in case of attack the fort be blown up and abandoned. An offensive against the Americans was the farthest thing from his mind.[8]

Bulger was an energetic, intelligent, and courageous officer whose chief fault was an obsessive jealousy of his own authority: "I did not come to this country with a nominal command," he announced.[9] By the end of his first month at Fort McKay, Bulger had driven the Michigan Fencibles, the backbone of his command, to mutiny. Bulger proclaimed martial law, and the mutiny was quelled with the prompt assistance of Robert Dickson and the officers of the Indian Department, but before many more days passed the captain also quarreled with Dickson.[10] Dickson had accompanied Bulger to Prairie du Chien, bringing badly needed supplies for the western Indians, but in the fall of 1814 the western Indian Department was made subordinate to the military command at Mackinac and on the Mississippi. Bulger resented Dickson's efforts to preserve the autonomy of his department, but both men made matters worse by displays of petty vanity and poor judgment. Bulger even refused to accept a loyal address of thanks from the villagers because it was addressed to Dickson as well as to himself.[11] Dickson, for his part, was far too much impressed by his own considerable services to the Crown, and took to styling himself "Superintendent of the Conquered Countries," a title for which he had no warrant and which enraged Bulger.[12]

A more substantial issue divided the soldier and the Indian agent. The western Indians were starving. As Bulger himself acknowledged, the tribes had been pushed to extremity by their service to the British. The ammunition the Indians needed for hunting had been expended in fighting the king's enemies and the travels required by campaigning had interfered with their corn harvest to the point where they could not feed their families. Hunger had reduced many of the Indians to "mere skeletons," some of them too weak even to walk. The war had destroyed the fur trade and the Indian goods Dickson had been able to bring to the Mississippi were pitifully inadequate. Bulger estimated that the supply of powder, for instance, was less than a quarter of what the tribes required to sustain life. Dickson's original instructions had authorized him to draw military stores as needed to supply the Indians "with the Knowledge & Concurrence of the Officer Comg H. M. Forces at the Post where the requisition is made." Now the two men clashed bitterly about what Bulger saw as Dickson's excessive generosity to the Indians and disregard for his own authority. Bulger was not without sympathy for the Indians, but his principal concern was for his own troops, whom he could scarcely manage to feed. Dickson tried to settle the quarrel, recognizing Bulger's authority over the military stores, and the two men might have resolved their differences had it not been for a series of intemperate letters from Lieutenant Colonel Robert McDouall at Mackinac, full of invective against Dickson. Also stirring the pot and pouring poison into Bulger's ear was Captain Thomas Anderson, who had remained at Prairie du Chien in command of a company of twenty men. Now he lurked about, a perfect Iago, who coveted Dickson's job and, in Dickson's words "acquired never fading Laurels in the school of deceit perfidy & Al Kinds of Villainey." To Captain Duncan Graham, Dickson appeared to have aged ten years within the space of three months.[13]

Although the Illinois frontier remained quiet during December and January, while the Indians engaged in their winter hunt, by late February Indian raids along the Ohio and Wabash Rivers began anew. Expecting such raids, Major Samuel Judy had already raised another company of volunteer rangers to protect the frontier,[14] but on March 1 Governor Edwards reported that "Within the last week some murders have been committed and several prisoners taken by the Indians in the County of Gallatin wh[ich] includes the U S. Saline."[15] What Edwards referred to was probably what became known as the Cannon-Stark Massacre. The Cannon family were newcomers to what is now southern Wabash County.[16] While in the woods cutting a bee tree, the family was attacked by a Kickapoo war party. Mr. Cannon was killed immediately and his fleeing son Samuel was overtaken, killed, mutilated, and beheaded. Mrs. Cannon, her daughter, and a son-in-law named Stark were led into captivity, but treated reasonably well and released after the war. The bodies of the father and son were wrapped in the skin of a horse and placed in a single grave, the first interment in the Painter Cemetery.[17] A company of Indiana Rangers pursued the Indians without overtaking them, but in what is now Wayne County one of the pursuing Rangers, named Hughes, was accidentally shot and killed by a comrade.[18]

Soon afterwards, two more men were murdered not far away. Along the Wabash River, in the southeastern part of what is now Wabash County, was a mixed French- and English-speaking community then known as Coffee Island, but now called Rochester.[19] On March 15 two Frenchmen, Joseph Burway and Joseph Pinchinaut went out in search of some stray horses. Hearing rifle fire, armed neighbors rode to their aid, but at the head of Baird's Pond, they found the bodies of the two men, "stripped, scalped, and mutilated." Pinchinaut, who had been unarmed, bore defensive wounds, and had been tomahawked, but not shot. Burway had been armed and the evidence showed that he had died fighting. Pursuing frontiersmen failed to overtake the attackers, but according to the story they did find the concealed bodies of five Indian warriors whom Burway had taken with him.[20] Responsibility for these and subsequent murders near Vincennes was never established, although Thomas Forsyth was told that they were the work of two separate war parties from Rock River, one composed entirely of Kickapoo warriors, the other of Kickapoo and Winnebago. The report was not improbable, for the Kickapoo held the French in lower regard than did the other Indian nations.[21]

More murders followed nearby in quick succession. On March 16, three days after Burway and Pinchinaut were killed, three more men were killed on the White River in Indiana. On March 20 another man was killed in Illinois, on the west side of the Little Wabash River.[22] On April 6, a farmer named James Baird (or Beard) was shot down by Indians while plowing his field in what is now Russell Township, Lawrence County.[23]

One other nearby Indian attack may date to the summer of 1815. In Lawrence County, directly across the Wabash River from Vincennes, dwelt a family named Bunton. One afternoon the mother and three daughters were surprised by Indians. The mother and two daughters were killed, but Jane, the third daughter, hid in a cornfield until nightfall, when she swam the river to safety in Vincennes. It is said that the Indians might have shot her, but spared the fleeing girl because her head was wrapped in a kerchief in the French manner.[24]

There is no special reason to doubt the Bunton killings, but the same cannot be said for a story that has entered the folklore of Coles County. In 1815, it is said, a team of government land surveyors, protected by soldiers, camped for the night on the Embarras hills, west of the later site of Blakeman's mill, a few miles southeast of the present Charleston. Indians attacked without warning and threw the camp into confusion, but the soldiers rallied and opened fire with their artillery. A bloody fight followed, in which the Indians got the worst and eventually withdrew.[25] Sadly, the story must be rejected. While it is true that in the dangerous days of 1815 surveying parties were sometimes guarded by Rangers,[26] the total silence of contemporary sources about such a dramatic event is a strong objection. An even stronger objection is that the earliest federal contract to survey what is now Coles County was not signed until January 27, 1821, and the survey was conducted during 1821 and 1822.[27] Like the battle of the Long Ridge, this source of local pride must be consigned to the realm of legend.

The Missouri frontier had long been the favorite target for raids by the Sauk. Raiding there resumed in dramatic fashion on March 7, 1815, with an attack on a detachment of Rangers led by Captain James Callaway. Returning from retrieving stolen horses, Callaway ignored the advice of Lieutenant Jonathan Riggs that he take a different route back to the fort. On the way back, Callaway and four of his men died in an Indian ambush. Other scattered murders followed throughout the month of March and into April.[28]

One of these incidents spilled over into Illinois Territory. On the western bank of the Mississippi was the little stockade known as Fort Independence, or Cap au Gris. After the destruction of Fort Johnson, this exposed post became the northernmost point along the river controlled by the United States. About the first week of April, Lieutenant John McNair[29] and a detachment of about six other Rangers were surprised while on a scout directly across the river from the fort, in what is now Calhoun County, Illinois. Only two soldiers escaped; four were killed on the spot in a firefight with the Indians. Curiously, the fort was unprovided with boats, so the helpless garrison watched in horror as the Indians mutilated the bodies and tauntingly waved the scalps about in full view of the fort. The wounded McNair was taken prisoner, but after two days march toward Rock River he could travel no farther and was tomahawked.[30]

Nevertheless, throughout the early part of the year, American efforts were directed more toward conciliation than retaliation, efforts complicated by the actions of some American soldiers. By the end of 1814, although the Kickapoo living alongside the Sauk on Rock River remained hostile, some of those nearer the Wabash were becoming weary of the war. In December the principal Kickapoo chief from the Vermilion River arrived at Fort Harrison, seeking aid for his naked and hungry people. Unfortunately a Ranger stationed there shot and killed the chief's wife as she stood beside him. Speedy arrest of the murderer, together with presents to the chief, helped smooth the matter over.[31]

Still to be resolved was the matter of the murder of friendly Potawatomi by Captain James B. Moore's Rangers. Gomo's moderation had prevented an immediate breach, and when Colonel Russell returned to Saint Louis after his winter march to Peoria, he correctly foresaw that the matter could be resolved by the Indian custom of "covering the dead," that is, by the giving of generous presents to the dead Indians' friends and relatives. In early March, as winter eased, Antoine LeClair journeyed to Peoria, escorting the Potawatomi woman and child who had been taken prisoner and the horses that had been seized by the Rangers. He also carried a message from Governor Clark, apologizing for the killings and promising to "cover the dead" with gifts. The chiefs returned a conciliatory answer.[32] Clark's promise to give presents was kept a month later by Indian agent Thomas Forsyth, who along with Captain Joseph Philips met the chiefs and the dead Indians' relatives outside the gates of Fort Clark, where Forsyth spread on the ground an assortment of trade goods. These he offered to the Indians with an eloquent speech, full of professions of friendship and regret for what had happened, tinged by just the slightest hint of menace.[33]

The Indians accepted the gifts—in truth they had no real choice—and Forsyth was able to report that the matter had been settled amicably.[34] The inquiry Colonel Russell had ordered into the conduct of Captain Moore ended with the captain's acquittal, when testimony made clear that the Indians had been killed contrary to Moore's orders. There was also a suggestion that the Indians had been hostile, a finding that was, as Edwards noted, somewhat inconsistent with giving gifts to their relations to atone for their murder.[35]

In settling this painful matter, LeClair and Forsyth dealt primarily with Black Partridge, who had now become the principal spokesman for the Potawatomi of the Illinois River valley. Sometime before March 15, Gomo had died, at the age of about fifty, depriving the Americans of a good friend and the Potawatomi of a skillful leader. Gomo was one of the most notable men, red or white, of his generation in Illinois, and it is sad to reflect that there is no memorial to him in the state except the name of a single short street in Peoria.[36] Gomo's own band was now led by his brother Senachwine, also known as Petchaho.[37] Senachwine, although not so able a man as his brother, was also a good friend to the Americans and continued Gomo's policy of peace. Many years later an old settler, who claimed that in his youth he had been "well and personally acquainted" with Senachwine, wrote that the chief "was a very honorable, high-minded man, scorning to do a mean act or even allow it to be done with his knowledge or consent. He, however, was like most other Indians, remarkably fond of intoxicating drink, but when sober [was] very intelligent and friendly to the white settlers." Place names in Bureau, Putnam, and Peoria counties pay tribute to Senachwine's memory.[38]

Ratifications of the Treaty of Ghent were exchanged at Washington on February 7, 1815.[39] News of peace reached Kaskaskia and Saint Louis by the first week of March, but official notice did not reach Mackinac Island until May 1. At the remote British post at Prairie du Chien, Captain Bulger did not receive official notice from his superiors until May 22, almost five months after the treaty had been signed at Ghent.[40] The hostile tribes were even slower to put down the tomahawk. A rumor of peace between Britain and the United States had trickled through to them, but when it did, some of the more hostile tribes ignored it. As a result, for many months only one side remained at war in the territories along the Mississippi and the Wabash. News of the Treaty of Ghent required a reluctant Colonel Russell to lay aside his plans for a major spring offensive, while the territories under his command suffered a series of Indian attacks to which he could not respond in kind. Russell found the situation "extreamly gawling," for it was his firm belief that "these hostile bands up the Mississippi must be humbled, for their own good and that of this country." Even more frustrating was that Russell was forced to endure public criticism for not responding more aggressively.[41]

Russell did take whatever defensive measures he could, calling on the governors to provide militia and sending gunboats up the Illinois, Mississippi, and Missouri Rivers. The gunboats served the dual purpose of preventing war parties from descending the rivers and, where possible, carrying news of peace to the Indian tribes. The boat Russell sent up the Mississippi was the *Governor Clark*, under the command of Major Taylor Berry.[42] Berry carried with him a letter from Clark addressed to "The British Officer on the Mississippi," enclosing a clipping from the *National Intelligencer* containing the text of the Treaty of Ghent. Berry's voyage was uneventful until just before he reached the mouth of Rock River. There a party of Indians under a white flag expressed joy at the news of peace and accepted presents, but before the boat had proceeded another mile, Indians fired on soldiers who were on the bank towing the boat against the current. One Ranger was killed. Stationed at Rock River was a small detachment of British troops under the command of Captain Graham. With Berry's boat anchored off the mouth of Rock River, Graham and Berry exchanged a series of courteous notes from April 14 through 16. Graham expressed his sorrow for the killing of the Ranger, regretting the difficulty of controlling the Indians. He had heard nothing about peace, but accepted the letter and newspaper clipping and promised to forward them to Captain Bulger at Prairie du Chien. Berry requested the release of two

American prisoners held by the Sauk, but Graham declined, explaining that his orders would not authorize him to do so. Graham did, however, assure Berry that the prisoners would be well treated and would no doubt be released as soon as possible.[43]

After Berry returned to Saint Louis, Graham decided to carry the American message to Fort McKay himself. Black Hawk and other Sauk warriors had preceded him, however, and, ignorant of the message Graham was carrying, they implored the British to send big guns to their village on Rock River, to protect their families and cornfields from the "Big Knives." The land and water of his country were red with Indian blood, Black Hawk said, and he pledged that his people would fight on until the Americans at last retired from the lands of the Sauk. Although it was still British policy to inform the Indians that the war was being carried on solely for their benefit, Captain Bulger's response was noncommittal. Perhaps he had an inkling of the message Graham was carrying to him. Possibly he had already seen it. Bulger merely told Black Hawk that his Great Father the king had placed the war club in the Indians' hands for their own good, and that when the king thought it necessary to lay the war club down, he would tell them. The next day, Bulger presented Black Hawk with the gift of a coat and pistols, with thanks for his fidelity.[44]

Graham's return to Prairie du Chien came at an awkward time. Soon after he arrived, Captain Bulger finally succeeded in removing Graham's friend and superior, Robert Dickson. The reason given was something Dickson had said to the visiting Sauk Indians that, when translated to him, Bulger declared "reprehensible" and calculated to undermine his own authority. Dickson was ordered to leave immediately for Mackinac, a bitter end to the superintendent's wartime service to King and Country. After seeing their chief on his way, some of Dickson's officers met in quarters to talk over what had happened. Graham, in the hearing of his colleague Thomas Anderson, incautiously made remarks supportive of Dickson and mildly critical of Bulger. Anderson immediately ran to Bulger to report what Graham had said, and so the victor of Credit Island was promptly arrested and sent to Mackinac in chains. Anderson, now senior officer, finally succeeded to command of the Indian Department.[45]

Once the treaty brought peace with the British, the Americans began planning to pacify the Indians. Predictably, governors Clark and Edwards were appointed commissioners to treat with the Indians of the Mississippi River and its tributaries.[46] As the third commissioner, the choice fell on Auguste Chouteau, usually known from a militia appointment as "Colonel Chouteau."[47]

Chouteau had been one of the original founders of Saint Louis, and through all the vicissitudes of Spanish, French, and American rule, he and his half-brother Pierre remained among the leading citizens of the city. Over the course of more than forty years, he had engaged in a variety of successful business ventures, including mining, banking, and land speculation in addition to his original activity in the fur trade. His extensive knowledge of the Indians beyond the Mississippi would make him a useful colleague. Secretary James Monroe's instructions to the commissioners were simple: They were to notify the tribes of the treaty of peace between the United States and Great Britain, invite their chiefs to a peace conference, and negotiate treaties of "peace and amity." The commissioners were told to confine the negotiations to the subject of peace, meaning that they were not to use the occasion to extort further land cessions from the Indians. They were to inform the Indians that the government intended to establish strong forts along the upper Mississippi and from the Mississippi to Lake Michigan, but also that the forts would be accompanied by trading-houses for the benefit of the Indians.[48] To back up the commissioners, and to protect the territories while negotiations were in progress, the secretary ordered 500 men under Colonel John Miller[49] to march from Erie, Pennsylvania, to Saint Louis.[50]

Secretary Monroe's instruction to contact the hostile tribes proved difficult to perform. While on his visit to Peoria to "cover" the dead Potawatomi, Thomas Forsyth had engaged Senachwine to carry a news account of the peace treaty to Rock River. The chief reported back to Fort Clark that, while the Kickapoo seemed receptive to the idea of peace, the Sauk and Winnebago were resolved to continue the war.[51] Now the commissioners sent out formal requests to the tribes to convene at Portage des Sioux, Missouri Territory, on July 6, 1815, to discuss treaties of peace. Some of the tribes were easy to reach, but with the Sauk actively blocking passage on the Mississippi, special arrangements had to be made to reach the tribes above the mouth of Rock River. Lieutenant George Kennerly volunteered to carry invitations to the Sioux by a long and circuitous route.[52] Trader Manuel Lisa, who had been appointed the previous summer as subagent to the tribes of the Missouri River, had done good service in keeping them friendly to the American cause and in holding the pro-British Sioux along the Mississippi close to home by threatening their rear. Now Lisa took charge of delivering invitations to the friendly tribes of the Missouri River and of escorting their chiefs to the conference.[53] Letters to most of the hostile tribes in Illinois and Wisconsin were entrusted to Forsyth, who again enlisted the amiable Senachwine to deliver them to the Sauk and Kickapoo of Rock River, as well as to the Menominee and Winnebago.[54]

The reception to these letters was mixed. Although the British authorities were now promoting peace, many Indians still remembered past British predictions that when spring came the Americans would try to lure them to Saint Louis, Fort Wayne, or Vincennes to make peace, but that it would be a trap. British traders who had been accustomed to operate in the United States accurately foresaw the end of their livelihood, and when puzzled Indian chiefs brought them the commissioners' letters for reading, the traders were not always cooperative. A letter from Edwards written in French was brought to Louis Buisson at Chicago. Although Buisson had helped redeem the captive survivors of Fort Dearborn, he now told the Indians, probably Menominee, that the letter was all lies. Even the interpreter at Fort Harrison was said to have warned the Indians that they would be ambushed and killed if they received presents at Fort Wayne, Vincennes, or Fort Clark.[55]

An even more serious obstacle was the resumption of hostilities around the borders of Illinois, although not in the territory itself. At the end of April and the early part of May, there had been a lull in the raiding, but in Indiana on May 13 a detachment of sixteen rangers under Lieutenant Morrison was surprised at dawn by a party of Indians, probably Potawatomi, at a place between Fort Harrison and Bussaron Creek, and dispersed with the loss of five killed.[56] On May 20, the Ramsey family was massacred near Charette in Missouri, about sixty miles from Saint Louis, by a war party from Rock River. Three young children caught playing in the yard were scalped and cut to pieces. The three commissioners rightly regarded this outrage as "additional evidence of the determined hostility of the Sauks & others of Rock River."[57] When the report of peace was finally confirmed by orders from Mackinac, Captain Bulger immediately sent Captain Francis Dease to Rock River to tell the Sauk to cease their attacks, but before Dease was even dispatched, a war party headed by Black Hawk had already left Rock River and could not be recalled. These warriors were probably responsible for the butchery at the Ramsey farm, and were certainly responsible for providing even more dramatic evidence of "determined hostility" four days later.[58]

Not far from the mouth of the Cuivre River, on the later site of Old Monroe in Lincoln County, Missouri, stood Fort Howard.[59] The fort was commanded by Captain Peter Craig.[60] About midday on May 24, a detachment of five Rangers was ambushed by Black Hawk's war party in full view of the fort. Craig led his men to the rescue, but rather than flee, the Sauk made a determined stand in a large sinkhole, from which the Rangers were unable to dislodge them. The fighting was fierce until nightfall, when the Rangers returned to the fort and the Indians slipped away in the darkness. The Indians left five dead on the field and a trail of bloodstains along their line of retreat. The loss to the Americans in this, the last land battle of the War of 1812, was seven killed, including Craig and another officer, five wounded, two of them mortally, and one missing, presumed dead. The next day, in response to a call for reinforcements, Captain Samuel Whiteside arrived with a company of Illinois Rangers. As he entered the fort, Whiteside saw the severed head of an Indian impaled on a stake. He immediately ordered the head taken down and buried.[61]

The same day that Rangers and Indians battled at the sinkhole, Captain Bulger and his British troops evacuated and burned Fort McKay and set out on the long journey to Mackinac. Receiving confirmation of the treaty on May 22, Bulger recognized the treaty for the betrayal it was. Fearing that the evacuation of Fort McKay might end in the same way as the evacuation of Fort Dearborn, Bulger called an immediate council the next day, before too many Indians could gather. Despite his haste, seventy chiefs gathered in the council house. For the British, only Bulger and Anderson attended the council, and the garrison in the fort was ordered to fire on the Indians if the captains gave a signal.[62]

Bulger and Anderson brought with them the long belt of wampum that had been used to call the tribes to war. Now it was dyed blue, to signify peace. They extolled the virtues of the treaty, telling the Indians that it guaranteed them the rights they had enjoyed before the war, and that Great Britain would now be the guarantor of those rights. Bulger had to admit, however, that the British promise that the lands north of the Ohio would be reserved for the king's red children could not be fulfilled. The Americans would not give them up. All the chiefs responded, many "in noble and affecting terms." An unnamed Sauk war chief spoke strongly against peace, but at last agreed to abide by the treaty. He warned Bulger, however, that he could make no promises for his people. In five hours, the conference was over and Indian messengers were sent to all the tribes.[63]

Unlike Heald at Fort Dearborn, Bulger acted swiftly and decisively. The day of the council he dispatched a letter to Governor Clark, telling him that he would evacuate the fort the next day. He then discharged the local militia, while permitting any who preferred to accompany him to Mackinac to do so. The next day, May 24, Bulger led his men out of Fort McKay, taking with them the public stores as well as the captured artillery, the latter to be restored to the Americans at Mackinac. Shortly after leaving, however, they met *batteaux* descending the Wisconsin River loaded with gunpowder, ammunition, and iron tools that McDouall had sent to the Mississippi as a last gift to the allies he was forced to abandon. The boatmen also carried letters of instructions from McDouall. Bulger returned to Prairie du Chien to distribute presents to the Indians still gathered there, and, in accordance with McDouall's orders, burned the fort. This was no mere act of spite, but instead a gesture of good faith toward the Indian allies. By the terms of the treaty, the Indians were to be restored to their rights before the war, and because there had been no American fort at Prairie du Chien before 1814, McDouall felt justified in ordering Fort McKay to be destroyed. As the fort burned, Bulger rejoined his troops, and the British army left the banks of the Mississippi River forever.[64]

The departure of the British removed an obstacle to the projected peace conference. A more important obstacle was the hostile attitude of many of the tribes, reflected by the continuing violence after the peace had been announced. Perhaps to make the point to the Indians that the government's patience was not inexhaustible, Illinois and Missouri territories were detached from the Eighth Military District, and added to that commanded by Major General Andrew Jackson, a signal to the tribes along the Mississippi that, if they failed to submit, the hard-handed general might treat them as he had done the Creeks. Jackson's orders were to pacify the Indians by conciliation if possible, but by force if necessary.[65] To command under him at Saint Louis, the War Department selected Daniel Bissell. When stationed there at the beginning of the war, Bissell had been so lethargic that an irritated Governor Howard had sought to have him removed. Once transferred to the eastern front, a new Daniel Bissell emerged. He served there with distinction and then returned to the Mississippi a brigadier general.[66]

Before Bissell even arrived at his new post, Colonel Russell had already resigned his command over to him. Russell had long been in bad health and he had not been continued in the peacetime army. Now, after bidding farewell to his troops, he brought an end to a military career that had begun by the side of Daniel Boone more than forty years before. Then the old Indian fighter began the journey back to Kentucky and a family he had not seen in nearly two years. He got as far as Kaskaskia before his health collapsed completely. Russell eventually recovered well enough to return home and to serve another term in the Kentucky state legislature.[67]

At Saint Louis, Bissell was met by a request from the commissioners that he provide a military force at the conference that would be sufficient not only to preserve order but also to impress the Indians with the power of the United States. The request was easier made than fulfilled. The government had already rushed to reduce the army to peacetime strength, a rush which caused much dissatisfaction in the territories, where the promised peace still seemed to be an illusion.[68] The Rangers had been disbanded. The regulars, many of whom had enlisted for the duration of the war, had been discharged almost *en masse*. In fact, Bissell found that in the two territories of Illinois and Missouri only a single officer, a lieutenant, had been kept in service. At Fort Clark, despite having been dropped from the rolls, Captain Philips remained in command simply because there was no other officer to take his place. Aside from Miller's troops, who would be in the district only temporarily, there remained in the two territories just 120 regular soldiers, including invalids, sixty of them on duty at Fort Clark and sixty assigned to Bellefontaine, although many of the latter were with Miller. The eastern frontier of Illinois Territory seemed to be entirely outside Bissell's ken. At least two of the forts along the Wabash, Fort Lamotte and the blockhouse on the Embarras River, were garrisoned not by federal or Illinois troops, but by Captain Hyacinth Lasselle's company of Indiana militia.[69]

The site the commissioners had chosen for the conference was the little French village of Portage des Sioux, on the west bank of the Mississippi just north of Saint Louis. During the war, the village had become a significant military encampment and supply depot. Its location, near the junction of the Mississippi, Missouri, and Illinois rivers, would provide easy access to Indians coming from all directions. Although close enough to Saint Louis and Kaskaskia for easy communication, it was nevertheless far enough away to keep the many hostile Indians who had been invited at a safe distance from the settlements. More than $20,000 in trade goods had been deposited there as presents.[70] As the Indians began arriving for the conference, so did a horde of traders, vendors, gamblers, and curiosity seekers. Also gathered at Prairie des Sioux were men who had taken an active role in the war and had now come to assist in the making of peace, and many of whom would witness one or more of the treaties. Among them were Indian agents Thomas Forsyth, Nicholas Boilvin, Maurice Blondeau, and John Johnson, as well as such soldiers as Samuel Whiteside, Jacob Short, James B. Moore, Alexander McNair, and Daniel Bissell. Contrasting effectively with the bustling color and gaiety of the scene were the long business-like rows of tents that housed Colonel Miller's regulars. To assist them in maintaining security, Bissell had asked each governor to provide a field officer and two companies of militia. Riding at anchor in the river nearby were the gunboats *Governor Clark* and *Commodore Perry*.[71]

The council was scheduled to open on July 6, but the commissioners delayed the opening four more days in order to permit more tribal representatives to arrive. By early June, Manuel Lisa had already brought in forty-three chiefs from the upper Missouri, but many of the more remote tribes to which the still-absent Kennerly had been sent were as yet unrepresented. Of the tribes in Illinois Territory, the Winnebago, Chippewa, and Menominee tribes had sent neither a representative nor an explanation of their failure to do so. The Kickapoo had sent a single chief. Thirty or forty Sauk had arrived from Rock River, but most were "mean and contemptible fellows," led by a single chief, who freely admitted that he had no authority to bind the tribe. Nevertheless, the Sauk swaggered about the village with "the most insufferable impudence." Bissell reported that many of the Indians "appear to attach much consequence to themselves, and hold the Americans in great contempt as warriors, little better than squaws." Few of the Illinois River Potawatomi had yet arrived, but when they did appear they were led by Black Partridge, Senachwine, and other principal chiefs.[72]

On July 10, William Clark, Ninian Edwards, and Auguste Chouteau walked to the council house to open the peace conference.[73] Clark began with a speech reviewing the conduct of each of the tribes since the beginning of the war. He purposely saved the Sauk and Kickapoo for last, and when he reached those tribes, he berated them for their recent violence. Clark expressed surprise at their failure to send proper delegations. The Sauk must immediately send off a messenger to Namoite and Black Hawk, he said, and if those chiefs did not appear at Portage des Sioux within thirty days, there would be war. He himself would ascend the Mississippi and find them. Seated around in the circle were many of the hereditary enemies of the Sauk: Shawnees, Delaware, Sioux, and Omaha. When Clark's threat was translated to them, they leapt to their feet, bellowing approval, a spectacle that would have filled Tecumseh's heart with sorrow. That night, after the Indians had retired to their camps, the commissioners heard a rumor that the other tribes were planning an attack on the Sauk and Kickapoo ambassadors. A strong guard was placed to protect them, but during the night the ambassadors eluded it and slipped away.[74]

A curious anecdote, quite possibly true, because related by a man who had been present, concerns John Moredock. Moredock attended the conference, as third lieutenant in a company of Illinois mounted volunteers commanded by Captain Short. After Clark had made each visiting chief the gift of a medal and an American flag, a three-gun salute was fired. Startled by the roar of the cannon, one of the chiefs, from a tribe that had previously been very refractory, but that was now suing for peace, fell down in terror, nearly dropping his flag. At this Moredock shouted, "See the villainous, cowardly, guilty rascal—he shows guilt and ought to be killed on the spot." The commissioners quieted Moredock and the moment passed, but Moredock was heard to say that the government might make peace if it pleased, but that he never would.[75]

Despite Moredock's objections and the defection of the Sauk, the three commissioners went right to work. On July 18 they concluded treaties of peace and friendship with the Potawatomi of the Illinois River and with the Piankashaw. The former presented no difficulty, at first. They had been seeking a formal peace treaty since Black Partridge and his warriors gave hostages to Clark at Saint Louis more than a year and a half earlier. Now they were the first to the treaty table. Obedient to their instructions, the commissioners made no mention of land cessions but limited the treaty to a mutual forgiveness of past injuries suffered by either side and to a general reaffirmation of past treaties between the parties. Senachwine, Black Partridge, and five other chiefs signed for the Potawatomi. One of the latter was a chief whose name the whites wrote as "Neggeneshek." If this was, as seems likely, the chief known as Nuscotnumeg, then the architect of the Fort Dearborn massacre was taking advantage of the general amnesty.

Conspicuous by his absence from the conference was Main Poc. That chief's health was failing. The following March, Thomas Forsyth encountered Main Poc and eight lodges of Potawatomi and Kickapoo along the Illinois River at the Grand Pass in modern Greene County. Much of the chief's hearing had been lost and he was generally unwell. Alcohol was destroying Main Poc, and the chief would die of it within months, still unreconciled to "those troublers of the earth," the Americans.[76] For their part, Senachwine, Black Partridge, and the rest were led to believe that by signing the Treaty of Portage des Sioux they had restored harmony with the Americans and would thereafter continue to live as they had done before the war. Only after they had returned home did the Potawatomi discover that the Americans now coveted their rich land along the Illinois River. Then they learned that the United States claimed their territory under Governor William Henry Harrison's disgraceful treaty of 1804, in which a few bewildered emissaries of the Sauk had purported to cede to the United States most of the future state of Illinois, including lands to which the Sauk had no shadow of a claim. Now Potawatomi land was to be included in the new military tract, west and north of the Illinois River, in which discharged soldiers would be rewarded with grants of land. Learning that American settlers would soon begin arriving on his people's hunting grounds, Black Partridge made a moving and noble protest, but the following year the Potawatomi were finally induced to sell all their lands south of Lake Michigan in exchange for a mess of pottage.[77]

The Piankashaw had once laid claim to land along both sides of the Wabash, including most of southeastern Illinois. As their numbers plummeted, however, they were unable to maintain this claim, until finally Harrison encouraged the tribe to move farther west, outside the orbit of the Prophet. Many of the tribe settled with the Kickapoo along the Illinois River, but after Edwards's and Russell's raid destroyed their village, they moved first to Rock River and then later across the Mississippi to the upper Missouri River. There they had remained during much of the war, until September 1814, when General Henry Dodge of Missouri, leading a mixed force of Rangers, militia, and friendly Shawnee warriors from the Apple Creek village near Cape Girardeau, found them in a fortified camp in what is now Saline County, Missouri. At his approach, the Indians first tried to flee but then quickly surrendered. The miserable remnant of the tribe numbered 31 warriors and 122 women and children, all reduced to abject poverty. After the surrender, the frightened Indians were surrounded by angry militiamen who blamed the Piankashaw, rightly or wrongly, for murders and depredations along the Missouri. Rifles were loaded and cocked; only the unflinching determination of General Dodge prevented a bloodbath that would have brought lasting shame to Missouri. In his old age, Dodge looked back at saving the Piankashaw as "one of the happiest acts of his life." Dodge brought the Piankashaw back to the neighborhood of Cape Girardeau, where they remained as prisoners of war until the peace conference. At Portage des Sioux their leaders signed a brief treaty of reconciliation similar to that reached with the Potawatomi. Although some of the Piankashaw preferred to remain in Missouri, others sought permission to return to the lands they still owned along the Embarras and Little Wabash rivers in Illinois. That request was granted, and for a few years longer their small village remained in Edwards County, near the present Albion.[78]

On July 19 there followed separate treaties with four bands of Sioux, and the next day a treaty with the Omaha, each containing a simple affirmation of oblivion for past injuries, with a promise of "perpetual peace and friendship" in the future. In each case, however, the commissioners added a provision not contained in the two earlier treaties. Each tribe was required to acknowledge that it was "under the protection of the United States, and of no other nation, power, or sovereign what so ever." Such language was a direct repudiation of Indian hopes that under the Treaty of Ghent the British would play a continuing role as guarantor of their rights.[79] The first seven treaties had all been easy to negotiate. The more difficult and important challenge would be to reach agreement with the tribes of Rock River. In order to give them time to appear, the commissioners adjourned the conference until after the running of the thirty-day interval they had given the Sauk and Kickapoo.[80]

Although not mentioned, another reason for the adjournment may have been that the commissioners were losing their military support. Colonel Miller's regiment had been detached from the department commanded by Major General Jacob Brown to guard the conference, but without consulting Jackson, who commanded the department in which they were now located, Brown now ordered Miller and his regiment to Detroit. Miller obeyed, marching his regiment away on March 29, stopping *en route* at Shawneetown to send a letter notifying Jackson at Nashville. Jackson learned with "regret and astonishment," that the northwestern frontier had been "left in the most defenseless state," but there was little he could do beyond urging the War Department to rush more regular troops to the Mississippi.[81] At the time, General Bissell was sick in bed at his farm near Saint Louis. Now his regular force had dwindled to about forty soldiers, many of them sick, at Fort Clark, and no more than fifty at Bellefontaine and Portage des Sioux. The enlistments of two companies of Missouri militia were expiring, and Bissell was required to discharge them. He immediately appealed to governors Edwards and Clark for four companies of militia to serve during the peace conference, and he himself left for Portage des Sioux to take command in person.[82]

Edwards feared, reasonably, that the departure of Miller's regiment would make the Indians less conciliatory,[83] but fortunately in trying to make peace the commissioners had an ally in the British. On July 3, Colonel Robert McDouall, still commanding at Mackinac, had sent Captain Thomas Anderson on a diplomatic mission to the allied tribes. McDouall hated the Treaty of Ghent, but as a soldier he considered it a matter of honor to comply. Anderson's instructions were to deliver presents, to urge the Indians to make peace with the Americans and with each other, and to encourage them to turn their attention to hunting and the cultivation of their lands. Whatever Anderson's deficiencies may have been with regard to humility, loyalty, and truthfulness, he did not lack courage. For two months, clad in the uniform of a British officer, he traveled alone or with a small party among restless and angry tribes, who were bitterly aware that they had been betrayed by his country once again. The crucial conference with the Sauk occurred at Prairie du Chien on August 3. Namoite, the aged principal civil chief of the tribe, was furious at the indignities shown to his delegates at Saint Louis. Anderson nevertheless insisted "that Your Great Father the King has made Peace with the Big Knives and that all his Red children are included in it [and] it is his absolute desire and command that you all bury the Tomahawk and live in harmony with them." He emphasized the importance of making peace among the tribes and of not harassing the traders on whom they must depend for their survival. Once a year they would be invited to Drummond Island, to which British headquarters would shift after Mackinac was returned to the Americans, and there the king would give them presents. Anderson assured the Sauk that the Americans would not injure them and advised them to smoke the pipe of peace with their agent, Boilvin.[84]

Black Hawk, whom McDouall considered "perhaps the ablest and bravest since the death of Tecumseh,"[85] reminded Anderson that the Sauk had gone to war the preceding year only after "the Red Head," Dickson, had threatened to set the other tribes against them if they did not. Moreover, the Sauk had been promised that if they sided with the British they would want for nothing. Now those promises had come to naught, and he had no choice but to heed Anderson's words and bury the hatchet. He hoped that the Americans would not force him to dig it up again.[86]

During the lull, the Americans also sent agents to the Indians who had not submitted. Forsyth journeyed to visit the Potawatomi and Kickapoo of the Kankakee and Vermilion Rivers. On the way he conferred with Senachwine, who told him he had heard no news from Rock River, except that Pemwatome, principal chief of the Kickapoo, would not attend the conference. Although the chief had not wanted war, he was now said to be "sulky." On the other hand, Little Deer, a hostile Kickapoo chief who had been active in raiding the Illinois frontier,[87] now strongly favored peace and promised that a delegation from his tribe would travel to Portage des Sioux. Another principal Kickapoo chief, "the

Otter" (Kiteta) visited Saint Louis, where Clark persuaded him to send a runner to his band on Rock River, urging them to attend. At Fort Clark, Captain
Philips also urged the Kickapoo to send a delegation. Three white captives
held by the tribe were sent to Peoria and delivered to Philips.[88] From Prairie
du Chien, Nicholas Boilvin reported that that village was in great commotion,
with the Indians divided among themselves on the subject of peace. The Sauk,
he believed, had ultimately decided not to make peace with the Americans
and had declared their determination to oppose any troops who might try to
build forts on the Mississippi River.[89]

When the conference resumed near the end of August, the Sauk of Rock
River were still absent, and so were the Menominee and the Winnebago.[90]
The Kickapoo, however, sent a delegation of chiefs and warriors. As predicted,
Pemwatome did not attend, but he did send a representative named Kenepaso,
or "The Bond Prisoner." The Otter appeared, but, for reasons not known,
Little Deer was not part of the delegation. On September 2, the tribe signed
a "treaty of peace and friendship," in four simple articles providing for mutual
amnesty, perpetual peace and friendship, mutual surrender of prisoners, and
reaffirmation of previous treaties.[91]

Also attending the conference was a delegation from those Sauk Indians
who had separated from the rest of the Sauk nation to live as wards of the
government on the Missouri River. Among the delegates was the friendly chief
Quashquame. For the most part, these Indians had kept faith and deserved
well of the United States, as the commissioners acknowledged. The preamble
to the treaty these Sauk were asked to sign praised the band's "proofs of their
friendship and fidelity" and affirmed the disposition of the United States "to
do them the most ample justice that is practicable." Because of their good
conduct, however, the Missouri Sauk had no bargaining power, and when
presented with an opportunity to do them justice, the commissioners instead
opted for a treaty that was entirely one-sided. The very first article required the
band to reaffirm the 1804 Treaty of Saint Louis and "to do all in their power
to re-establish and enforce the same." By the second article, the Missouri band
bound themselves to keep separate from their brethren on the Rock River and
to give them "no aid or assistance whatever." By the third and final article, the
government promised to give the band "all the rights and privileges secured to
them by the Treaty of St. Louis," and "as soon as practicable" to pay them "a just
proportion" of the tribe's annuity. The treaty was signed on September 13, 1815,
hardly the proudest day in the lives of William Clark and Ninian Edwards.[92]

The commissioners next turned their attention to the Fox. Despite their close ties to the Sauk, the Fox had by and large sat out the war, preferring to concentrate on exploiting their lead mines along the western bank of the Mississippi River. They were also reluctant to antagonize the Americans, whom they saw as potentially useful allies in some future war with their hereditary enemies, the Winnebago. To them the commissioners offered the usual treaty of mutual amnesty, perpetual peace and friendship, and exchange of prisoners. A fourth article, however, required the Fox to recognize the Treaty of Saint Louis.[93] Treaties with the Osage and the Iowa completed the work of the commissioners. Having negotiated and signed a dozen treaties, they dismissed the remaining Indians. The commissioners adjourned to Saint Louis and the troops who had guarded them sailed down the river to Bellefontaine.[94]

No treaty was concluded that year with the Sauk. In late August, Nicholas Boilvin with an escort of Sioux warriors had visited the tribe at Rock River. He explained to Namoite that the commissioners were waiting at Portage des Sioux in hopes of making peace with the tribe, but the old chief referred the matter to a council of chiefs and warriors for decision. The Sauk council told the Indian agent that they wished to remain "tranquil" in their village, but Boilvin replied that this was not an option and insisted the tribe send a delegation to Portage des Sioux to "settle all differences." The council balked at this suggestion; a British officer, they claimed, had told them to live in peace with the Americans but had discouraged them from going to Saint Louis to enter into a treaty. Moreover, those of their young men who had gone to the conference in July had been mistreated. The chiefs told Boilvin that "they were masters of their own villages and knew what was best for them to do, and that they would not attend the treaty." Possibly because of his Sioux bodyguard, Boilvin was treated civilly, but he had to report that the tribe's hostility to the United States was unchanged. In fact, there were war parties still in the field.[95] Certainly the Sauk had no reason to feel that they had been defeated. Between the Des Moines and Wisconsin rivers they were the masters of the Mississippi Valley and they had twice sent American invaders running for their lives. The tribe had proven its ability to raid the Missouri frontier at will, and at the Sinkhole Black Hawk's war party had battled two companies of Rangers to a standstill.

All the same, wiser heads must have understood that they could not stand alone against the power of the United States, for despite the council's answer to Boilvin, the tribe soon changed its mind. The story Black Hawk told years later was that Namoite finally decided for peace and led a delegation that accompanied the Fox part of the way down the river toward Portage des Sioux. At the mouth of Henderson Creek, however, the old chief became sick and died. His brother succeeded him, but he was seized by a superstitious fear that if he continued the journey he too would die, a fear Black Hawk considered "reasonable," so the delegation returned to Saukenuk. In mid-October, however, a delegation from the Sauk of Rock River arrived at the nearly deserted Portage des Sioux. The Sauk had finally decided for peace but had arrived too late. The conference was over. The Sauk delegates were sent home and told to return to Saint Louis in the spring.[96]

In April 1816, the three commissioners reassembled at Saint Louis to renew the council. Again Indians from throughout the Mississippi River region assembled, to the number, it was estimated, of 1,800. Defiant to the end, the delegates from Rock River did not arrive until May. They met a stern reception. Although recognizing that the Treaty of Ghent had secured the tribes the rights they had enjoyed before the war, the commissioners were resolved to exact a penalty from the Rock River Indians for the acts of violence they had committed after the treaty had become known.[97] At first the tribesmen were insolent and defiant, but Clark, especially, knew how to deal with recalcitrant Indians. Even those who conducted themselves with mildness were regarded sternly. A young man visiting from the East commented to Clark that a chief in attendance had a countenance that proclaimed "mildness and mercy." Clark replied that "under this mild and insinuating exterior, were concealed uncommon degrees of cunning, courage, revenge, and cruelty; that in fact he had been the most bloody and troublesome partisan against us, during the war, of the whole tribe."[98]

Two anecdotes left by visiting easterners give a window into the negotiations at Saint Louis. After meeting in his council house with representatives of other tribes, Clark at last received eight chiefs of the Sauk. The chiefs began with apparent humility: "White Chief, we have come down to have a friendly talk with you. There is no more war in our hearts. . . . We are poor and needy, cold and hungry. We want something to eat, and ammunition to hunt game or we shall starve next winter. We will behave like dutiful children and never again molest our white brethren." Clark interrupted the speaker, "Who are you, you rascal? . . . I think I know you." The chief then immediately changed his tone, boasting: "I am the first man who broke into the settlement on the breaking out of the last war. I killed and scalped two women and a child. Here are the scalps!" He then took the scalps from a bag and brandished them before the governor. The chief went on to say that he now wished for peace, but added that "if you refuse me these presents the next time I will come like the Missouri in flood . . . like a prairie on fire . . . like a herd of buffalo when they rush." Clark heard him and the other chiefs out, then told them he would neither smoke with them nor give them presents, and ordered them to go home: "you are rogues, liars, and murderers." When they had gone, Clark called two of the Sauk chiefs back to the council chamber, offering them the pipe of peace. He also gave the senior chief a rope, telling him to take it to the chief who had threatened him, with a message that if he were ever again found in Missouri, Clark would hang him.[99]

Another session with the Sauk was proceeding more cordially until the Indians stated their expectation that British traders would still be allowed to visit them. Clark replied firmly that that could not be permitted. The chiefs and warriors grunted with anger, and a speaker rose to tell the commissioners that what they asked for had already been promised and that "the American people had two tongues." At the insult, Clark broke off the council. That afternoon, a company of U.S. artillery was moved alongside the Sauk camp on the riverfront to parade and fire its big guns. This impressed the Sauk; the next morning they humbly sought to reopen the council. The commissioners granted the request, and, when the session began, the former speaker apologized that his awkward choice of words had led to misunderstanding: that he had only meant to say that the Americans used two languages, English and French. The ruse was transparent, but Clark, usually easygoing and always practical, accepted the explanation and the conference proceeded.[100]

On May 13, 1816, the Sauk of Rock River finally submitted, signing a treaty that contained a preamble reciting the tribe's misdeeds since the Treaty of Ghent. By the treaty itself they explicitly recognized and confirmed the hated Treaty of 1804 by which they had been stripped of their lands in Illinois. They promised that by July 1, 1816, they would deliver to the commanding officer at Cantonment Davis (a temporary fortification that had been erected at the present Warsaw)[101] all the property that they had stolen or plundered from Americans since the announcement of peace. If they did not comply, they would forever forfeit their annuities under the 1804 treaty. Twenty-two chiefs and warriors signed the treaty, including Black Hawk, who afterwards claimed that he had not understood that the Sauk were giving up their village and that he would never have signed the treaty if he had known. Possibly that was true.

The Sauk then departed for Rock River, humiliated, but not humbled, and, it might be said, cheated, but not defeated. The treaty of 1816 stored up trouble for the future, which would erupt in tragedy sixteen years later.[102]

During the late spring and early summer of 1816, the commissioners reached additional treaties of peace with other tribes, including the Sioux and a small band of Winnebago on the Wisconsin River. The Menominee did not come to Saint Louis to make peace until March 1817, and the Winnebago of Rock River never entered into any formal treaty to end the war.[103] Nevertheless, the war was over. Peace, of a sort, had been restored, and the government could now turn its attention to acquiring more land. When he first saw the text of the Treaty of Ghent, Lieutenant Colonel McDouall had predicted bitterly that within fifty years there would not be an Indian left between the Great Lakes and the Rocky Mountains.[104] He was wrong, of course, but had he been referring to what would soon be the state of Illinois, he would not have been far from the mark. The land area of Illinois exceeds 55,000 square miles, and in all that vast fertile expanse no room could be found for 10,000 Indians. With his customary cynicism, Ninian Edwards recommended a policy of liberality "for two or three years" to keep the tribes "in a good humor" until they could be rendered powerless by the growth of the white population.[105] He was correct. With reduction of the Indian threat and sale of the public lands, American settlers poured into the state. The population of the territory, less than 13,000 in 1810 and falling during the war, grew to 55,211 in 1820, 157,445 in 1830, and 476,183 in 1840, by which time the last of the Indians was gone.

What happened to the Indians was tragic, to be sure, but it was also inevitable, and the heroism of the generation of pioneers that subdued them must not be overshadowed by the darker aspects of the story. Where the hard-handed men and women of 1812 had destroyed, they also planted and built. It is all too easy, two hundred years later, for those who enjoy the wealth and security of the state they made, to condemn them for doing what they had to do to make it. It is also unbecoming. Were they able to speak, they might reply in the words of Edgar Lee Masters:[106]

> We cut the buffalo grass,
> We felled the forests,
> We built the school houses, built the bridges,
> Leveled the roads and tilled the fields
> Alone with poverty, scourges, death.

NOTES

Chapter 1. Morning

1. On the War of 1812, see Hickey, *War of 1812*; Mahon, *War of 1812*.

2. *Illinois in 1837*, 10–15; Peck, *New Guide*, 258–63; Flint, *Recollections*, 120–21; Flower, 64–65; Howard, *Illinois*, 1–7.

3. Flint, *Recollections*, 121.

4. Musselman, "History of the Birds," 2–6, 16–18; Audubon, *Writings and Drawings*, 260–69.

5. Hoffmeister, *Mammals*, 27–31, 316–17; Matson, *Reminiscences*, 313–15; *Illinois in 1837*, 38–39; Reynolds, *My Own Times*, 54–55, Flower, 358.

6. Hoffmeister, *Mammals*, 313–5; Husband, *Old Brownsville Days*, 3–5; *Illinois in 1837*, 39–40; Blanchard, *Roar of God's Thunder*, 28–29 (pp. 33–34 in "Deluxe Edition").

7. On what he called "The Period of the City States," see Alvord, *Illinois Country*, 358–78.

8. Mason, 56.

9. Darby, *Emigrant's Guide*, 213.

10. Buck, *Illinois in 1818*, 80–82.

11. Esarey, *Messages and Letters*, 1: 349–55; Mason, 55–56; Allen, *Legends and Lore*, 215–16; Koeper, *Illinois Architecture*, 20–24; Baldwin, *Echoes*.

12. Reynolds, *My Own Times*, 37–39; Carrière, "Life and Customs," 38–47; Esarey, *Messages and Letters*, 1: 349–55.

13. James, "Account of an Expedition," 101.

14. On the New Design settlement, see *Combined History of Randolph*, 66–67, 75–82, 330–32; Klein, *Arrowheads*, 575–80.

15. On the Goshen settlement, see *History of Madison*, 71–80; Reynolds, *Pioneer History*, 280, 314.

16. Caldwell, "Shawneetown"; Croghan, 137–38.

17. *TP*, 16: 357–60; *Weekly Register*, 5: 322–23 (January 15, 1814); Cuming, "Sketches," 270–71; Woods, *Two Years*, 94–97, quotation, 97; Flower, 108–9; *History of Gallatin*, 92–96; 2 U.S. Stat. 590–91, §6.

18. Myers, "Gallatin County Salines"; Smith, "Salines"; Buck, *Illinois in 1818*, 71–72; *TP*, 16: 296–97; Cornelius, "John Hart Crenshaw," 13–36. American authorities also turned a blind eye to the persistence of slavery among the French inhabitants. Unfortunately, the transparent ruse of "indentures" was adopted to disguise slavery in places other than the Salines. Harris, *History of Negro Servitude*, 7–15, 22–23.

19. *TP*, 16: 244–47.

20. Flower, 120–21.

21. *TP*, 14: 518–20; Reynolds, *Pioneer History*, 395; Hulme, "Journal," 48; Flower, 65.

22. *TP*, 14: 258, 16: 296–97, 319–20, 428–29; 3 U.S. Stat. 318.

23. *TP*, 14: 563–69.

24. Flint, *Recollections*, 91.

25. *ASP: Military Affairs*, 1: 320; Fisher, "Western Prologue," 278–79.

26. Cuming, "Sketches," 276–77; Babson, "Architecture," 28–31. For the history of Fort Massac, see Caldwell, "Fort Massac," *JISHS* 43: 100–19, 265–81, 44: 47–60. The site is now a state park.

27. Fisher, "Western Prologue," 278–79.

28. *TP*, 16: 162–66.

29. Philbrick, *Pope's Digest*, 30: 396–442.

30. Nathaniel Pope was born at Louisville, Kentucky, on January 5, 1784. After study at Transylvania College, he moved to Saint Genevieve, Missouri, where he began to practice law. Appointed secretary of Illinois Territory, served from March 1809 until he resigned September 5, 1816. Delegate from Illinois Territory to 14th and 15th congresses, 1816–18. As delegate, Pope persuaded Congress to move the upper boundary of the new state northward, in order to give Illinois an outlet on Lake Michigan, thereby placing Chicago in Illinois instead of Wisconsin. First U.S. district judge for the District of Illinois, from March 3, 1819, until his death. Unsuccessful candidate for U.S. Senate, 1824. Died at Saint Louis, January 22, 1850. Pope County, Illinois, is named for him. *BDUSC*, 1751–52; Angle, "Nathaniel Pope"; Meese, "Nathaniel Pope"; Philbrick, *Pope's Digest*, 28: ix–xxi. Pope's appointments as acting governor are in *TP*, 17: 619–24.

31. Ninian Edwards was born in Montgomery County, Maryland, on March 17, 1775. Moved to Kentucky in 1795 and served in the legislature 1796–97. Admitted to the bar in 1798. Judge of the general court of Kentucky, 1803, circuit court, 1804, and court of appeals, 1806. Chief justice of the Kentucky Supreme Court 1808–9. Governor of Illinois 1809–18 and U.S. senator 1818–24. Resigned from Senate to accept appointment as U.S. minister to Mexico, 1824, but never served. Third governor of the State of Illinois 1826–30. Unsuccessful candidate

for U.S. House of Representatives, 1832. Died Belleville, Illinois, July 20, 1833. Interred in Oak Ridge Cemetery, Springfield. *BDUSC*, 1006; *DAB*, vol. 3, pt. 2, 41–42. No fully satisfactory biography of Ninian Edwards has ever been published. That by his son, Ninian Wirt Edwards, contains much valuable material but is ill-organized and, as might be expected, uncritical. Other studies that discuss Edwards's career are Bakalis, a Ph.D. dissertation; Holden; Wixon, also a Ph. D. dissertation; and Simeone.

32. Reynolds, *My Own Times*, 56–57.

33. Davis, *Frontier Illinois*, 105–6.

34. *TP*, 16: 199–203.

35. Buck, *Illinois in 1818*, 40–60; Hammes, "Squatters," 59: 319–23; 2 U.S. Stat. 797–98.

36. Buck, *Illinois in 1818*, 164–67, Reynolds, *My Own Times*, 58–59; Reynolds, *Pioneer History*, 357–58.

37. Reynolds, *My Own Times*, 40–44; Smelser, "Material Customs."

38. Smelser 22–24; Mason, 51; Reynolds, *My Own Times*, 40; Buley, *Old Northwest*, 1: 240–56, 308–10.

39. Van Voorhis, *Notes*, 144–45.

Chapter 2. Evening

1. Tanner, *Atlas*, 97–100.

2. On the Illinois Indians, see Temple, *Indian Villages*, 11–56; Blasingham, "Depopulation"; Stout, "Report," 349–93; Owens, "Jean Baptiste Ducoigne."

3. Kappler, *Indian Affairs*, 2: 67–68; Esarey, *Messages and Letters*, 1: 76–84; Owens, *Mr. Jefferson's Hammer*, 80–81. One reservation lay three miles north of the village of Kaskaskia, in T6S, R8W, and the other near the present village of Sand Ridge, in T9S, R3W. Throop, *Last Village*, 11–14; Bonnell, *Illinois Ozarks*, 107–9.

4. On the Piankashaw, see Anson, *Miami Indians*; Libby, "Anthropological Report"; Jablow, "Study of Indian Tribes," 335; Temple, *Indian Villages*, 57–82; Hodge, *Handbook*, 2: 240–41; Kappler, *Indian Affairs*, 2: 72–73, 89; Esarey, *Messages and Letters*, 1: 25–31, 41–46, 422–30; 2: 20–21, 696–97.

5. Reynolds, *Pioneer History*, 20; Esarey, *Messages and Letters*, 1: 25–31, 349–55; Forsyth to Clark, July 20, 1813, in Forsyth Papers; Forsyth to Eaton, September 18, 1814, in *WHC* 9: 331–36. (The latter contains an evident misprint giving the number of Kickapoo warriors as 40, rather than 400, the number needed to reach Forsyth's grand total.)

6. On the Kickapoo, see Temple, *Indian Villages*, 156–72; Stout, "Report," 305–47; Hodge, *Handbook*, 1: 684–86; Tanner, *Atlas*, 98–100. Gibson, *The Kickapoos*, is

unreliable and should be used with caution. On the Grand Village, see Smith, *Grand Village*; Berkson, "Cultural Resistance," 4: 107–205. On the presence of the Kickapoo in DeWitt County, see *History of DeWitt County*, 43. On depredations committed by the Prairie Kickapoo, see Esarey, *Messages and Letters*, 1: 211–14, 217–18, 222–25; *TP*, 16: 51–52, 115; Reynolds, *Pioneer History*, 21.

7. The leading history of the Potawatomi is Edmunds, *The Potawatomis*. Clifton, *Prairie People*, contains many perceptive insights and a few somewhat questionable ones. Also useful are Edmunds, "Illinois River Potawatomi," 63: 341–62; Temple, *Indian Villages*, 126–55; Conway, "Potawatomi Politics," 65: 395–418; Clifton, "Chicago Was Theirs"; Jablow, "Study of Indian Tribes," 404.

8. Edwards, *History*, 315–18; Forsyth to Clark, July 20, 1813; Tanner, 98–100; Clifton, *Prairie People*, 160–61; Wheeler-Voegelin, "Anthropological Report," 222–31. On the villages along the Kankakee River, see Vierling, "The Fur Trade in Illinois," vol. 18, no. 2, 6–10.

9. McAfee, *History*, 298.

10. Forsyth, "Main Poc & Tecumseh," DM, 4 T 50–56, Wisconsin Historical Society, Madison; Edmunds, "Main Poc," 9: 259–72; Franz, "To Live by Depredations," 102: 238–47; Clifton, *Prairie People*, 194–97.

11. On his return from Washington, Wells, who had been raised among the Indians and knew them well, reported that "The Marpocks conduct is insufferable. He exceeds everything I ever saw. He has even attempted to eat his wife. He cannot be kept sober and it is doubtful if he ever reach his home as he continually threatens the other chiefs and has mad[e] frequent attempts to kill his wife and I am certain that if he attempts to put his threats in execution that he will be put to death." Wells to Secretary of War, January 16, 1809, NA, RG 107, LRSW, M 221, Roll 33, 1317.

12. The Fox described themselves as "Mesquakie," while the French called them Renards. The names Sauk and Fox are the ones in most common use and have been adopted here as the most recognizable to the general reader.

13. The origin of the name "Saukenuk" is uncertain. There is apparently no record of the Indians or anybody else using the name until long after the Sauk had been removed from Illinois. See: *Historic Rock Island*, 11–12. The name has entered common historical usage, however, and is also convenient, so it will be used here.

14. On the Sauk and Fox, see Temple, *Indian Villages*, 83–125; Hagan, *Sac and Fox*; Gussow, "Anthropological Report," 1: 29–20; Gussow, "Ethnological Report," 1: 121–84.

15. Hagan, *Sac and Fox*, 5–6, 9–12; *Historic Rock Island*, 10–11; Trask, *Black Hawk*, 33–43.

16. Kappler, *Indian Affairs*, 2: 74–77; *ASP: Indian Affairs*, 1: 695; *TP*, 13: 76–80, 164–72; Wallace, *Prelude*, 5–7, 13–21; Owens, *Jefferson's Hammer*, 86–92; Stout, "Anthropological Report," 2: 234–39; Hagan, *Sac and Fox*, 16–25; Jackson, *Black Hawk*, 53–54.

17. At the present site of Fort Madison, Iowa.

18. Black Hawk (Black Sparrow Hawk) was born at Saukenuk on the Rock River in 1767. Although he was never a civil chief of the Sauk, his youthful exploits against the Osage and Cherokee made him an influential war leader. A vocal opponent of the treaty of 1804, Black Hawk sided with the British during the War of 1812. The faction of the Sauk he led thereafter became known as "the British Band." In 1832 Black Hawk led a portion of the Sauk from Iowa in attempt to reclaim their old home on the Rock River. In the ensuing war, Black Hawk was captured and his band almost annihilated. After touring the East as a prisoner of war, he returned to Iowa and died on the Des Moines River on October 3, 1838. Hodge, *Handbook*, 1: 150–2; Trask, *Black Hawk*.

19. Hagan, *Sac and Fox*, 33–4, 39–40; Jackson, *Black Hawk*, 55–57; Jackson, "Old Fort Madison," 47: 16–19.

20. Temple, *Indian Villages*, 188–95; Tanner, *Atlas*, 98–100; Bent, *Whiteside County*, 38, 363–64.

21. Forsyth to Clark, December 23, 1812, in Forsyth Papers, Missouri History Museum, Saint Louis; *TP*, 16: 218; *WHC* 9: 152, 11: 300; Edwards, *History*, 315–18; *Illinois in 1837*, 31–32.

22. Temple, *Indian Villages*, 196–99; Tanner, *Atlas*, 98–100; Keesing, *Menomini Indians*; Ourada, *Menominee Indians*; Forsyth to Clark, July 20, 1813; *WHC* 11: 331–36.

23. Stout, "Report," 285–303; Clifton, *Prairie People*, 216–19; Edmunds, *Shawnee Prophet*, 3–7, 22–27.

24. Esarey, *Messages and Letters*, 1: 69–73.

25. William Henry Harrison, born February 9, 1773, in Charles City County, Virginia. Commissioned ensign in the 1st U.S. Infantry, August 16, 1791. Promoted lieutenant, June 2, 1792, and captain, May 15, 1797. Resigned June 1, 1798. Secretary of the Northwest Territory, 1798–99, delegate to Congress from Indiana Territory, 1799–1800, governor of Indiana Territory, 1801–13. Appointed major general in U.S. Army, March 2, 1813, and resigned May 31, 1814. Representative in Congress from Ohio, 1816–19, Ohio state senator 1819–22, U.S. senator for Ohio, 1825–28, and U.S. minister to Colombia, 1828–29. Elected ninth president of the United States, 1840, he served from March 4, 1841, until his death on April 4, 1841. Buried at William Henry Harrison Memorial State Park, opposite Congress Green Cemetery, North Bend, Ohio.

Heitman, *Historical Register*, 1: 505–6; *BDUSC*, 1207. Biographies: Cleaves, *Old Tippecanoe*; Owens, *Mr. Jefferson's Hammer*.

26. Kappler, *Indian Affairs*, 2: 64–68, 70–73, 74–79, 80–82, 89, 101–5; Cleaves, *Old Tippecanoe*, 31–38, 60–68.

27. Tenskwatawa, better known as "The Prophet," was born about 1775 at Old Piqua in Ohio, the son of a Shawnee warrior and a Creek woman. He lost an eye in an accident with an arrow. Visions beginning in 1805 made him the first leader of the Indian revival, but after defeat at the battle of Tippecanoe the Prophet faded into the background while his brother Tecumseh took control of the movement. Tenskwatawa was present at the battle of the Thames (1813), but he escaped with the British while Tecumseh died fighting. He remained in Canada until 1825, when he returned to the United States and took part in the removal of the Shawnee west of the Mississippi. In 1826 he established a small village near Kansas City, Kansas, and died there in November 1836. *ANB*, 21: 448–50. Biography: Edmunds, *Shawnee Prophet*.

28. Edmunds, *Shawnee Prophet*, 33–39; Forsyth to Clark, December 23, 1812.

29. Esarey, *Messages and Letters*, 1: 182–84.

30. Edmunds, *Shawnee Prophet*, 47–49; Drake, *Life of Tecumseh*, 91.

31. Tecumseh was born in Ohio, probably about 1768. His reputation as a warrior was earned in the border wars and at the battle of Fallen Timbers. At first he remained in the background of the Indian revival movement initiated by his younger brother Tenskwatawa, but he gradually came to the fore and was the acknowledged leader after Tenskwatawa's defeat in the battle of Tippecanoe. Tecumseh commanded a mixed Indian force during the operations that ended in the surrender of Detroit (1812). He was absent, recruiting on the Wabash, during the battle on the River Raisin (January 1813), but that summer he took part in the siege of Fort Meigs, where his personal influence halted the massacre of American prisoners. After the American victory at Lake Erie, Tecumseh accompanied the British retreat into Canada and died fighting at the battle of the Thames, October 5, 1813. *ANB*, 21: 422–25. Biographies: Sugden, *Tecumseh*; Drake, *Life of Tecumseh*.

32. Esarey, *Messages and Letters*, 1: 548–51.

33. Forsyth, "Main Poc and Tecumseh," DM, 4T50–56.

34. Shabbona (Shabonee, Shaubena, Chambly) was probably born in Ohio about 1775. Having married the daughter of a Potawatomi chief, he thereafter became a member of that tribe. Upon the death of his father-in-law, Shabbona became recognized as a chief. For many years his principal home was at a place known as Shabbona Grove (now Chief Shabbona Forest Preserve) in southern DeKalb County, Illinois. Shabbona fought alongside Tecumseh and the British during

the War of 1812, but after the death of Tecumseh he returned to Illinois and made his peace with the Americans. During the Black Hawk War of 1832 he sided with the United States and is credited with saving lives by his warnings to settlers. In 1837 Shabbona accompanied his tribe to their new home in Missouri but soon returned to Illinois. In 1849 an ungrateful country evicted Shabbona and his family from their home at Shabbona Grove and the old chief spent his last years in poverty. He died July 27, 1859, and is buried in Evergreen Cemetery, Morris, Illinois. Several place names in DeKalb County preserve Shabbona's memory. Vogel, *Indian Place Names*, 132–35; Walters, "Shabonee"; "Historical Notes." Biographies: Matson, *Memories of Shaubena*, is said to have been based on the author's conversations with the chief himself. Hatch, *Indian Chief Shabbona*, and Dowd, *Built like a Bear*, contain little of independent value.

35. Edmunds, *Potawatomis*, 172; Matson, *Memories of Shaubena*, 19–20.

36. Hickey, *War of 1812*, 73; *MPHC* 15: 47–49, 53; Wood, *Select British Documents*, 1: 164, 271–78; Stanley, "Indians."

Chapter 3. Rumors of War

1. On the killing of Elijah Cox, see "Deposition of Rebecca Cox," June 13, 1814, NA, RG 107, LRSW (M 221, Roll 36, Frame 3283); *Louisiana Gazette*, June 27, 1811; *Reporter*, July 13, 1811, 3; Edwards, *History*, 29, 46, 285–87; Esarey, *Messages and Letters*, 1: 512–17, 530–31; Bissell to Secretary of War, June 28, 1811, in Daniel Bissell Papers, Folder 3, Missouri History Museum, Saint Louis; *ASP: Indian Affairs*, 1: 803–4; *TP*, 8: 134–35; Forsyth to Clark, July 20, 1813, Thomas Forsyth Papers, Missouri History Museum, St. Louis; Reynolds, *Pioneer History*, 404; Reynolds, *My Own Times*, 78; Alex Wells, DM, 20S136–37; Smith, *History of Southern Illinois*, 1: 432–33; *Bond County History*, 12; Wilson and Kaegy, *Tales of Hill's Fort*, 79–81.

2. William Pruitt (also Preuitt, Prewitt) came to Illinois as part of a large family who settled in Madison County in 1806. Appointed captain of militia May 3, 1809, and again January 2, 1810. He was promoted to major in the Second Regiment of militia April 24, 1811. He may subsequently have enlisted as a private soldier in Captain Jacob Short's company of U.S. Rangers, but his career is difficult to trace because of confusion with a cousin of the same name. He was dead by December 6, 1814, when his brother Abraham appeared in court as administrator of his estate. *TP* 17: 622, 630, 636; Wilson and Kaegy, *Tales of Hill's Fort*, 33, 35, 56–55; Wilson and Kaegy, *Hill's Fort*, 34–36; *History of Madison*, 78, 87, 130, 218.

3. Reynolds, *Pioneer History*, 404.

4. The accounts of the pursuit of the Cox murderers contain many discrepancies

and inaccuracies. A contemporary account says that the pursuers were led by "capt. Whitesides" (presumably William Bolin Whiteside) and that the kidnapped girl was found tomahawked, but alive, in a camp the Indians had vacated. *Western Sun*, June 15, 1811, 3. Two weeks later the same newspaper printed a different version, closer to, but not identical with, the traditional account. *Western Sun*, June 29, 1811, 3. Another version, in DM, 20S137, claims that Pruitt led his party home without a fight, leaving the girl in the hands of the Indians until a Frenchman subsequently ransomed her. This is simply wrong, as Rebecca's own affidavit establishes. Another erroneous tradition holds that the murderers were pursued by a company led by Samuel Whiteside, which tracked them through Macoupin County, killing almost all of them at specifically identified locations. Blevins, "Historical Sketch"; Strange, *History of Montgomery County*, 432–33. That story must also be rejected. There is no reason to believe that more than possibly one Indian was killed. Blevins was one of the first white children born in Macoupin County, but he may have confused this pursuit with the one actually led by Captain Samuel Whiteside after the Wood River massacre in 1814.

5. The couple was married in Saint Clair County on July 7, 1812. Illinois Statewide Marriage Index, Office of the Illinois Secretary of State.

6. The monument stands on the north side of Cox Monument Road, 450 E, 800 N, about two miles northeast of the village of Pocahontas. The monument identifies the young man by last name only, but the deposition of his sister established that his name was Elijah.

7. Edwards, *History*, 286–87; *Western Sun*, June 29, 1811, 3; *Reporter*, July 13, 1811, 3.

8. According to one account, the second man was named Hodgen and according to another he was Price's son. Ellis, however, is the name by which Governor Edwards identified him immediately after the attack and is most likely to be correct.

9. The spring then flowed at what is now the northeast corner of Second and Spring Streets. "Historic Sites of Alton"; Norton, *Centennial History*, 37–38. Price was reportedly buried near the spring.

10. *Louisiana Gazette*, June 27, 1811; *Reporter*, July 13, 1811, 3; William Whiteside to Edwards, June 21, 1811, NA, RG 107, LRSW (M 221, Roll 36, 3285); Edwards, *History*, 39, 46, 287; Bissell to Secretary of War, June 28, 1811; *TP*, 14: 536–36; Forsyth to Clark, July 20, 1813; *History of Madison County*, 80; "Madison County in the Days of the Indians and Pioneers," *Greenville Advocate*, July 4, 1889; "Speck of Indian Warfare."

11. Whiteside to Edwards, June 21, 1811; *TP*, 16: 162.

12. That is the story Captain William Wells heard from Indians at Fort Wayne

and reported to the War Department. *TP*, 8: 134–5. Governor Harrison emphatically disagreed with this account. Esarey, *Messages and Letters*, 1: 604–5.

13. Esarey, *Messages and Letters*, 1: 526–28, 631–32; *TP*, 16: 164–66, 169–71.

14. *TP*, 16: 164–66.

15. *TP*, 16: 162–63; Petition for a License for a Ferry across the Mississippi River, March Term, 1809, Perrin Collection, Illinois State Archives, Springfield; Hammes, "Squatters," 375.

16. *TP*, 16: 162–63.

17. *Missouri Gazette* [Saint Louis], March 20, 1813.

18. For details, see Wilson and Kaegy, *Forts*, 120–207.

19. *TP*, 16: 257–58.

20. Fort Russell stood in NE ¼, SE ¼, NE ¼ section 34, T5S, R8W, just west of present Highway 59. *History of Madison*, 81, 217, 475; Smith, *History of Southern Illinois*, 1: 111; Wilson and Kaegy, *Forts*, 152–55.

21. Reynolds, *My Own Times*, 82; *TP*, 16: 265–66, 312–15, 362–63.

22. Whiteside's Station stood about halfway between Waterloo and Columbia, in what is now Monroe County.

23. On the Whiteside family see Bateman, *Historical Encyclopedia*, 586; Reynolds, *Pioneer History*, 185–90; Baldwin, *Echoes*, 139–42, 351–53.

24. Edwards, *History*, 294–95.

25. The Second Regiment, as it was numbered, was organized into three battalions, commanded by Majors John Moredock, Samuel Judy, and William Pruitt. Stevens, "Illinois," 174–75.

26. Before division, Colonel William Whiteside held appointive military positions in Indiana Territory. In Illinois he was appointed major (May 2, 1809), colonel (December 22, 1809), and treasurer of Saint Clair County (March 9, 1815). He died soon after the last appointment, between March 9 and April 8, 1815. Reynolds, *Pioneer History*, 185–90; *TP*, 17: 621, 630, 651; Philbrick, *Laws of Indiana Territory*, ccxlviii, cclxi, n. 40; Woollen et al., *Executive Journal*, iii, 130.

27. William Bolin Whiteside was born in North Carolina, December 27, 1777, and came to Illinois with the family in 1793. Appointed captain of Illinois territorial militia May 2, 1809, and major April 19, 1810. Resigned as major to accept federal appointment as captain of U.S. Rangers, March 1812. Honorably discharged, June 15, 1815. Sheriff of Madison County, 1818–22. During the Black Hawk scare of 1831, he took the field one last time as captain of a mounted company of spies. William Bolin Whiteside died at his home in Madison County, Illinois, November 18, 1835. He was buried in a family graveyard, known as Whiteside Cemetery, very near the present stadium of Southern Illinois University at Edwardsville. John Reynolds, who served as a Ranger under Whiteside's

command, said of him, "He was raised on the frontiers and without much education, but possessed a strong and sprightly intellect and a benevolence of heart that was rarely equaled. All his talents and energies were exerted in the defense of his country." *TP*, 16: 197, 17: 621–22, 632, 641; Reynolds, *Pioneer History*, 416–17; *History of Madison*, 76, 81, 83, 130, 132, 139, 140; Heitman, *Historical Register*, 1: 1029; Whitney, *Black Hawk War*, 1: 101–2, 2: 69, n. 18.

28. Edwards, *History*, 299.

29. Samuel Whiteside was born in North Carolina April 12, 1783, and moved to Illinois with the family in 1793. His father John Whiteside, a Revolutionary soldier, settled near Bellefontaine, now Waterloo. Samuel rose steadily in the militia: ensign January 2, 1810, captain June 27, 1811, major February 26, 1817, colonel May 22, 1817, and brigadier general 1819. He also saw federal service as captain of U.S. Rangers (August 1, 1813), from which he was honorably discharged, July 30, 1814. Member of first Illinois General Assembly (1818–20). Served as brigadier general of volunteers at outset of Black Hawk War, but when the army he commanded was dissolved, Whiteside reenlisted as a private in Captain Adam Snyder's company. In 1854 Whiteside sold his farm in Madison County and moved to Christian County, Illinois, where he died January 13, 1866. He is buried in Hunter Cemetery, Mosquito Township, Christian County. Carter, *TP*, 17: 630, 636, 659, 662; *History of Madison*, 76, 131, 167, 217–18, 454; Whitney, *Black Hawk War*, 1: 235–39, 2: 69, n. 15; Pease, *Illinois Election Returns*, 185, 189; Callary, *Place Names*, 374–75.

30. *WHC* 7: 325; *History of Jo Daviess County*, 284, 293. The story is vividly retold in Baldwin, *Echoes*, 352–53. There is a somewhat different version of the story in Ford, *History*, 124–25.

31. Edwards, *History*, 284–85, 287–88.

32. Ibid., 284–85, 286–87.

33. *TP*, 16: 162–63, 164–66; Esarey, *Messages and Letters*, 1: 526–28. Which three companies Edwards ordered out is uncertain, but they were probably those commanded by Captains William Bolin Whiteside, Samuel Whiteside, and William Alexander. Only the muster roll of Alexander's company appears to have survived. *RAGI*, 9: 320; Corrigan and Temple, "Illinois Volunteer Officers," 236.

34. *TP*, 16: 162–66, 169–71, 178.

35. The "Illinois River Blockhouse," as it was known, stood just above Grafton, near the spot where a concrete cross now commemorates the passage of Marquette and Jolliet. The blockhouse was abandoned after the war and in 1819, a settler named George Finney appropriated timbers and foundation stones to build his house. *History of Greene and Jersey*, 71; Postlewait, *History of Jersey County*, T164;

Hair, *Gazetteer*, 282; "See Mound Builders as Early Grafton Settlers," *Democrat News* (Jerseyville, Illinois), September 23, 1965; "River City's History," *Democrat News*, June 29, 1978; "Map of Jersey County," c. 1906, and accompanying letter of W. E. Carlin to Jessie Palmer Webber, November 15, 1906, in Abraham Lincoln Presidential Library, Springfield.

36. Washburne, *Edwards Papers*, 63–67; Stevens, "Illinois," 75–76; W. B. Whiteside to Edwards, August 4, 1811, Ninian Edwards Papers, Box 1, Folder 2, Chicago History Museum.

37. Houck, 3: 98–100; Edwards, *History*, 37, 321; Washburne, *Edwards Papers*, 56–57; *TP*, 14: 412–15, 16: 250–53; *WHC* 11: 320; Samuel Cole, DM, 23S65–76; James Cole, DM, 23S94–99. *Louisiana Gazette*, July 4 and 18, 1811.

38. Conway, "Potawatomi Politics." Gomo told his friend, trader Thomas Forsyth, that he himself was willing to surrender the murderers, but that he could get no support from the other chiefs and warriors, and that if he went to apprehend the murderers himself he would be killed. Forsyth to Clark, August 20, 1811, Forsyth Papers.

39. Robert Forsyth, DM, 22S107.

40. Samuel Levering was born in Philadelphia, September 13, 1778. He is said to have been a ship carver by trade. As an adult Levering moved to the Illinois Territory and settled at Kaskaskia. The governor appointed Levering a lieutenant in the Randolph County militia on June 26, 1810, and promoted him to captain May 20, 1811. Shortly after his return from this diplomatic mission, Captain Levering died at Kaskaskia sometime between September 2, 1811, when he wrote a letter to General William Clark, and September 18, when the vacancy caused by his death was filled by the governor. *TP*, 17: 633, 636, 637; Levering to Clark, September 2, 1811, William Clark Papers, Box 12, Folder 2, Missouri History Museum; Levering, *Levering Family*, 172, 896–99.

41. For the story of Levering's mission, see Edwards, *History*, 38–55; Stevens, "Illinois," 74–95; *TP*, 16: 169–72, 175–79; Executive Records, RS 100.003, Folder 11, Illinois State Archives, Springfield; Reynolds, *My Own Times*, 78–79. The picturesque account of Matson, *French and Indians*, 195–97, belongs to the realm of romance. For the "Prairie Marcot" blockhouse, see *ASP: Indian Affairs*, 4: 800; Reynolds, *Pioneer History*, 405; Edwards, *History*, 38; Campbell to Clark, July 30, 1811, William Clark Papers, Box 12, Folder 2, Missouri History Museum; Stevens, "Illinois," 72, 74; *Louisiana Gazette*, July 18, 1811. The blockhouse was apparently not of long duration and may have been the one from which the Indians bragged the whites had run when they learned of a war party coming downriver. Forsyth to Clark, November 1, 1811, Forsyth Papers. (The original letter has been damaged, and this reading is in part conjectural.)

42. The Little Chief would die sometime before May 1812, and be succeeded on Aux Sable Creek by a chief named Pepper. Edwards, *History*, 315–18.

43. *Ibid.*, 47–49.

44. *Ibid.*, 49–50.

45. "Journal of Captain Hebert," NA, LRSW (M 221, Roll 36, 3304–5); Reynolds, *My Own Times*, 78–79; Stevens, "Illinois," 95. Trotier had accompanied Levering as a boatman. Edwards, *History*, 38. There was a French Canadian named Joseph Trotier who settled in Cahokia about 1776 and engaged in trade between the Illinois country and New Orleans. *History of St. Clair*, 49, 80–81.

46. *TP*, 16: 174–75; Reynolds, *My Own Times*, 79. According to Reynolds, Levering died from exposure along the river.

47. Forsyth to Clark, September 15, 1811, Forsyth Papers.

48. Esarey, *Messages and Letters*, 1: 554–55; *TP*, 16: 169–71; Mahon, *War of 1812*, 22.

49. Esarey, *Messages and Letters*, 1: 542–46.

50. D. L. McCawley to Draper, June 9, 1884, DM, 5YY40; J. J. McCawley to Draper, June 16, 1884, DM, 5YY41.

51. Hubbs, *Pioneer Folks*, 192; Hale, *Williamson County*, 42.

52. This was a crossing place frequently used by Indians. Perrin, *History of Alexander*, 268; [Wall], *Moyers' Brief History*, 11–12.

53. The literature on the Tippecanoe campaign is extensive. For the essentials, see the documents, mostly letters and orders, reprinted in Esarey, *Messages and Letters*, 1: 589–675. See also Cleaves, *Old Tippecanoe*, 98–104; McAfee, *History*, 17–38; Beard, *Battle of Tippecanoe*; Pirtle, *Battle of Tippecanoe*. For Indian perspectives on the battle, see Wood, *Select British Documents*, 1: 280–83; Whickar, "Shabonee's Account."

54. Isaac White was born in Prince William County, Virginia, about 1776. Moved to Vincennes, Indiana, 1800. Appointed by Governor Harrison to be agent of the U.S. Salines, near the present Equality, Illinois, 1805. Appointed major (December 22, 1809) and colonel of the newly organized Third Regiment (June 27, 1810). Killed in action at Tippecanoe, November 7, 1811. Whether White County was named for Isaac White or for General Leonard White remains uncertain. *TP*, 17: 630, 633; White, *Sketch*; Sandham, "Colonel Isaac White"; Beard, *Battle of Tippecanoe*, 66, 112; Pirtle, *Battle of Tippecanoe*, 123; Callary, *Place Names*, 373–74.

55. Hamlet Ferguson was born in South Carolina in 1772 or 1773. He came to Smithland, Kentucky, in 1796, but by 1806 he had crossed the Ohio River into what is now the southern part of Pope County, Illinois. He served as a justice of the peace under the laws of first Indiana Territory (1806) and later of Illinois Territory (1809). He was appointed captain in the Illinois Territorial

Militia (January 2, 1810) and was promoted to major in the new Third Regiment (January 27, 1810). Ferguson served as a judge of the first county court of Johnson County (1813), sheriff of Johnson County (1815), first sheriff of Pope County (1816), and judge of the county court of Pope County (1817). He was a member of the convention that wrote the first state constitution for Illinois (1818). Colonel Ferguson died in Livingston County, Kentucky, December 11, 1840, and lies buried in the Ferguson Cemetery near Smithland. Ferguson, "He Acted Well"; McCormick, "Ferguson and O'Melveny."

56. Philip Tramell resided at the U.S. Salines, near the present Equality, Illinois. Represented Gallatin County in the first and second territorial legislatures (1812–16). Appointed captain of militia (January 2, 1810), major in Third Regiment (June 27, 1810), and lieutenant colonel of Fourth Regiment (November 28, 1811). Resigned his commission March 1814. *TP*, 17: 630, 633, 638, 648; *List of State Officers*, 137.

57. Stevens, "Illinois," 175–76; *TP*, 17: 633, 638; Tramell to Edwards, January 4, 1812, and Tramell to Edwards, January 18, 1812, in Executive Records, RS 100.002, Illinois State Archives. No record of Ferguson's promotion to lieutenant colonel has been found, but that it was made is established by Militia Muster Roll, Records of the Illinois Territory, RS 100.013, Illinois State Archives.

58. According to Alexander Robinson, Waubansee was a younger brother of Black Partridge, one of the principal chiefs of the Illinois River Potawatomi. There are different versions of his exploit, which on another occasion he tried to repeat with less success, receiving a bayonet wound in the shoulder. His principal residence is said to have been along the west bank of the Fox River, in the north part of the present Aurora, Illinois, with another at Oswego, near the mouth of Waubonsie Creek. Waubansee is commemorated today in Kane, Kendall, and DuPage counties by Waubonsie Creek, Waubonsie Valley High School, and Waubonsee Community College, in Grundy County by the village and township of Wauponsee, and in Chicago by Wabansia Avenue. Esarey, *Messages and Letters*, 606–7; Reynolds, *My Own Times*, 85–86; Alexander Robinson, DM, 21S279–80; Robert Forsyth, DM, 22S105; Joseph N. Bourassa, DM, 23S190; Vogel, *Indian Place Names*, 160–62, 164; Beckwith, *Illinois and Indiana Indians*, 172 n.; Hicks, *History of Kendall County*, 48–49; *Past and Present of Kane County*, 225, 276. A biography, based on uncritical use of sometimes unreliable sources, is Zeman, *Wabansi*.

59. McAfee, *History*, 34; Cleaves, *Old Tippecanoe*, 95; *Louisiana Gazette*, April 25, 1812.

60. Esarey, *Messages and Letters*, 1: 656–58; *National Intelligencer*, January 25, 1812, in Knopf, *Document Transcriptions*, 5: pt. 1, 44–46.

61. Edwards, *History*, 289–91.

62. Grand Pass is in Patterson Township, in the northwest corner of the present Greene County. The place took its name from a narrow channel that once connected a chain of small lakes, below the bluffs near the river. *History of Greene County*, 223–24.

63. William Whiteside to Edwards, December 4, 1811, NA, RG 107, LRSW (M 221, Roll 44, 9314); Forsyth to Clark, November 1, 1811, Forsyth Papers; *Louisiana Gazette*, November 16, 1811.

64. Whiteside to Edwards, December 4, 1811; Edwards, *History*, 294–95.

65. Clark to Secretary of War, March 22, 1812, NA, RG 107, LRSW (M221, Roll 43, 8517); *TP*, 16: 193–94; Matson, *Memories of Shaubena*, 19–20; Sugden, "Tecumseh's Travels," 164–65.

66. Hebert was born in Québec about 1772 but was in Cahokia by 1797, when he entered into a marriage contract in that village. Governor Edwards appointed Hebert captain in the Second Regiment of militia on July 2, 1811. Carter, *TP*, 17: 637; Edwards, *History*, 38, 44; *History of St. Clair*, 130; "Marriage Contract between Heberd and Baron," in Marriage Contracts, 1797–1802, 65, Perrin Collection, Illinois State Archives, Springfield.

67. Edwards, *History*, 292–95, 300–02; *Reporter*, March 21, 1812, 2; *Louisiana Gazette*, June 20, 1812.

68. *TP*, 14: 506–7, 518–20, 16: 186–8; *ASP: Indian Affairs*, 1: 806.

69. *TP*, 14: 518–20; *History of Lincoln County*, 223–24.

70. Edwards, *History*, 311; *TP*, 14: 531–34; *ASP: Indian Affairs*, 1: 807; *National Intelligencer*, April 14, 1812, in Knopf, *Document Transcriptions*, 5: pt. 1, 63.

71. *Louisiana Gazette*, April 25, 1812.

72. Edwards, *History*, 305, 321; *TP*, 14: 518–20, 16: 193–94; Forsyth to Clark, July 20, 1813; *Reporter*, March 14, 1812, 3; *History of Lincoln County*, 223–24.

73. Daniel Bissell was born in Connecticut, August 15, 1769. He served in the Revolution as a drummer in the Connecticut Militia. As a sergeant at St. Clair's defeat (1791) Bissell received a battlefield commission as ensign, and was afterwards regularly commissioned ensign April 1792 and lieutenant January 3, 1794. Assigned to First Infantry 1796. Promoted captain (January 1, 1799), lieutenant colonel (August 18, 1808), and colonel (August 15, 1812), at which time he was transferred to Fifth Infantry. Promoted brigadier general March 9, 1814. With reduction of army after war, Bissell was retained in service (May 17, 1815) as colonel of First Infantry, with brevet as brigadier general. Honorably discharged June 1, 1821. General Bissell died December 14, 1833, at his home Franklinville Farms, near Saint Louis. Heitman, *Historical Register*, 221; Christensen et al., *Dictionary*, 76–77; *Missouri Historical Review*, 8: 119 (January 1914).

74. Fort Mason was built near the present Saverton, Missouri, just south of Hannibal, to guard a favorite Indian crossing place on the Mississippi. Lieutenant John Campbell of the regular army commanded a small garrison. *TP*, 14: 520–21, 551, 563–69, 573–74; "Missouriana," 284.

75. *TP*, 14: 522–23, 530, 593–94; Knopf, *Document Transcriptions*, vol. 6, pt.i, 108–10; Caldwell, "Fort Massac since 1805."

76. *TP*, 14: 520–23.

77. *TP*, 14: 523. Shortly after the incident, Captain Levering met Whiteside and his command at Portage des Sioux, the company having apparently been withdrawn from the blockhouse. Edwards, *History*, 38.

78. *TP*, 14: 551–52.

79. 2 U. S. Stat. 670; Knopf, *Document Transcriptions*, 8: 11; *TP*, 8: 168–69, 14: 529.

80. Knopf, *Document Transcriptions*, 8: 11; *TP*, 14: 541–42; Reynolds, *My Own Times*, 84.

81. Edwards, *History*, 299–300, 311–12; Knopf, *Document Transcriptions*, 6: pt. 1, 53; *TP*, 16: 197–98. Whiteside's nomination was confirmed on March 13, 1812. Senate, Exec. Journal, II, 234, 236.

82. *National Intelligencer*, April 4, 1812, transcribed in Knopf, *Document Transcriptions*, 5: pt. 1, 61.

83. Edwards, *History*, 303–6, 311; *TP*, 16: 193–94. The muster rolls of these three companies are in *RAGI*, 9: 326–27, and Stevens, "Illinois," 79–80. An apparent discrepancy between the two lists is explained by the promotion of Lieutenant Henry Cook to command the third company following Samuel Judy's promotion to major, April 12, 1812, *TP*, 17: 641.

84. John Scott was an old resident of Saint Clair County who had settled there before 1799. Appointed captain of militia (May 3, 1809), captain Second Regiment (January 2, 1810), and major of Second Regiment, August 15, 1814. In 1814 he entered 320 acres in S 1/2 section 1, T1N, R8W, between the present Belleville and O'Fallon. *History of St. Clair*, 34, 74, 132; *TP*, 17: 622, 630, 649. He must not be confused with another, younger John Scott of Saint Genevieve, Missouri, who represented Missouri in Congress.

85. Edwards, *History*, 311. It is by no means clear that all three companies remained on active duty for the full three months. On March 23 Edwards spoke in terms of having one company in the field. *Ibid.* Eventually the government agreed to pay all the militia Edwards called out as if they were Rangers. Knopf, *Document Transcriptions*, 8: 34.

86. Edwards, *History*, 310.

87. *Ibid.*, 55–56.

88. *ASP: Indian Affairs*, 1: 807; Clark to Edwards, April 11, 1812, Edwards Papers,

Box 1, Folder 3, Chicago History Museum; *Louisiana Gazette*, April 11, 1812; *Reporter*, April 25, 1812, 3; Edwards, *History*, 63; Edmunds, *Potawatomis*, 179.

89. For the council of Cahokia, see Edwards, *History*, 56–65; Stevens, "Illinois," 100–112; *Louisiana Gazette*, April 18 and 25, 1812; *Reporter*, May 16, 1812, 3; Reynolds, *My Own Times*, 83.

90. The name is given by Edwards as "Black Bird," but he probably meant Black Partridge (Mucketypoke), who later opposed the Fort Dearborn massacre and helped save some of those who survived, rather than Black Bird (Siggenauk or LeTourneau), a war chief of Pepper's band who led the Indians in that battle and took the surrender of the Americans. (See, generally, chapter 4.) The two chiefs have sometimes been confused with one another (DM, 3Q38–39). Black Partridge was too important a chief to have been excluded from the council at Cahokia, while Black Bird, although part of Pepper's band, was an Ottawa. The list of chiefs attending also refers to an Ottawa chief named Black Bird, who did not attend, but sent a substitute. Edwards, *History*, 315–18.

91. In fact, less than a month later Congress would set aside more than 2 million acres north of the Illinois River as military bounty lands. 2 U.S. Stat. 728.

92. Forsyth to Clark, May 6, 1812, Thomas Forsyth Papers.

93. *TP*, 16: 215–16.

94. Twice in March Edwards reported news of murders in the territory, first of two men, then of one man. *TP*, 16: 193–94, 202–3. No other mention of these killings has been found. The frontier was constantly swept by rumors of Indian atrocities, sometimes true, sometimes false. Whether the murders Edwards reported in March actually happened is an open question.

95. Kirkland, *Story of Chicago*, 54; Jensen, *Historic Chicago*, 50.

96. On the Lee's place murders see *Louisiana Gazette*, May 30, 1812; Knopf, *Document Transcriptions*, 6: pt. 1, 134, 142, 164–65; *TP*, 16: 212–13; *Reporter*, June 13, 1812, 1; Quaife, *Chicago and the Old Northwest*, 212–13; Quaife, *Checagou*, 117–19. There is a vivid, but partly fictionalized, account of the killings in Kinzie, *Wau-Bun*, 205–9.

97. For the Hutson massacre, see Esarey, *Messages and Letters*, 2: 31–34; Knopf, *Document Transcriptions*, 6: pt. 1, 191; *Reporter*, April 25, 1812; *Louisiana Gazette*, May 16, 1812; *Missouri Gazette*, August 5, 1815; *National Intelligencer*, June 4, 1812, transcribed in Knopf, *Document Transcriptions*, 5: pt. 1, 83–85; Perrin, *History of Crawford*, 33–34, 220; Bateman, *Illinois Historical*, 619, 635–36, 676–79; Hutson, "Killed by the Indians."

98. Forsyth to Clark, July 20, 1813.

99. Part of the lore of the Hutson massacre is the story that before the house was burned the murderers threw the young Hutson baby into a boiling cauldron

(e.g., Hutson, "Killed by the Indians," 102). The story was in circulation within at least three years after the murders (*Missouri Gazette*, August 5, 1815) but is unlikely to be true. A newspaper account written immediately after the massacre judged from the appearance of the remains that the mother died "holding the youngest child in her arms, and the others clinging to her for protection." *Western Sun*, April 18, 1812. A similar story was told in connection with the massacre of the O'Neal family: *History of Lincoln County*, 223. Whether true or not, the boiling of babies seems to have been a stock atrocity charged to the Indians. Compare Flint, *Recollections*, 160.

100. Perrin, *History of Crawford*, 34. Either or neither (but not both) of two references may record something about Hutson's subsequent life. He may have been the "Mr. Huston" whose death is reported in Knopf, *Document Transcriptions*, 6: pt. 1, 191. Alternatively, he may instead have been the brave "Mr. Hutson" who in September 1812 accompanied Ensign Floyd of Captain Dubois's company in an attempt to break through to the besieged Fort Harrison, after the rest of the company had turned back. *Western Sun*, September 8, 1812, 3; *Reporter*, September 12, 1812, 1.

101. Callary, *Place Names*, 168; Tolle, "Hutsonville."

102. For the Harriman massacre, see Esarey, *Messages and Letters*, 1: 707–8, 2: 41–44; *National Intelligencer*, June 4, 1812, transcribed in Knopf, *Document Transcriptions*, 5: pt. 1, 83–85; *Louisiana Gazette*, May 16, 1812; *Western Sun*, April 25, 1812; *Combined History of Edwards*, 71; Cleaves, *Old Tippecanoe*, 110. The family's surname was often spelled Harryman or Haryman. Mussel Shoals was located where the Vincennes-Illinois Trace crossed the Embarras River, one mile south of the mouth of Indian Creek, at the SW corner of NW1/4, Section 21, T3N, R11W. White, "Historical Notes," 367; personal communication from John M. King.

103. Thomas Forsyth believed that these Indians were the same ones who had killed the Hutson family a few days earlier. Forsyth to Clark, July 20, 1813.

104. James Miller was born in New Hampshire, April 25, 1776. Commissioned as a major in the Fourth Infantry July 8, 1808. Promoted lieutenant colonel November 30, 1810. Fought at Tippecanoe and succeeded to command of regulars in Indiana Territory after transfer of Colonel John Boyd, January 1812. Brevetted colonel August 9, 1812, for distinguished service at battle of Brownstown, promoted colonel March 9, 1814. Brevetted brigadier general July 25, 1814, for distinguished service at Niagara Falls. Thanks of Congress, November 3, 1814. Resigned from army, June 1, 1819. Governor of Arkansas Territory, 1819–23. Collector of the Port of Salem, Massachusetts, 1825–49. Died at Temple, New Hampshire, July 7, 1851, and buried in Harmony Cemetery,

Salem, Massachusetts. Miller County, Arkansas, is named for him. Drake, *Dictionary*, 621; Heitman, *Historical Register*, 1: 46, 48, 710–11; Esarey, *Messages and Letters*, 2: 17.

105. *National Intelligencer*, July 4, 1812, transcribed in Knopf, *Document Transcriptions*, 5: pt. 1, 69. It may have been about this time that a blockhouse was erected at Mussel Shoals, on the Embarras River, where the Harriman family had been murdered. Lewis, *Fort Allison*, 3.

106. On Coffee Island, see *Combined History of Edwards*, 331–35.

107. Tramell to Edwards, May 16, 1812, *TP* 16: 224.

108. William McHenry settled on the Wabash in 1810 but the next year moved inland, where he built a horse mill and a blockhouse. He served as first lieutenant in Willis Hargrave's militia company and as captain of his own company. Mustered into federal service as third lieutenant of U.S. Rangers August 1, 1813, and honorably discharged June 15, 1815. In 1818 represented White County in the convention that wrote the first Illinois constitution, and subsequently served as its representative in the First, Fourth, Fifth, and Ninth General Assemblies, and as senator in the Sixth and Seventh. He took the field once more as major of Illinois Volunteers during the Black Hawk War of 1832. Died at Vandalia, February 3, 1835, and lies buried there in South Hill Cemetery. *History of White County*, 221–22, 450; *RAGI*, 9: 238; Corrigan and Temple, "Illinois Volunteer Officers," 238; Heitman, *Historical Register*, 1: 668; *TP*, 17: 637, 639; *Illinois Advocate & State Register* [Vandalia], February 5, 1835; Bateman, *Historical Encyclopedia*, 364; Clayton, *Illinois Fact Book*, 197, 199–201, 204.

109. *TP*, 16: 223–25; Esarey, *Messages and Letters*, 2: 48–49.

110. Willis Hargrave was a native of Kentucky who settled in what is now White County, Illinois. He served in the Third Territorial Legislature (1817–18), the convention that drafted the first state constitution (1818), and the first Illinois Senate (1818–20). Hargrave eventually reached the rank of major general in the Illinois militia, a position he resigned in 1827. In later life he lived in Gallatin County, where he was superintendent of the Salines and served as president of the Board of Trustees of Equality. During the Black Hawk War of 1832, he served as colonel of a regiment of Illinois Mounted Volunteers and took part in the Battle of Bad Axe. General Hargrave is buried in an unmarked grave in the Village Cemetery at Equality. Bateman, *Historical Encyclopedia*, 221; Pease, *Illinois Election Returns*, 185, 187; Whitney, *Black Hawk War*, 1: 245 and 2: 628, n. 3; *History of Gallatin*, 122–23; Miner, *Gallatin County*, 1: 9.

111. The names of the men Hargrave led on this campaign are probably included in the company roster printed in *RAGI*, 9: 328.

112. Philbrick, *Pope's Digest*, 2: 145–46.

113. Washburne, *Edwards Papers*, 68–69; *TP*, 16: 223–25.

114. Edwards, *History*, 319–21.

115. Nathan Boone was the youngest son of Daniel Boone, the famous pioneer of Kentucky. Born in Kentucky, 1781. In Missouri engaged in salt-making and surveying. Appointed Captain U.S. Rangers, March 25, 1812, and promoted major, December 10, 1813. Honorably discharged in June 1815. Delegate to first Missouri Constitutional Convention, 1820. Reenlisted as captain of mounted Rangers, June 16, 1832. Assigned to First Dragoons as captain, August 15, 1833. Promoted major, February 16, 1847, and lieutenant colonel, Second Dragoons, July 25, 1850. Resigned July 15, 1853. Died January 12, 1856, and buried in a family cemetery near his home at Ash Grove, Missouri. His home is now a Missouri state historic site. Heitman, *Historical Register*, 230. Biography: Hurt, *Nathan Boone*. See also Hammon (ed.), *My Father, Daniel Boone*.

116. Edwards, *History*, 312–15, 328–29.

117. Ibid., 328–29.

118. James Biggs Moore, born October 8, 1780, was the third son of Captain James Moore, one of the founders of Bellefontaine, now Waterloo, Illinois. As a young man, James B. ran a keelboat between Illinois and New Orleans before going into the tanning business. When war broke out he was frequently in service as captain of militia. When Congress authorized three additional companies of militia in 1813, Moore was commissioned one of the captains and was in federal service between August 1, 1813, and June 15, 1815. In 1816 Moore was appointed first sheriff of Monroe County. Although he reached the rank of major general in the state militia, Moore's Whig and antislavery views limited his political success, as in his futile run for governor in 1824. After numerous defeats, he was elected as a state senator in 1837, serving in the Tenth and Eleventh General Assemblies. General Moore died July 10, 1840, and is buried in the Moore Cemetery, section 36, T2S, R10W, Monroe County, Illinois. Klein, *Arrowheads*, 598–603; Bateman, *Historical Encyclopedia*, 382–83; *TP*, 17: 630, 653, 658; Pease, *Illinois Election Returns*, 7, 14–17, 81 n. 1, 220, 231, 265, 304, 332; Alvord, *Governor Edward Coles*, 51, 318; Heitman, *Historical Register*, 1: 722; *RAGI*, 9: 324, 330–31, 335, 339–40; *Selected Monroe County, Illinois Cemetery Inscriptions* (Millstadt, Illinois, 1972?) in Abraham Lincoln Presidential Library, Springfield; Baldwin, *Echoes*, 323.

119. Jacob Short, born in Kentucky about 1775, was an early settler near Turkey Hill in Saint Clair County. In January 1810 Short was appointed captain in the Saint Clair County militia. He and his company were frequently in service during the early part of the war. When Congress in 1813 approved three additional companies of U.S. Rangers, Short was appointed captain of one of them, and

he was in federal service from August 1, 1813, until June 15, 1815. He also served in the lower house of the first territorial legislature but resigned the position in October 1813, being succeeded by John Moredock. In 1822 Short moved to Menard County, Illinois, where he died, March 28, 1825, aged fifty years. He was buried in the Old Concord (Goodpasture) Cemetery, north of Petersburg, in Section 3, T18N, R7W. *History of St. Clair*, 49; Miller, *Past and Present of Menard County*, 89; *TP*, 16: 300–302, 17: 630, 647; *RAGI*, 9: 324, 326, 335–36; Heitman, *Historical Register*, 1: 884; Allers et al., *Menard County*, 33.

120. *RAGI*, 9: 330; Stevens, "Illinois," 181.

121. *TP*, 16: 236–38.

122. *TP*, 16: 226–28.

123. *TP*, 16: 234–36.

124. *TP*, 16: 232–34.

125. Edwards, *History*, 327–29.

126. *TP*, 8: 179, 16: 217.

127. William Russell was born in Culpeper County, Virginia, March 6, 1758. In 1774, he accompanied Daniel Boone on an expedition against the southern Indians and was thereafter continually engaged in Indian warfare until 1779. During the Revolution, Russell fought at King's Mountain, Whitsell's Mill, and Guilford Courthouse. Afterwards settled in what is now Fayette County, Kentucky. Served under Governor Charles Scott and General James Winchester in their campaigns against the Indians and in 1793–94 commanded a regiment of Kentucky volunteers under General Anthony Wayne. Served in state legislatures of Virginia (1789, 1791) and Kentucky (1792, 1796–1800, 1802–7, and 1823). Appointed colonel of Seventh U.S. Infantry Regiment May 3, 1808, and honorably discharged June 15, 1815. Unsuccessful candidate for governor of Kentucky, 1824. Colonel Russell died at his home, Mount Brilliant, in Fayette County, Kentucky, on July 3, 1825, and was buried nearby. Russell County, Kentucky, is named for him. Allen, *History of Kentucky*, 51–53; Collins, *History of Kentucky*, 1: 366, 2: 170, 695–96; Draper, *King's Mountain*, 406–7; Heitman, *Historical Register*, 1: 854; Des Cognets, *William Russell*, 43–48; Reynolds, *My Own Times*, 86. It has been stated (by Collins and others) that Colonel Russell fought in the battle of Tippecanoe, but that is incorrect. No account of the battle mentions him.

128. Knopf, *Document Transcriptions*, 6: pt. 1, 207, 235, pt. 2, 47; *TP*, 16: 240, 256–58.

129. Esarey, *Messages and Letters*, 2: 58–59, *TP*, 14: 570–71, 16: 228–30.

130. Edwards, *History*, 315–18.

131. Edwards, *History*, 321, 325–26; Knopf, *Document Transcriptions*, 6: pt. 2, 7–10; *TP*, 14: 571–72; *TP*, 14: 570–71, 16: 228–30.

132. *TP*, 14: 570–71, 16: 228–30. The chronic shortage of gunpowder among the tribes of central Illinois may provide a better explanation than "cultural resistance" for the continued use of bows and arrows by the Kickapoo of the Prairie. See Berkson, "Cultural Resistance."

133. Mahon, *War of 1812*, 31.

134. *TP*, 16: 228–30; Edwards, *History*, 332–35; *Reporter*, August 29, 1812, 2.

135. *TP*, 14: 578–80; Edwards, *History*, 332–35; *Reporter*, August 1, 1812.

136. *TP*, 16: 253–55.

137. *TP*, 16: 212–13; Quaife, *Chicago and the Old Northwest*, 213.

138. Edwards, *History*, 326.

139. Allen, *Pope County Notes*, 10–11.

140. John McCawley was born in Jefferson County, Kentucky, December 24, 1782. He moved to Illinois in 1810. After being warned off his farm in 1812, he retired to Kentucky but returned to Illinois in 1816. McCawley's home served temporarily as the first Clay County courthouse. He later served as a judge of the County Commissioners' Court. He died May 25, 1854, and is buried in the McCawley Cemetery, in the NE ¼ of section 28, T3N, R8E. *History of Clay and Wayne*, 307, 391–92; Tanner, *Cemetery Inscriptions*, 2.

141. *History of Clay and Wayne*, 391–92; D. L. McCawley to Draper, June 9, 1884, DM, 5YY40; J.J. McCawley to Draper, June 16, 1884, DM, 5YY41.

142. Edwards, *History*, 332–35; Knopf, *Document Transcriptions*, 6: pt. 3, 4–5. Not all the units called out by Edwards during this period can be identified. Three that can are Captain James B. Moore's "Second" company, from July 27 to August 11, 1812, a detachment of mounted riflemen commanded by Ensign Samuel Whiteside, from August 7 to August 22, 1812, and Captain Samuel Whiteside's volunteer company of mounted riflemen, from August 22 to November 13, 1812. *RAGI*, 9: 330–31; Stevens, "Illinois," 181–83.

143. Edwards, *History*, 332–35.

Chapter 4. Chicago

1. Porter Hanks of Massachusetts was commissioned second lieutenant of artillery, January 17, 1805, and promoted to first lieutenant, December 31, 1806. Killed at Detroit, August 16, 1812. Heitman, *Historical Register*, 1: 497.

2. Of the British summons to surrender Hanks later stated: "This, sir, was the first information I had of the declaration of war." Brannan, *Official Letters*, 34–35; Wood, *Select British Documents*, 1: 432–34; Gilpin, *War of 1812*, 89–91, Kellogg, "Capture of Mackinac," 124–45.

3. Charles Roberts, born in England about 1772, commissioned ensign in 1795 and served for about ten years in the West Indies, where he was promoted captain

(1801) and became subject to recurrent attacks of fever. In 1806, being no longer capable of regular service, Roberts was transferred to the Tenth Royal Veteran Battalion and arrived in Canada in 1807. In 1811 he was placed in command of the remote post of Fort Saint Joseph (Saint Joseph Island, Ontario) on Lake Huron. After capturing Mackinac, Roberts remained in command there until ill health forced him to take leave in September 1813. He returned to England in 1815 and died at London on May 4, 1816. Irving, *Officers*, 235 and 236 n. 15; *Dictionary of Canadian Biography*, 5: 713–14.

4. The exact size of the British force is impossible to determine. Hanks estimated it as 46 regulars, 260 Canadian militia, and 715 Indians of various tribes. Brannan, *Official Letters*, 34–35. Roberts reported his force as "a few" regulars, 180 Canadian *voyageurs*, and about 300 Indians. Wood, *Select British Documents*, 1: 432–33. Askin's estimate was 200 Canadians in addition to the regulars, 113 Sioux, Menominee, and Winnebago commanded by Dickson, and 280 Chippewa and Ottawa commanded by himself. Wood, *Select British Documents*, 1: 436–37. Matthew Irwin, the U.S. factor at Chicago, who had arrived at Mackinac the day before the surrender, gave the British forces as 46 regular officers and men, 350 Canadian boatmen, 122 Sioux, Menominee, and Winnebago, and 80 to 100 Chippewa and Ottawa. Knopf, *Document Transcriptions*, 6: pt. 3, 10–11.

5. Capitulation, July 17, 1812, in Wood, *Select British Documents*, 1: 435–36.

6. Wood, *Select British Documents*, 1: 436–37. Matthew Irwin was of the same opinion: "The least resistance from the Fort would have been attended with the destruction of all the prisoners who fell into the hands of the British, as I have been assured by some of the British Traders, & the same fate, as I have been further assured, would have attended the officers & soldiers had a single Indian been killed. Nothing else, it is said, would have satisfied the Indians, & it was not without great difficulty they were prevented from taking the lives of several Americans, after the Fort capitulated." Knopf, *Document Transcriptions*, 6: pt. 3, 10–11.

7. Knopf, *Document Transcriptions*, 6: pt. 3, 30, 35; McAfee, *History*, 88; *National Intelligencer*, September 8, 1812, transcribed in Knopf, *Document Transcriptions*, 5: pt. 1, 195–96.

8. McAfee, *History*, 70.

9. Hull, *Defense*, 64–68.

10. General John E. Hunt, DM, 21S63–64.

11. For Hull's campaign and surrender, see Brannan, *Official Letters*, 44–49; *MPHC*, 15: 132; McAfee, *History*, 50–90; Casselman, *Richardson's War*, 47–85; Gilpin, *War of 1812*, 63–125.

12. Knopf, *Document Transcriptions*, 6: pt. 3, 4–5; Edwards to Scott, August 4, 1812, in Ninian Edwards Papers, SC 447, Folder 1, Abraham Lincoln Presidential Library, Springfield; Edwards, *History*, 332–34.

13. The actual site of the fort was about fifty feet north of the intersection of Wacker and Michigan Avenues, partly in the present channel of the river. Angle, "Fort Dearborn," 99.

14. Quaife, "Fort Dearborn Massacre," 566–70. On the design of Fort Dearborn, see Babson, "Architecture," 35–37.

15. Quoted in Frazier, "Military Frontier," 82.

16. Knopf, *Document Transcriptions*, 6: pt. 1, 92.

17. *TP*, 17: 430–37. The War Department thought that Chicago was in Indiana Territory: *ASP: Military Affairs*, 1: 430.

18. Quaife, *Chicago and the Old Northwest*, 145–48.

19. For an account of this sorry quarrel, see *ibid.*, 172–75; *TP*, 16: 66–68.

20. Nathan Heald was born at Ipswich, New Hampshire, September 24, 1775, commissioned second lieutenant March 3, 1799, first lieutenant November 1, 1799, and captain January 31, 1807. After the massacre, he was promoted major as of August 26, 1812, but his wounds prevented further active service. Heald was honorably discharged June 1, 1814, and died at O'Fallon, Missouri, April 27, 1832, still suffering from wounds he had received at Fort Dearborn. Heitman, *Historical Register*, 1: 518; Quaife, *Chicago and the Old Northwest*, 176–77, 244–45, 402–5; DM, 17U29.

21. Linai Taliaferro Helm was born in Virginia about 1783. He was commissioned ensign December 9, 1807, second lieutenant December 8, 1808, first lieutenant January 20, 1813, and captain April 15, 1814. He resigned his commission September 27, 1814. Helm and his wife Margaret were divorced in 1829. He returned to Virginia, where he remarried. Although Heitman gives the date of Helm's death as 1838, he was in fact still living, on a farm in Fauquier County, Virginia, in September, 1850. Heitman, *Historical Register*, 1: 521; Quaife, *Chicago and the Old Northwest*, 177, 276; 1850 U.S. Census, Fauquier County, Virginia, Turners District, 318.

22. George Ronan, of New York, graduated from the U.S. Military Academy at West Point, March 1, 1811. He was commissioned ensign in the First Infantry and ordered to Fort Dearborn. Killed in action August 15, 1812. Ronan Park, 3000 W. Argyle Street, Chicago, honors his memory. Heitman, *Historical Register*, 1: 844; Quaife, *Chicago and the Old Northwest*, 177, 223; Cullum, *Biographical Register*, 100.

23. Isaac Vail Van Voorhis, born Fishkill, New York, February 22, 1790, was appointed surgeon's mate March 1, 1811, and assigned to Fort Dearborn. Killed

in action, August 15, 1812. Heitman, *Historical Register*, 1: 984; Van Voorhis, *Notes*, 143–45; Quaife, *Chicago and the Old Northwest*, 177, 196, 386–87.

24. Knopf, *Document Transcriptions*, 6: pt. 1, 220–21.

25. In this instance, the portrait that emerges from Kinzie, *Wau-Bun*, 207, 212, 225, 228, may have some validity, agreeing as it does with the depiction of Ronan in the letters of Van Voorhis and Irwin.

26. See Quaife, *Chicago and the Old Northwest*, 196.

27. Matthew Irwin was born in Philadelphia about 1770. He served as U.S. factor at Chicago 1809 to 1812, assistant commissary of purchases for U.S. Army, May 1813 to June 1815, U.S. factor at Green Bay, 1816 to 1821, and chief justice and judge of probate for Brown County, Wisconsin, 1818 to 1820. In 1821 Irwin returned to Pennsylvania, settling at Uniontown, Fayette County, where he engaged in commerce and served as postmaster. Irwin died about 1845, at the age of nearly 75. *WHC* 7: 269–70; Quaife, *Chicago and the Old Northwest*, 298–99.

28. *TP*, 16: 184–85, 195–96, 212–13, 219–22; Knopf, *Document Transcriptions*, 6: pt. 1, 220–21, 6: pt. 2, 1, 67, 69–71; Quaife, "Fort Dearborn Massacre," 1: 566–70.

29. See pages 46–47, supra.

30. *TP*, 16: 212–13, 221–12; Knopf, *Document Transcriptions*, 6: pt. 1, 220–21.

31. Knopf, *Document Transcriptions*, 6: pt. 2, 67, 69–71.

32. See, for instance, Gordon, "John Kinzie," 60–62. Kinzie's son saw his father sharpen a knife and conceal it under his coat before going to the fort. LaLime, he claimed, fired first and his bullet struck a scarf at Kinzie's neck without injuring him. Arthur Kinzie to Hubbard, February 5, 1884, in John Kinzie Collection, Chicago History Museum. For a contrary view, see "Historical Sketch No. 1: The Death of John LaLime at Fort Dearborn," in William R. Head Papers, Chicago History Museum, Chicago.

33. LaLime's body was buried in the vicinity of Cass (now Wabash) and Illinois streets. In 1891 a skeleton believed to be that of LaLime was unearthed by workmen and donated to the Chicago Historical Society. Kirkland, *Chicago Massacre*, 185–95.

34. Knopf, *Document Transcriptions*, 8: 20; *ibid.*, 6: pt. 2, 69–71; Heald to Irwin, June 26, 1812, NA, RG 107, LRSW (M 221, Roll 46, 871). (Heald's letter is wrongly dated "12th April 1812" in Knopf, *Document Transcriptions*, 6: pt. 1, 126.)

35. Billy Caldwell, son of a British officer and a Mohawk woman, was born near Niagara on March 17, 1780. Among the Indians he was known as "The Sauganash," meaning the "Englishman." As a young man he worked as a clerk for the trading firm of Kinzie & Forsyth, normally at Peoria. After war broke out in 1812, Caldwell was commissioned a captain in the British Indian Department. He fought at the River Raisin, where he was severely wounded while trying to

save the life of a wounded American officer. Caldwell also saw action at Fort Meigs, Fort Stephenson, the Thames, and along the Niagara frontier. Toward the close of the war, he was briefly head of the British Indian Department. About 1820 Caldwell drifted to Chicago, where, in 1829, the Americans appointed him a chief of the Potawatomi tribe. On behalf of the tribe Caldwell signed the 1833 Treaty of Chicago that surrendered their lands east of the Mississippi, and in 1835 he led their migration to Iowa. During the last years of his life, Caldwell stoutly defended the rights of the Potawatomi against further American demands and encroachments. He died at Council Bluffs, Iowa, on September 27, 1841. Clifton, "Merchant, Soldier"; Irving, *Officers*, 210.

36. *TP*, 16: 248–50, 256; Knopf, *Document Transcriptions*, 6: pt. 4, 10–11; Quaife, "Fort Dearborn Massacre," 566–70.

37. Any study of the Fort Dearborn massacre must begin with the work of Milo M. Quaife: "Some Notes," and *Chicago and the Old Northwest*. The latter remains indispensable, although discovery of additional source material, some of it by Quaife himself, prompted the author to revise some of his conclusions: Quaife, "Fort Dearborn Massacre"; Quaife, *Checagou*, 121–22, 135, 147–50. Despite its age, Kirkland, *Chicago Massacre*, contains a good deal of useful material, although the author gives too much credence to Juliette Kinzie's fanciful account in chapters 18 and 19 of *Wau-Bun*. The unreliability of Mrs. Kinzie's account was amply demonstrated by Quaife, *Chicago and the Old Northwest*, 382–88. (See also Hurlbut, *Chicago Antiquities*, 347–55.) Most histories of the city of Chicago contain accounts of the massacre. Among the most sensible, although still influenced by *Wau-Bun*, are Andreas, *History of Chicago*, 1: 80–83; Kirkland, *Story of Chicago*, 1: 57–77; Hamilton, *Epic of Chicago*, 45–61. All these books contain something of value, despite what are sometimes significant inaccuracies. Books that merely follow *Wau-Bun* uncritically—such as McClure, *Stories and Sketches*, 130–41; Blanchard, *Discovery and Conquests*, 386–412; and Currey, *Story of Old Fort Dearborn*—have little value. Fort Dearborn has been the subject of at least four novels: Myrtle Reed, *The Shadow of Victory: A Romance of Fort Dearborn* (New York: Grosset & Dunlap, 1903); Randall Parrish, *When Wilderness Was King* (Chicago and New York: A. C. McClurg, 1904); Edward Sylvester Ellis, *Black Partridge, or the Fall of Fort Dearborn* (New York: E. P. Dutton, 1906); Jerry Crimmins, *Fort Dearborn* (Evanston, Ill.: Northwestern University Press, 2006); and even a children's book: Leon E. Burgoyne, *Ensign Ronan, a Story of Fort Dearborn* (Philadelphia: Winston, 1955).

38. Heald to Cushing, October 23, 1812, in Brannan, *Official Letters*, 84–85. Heald's original handwritten autobiography is in DM, 17U29. The autobiography and report are also printed in Quaife, *Chicago and the Old Northwest*, 402–8.

Although Quaife had a high opinion of Heald's veracity, the extreme brevity of the report suggests that there may also have been aspects of the event that Heald preferred not to mention. Two secondhand accounts are quite valuable because written very soon after the event. One is an account of the massacre entered into his diary by Charles Askin at Mackinac on September 22, 1812, immediately after a conversation with Heald. Quaife, "Fort Dearborn Massacre," 563–65. The other is an account purporting to be that of Captain and Mrs. Heald that appeared in the *Crawford Weekly Messenger* [Meadville, Pennsylvania], October 21, 1812, 2, and was reprinted in *Reporter*, November 18, 1812, 3. Fuller, but much farther separated from the events in time, is the account of the massacre preserved by their son, Darius Heald, as he had heard his mother tell the story "a hundred times." Rebecca Heald had herself been a participant in the battle, wounded in no fewer than five places during the fight near the wagons. Some of her information, though, must necessarily have come from her late husband. Darius told the story twice: to Lyman Draper in 1868 and to Joseph Kirkland and a stenographer in 1892. Draper's notes of his interview are contained in DM, 23S41–57, and are printed in Quaife, *Chicago and the Old Northwest*, 409–13. The 1892 version is printed in Kirkland, "Chicago Massacre" (1882), and quoted extensively in Kirkland, *Chicago Massacre*, 31–38 (1893).

39. Helm's narrative is printed in Quaife, *Chicago and the Old Northwest*, 415–21, and in Gordon, *Fort Dearborn Massacre*, 13–26. Helm's narrative, although longer and more detailed than Heald's, is a dishonest document, evidently written with the aim of destroying Heald's reputation and enhancing that of Helm. Helm himself admitted his antipathy to Heald. *MPHC*, 12: 661 ("the history cannot possibly be written with truth without eternally disgracing Major Heald"). See Quaife's discussion in *Chicago and the Old Northwest*, 388–91. Helm later supplemented his account with an affidavit he wrote in support of the pension application of Corporal Joseph Bowen. That affidavit is printed in Milo M. Quaife, "Fort Dearborn Massacre," 561–73. Finally, and most destructively, Helm's version of events, conveyed through his wife Margaret, formed the basis of Juliette Kinzie's vivid and unreliable account of the massacre in *Wau-Bun*. Mrs. Kinzie was John Kinzie's daughter-in-law, but she never met him. Her account is derived principally from her conversations with other members of the family, especially Mrs. Helm, but also owes much to the author's own romantic imagination. It first appeared as an anonymous pamphlet in 1844, and was afterwards incorporated into her book. After its publication, *Wau-Bun* quickly became the accepted version of events. It would perhaps have been better had Mrs. Kinzie's account of the massacre never been written. See the demolition of Mrs. Kinzie's version in Quaife, *Chicago and the Old Northwest*, 382–88.

40. Corbin's affidavit is printed in Quaife, "Story of James Corbin." Corbin's account gives no indication that he was interested in any of the controversies surrounding the evacuation and massacre and appears to be the straightforward recollection of a private soldier, as dictated from memory in 1826.

41. Two years after the end of the war, a pamphlet appeared under the name of *Narrative of the Captivity and Sufferings of James Van Horne*, purporting to contain Private Van Horne's firsthand recollections of his capture and captivity. After some introductory matter, obviously not the work of the soldier himself, there follow a very brief account of the battle and a much more detailed and interesting account of the aftermath. Those two sections of the narrative are written in the first person and the latter, at least, bears all the marks of authenticity. Van Horne provides details found nowhere else. The little work is all the more valuable for its early date, having been published long before controversy had poisoned the well.

42. Kinzie to President Monroe, April 4, 1817, in Haydon, "John Kinzie's Place," 185–87. The account of the massacre in Kinzie's own letter is very brief, but there also survive three other versions of events as related by people who had heard the story from Kinzie's own mouth. The earliest is in a letter written less than three weeks after the massacre by Kinzie's half-brother, Thomas Forsyth. Forsyth to Howard, September 7, 1812, in *TP*, 16: 261–65. This letter seems to have been overlooked by most historians. In 1820 Kinzie told the story of the massacre to Henry Rowe Schoolcraft and Captain David Bates Douglass. Schoolcraft blended what Kinzie had told him with what he himself had read in other sources to produce a brief composite account. Douglass's notes are more detailed and appear to be closer to a *verbatim* record of Kinzie's own story. Schoolcraft, *Schoolcraft's Narrative*, 255–58; Williams, "John Kinzie's Narrative" (printing and discussing Captain Douglass's notes).

43. There exist two curious letters purporting to have been written by Corporal Walter K. Jordan: Jordan to "Betsey" [his wife], October 12, 1812, and Jordan to Joseph Hunter, December 17, 1812. The first letter appears in Esarey, *Messages and Letters*, 2: 165–67. According to these letters, Jordan accompanied Captain Wells and 100 friendly "Confute" Indians to the relief of Fort Dearborn, where he took part in the battle, witnessed the death of Wells, and was taken prisoner before escaping back to Fort Wayne. Versions of the letter appeared in *The National Intelligencer* of April 22, 1813, and another in *Niles Register*, May 8, 1813, but differ from the original, reprinted in D. Barnhart, "New Letter." The second letter is also printed in Barnhart's article. Despite its early date, Quaife and Kirkland both branded the first letter a hoax (Quaife, *Chicago and the Old Northwest*, 394–96; Kirkland, *Chicago Massacre*, 116–18), although Quaife

later softened his views. At the time Quaife originally wrote, there was good reason to doubt the authenticity of the Jordan letters. Neither Heald, Helm, Griffith, Kinzie, nor any other participant in the massacre mentions Jordan, or that Wells was accompanied by an American soldier. Moreover, Captain Rhea, commanding at Fort Wayne, in one of the first reports of the massacre, omitted to mention that one of his own noncommissioned officers had accompanied Wells and would then have been missing. Knopf, *Document Transcriptions*, 6: pt. 3, 40. This concern is laid to rest by two contemporary references that were unknown to Quaife but have since come to light. The first reference is contained in a brief account of Wells's mission in *Reporter*, September 5, 1812, p. 2. ("Wells . . . went from Ft. Wayne to Chicago with one white man and about 30 or 40 Miami Indians, in order to escort the garrison in.") The second is contained in a letter written by an officer at Fort Wayne the following October, which states that "on the 8th Captain Wells, with a party of thirty-five Miami Indians with their pack horses, and one of our soldiers with five of the public horses, started to assist Captain Heald in the evacuation of Chicago." Palmer, *Early Days*, 880–85. Quaife's other objection still stands: Jordan's two letters are so full of errors that it is difficult to believe that they were written by an actual eyewitness. Even Barnhart, who ably defended the letters' authenticity, had nothing to say in defense of their accuracy or reliability. Little use will be made of them here.

44. Isabella Cooper was nine years old at the time of the massacre, stepdaughter of settler Thomas Burns. After the war she lived in Ohio with the family of Major Abraham Edwards, whose son many years later related what he recalled of her story. John Wentworth, *Early Chicago*, 54–59. See also Quaife, *Chicago and the Old Northwest*, 252–53.

45. Simmons, *Heroes and Heroines*. This book was written by a relative of Mrs. Susan Millhouse Simmons, herself a survivor and the widow of a soldier who fell in the battle. The account of the massacre appears to be taken almost entirely from published secondary sources, although the statement that Mrs. Simmons witnessed the death of her husband, fighting with clubbed rifle in defense of the wagons, may represent a genuine family tradition. Even this is suspect, for Thomas Forsyth reported that Private Simmons died not in the battle but in captivity the following winter. Knopf, *Document Transcriptions*, 7: pt. 2, 181. The only real value of the book lies in its moving account of the captivity of Mrs. Simmons and her infant daughter. See Quaife, *Chicago and the Old Northwest*, 247, n. 635.

46. After release from captivity Griffith returned to active duty, serving with McAfee, who used Griffith's reminiscences in his own *History*, 98–101. McAfee's account is regrettably brief, running to no more than three pages.

47. During the period 1854 to 1858, amateur Chicago historian William R. Head lived in Carlinville, Illinois, where he became acquainted with Moses Morgan, a carpenter who in 1816 had assisted in the building of the second Fort Dearborn. According to Morgan, far up the north fork of the Chicago River, a soldier of Heald's command, who had been wounded and taken prisoner by the Indians, was found living in a hut with three Indian wives. The "wounded soldier" was interviewed in depth by Dr. Gales, the new post surgeon, but his report was lost when the troops moved from their temporary camp into the newly completed fort. Nevertheless, the soldier's account was discussed at the time and became common knowledge among the builders of the fort. According to Head, Morgan told him what he remembered of it, and many years later Head wrote an account of what he had heard from Morgan, using notes now destroyed. Head's handwritten account is contained in the William R. Head Papers in the Chicago History Museum. Head's narrative has never been published in full but is summarized by Quaife, *Chicago and the Old Northwest*, 260–61, 400–401. Needless to say, it would be unwise to place much credence in an account preserved under such circumstances, but the "wounded soldier's" story does contain details found nowhere else.

48. DM, 21S274–90.

49. Hamilton to Bissell, August 24, 1812, NA, RG 94, RAGO, LRAG (M 566, Roll 7, 107). Hamilton's account of the massacre is one of the earliest. He received it directly from an Indian chief he believed to be reliable, and the contents of the story support Hamilton's assessment. The chief had with him a piece of the garrison's flag. Because Hamilton had no other source of information, his letter represents an undiluted Indian viewpoint, albeit at secondhand.

50. Jackson, *Black Hawk*, 66–67. Black Hawk was not present at the massacre but passed the site not long afterwards on his way to Detroit.

51. Unfortunately Pokagon had also read and been influenced by published accounts of the massacre, including *Wau-Bun*. Simon Pokagon: "The Massacre of Fort Dearborn," 98: 649–56; "Fort Dearborn Massacre from an Indian's Point of View," *Chicago Tribune*, February 7, 1897, 37. See also "Flaws in Pokagon Tale," *Chicago Tribune*, February 8, 1897, 9.

52. Brannan, *Official Letters*, 84. What purports to be Hull's original order is contained in the DM, 8U69. The text is printed in Quaife, *Chicago and the Old Northwest*, 216.

53. So Wells suspected. Kirkland, *Story of Chicago*, 115–16.

54. Forsyth to Clark, July 20, 1813, in Forsyth Papers, Missouri History Museum, Saint Louis; Tanner, *Atlas*, 106–7; Wheeler-Voegelin, "Anthropological Report," 232. The precise location of Main Poc's village on the Fox River remains to be

established. Forsyth described the village as "about 30 or 36 miles from the mouth of sd. River by water, and not more than 18 or 20 miles across the Piarie [sic] from Sandy Creek," which suggests a location approximately along the stretch of river between Meramech Hill and Yorkville. Wheeler-Voegelin, however, places the village "at the Great Rapid on the Fox River . . . 30–36 miles from the river's mouth." This description is self-contradictory, because the Rapids were only five miles above the river's mouth. *Illinois in 1837*, 36.

55. Brannan, *Official Letters*, 84. By contrast, Juliette Kinzie in her 1844 account claimed that the Indians became "unruly," walking as they pleased into the fort and even into the officers' quarters, in defiance of the sentinels. *Wau-Bun*, 215. Mrs. Kinzie had no firsthand knowledge, however, and the inherent improbability of her account places it in the same category as her other efforts to blacken the memory of Captain Heald. Heald's son Darius said later that after reading *Wau-Bun* his mother described its account of the massacre as "exaggerated & incorrect," specifically identifying the account of "troublesome" Indians crowding into the fort as false. Quaife, *Chicago and the Old Northwest*, 413.

56. Williams, "Kinzie's Narrative," 347–48.

57. McDonald, *Biographical Sketches*, 183–96; Hutton, "Two Worlds," 33–41; General John E. Hunt, DM, 21S42–45; Judge James Wolcott (Wells's son-in-law), DM, 21S45–93.

58. On Wells's checkered career as Indian agent, see Woehrmann, *Headwaters*, 116–27, 142–70, 275–77.

59. Helm's later story that Heald reluctantly agreed to destroy the ammunition only after Kinzie offered to forge an order from Hull requiring him to do so is contradicted by the language of the order itself. Gordon *Fort Dearborn Massacre*, 17; Gordon, "John Kinzie: A Sketch," 62. John Kinzie himself said afterwards that Heald had been entirely willing to destroy the ammunition and liquor. Williams, "Kinzie's Narrative," 46: 348. For the order itself, see DM, 8U69.

60. *ASP: Claims*, 424–25.

61. *TP*, 16: 244–55.

62. Black Hawk, who was not present, believed that the Indians' anger over destruction of the powder triggered the massacre. Jackson, *Black Hawk*, 66–67. Pokagon agreed that the attack was sparked by the Indians' belief that Heald had reneged on a promise to distribute gunpowder and whiskey along with the other goods. "Massacre at Fort Dearborn," 98: 652, 654; *Chicago Tribune*, February 7, 1897, 37.

63. Certificate of Nathan Heald, December 2, 1817, Draper Manuscripts 1T6.

64. Kirkland, *Story of Chicago*, 116.

65. *TP*, 16: 261–65.

66. Quaife, *Chicago and the Old Northwest*, 410.

67. This belief derived from Juliette Kinzie's assertion that Hull's order had been to evacuate the fort "if practicable." *Wau-Bun*, 211. Mrs. Kinzie presumably had this information from her sister-in-law, and anything she knew about the terms of the order could only have come in turn from her husband, Lieutenant Helm. The eventual discovery of Helm's own account of the massacre in the collections of the Detroit Public Library establishes him as the source of the "if practicable" language. Kinzie, *Wau-Bun*, 211; Gordon, *Fort Dearborn Massacre*, 38.

68. "I shall immediately send an express to Fort Dearborn with orders to evacuate that post and retreat to this place or Fort Wayne, provided it can be effected with a greater prospect of safety than to remain. Captain Heald is a judicious officer, and I shall confide much to his discretion." Hull to Secretary of War, July 29, 1812, NA, RG 107, LRSW, M 221, Roll 45, 380; Knopf, *Document Transcriptions*, 6: pt. 3, 309–10; Quaife, "Some Notes," 125.

69. DM, 8U69. The text of the order is given in Quaife, *Chicago and the Old Northwest*, 216.

70. Quaife, *Checagou*, 121; Gordon, *Fort Dearborn Massacre*, 17. For a sample of Kinzie's handwriting, see Kinzie to Cass, July 1, 1820, John Kinzie Collection, Chicago History Museum. For Heald's handwriting, see Heald's Journal, DM, 17U33, Heald to Tucker, DM, 24U9, or Heald to Forsyth, DM, 24U15. It was Milo Quaife who first noticed Hull's order in the Draper Manuscripts. Over time Quaife softened somewhat his originally firm conviction that the order was genuine.

71. Quaife, *Chicago and the Old Northwest*, 413–4; Williams, "Kinzie's Narrative, 46: 350, fn.

72. Black Partridge (Mucketypoke, Muck-a-da-puck-ee) was chief of a band of Potawatomi who lived along the Illinois River. His village appears to have been mobile, located at various times in northwest Tazewell County, at the mouth of Aux Sable Creek, east of Morris, and at the present site of Metamora. Although Black Partridge opposed the Chicago massacre, he afterwards took up the tomahawk, leading an abortive raid down the Illinois River in September and taking part in the battles on the River Raisin in January 1813. After the death of Gomo in early 1815, Black Partridge emerged as the principal chief of the Illinois River Potawatomi. He was remembered as a large man and very intelligent. Black Partridge died about 1820, at Gomo's village near the present Chillicothe, Illinois. Partridge Township and Partridge Creek in Tazewell County are named for him. Alexander Robinson, DM, 21S281; Robert Forsyth, DM, 22S105; Smith, *Metamora*, 21–59; Callary, *Place Names*, 269.

73. Topinebee was a chief of the Saint Joseph River Potawatomi in southwestern Michigan. As a young man he had fought the Americans in St. Clair's defeat (1791) and had signed the Treaty of Greenville (1795) that put an end to the war. He took no part in the War of 1812. Through his influence, and that of Five Medals, many of his people remained neutral. In later years Topinebee represented his people in a series of treaties that led to the loss of their land in Indiana and Illinois. In old age, he was ruined by drink, and died in southern Michigan in August 1840. Alexander Robinson, DM, 21S280; Barce, "Topenebee," 14: 3–12.

74. Nuscotnumeg was sometimes said to have been the brother-in-law of Main Poc. He was remembered as "the bravest of the brave," but also as barbarously cruel, known for taking children by their heels to knock their brains out. Nuscotnumeg fought at the River Raisin, at Fort Meigs, and at the Thames. He signed a treaty in October 1818 but died about 1820, either killed by friends of a warrior he himself had slain, or killed in a drunken frolic by "an old squaw," at "Terre Coupée," south of the present Niles, Michigan. Alexander Robinson, DM, 21S288–9; Joseph N. Bourassa, DM, 23S191.

75. Alexander Robinson, DM, 21S285–7; *TP*, 16: 261–5; *Missouri Gazette*, September 19, 1812, October 24, 1812.

76. Smith, *Metamora*, 25.

77. McAfee, *History*, 98; Gordon, *Fort Dearborn Massacre*, 23–24; Quaife, *Chicago and the Old Northwest*, 220–21.

78. See Quaife's careful effort to number and identify the members of the party in *Chicago and the Old Northwest*, 425–36. The version of the "wounded soldier" says that there were only two wagons, one carrying the women and children and the other carrying the ammunition and provisions. William R. Head Papers.

79. Haydon, "John Kinzie's Place," 185–87; Kinzie, *Wau-Bun*, 174–75. We may discount Irwin's suggestion that Kinzie accompanied the troops in order to guarantee that no witness to the murder of LaLime would survive the massacre. Quaife, "Fort Dearborn Massacre," 1: 566–70.

80. Brannan, *Official Letters*, 84–85; Williams, "Kinzie's Narrative," 349; Quaife, *Chicago and the Old Northwest*, 411, 413; *Chicago Tribune*, February 7, 1897, 37; Schoolcraft, *Schoolcraft's Narrative*, 257.

81. Schoolcraft, *Schoolcraft's Narrative*, 256; Brannan, *Official Letters*, 84–85.

82. The evidence for Eighteenth and Prairie is set out in Kirkland, *Chicago Massacre*, 207–10. The case for Roosevelt and Michigan is made in Musham, "Battle of Chicago."

83. The less trustworthy account of the so-called "wounded soldier" relates that the halt was caused when two young Potawatomi boys began shooting at the animals pulling the wagons, wounding a horse and causing two oxen to turn,

breaking the wagon pole and nearly overturning the wagon. It was while the troops stood patiently waiting for repairs to be made that the attack began. William R. Head Papers; Quaife, *Chicago and the Old Northwest*, 401.

84. See Kirkland, *Story of Chicago*, 1: 66; Frank E. Stevens, "Illinois," 121.

85. Williams, "Kinzie's Narrative," 46: 349; Kinzie, *Wau-Bun*, 177. Ronan was the first graduate of the U.S. Military Academy to be killed in action. Cullum, *Biographical Register*, 100.

86. Brannan, *Official Letters*, 84–85; Williams, "Kinzie's Narrative," 46: 349.

87. Pokagon, "Massacre at Fort Dearborn," 653; Simmons, *Heroes*, 48–49.

88. Juliette Kinzie preserves a story, evidently derived from Margaret Helm, that during the fighting a terrified Van Voorhis ran up to Mrs. Helm, pouring out his fear of dying without spiritual preparation. Moments later he was cut down, and she was dragged off to the lake by Black Partridge. *Wau-Bun*, 225–26. That Van Voorhis would, at the height of the battle, begin a theological conversation with a seventeen-year-old young woman who was the wife of one bitter personal enemy and the stepdaughter of another is hard to credit. John Cooper, a friend and classmate of Van Voorhis, and his predecessor as surgeon's mate at Fort Dearborn, vouched for Van Voorhis's personal courage and fiercely disputed the account of his death in *Wau-Bun*. See Wilson, "Chicago," 13. Historian Milo Quaife also rejected the story (Quaife, "Some Notes," 126; Quaife, *Chicago and the Old Northwest*, 387), although his rejection of the story was influenced by his belief, later revised, that Mrs. Helm's rescue by Black Partridge was also a fiction. Quaife, "Fort Dearborn Massacre," 564, n. 13. See also Hurlbut, *Antiquities*, 352–53. Quaife was unaware of the mutual hatred that had existed between Van Voorhis and the Helm/Kinzie faction. Certainly the Helm/Kinzie account of Van Voorhis's death may have been another instance of score-settling, but on present evidence it is impossible to erase definitively this stain on the doctor's memory. In December 1812, E. M. Van Voorhis of Fishkill, New York, wrote the adjutant general seeking information about his brother's death. His letter was referred to Heald for a response. Heald's own letter, should it ever be discovered, might prove illuminating. Adjutant General's Office to Van Voorhis, December 23, 1812, and Adjutant General's Office to Heald, December 23, 1812, both in NA, RG 94, RAGO, Letters Sent (M 565, Roll 4, 254).

89. Stevens, "Illinois," 124–25. Another version, that of the "wounded soldier," claimed that an Indian boy bound Cicely's feet and carried her home to be his "wife." William R. Head Papers.

90. *Niles Weekly Register*, 6: 221 (June 4, 1814); [Van Horne], *Narrative*, 8.

91. Benac was part Indian and part French. He was still living as late as 1854, when General Hunt saw him passing through Toledo on his way to Montreal

and spoke with him in French. General John E. Hunt, DM, 21S57; Pokagon, "Massacre at Fort Dearborn," 653.

92. Wentworth, *Early Chicago*, 54–59; Quaife, *Chicago and the Old Northwest*, 252–53.

93. According to another version, the Miami joined the attackers. McAfee, 99. Apparently after returning home, the Miami covered themselves by pretending that they had suffered grievously in the battle, claiming that "Several of their chiefs were killed." *Reporter*, September 5, 1812, 2.

94. That Rebecca Heald witnessed the death of her uncle is confirmed not only by the much-later recollection of her son Darius, but by the nearly contemporaneous account attributed to her in the *Crawford Messenger* [Meadville, Pennsylvania], October 21, 1812, 2, and by the later account of John Kinzie. Williams, "Kinzie's narrative," 349–50.

95. There are numerous alternative versions of Wells's death. According to *Wau-Bun*, when he learned of the massacre of children at the wagons, Wells galloped back in the direction of the Indians' village, either to retaliate against their women and children or to lure the warriors away from the wagons. Lying low on the back of his horse and firing at his pursuers, he was finally wounded and his horse brought down. Wells was extricated from under his horse by Winnemeg and Waubansee, who tried to save him, but he was stabbed in the back by an Indian named Pesotum. Kinzie, *Wau-Bun*, 230. According to another version, Wells, wounded and dismounted, was surrounded by Indians. With capture and torture inevitable, Wells taunted and jeered at the Indians until a young warrior, enraged at being called a "squaw," shot him. Lossing, "Kinzie House," 6: 325; Blanchard, *Discovery and Conquests*, 394–95, n. According to yet another version, Wells appealed to Topinebee, who was restraining his own warriors as best he could: "Father, I want to live." Topinebee replied: "My son, you can live," but other warriors killed Wells despite the chief's efforts to save him. Joseph N. Bourassa, DM, 23S194–5. A Potawatomi chief named White Hair later went to Detroit to collect a reward from the British for killing Wells. *TP*, 16: 312–15.

96. It is said that the day after the massacre the scattered pieces of Wells's body were collected and buried in the sand by his friend, Billy Caldwell. DM, 9YY109 (11); Brown *History of Illinois*, 316, n. 2. According to another version, the body was buried by Black Partridge. Matson, *Memories of Shaubena*, 21–22. The bodies of the other Americans killed in the massacre were left lying where they had fallen until soldiers returned in 1816 to rebuild the fort. The soldiers then gathered and boxed the remains and buried them in a pit, at a place previously used as a graveyard, between one-half and three-fourths of a mile southwest of the fort

and about one-half mile west of what was then the lakeshore. "Narrative of Moses Morgan: Annals," under date July 6, 1816, in William R. Head Papers.

97. Kinzie, *Wau-Bun* (1856), 226–27. The essentials of the story were confirmed by Heald in an account related soon after the massacre. Quaife, "Fort Dearborn Massacre," 564. Oddly enough, neither Helm nor John Kinzie mentioned this incident, and Kinzie in fact told a contradictory story, saying that when a friendly warrior approached them to offer protection Mrs. Helm ran away to the lake for safety, but soon afterwards returned on her own. Williams, "Kinzie's Narrative," 46: 350.

98. Quaife, *Fort Dearborn Massacre*, 564, 573; Quaife, "Story of James Corbin," 222; McAfee, *History*, 99.

99. This is Heald's account, and Helm does not disagree that it was Heald who conferred with Black Bird, although he tries to put that fact into the worst possible light for Heald. McAfee, 99, states that it was Sergeant Griffith who negotiated with LeClerc. (The surname is often listed as "LeClaire," which would be similarly pronounced.) The "wounded soldier" said that it was Heald and Griffith together who surrendered to Black Partridge. William R. Head Papers.

100. After the war, LeClerc worked as an interpreter, and the 1829 Treaty of Prairie du Chien reserved a section of land for him at Paw Paw Grove. LeClerc was still living in the vicinity of Chicago when the Black Hawk War broke out in 1832, for during that conflict he was stationed at Fort Dearborn as a private in Captain Boardman's company and was afterwards a member of a company of Potawatomi warriors in the service of the United States. LeClerc migrated west with the tribe, and when bounty land warrants were issued to Boardman's company in 1855, he was listed as being in "Indian Country." In 1866 Alexander Robinson spoke of LeClerc as already dead. Whitney, *Black Hawk War*, 1: 448, 449 n., 560; 2: 584 n. 2; Kappler, *Indian Affairs*, 2: 298; DM, 21S285.

101. Black Bird was by birth an Ottawa, but he had married a Potawatomi woman and was accepted as a chief of her tribe. He did not attend the conference at Cahokia with Edwards, but sent a representative. His name is also given as Siggenauk and LeTourneau. Knopf, *Document Transcriptions*, 6: pt. 1, 199–203; Edwards, *History*, 39, 56, 315–18; WHC 10: 110 n. He has sometimes been confused with a Chippewa chief of the same name who lived near Mackinac and also sometimes with Black Partridge. DM, 3Q38–9, 21S274–5. It is possible, though, that the Black Bird who led the Indians in the battle may be identical with a chief of that name who lived on the Saint Joseph River and died about 1834, at more than eighty years of age. Peter Navarre, DM, 21S82.

102. Brannan, *Official Letters*, 84–5; Quaife, "Fort Dearborn Massacre," 564. The

circumstances of the surrender provide one of the most glaring contradictions between the versions of Heald and Helm. Although his two accounts are not entirely inconsistent, Helm asserts that Heald surrendered only himself, leaving Helm effectively in command of the troops on the hillock. As Helm tells the story, on advice of the interpreter, he and the men refused Heald's call on them to surrender, waiting fully two hours while the Indians held a council about the terms of surrender, and only agreeing to terms after they learned that John Kinzie had been spared and they had been assured of their own safety. Gordon, *Fort Dearborn Massacre*, 19–21; Quaife, "Fort Dearborn Massacre," 573. Besides magnifying his own role, the thrust of Helm's account is to imply that his former commander was either a coward or a traitor. To some extent, Helm's story of his taking command is corroborated by a very brief affidavit of the interpreter, submitted in support of Helm's application for a pension, stating that Helm was initially resistant to Heald's call to surrender and that Helm's courage and firmness saved the lives of the remaining men. Nevertheless, the story must be rejected. Perhaps needless to say, Heald does not mention Helm playing any such role, but more significantly neither do the accounts of Corbin, Van Horne, and Griffith, all of whom were among the soldiers on the knoll. Quaife, "Story of James Corbin," 222; [Van Horne], *Narrative*, 5; McAfee, *History*, 99–100. Neither does the account of the so-called "wounded soldier," which stated that it was Heald and Griffith together who surrendered to Black Bird and added that Helm was so drunk on the day of the massacre that he could not retain his place in line. Quaife, *Chicago and the Old Northwest*, 401.

103. Gordon, *Fort Dearborn Massacre*, 22.

104. See the careful analysis in Quaife, *Chicago and the Old Northwest*, 428–36.

105. Heald's report estimated the Indian loss as "about fifteen." Brannan, *Official Letters*, 84–85. Thomas Forsyth, who arrived at Chicago the day after the battle, gave the Indian loss as three killed and three wounded. *TP*, 16: 261–65. A friendly chief told Lieutenant Hamilton that the Indians lost only three killed. Hamilton to Bissell, August 24, 1812. Alexander Robinson put the Indian loss at two killed and two wounded. DM, 21S287. On the other hand, based on Indian tradition, Simon Pokagon made the unlikely claim that the Indian loss "must have been" twice that of the Americans. Pokagon, "Massacre," 653.

106. *MPHC*, 15: 159–61 (at least five); Quaife, "Fort Dearborn Massacre," 564 (seven soldiers); Quaife "Story of James Corbin," 222 (two wounded soldiers and five unwounded); McAfee, *History*, 100 (three or four); Gordon, *Fort Dearborn Massacre*, 23, 26; Williams, "Kinzie's Narrative,"120; Kinzie, *Wau-Bun* 178–79; DM, 21S287, 8U88. Van Horne, the only eyewitness to list those killed immediately after the battle, says that there were six, all wounded, and

gives their names as James Lata, Jacob Landon, Richard Gardner, Prestly Andrews, Micajah Dennison, and Thomas Burns. [Van Horne], *Narrative*, 5–6. Pokagon, "Massacre," 654, believed that the killings may have been a mistake by braves who were unaware of the surrender. There may be a slender basis of truth in this. Kinzie told Douglass that three soldiers were killed by an Indian volley fired into their group when one of their number had drawn a knife after mistaking the intentions of warriors who were firing in the air to celebrate their victory. Heald's report to his superiors inexplicably makes no mention of his men having been murdered after the surrender, although both the account he gave to Askin at Mackinac and the account printed in the *Crawford Weekly Messenger* show that he knew of it. Brannan, Official Letters, 84–85; Quaife, "Fort Dearborn Massacre," 563–65; *Crawford Weekly Messenger*, October 21, 1812.

107. When British Indian agent Robert Dickson visited Chicago the following March, he found the powder magazine and the houses around the fort still in a good state of preservation and told the Indians not to destroy them since their British Father's troops might be able to use them. Dickson also saw two brass three-pound cannon, one on wheels that had been dumped into the river and the other dismounted. He hoped to have them brought to Mackinac. *MPHC* 15: 262. Dickson was not wholly successful in recovering the artillery, however, for one of the fort's cannons was dredged from the river about forty years later and sold for scrap. Hurlbut, *Antiquities*, 21, 128–43.

108. Heald to Cushing, October 23, 1812; Kirkland, "Chicago Massacre in 1812," 28: 120–21; Quaife, *Chicago and the Old Northwest*, 412–13; DM, 21S288. Heald was in great danger until his escape. Many of the Indians believed he had deceived them by destroying the whiskey and gunpowder and wanted to kill him. Williams, "Kinzie's Narrative," 46: 350–51; Pokagon, "Massacre," 654.

109. Gordon, *Fort Dearborn Massacre*, 23; Burton, "Fort Dearborn Massacre," 15: 89; Forsyth to Heald, January 2, 1813, DM, 24U10; Quaife, *Chicago and the Old Northwest*, 246. Although Matson, *French and Indians*, 206–9, credits Black Partridge with a role in ransoming Helm, there is no contemporary mention of involvement by Black Partridge, and Matson's chronology cannot be correct.

110. Kinzie did not name his rescuer, but according to Alexander Robinson, Kinzie's life was saved by Nuscotnumeg himself. DM, 21S287.

111. Haydon, "Kinzie's Place," 185–87; Williams, "Kinzie's Narrative," 46: 350–51; Kinzie, *Wau-Bun*, 184–88; Alexander Robinson, DM, 21S283. Not only did Kinzie himself not mention the dramatic rescue of his family by Billy Caldwell, but there is no contemporary documentation of the story whatever. Moreover, it seems unlikely that murderous Potawatomi warriors so intent on bloodshed

as to disregard the protection that Black Partridge and Waubansee had afforded the family would have been swayed by the sudden arrival and intercession of Kinzie's half-Mohawk clerk. Although Caldwell himself was apparently given to telling the story in his later years, it has come to be doubted by some historians. Clifton, "Merchant, Soldier," 196; Vierling, "Fur Trade," 15.

112. See, e.g., Forsyth to Heald, January 2, 1813, DM, 24U6.

113. Simmons, *Heroes*, 53–55; Quaife, *Chicago and the Old Northwest*, 247–51.

114. Quaife, *Chicago and the Old Northwest*, 235–36; *Niles Weekly Register*, 6: 221 (June 4, 1814); [Van Horne], *Narrative*, 11. Van Horne encountered Mrs. Needs along the Fox River while both were in captivity and had the story of the child's death directly from her.

115. Forsyth to Heald, April 10, 1813, DM, 24U10; *TP*, 16: 324–27; Knopf, *Document Transcriptions*, 7: pt. 2, 181.

116. Knopf, *Document Transcriptions*, 7: pt. 1, 181.

117. Wood, *Select British Documents*, 1: 514–16, 520–21.

118. *MPHC* 15: 159–61, 163–64, 172. Woodward's information can only have come from Heald. He says at the beginning of his letter that three survivors had reached Detroit, an obvious reference to the Healds and Sergeant Griffith.

119. *MPHC*, 15: 218–21, 258–59.

120. Louis Buisson (or Bisson, Bieson, or Besson), c. 1758 to c. 1830, a Canadian fur trader who was frequently at Chicago and owned property at Peoria. His wife was a full-blood Potawatomi Indian. It has been claimed that Buisson was at his cabin north of the river in Chicago on the day of the massacre but kept himself and his family indoors and unharmed. In 1818 he was at Peoria as agent for the American Fur Company. At that time Buisson was described as "a large, portly, gray-headed man, who was then about sixty years of age, and for more than forty years had been an Indian trader on the Ohio, Mississippi, and Illinois Rivers." Hubbard, *Autobiography*, 28–29; Franke, *French Peoria*, 54–55, 101, 105; Danckers, *Compendium*, 76, 89.

121. François DuPin (also Le Moyne, Des Pins, DuPain), a fur trader originally from Montreal who was frequently at Chicago and in the Illinois River Valley. Danckers, *Compendium*, 129; Matson, *French and Indians*, 229–30; Carter, *TP*, 14:654; 16:.310.

122. *Niles' Weekly Register*, 6 (June 4, 1814): 221.

123. Mrs. Lee had been widowed, but not by the massacre at Chicago. By chance, her husband was at Mackinac during the events of August 15, thereby evading death a second time, only to fall in the battle at the River Raisin, January 22, 1813. Forsyth to Clark, July 20, 1813, Forsyth Papers. On the rescue of other prisoners, see Forsyth to Heald, January 2, 1813, DM, 24U6; Quaife, "Story

of James Corbin," 223–24; Quaife, *Chicago and the Old Northwest*, chapter 11; Matson, *French and Indians*, 229–30.

124. On "Peter Bell," see Quaife, *Chicago and the Old Northwest*, 254; *WHC* 12: 108–10; Esarey, *Messages and Letters*, 2: 279–80, 643–44, 655.

125. McAfee, *History*, 101–2.

126. Zachary Taylor was born in Orange County, Virginia, November 24, 1784. He joined the U.S. Army as first lieutenant in 1808, was promoted captain November 30, 1810, and brevetted major as of September 5, 1812, for his gallant defense of Fort Harrison. He was promoted to major (May 15, 1814), lieutenant colonel (1819), colonel (1832), and major general (1846). He saw active service in the War of 1812, Black Hawk War, and Second Seminole Wars, before becoming a national hero in the Mexican War, in which against great odds he won the decisive battle of Buena Vista. Taylor was three times voted the thanks of Congress. As a Whig, he was elected twelfth president of the United States, serving from March 4, 1849, until his death July 9, 1850. He rests in Zachary Taylor National Cemetery, Louisville, Kentucky. Heitman, *Historical Register*, 1: 46, 949. Biography: Hamilton, *Zachary Taylor*.

127. Esarey, *Messages and Letters*, 2: 125–28, 134; *Western Sun*, September 15 and 22, 1812; *Reporter*, September 26 and October 10, 1812; Taylor to Lear, December 15, 1814, Zachary Taylor Papers, Series 2, Library of Congress; McAfee, 153–54; Duddleston, "Fort Harrison"; Hamilton, *Zachary Taylor*, 40–44; Bradsby, *Vigo County*, 118–22.

128. The fort was originally called Fort Bellevue.

129. Thomas Hamilton, of New York, served in the army as an enlisted man 1802–6; promoted ensign, March 6, 1806; 2d lieutenant, June 1, 1807; first lieutenant, December 15, 1808; captain, February 21, 1814; honorably discharged June 15, 1815. Hamilton was reinstated May 17, 1816; brevet major February 21, 1824; resigned August 16, 1828. Heitman, *Historical Register*, 1: 494.

130. Brannan, *Official Letters*, 63–65; *Missouri Gazette*, September 19 and 26, 1812; Jackson, "Fort Madison."

131. James Rhea, of New Jersey, lieutenant 1791; ensign January 8, 1799; transferred to First Infantry April 1, 1800; first lieutenant June 15, 1800; captain July 29, 1807; resigned December 31, 1812. Heitman, *Historical Register*, 1: 826.

132. Philip Ostrander, of New York, sergeant, First infantry; promoted ensign November 14, 1806; 2d lieutenant May 1, 1808; first lieutenant October 30, 1812; died at Fort Wayne July 30, 1813. Lieutenant Ostrander was in temporary command of Fort Dearborn for nine months, during the absence of Captain Heald, 1810–11. Heitman, *Historical Register*, 1: 762; Quaife, *Chicago and the Old Northwest*, 109.

133. Daniel Curtis, born New Hampshire, taught school in Detroit before enlisting in First Infantry as ensign January 3, 1812; promoted second lieutenant December 31, 1812; first lieutenant April 15, 1814; regimental adjutant August 1814 to June 1815; captain October 17, 1820, dismissed October 16, 1821; reinstated April 8, 1822; dismissed January 8, 1823. Curtis resumed teaching school, first at Green Bay and then at Prairie du Chien, Wisconsin, where he died in the winter of 1833–34. Heitman, *Historical Register*, 1: 346; *WHC* 2: 174–75; 5: 325 and note, 332; 7: 228; 12: 461–63.

134. Palmer, *Early Days*, 880–85; McAfee, *History*, 126–28; *Missouri Gazette*, October 10, 1812; Brice, *History*, 212–26; Woehrmann, *Headwaters*, 225–48; Alexander Robinson, DM, 21S281. According to Robinson, the log cannons were devised by Aubenaw, a war chief who led 50 Potawatomi warriors from the Wabash against Fort Wayne.

135. Wood, *Select British Documents*, 1: 592–94; *MPHC*, 15: 147–48; McAfee, *History*, 102, 125–28. For Muir's expedition, see Casselman, *Richardson's War*, 93–103, 296–300.

136. Palmer, *Early Days*, 880–85; McAfee, *History*, 136; Smith to Patterson, September 13, 1812, DM, 27C87; *Missouri Gazette*, October 10, 1812; Cleaves, *Old Tippecanoe*, 119–20.

137. *MPHC*, 15: 151–52, 157–58; Woehrmann, *Headwaters*, 246–48.

138. Shequenebec's visionary dreams had recently raised him to influence as a kind of prophet. He was leader of a band of Potawatomi that Thomas Forsyth considered to be "composed of the very worst Indians in all this Country." Forsyth to Clark, September 15, 1811, Forsyth Papers; *Missouri Gazette*, October 24, 1812.

139. The abortive September raid is not well documented. The principal sources are Knopf, *Document Transcriptions*, 6: pt. 3, 143; Edwards, *History*, 343; *TP*, 16: 261–65, 310–12, 379–81; Forsyth to Clark, July 20, 1813, in Forsyth Papers; *Missouri Gazette*, September 16, October 10, and October 24, 1812; *National Intelligencer*, October 27, 1812, transcribed in Knopf, *Document Transcriptions*, 5: pt. 1, 268; *National Intelligencer*, March 24, 1813, transcribed in Knopf, *Document Transcriptions*, 5: pt. 2, 49.

140. Knopf, *Document Transcriptions*, 6: pt. 3, 51.

141. *TP*, 8: 197–99, 16: 257–58, 265–66; Knopf, *Document Transcriptions*, 6: pt. 3, 143; *Missouri Gazette*, September 5, 1812.

142. McAfee, *History*, 108–9, 156; Shelby to Edwards, August 28 and November 2, 1812, Governor Isaac Shelby (Second Term), Letter Book A, 82–83, 83–85, Kentucky Department of Libraries and Archives, Frankfort; *National Intelligencer*, September 24, 1812, transcribed in Knopf, *Document Transcriptions*,

5: pt. 1, 231–32. In fairness to Gibson, it must be acknowledged that he appears to have been motivated in large part by a desire to lift the siege of Fort Harrison. *Indiana Magazine of History*, 1: 128–31.

143. Edwards, *History*, 340.

144. Captain Risdon H. Price, a native of Maryland, came to Saint Louis in 1807 and set up shop as a merchant. He also served as a director of the Bank of Saint Louis. In 1808 Price was elected lieutenant of a volunteer company from Saint Louis and sometime thereafter, probably 1810, he acquired the title of captain. The years before his death in 1847 were darkened by business reverses and ill health. He was a son-in-law of General Daniel Bissell. Billon, *Annals of Saint Louis*, 89, 269–70; *Price's Heirs v Evans*, 26 Mo. 30, 48 (1857).

145. Two men named Musick, David and James, bore the title of captain in the Missouri militia during the war of 1812. Which of them commanded a gunboat in this operation remains to be discovered.

146. *Missouri Gazette*, September 16 and October 10, 1812.

147. Henry Dodge was born at Vincennes, Indiana, October 12, 1782, but moved with his family to Saint Genevieve, Missouri in 1796. Sheriff of Saint Genevieve County, 1805–21. Served in Missouri militia in War of 1812, reaching rank of brigadier general. Moved to Dodgeville, Wisconsin, area in 1827 and commanded mounted Rangers in both the Winnebago War of 1827 and the Black Hawk War of 1832. In the latter he was engaged in several skirmishes and in the concluding battle of Bad Axe. Governor of Wisconsin Territory (1836–41, 1845–48), Wisconsin's delegate to Congress (1841–45), and U.S. senator (1848–57). Died Burlington, Iowa, June 19, 1867, and buried Aspen Grove Cemetery. *ANB*, 6: 683–84; *BDUSC*, 968.

148. *Missouri Gazette*, October 10 and 17, 1812.

149. *TP*, 16: 261–65; *Missouri Gazette*, October 10 and 24, 1812; *TP*, 14: 614–22; *National Intelligencer*, March 24, 1813.

150. Knopf, *Document Transcriptions*, 6: pt. 3, 187; Lewis, *Fort Allison*, 3–4. On Fort LaMotte, see Reynolds, *My Own Times*, 84, 93; Perrin, *History of Crawford*, 31–32; Selby, *Illinois Historical*, 635, 677; Wilson and Kaegy, *Forts*, 190–93. On Fort Allison, see Chapter 7, note 34.

151. On Hill's Fort, see *History of Bond and Montgomery*, 13–14, 19, 21–23, 73, 140, 152; *Bond County History*, 9; Wilson and Kaegy, *Tales of Hill's Fort*; "Granite Boulder Marks the Spot," *Greenville Advocate*, August 15, 1921, 3.

152. Edwards, *History*, 343; Edwards to Shelby, October 4, 1812, DM, 5X17; John Reynolds, *My Own Times*, 83; Reynolds, *Pioneer History*, 407; Wilson and Kaegy, *Tales of Hill's Fort*, 81–82.

153. Stevens, "Illinois," 142–43; *History of White County*, 293–95. Based on oral

information, Stevens dated the Pond Settlement Massacre to October 1812, but a more recent researcher argues for a date of 1817 or later. Musgrave, *Handbook*, 167, n. 206.

154. *TP*, 16: 265–66; Edwards, *History*, 343; McAfee, *History*, 156.

Chapter 5. Peoria

1. *TP*, 16: 265–66; Edwards to Secretary of War, October 4, 1812, DM, 5X17.

2. *RAGI*, 9: 333. Also serving on Edwards's staff was Lieutenant Robert Todd of Kentucky, a regular army officer stationed at Fort Russell. Heitman, *Historical Register*, 1: 964.

3. Reynolds, *My Own Times*, 86; Reynolds, *Pioneer History*, 354, 407. In *My Own Times* Reynolds says that the second regiment was commanded by *Elias* Rector, but in *Pioneer History* he says it was commanded by *William*. It is surprising that there seems to be no way to determine which version is correct. Edwards's own report is silent. Elias was Edwards's adjutant general, while William, the oldest of the brothers, was a brigadier general of militia. In later years, however, Elias was known as "Colonel Rector," and it may have been at this time that he acquired the title.

4. Stephenson died at Edwardsville, October 10, 1822. *BDUSC*, 1972; Reynolds, *Pioneer History*, 411; *TP*, 16: 47–48, 17: 338, 626.

5. Reynolds, *Pioneer History*, 353–54; Shinn, *Pioneers*, 397–98; Salmans, *History*, 207–11; Bateman *Historical Encyclopedia*, 443–44. The Rectors were of German descent; the family name was originally Richter.

6. William Rector was born in Fauquier County, Virginia, before 1785, moved to Kaskaskia 1806; deputy surveyor, 1806–13; brigadier general of Illinois militia, 1811–13; appointed principal deputy surveyor of Missouri Territory and moved to Saint Louis, October 1813; surveyor-general for Illinois and Missouri, 1816–24; delegate to first Missouri Constitutional Convention, 1820; died at his home in Illinois, June 6, 1826. Philbrick, *Laws of Indiana*, ccxxxiii; U.S. Senate, *Executive Journal*, 2: 165–66; *TP*, 16: 373; Houck, *History*, 3: 249; Billon, *Annals*, 32; Shinn, *Pioneers*, 380–82, 387–93; *Missouri Intelligencer* [Franklin, Missouri], June 16, 1826; *Missouri Historical Review*, 90: 21, n. 41.

7. *TP*, 16: 113, 160, 373, 378.

8. Elias Rector was born in Fauquier County, Virginia, 1785; moved to Kaskaskia, 1806; deputy surveyor 1806–13; adjutant general of Illinois militia, May 3 to July 18, 1809, and May 28, 1810, to October 25, 1813; clerk of Court of Common pleas, January 28 to October 25, 1813; moved to Saint Louis about October 1813; postmaster of Saint Louis, 1819–22; elected to Missouri State Senate, 1821, but died in office, August 7, 1822. Philbrick, *Laws of Indiana*, ccxxxiii; *TP*, 16: 389,

17: 622, 632, 646, 647; *Missouri Intelligencer* [Franklin, Missouri], September 3, 1822; Billon, *Annals*, 54; Shinn, *Pioneers*, 380, 382–83, 382–92; *Missouri Historical Review*, 90: 8, n. 16 (with portrait).

9. Nelson Rector was born in Fauquier County, Virginia, but was acting as a deputy surveyor in Illinois Territory by 1810; appointed aide de camp to Governor Edwards, November 10, 1812; severely wounded while surveying, March 1, 1814; commanded company in battle of Credit Island, September 6, 1814; died a suicide while surveying on the Arkansas River, about December 1815. *TP*, 16: 76–80, 169–70, 397–99, 401–2, 17: 276–78, 284–85, 320, 645; Reynolds, *My Own Times*, 101–2; *RAGI*, 9: 333.

10. Hall, *Romance*, 343–46; Reynolds, *My Own Times*, 138; *Combined History of Randolph, Monroe and Perry Counties*, 333–35. Author Herman Melville sent this story around the world by retelling it in chapter 27 of his novel *The Confidence Man* (1857). See Russell, "Indian Hater," 13.

11. Brady, "Moredock," 6–10; Piggott, DM, Z36–7; Patterson, DM, Z58; Scott to Draper, January 14, 1863, DM, Z102; Scott to Draper, January 29, 1863, DM, Z103; Lemen to Draper, February 12, 1863, DM, Z108.

12. See the admiring sketch of Moredock in Reynolds, *Pioneer History*, 146–50; Cass County: Barge, "Rejected County Names" 11: 122; Saline County: Ferguson, "Perilous Infancy," 10: 52, n. 8.

13. The muster roll of Samuel Whiteside's company, in service between August 22 and November 13, 1812, is printed in *RAGI*, 9: 324–26.

14. The names of the soldiers Hargrave led to Peoria are in Felty, "Illinois Territorial Militia," 138–9.

15. Nathaniel Journey (often spelled "Jurney") came to Illinois from Kentucky sometime between 1804 and 1809. He was appointed a captain in the territorial militia May 2, 1812, and promoted to major on February 18, 1813. He was the builder and proprietor of Journey's Fort near the present Aviston, and his company patrolled the frontier in the neighborhood of Clinton County. On August 1, 1813, Journey was commissioned 1st lieutenant in the U.S. Rangers and was honorably discharged June 15, 1815. He is believed to have died at Saint Charles, Missouri, apparently of illness, between January 23, 1816, when his will was signed, and the following June 29, when the will was recorded. *TP*, 17: 641; Corrigan and Temple, "Illinois Volunteer Officers," 238; *TP*, 16: 300–302; *History of Marion and Clinton*, 50; Reynolds, *My Own Times*, 86 (wrongly giving his name as "Janney"); Heitman, *Historical Register*, 1: 585; personal communication from Teran Buettel of Morning Sun, Iowa.

16. Judy was born in Switzerland in 1774 but as a boy came to Illinois. He became one of the leaders of the Goshen settlement, which he represented in the upper

house of the territorial legislature. He also served as judge of common pleas and county judge of Madison County, and in March 1815 he succeeded William Whiteside as colonel of the Second Regiment of militia. Judy died January 12, 1838, and is buried in the Nix-Judy Cemetery, near Glen Carbon. *TP*, 17: 644, 651, 654; Reynolds, *Pioneer History*, 319–22; *History of Madison County*, 71; Norton, *Centennial History*, 173–74; Detmer, "Goshen Settlement," 2; Baldwin, *Echoes*, 339–42. The muster roll of Judy's company of spies is printed at *RAGI*, 9: 329.

17. The names of the men in Cox's detachment are given at *RAGI*, 9: 329–30. Cox was one of the leaders of a party that came in 1804 from Abbeville, South Carolina, to Randolph County's "Irish Settlement," where Cox operated a ferry across the Kaskaskia River, about six miles above the present village of Evansville, Illinois. On January 2, 1810, the governor appointed Cox a captain in the militia. Cox died in Randolph County on the farm where he had settled. Montague, *Directory*, 85; Allen, *Randolph County Notes*, 5; *TP*, 17: 630.

18. For Captain Dudley Williams's company, see *RAGI*, 9: 332.

19. Knopf, *Document Transcriptions*, vol. 7, pt. 1, 4.

20. *Missouri Gazette*, October 17, 1812; *The Western Sun* [Vincennes], October 13, 1812, 3; *TP*, 16: 268–69.

21. Reynolds, *My Own Times*, 86–87; Edwards, *History*, 69–72; Washburne, *Edwards Papers*, 86–90.

22. Stevens, "Illinois," 134–38; Brannan, *Official Letters*, 88–89; Knopf, *Document Transcriptions*, 6: pt. 4, 78.

23. At the time of the raid, John Reynolds (1788–1865) was just beginning a career that took him to some of the highest offices of the state, including associate justice of the first Supreme Court of Illinois, fourth governor of Illinois, and representative in Congress. Although Reynolds was a college graduate and lawyer, his political success owed much to his cultivation of a folksy image as "the Old Ranger," based on his service in the War of 1812. However far his political career may have fallen short of the highest ideals, there can be no doubt of the debt that historians of the state's early days owe to his two books: *The Pioneer History of Illinois* and his memoir, *My Own Times*. BDUSC, 1800. Biography: Harper, "John Reynolds."

24. Reynolds, *My Own Times*, 86–87.

25. Reynolds, *My Own Times*, 87; Stevens, "Illinois," 134–38; *Missouri Gazette*, November 7, 1812. Edwards and the *Missouri Gazette*, which obtained its information from the governor, place the two villages on the Saline Fork, while Reynolds mentions only one village and says it was on Sugar Creek. Stringer, *History*, 1: 46–48, places the principal village of the Kickapoo on the north side

of Salt Creek, near the present city of Lincoln. The village or villages have been conjecturally identified with the Rhodes site, an archaeological site excavated by the Illinois State Museum in the 1970s with results that have never been published. Mazrim, *Sangamo Frontier*, 125 & n. 4, 131–32 & n. 17.

26. *History of Tazewell County*, 197.

27. Thomas Carlin (1786–1852) served as first sheriff of Greene County (1821), state senator (1825–33), and governor of Illinois (1838–42). Howard, *Illinois Governors*, 52–57.

28. Indian villages moved frequently so identification is not always certain. Both Edwards and Russell reported that the village they destroyed at the head of Lake Peoria had been headed by Pemwatome. A few months earlier, however, Edwards reported to the War Department that the Kickapoo village being built at the head of Peoria Lake was that of Little Deer and that Pemwatome was building his village on the lake three leagues (nine miles) from Peoria. Edwards, *History*, 315–18. On the legend that the village at the head of the lake was that of Black Partridge, see note 31, below.

29. Libby, "Anthropological Report," 216–19; Forsyth to Gibson, July 26, 1812, Chicago History Museum.

30. Stevens, "Illinois," 136–37; *TP*, 16: 244–47.

31. The monument stands at the intersection of Illinois Highway 26 and Bricktown Road, near the extreme southwestern corner of section 11, T28N, R3W. The area around the monument meets various descriptions as near "the head of the lake," "at the foot of a hill," and "near a muddy creek" and at the time it was separated from the Illinois River by a wide marsh. Early settlers saw remains of Indian houses at the location. "Death of Woodford County Man Recalls Colorful History of Ancient 'Black Partridge Village,'" *Peoria Star*, July 19, 1936; Spooner, "Historic Indian Villages," 1: 15–18; "Peoria Historian Defen[ds] Location of Monument as Indian Village Site," *Lacon Home Journal*, November 17, 1955, 14. Although Edwards plainly stated that the village he destroyed at the foot of the bluffs was "inhabited by Kickapoos and Miamies," the continual misidentification of the village as that of the Potawatomi chief Black Partridge derives from the much-later memoir of John Reynolds, *My Own Times*, 87. Reynolds's error was followed and amplified in the vivid narratives of Matson, *French and Indians*, 200–209, and Ellsworth, *Records*, 574–78. The discrepancy has not gone unnoticed, but so strong a hold has the Matson-Ellsworth version taken on the imagination of local historians that it has been glibly assumed that "Edwards evidently was mistaken." C. Henry Smith to Harry L. Spooner, April 1, 1947, in Peoria Historical Society Collection, Special Collections Center, Davis-Cullom Library, Bradley University, Peoria. That seems unlikely. Edwards

commanded the expedition and his official report was written immediately after the event. Reynolds, by contrast, had ridden as a private soldier and wrote from memory more than forty years later. Probably "The Old Ranger" confused the Kickapoo village at the base of the bluff with a separate Potawatomi village nearer the river, which the army attacked immediately afterwards and which his account does not mention.

32. Wright (often spelled "Right") had settled in the western part of Wood River Township, Madison County, in 1806. Although he held the rank of captain in the militia, he had volunteered to ride with Judy as a private soldier. At first the wound was not thought to be mortal, but after the army returned, Wright died of it at the Wood River Fort. Five minor children survived him. *TP*, 17: 630; *RAGI*, 9: 328; Knopf, *Document Transcriptions*, vol. 6, pt. 4, 78; Edwards, *History*, 343–45; Norton, *Centennial History*, 176; "Madison County Records and Indentures, 1812–1815," 8, 12, 13, 27, Illinois State Archives, Springfield.

33. *History of Jackson County*, 34; Matson, *French and Indians*, 202–3, n. ("He described some acts of the soldiers, which for the sake of humanity ought not to be recorded in history.")

34. Stevens, "Illinois," 134–38; Reynolds, *My Own Times*, 88–89.

35. Reynolds, *My Own Times*, 88–89; Stevens, "Illinois," 134–38; *TP*, 16: 268–69; Knopf, *Document Transcriptions*, 6: pt. 4, 78, 7: pt. 1, 94; *Missouri Gazette*, November 7, 1812; McVicker, "Chapter."

36. If the village was indeed that of Shequenebec, the inhabitants were hardly innocents. Thomas Forsyth considered Shequenebec's band to be "composed of the very worst Indians in all this Country." They had committed many depredations against the unoffending people of Peoria. Forsyth to Clark, November 1, 1811, Thomas Forsyth Papers, Missouri History Museum, Saint Louis.

37. Stevens, "Illinois," 134–38; *Missouri Gazette*, November 7, 1812; Matson, *French and Indians*, 209. It is by no means impossible that both Shequenebec and Black Partridge lived at this village. In September they had been associated in the abortive raid on the settlements. *Missouri Gazette*, October 24, 1812.

38. *Missouri Gazette*, December 12, 1812. ("A friend of ours who was on that expedition says: 'When our men found six white scalps on one of the Indian houses, and recognized them to belong to O'Neil's wife and children, they were on the verge of retaliation, but more generous feelings gave place to revenge, and only one squaw was put to death.'")

39. Matson, *Reminiscences*, 236–37.

40. Norton, *Centennial History*, 1: 40; Reynolds, *My Own Times*, 89.

41. *TP*, 16: 268–69; *Missouri Gazette*, November 7 and December 12, 1812; Stevens, "Illinois," 137.

42. Stevens, "Illinois," 134–38; Knopf, *Document Transcriptions*, 6: pt. 4, 78, 7: pt. 1, 90; Edwards, *History*, 343–45; *Missouri Gazette*, November 7, 1812; *TP*, 16: 268–69, 17: 33–35; *RAGI*, 9: 325. Captain Wright died at Wood River Fort about six weeks after being wounded. *History of Madison County*, 416. One local historian later claimed, apparently based on oral sources, that two soldiers named Patrick White and John Shur were also killed in the raid. Ellsworth, *Records*, 576. No record of such soldiers has been found, and the reports of Edwards and Russell make it clear that Wright was the only fatality among the attackers.

43. Stevens, "Illinois," 134–38; Reynolds, *My Own Times*, 89; Smith, *Metamora*, 45.

44. Reynolds, *My Own Times*, 89–90; Reynolds, *Pioneer History*, 407.

45. Edwards, *History*, 69–76. John Moredock's conduct on the expedition later became an issue. A month after the militia had been discharged, the first territorial legislature recommended to Congress that additional companies of U.S. Rangers be organized in the territory and that Moredock be appointed to command them. Among the qualities and achievements cited to support the appointment was that he had "held a Distinguished rank and acted a Meritorious part in the late campaign under Governor Edwards." Edwards duly transmitted the petition to Washington, but in April, when the raising of the new companies had become a reality, Edwards objected to the appointment and recommended that his friend Stephenson be appointed instead. Edwards claimed that on the march to Peoria Moredock's "conduct was so exceptionable, violating positive orders that he was arrested by Colo Russell." In addition, he claimed Moredock had become separated from his battalion so that it could not carry out its mission to attack the Indians' left flank, in contrast with Edwards's earlier report to the War Department that his officers and men "were uniformly obedient to my orders." Two members of the legislature, Jacob Short and Samuel Judy, had served with Moredock on the Peoria campaign, and Judy was part of the committee that drafted the resolution that recommended Moredock, which becomes puzzling if his conduct really was so objectionable. Alex Wells, an old soldier who had served on the expedition, afterwards recalled that on the march Moredock had been briefly placed under arrest for shooting a deer in violation of the order of silence. When the deer bounded out, Edwards called out "Don't shoot Moredock!" but Moredock fired anyway. He later explained that knowing the men needed meat he had thought the governor said: "Shoot, Moredock!" After apologies, Moredock's sword was returned to him. *TP*, 16: 271–72, 316–18; "Journals of Legislative Council," December 1 and 4, 1812, Record Group 100.10, Illinois State Archives, Springfield; Alex Wells, DM, 20S136.

46. For a dissent, see Ballance, *History of Peoria*, 32–40.

47. *TP*, 16.285–89, 312–15.

48. Matson, *French and Indians*, 209–11, followed by Smith, *Metamora*, 48–49.

49. *National Intelligencer*, October 10, 1812, in Knopf, *Document Transcriptions*, 5: pt. 1, 255, 257; *Reporter*, September 12, 1812, 2.

50. Shelby to Hopkins, September 8 and 12, 1812, Governor Isaac Shelby (Second Term), Letter Book A, Kentucky Department of Libraries and Archives, 16–18, 19–21; Esarey, *Messages and Letters*, 2: 121–22, 153–55, 192–93; *National Intelligencer*, October 10, 1812, in Knopf, *Document Transcriptions*, 5: pt. 1, 257; Butler, *History*, 360–61. There is a good brief account of Hopkins's expedition in McAfee, *History*, 157–60.

51. Heitman, *Historical Register*, 300; *BDUSC*, 1276; *DAB*, vol. 5, pt. 1, 218–19; Collins, *History of Kentucky*, 2: 343–45; Baskett, "General Samuel Hopkins;" Starling, *History*, 54, 99, 103, 255, 796.

52. *TP*, 8: 209–10.

53. Knopf, *Document Transcriptions*, vol. 6, pt. 3, 187, vol. 6, pt. 4, p. 2, 13; Walker to [unidentified], November 1, 1812, DM, 9U14. George Walker served on the campaign with the title of judge advocate general and was well placed to observe the events he describes.

54. Walker to [unidentified], November 1, 1812; "Letters of Captain Hamilton," 43: 395.

55. Knopf, *Document Transcriptions*, 6: pt. 4, 13; Esarey, 2: 162–63.

56. For the Shakers in general, see Andrews, *People Called Shakers*; Stein, *Shaker Experience*; Ferguson, "Central Themes."

57. Boice, *Maps*, 65–73; McClelland, "Memorandum of Remarkable Events," 281, 287–91, 338, 346. Busro was as far west as the Shakers ever spread, except for a short-lived community in Lawrence County, Illinois. *Combined History of Edwards*, 342–43. For the friendship that existed between the Shakers and Tecumseh, see Sugden, *Tecumseh*, 138–42, 221.

58. *TP*, 8: 384–87; Flower, *History*, 57–58. The Shakers' subsequent petition to Congress for redress was denied on the specious ground that the army's depredations had not been ordered by the commanding officer. *ASP: Claims*, 419.

59. *Reporter*, November 11, 1812; Stevens, "Illinois," 128–31; "Letters of Captain Hamilton," 43: 396–99; Knopf, *Document Transcriptions*, 6: pt. 4, 14, 67; Walker to [unidentified], November 1, 1812; *Missouri Gazette*, January 16, 1813.

60. *Reporter*, November 11, 1812; Knopf, *Document Transcriptions*, 6: pt. 4, 67; "Letters of Captain Hamilton," 43: 395.

61. The following account is drawn from Hopkins to Shelby, October [2]6, 1812, Stevens, 128–31; Hopkins to Gibson, October 26, 1812, Knopf, *Document*

Transcriptions, 6: pt. 4, 67; Walker to [unidentified], November 1, 1812, DM, 9U14; Shelby to Harrison, November 1, 1812, Esarey, *Messages and Letters*, 2: 192–93; John H. Morris to [unidentified], January 13, 1813, in Governor Isaac Shelby (Second Term), Military Correspondence, Folder 73, Kentucky Department of Libraries and Archives, Frankfort; and "To the Public," [Narrative of Jechonias Singleton and supporting affidavits], in *Reporter*, December 26, 1812, p. 1. These documents are the primary sources for Hopkins's campaign in Illinois. Hopkins, Walker, Morris, and Singleton were participants, while Governor Shelby obtained his information from Captain Anthony Crockett, one of Hopkins's officers. Also useful, although secondhand, is "Extract of a Letter Written at Fort Harrison," in *Reporter*, November 21, 1812, 1.

62. McAfee, *History*, 155; Esarey, *Messages and Letters*, 2: 406–8; Dillon, *History*, 491.

63. Jechonias Singleton, of Woodford County, Kentucky, appointed captain in Lieutenant Colonel James Allen's Regiment of Kentucky Mounted Volunteer Militia, September 18, 1812. Promoted to major, September 29, 1812. By September 1, 1815, he had attained the rank of colonel in command of 11th Regiment, Kentucky Militia. *Report of the Adjutant General of the State of Kentucky*, 248, 250; Railey, *History*, 14, 380.

64. John H. Morris to [unidentified], January 13, 1813.

65. Cunningham, *History of Champaign County*, 656.

66. *Reporter*, November 11, 1812; Walker to [unidentified], November 1, 1812.

67. Beckwith, *History*, 55.

68. *Missouri Gazette*, January 16, 1813.

69. Ibid.

70. On the way home, the troops stopped at Bussaron Creek to loot the Shaker community one more time.

71. Esarey, *Messages and Letters*, 2: 201–2; Shelby to Hopkins, November 9, 1812, in Governor Isaac Shelby (Second Term), Letter Book A, Kentucky Department of Libraries and Archives, Frankfort, 35–37; Knopf, *Document Transcriptions*, 6: pt. 4, 139; *Missouri Gazette*, January 16, 1813; McAfee, *History*, 160.

72. Esarey, *Messages and Letters*, 2: 201, 231–34; Brannan, *Official Letters*, 95–97; Knopf, *Document Transcriptions*, 6: pt. 4., 139; Butler, *History*, 362–64; *Western Sun*, December 9, 1812; Dillon, *History*, 501–5.

73. *Reporter*, May 11, 1813, 2; BDUSC, 1276. Hopkins should not be confused with his son, Captain Samuel Goode Hopkins, who served in the regular army during the war. Heitman, *Historical Register*, 1: 542.

74. Craig's company had enlisted September 5, 1812, and served until discharged on December 2, 1812. The muster roll is printed in *RAGI*, 9: 323.

75. *TP*, 17: 639; Knopf, *Document Transcriptions*, 6: pt 1, 50.

76. *RAGI*, 9: 331. This was not the only time Tramell was called on to guard valuable public property. See Steinhuss to William Clark, August 28, 1813, William Clark Papers, Box 12, Folder 5, Missouri History Museum, Saint Louis. ("You will receive from Col. Philip Trammel a box containing two thousand dollars specie, concerning which further particulars are unnecessary.")

77. Washburne, *Edwards Papers*, 86–90. Craig's statement that he arrived at Peoria on November 5 and departed on November 9 is difficult to accept at face value. The events as he describes them must have taken more than four days to unfold, and his own account claimed that he and Forsyth were on friendly terms "for six or seven days" before the breach.

78. See Edward Coles's 1820 report on the land claims at Peoria, in *ASP: Public Lands* 3: 421–31. Coles's map is on page 423. The report, without the map, is also printed as an appendix to Alvord, *Governor Edward Coles*, 222–53. The estimate of 200 to 300 inhabitants is that of Edwards, *History*, 66. A good brief history of the French village is Franke, *French Peoria*, 44–45.

79. The principal contemporary accounts of Craig's expedition are Craig to Edwards, December 10, 1812, in Washburne, *Edwards Papers*, 86–90, and Thomas Forsyth, "A true account of the expedition under Thomas E. Craig of Shawanoe town to Peoria," DM, 1T11. Craig and Forsyth hated each other, and while their accounts relate a somewhat similar sequence of events, they are impossible to reconcile in detail. Another eyewitness account is "Memorial to Congress from inhabitants of Peoria," December 20, 1813, in *TP*, 16: 379–87. The "Memorial" supports Forsyth's version, but was obviously heavily influenced by Forsyth, who was one of the signers. An account basically favorable to Craig appeared in *National Intelligencer*, December 24, 1812 (in Knopf, *Document Transcriptions*, 5: pt. 1, 294). Other early accounts at one remove from eyewitness testimony are Reynolds, *My Own Times*; Matson, *French and Indians*; and Edward Coles's 1820 report. Reynolds did not witness the destruction of Peoria, but he was later married to Mme. LaCroix, who did, and his brief account is due some credit for that reason. Matson's account is based on interviews with old men who had been present at the event as boys, as well as with Forsyth's son Robert, but his account is in certain respects contradicted by the contemporary sources and should be used with caution. Coles had the advantage of either interviewing or obtaining affidavits from all the surviving adult residents only eight years after the event, but his concern was with the land claims, and his report contains little detail about Craig's actions. All subsequent accounts descend from one or more of these sources.

80. Strictly speaking, Forsyth and the other men in the field were considered subagents, who reported to the actual Indian agent, General William Clark at Saint Louis.

81. Edwards, *History*, 289–90.

82. One of these men was Louis Buisson, who was afterwards instrumental in rescuing the survivors of the Fort Dearborn garrison from captivity. See page 246, note 120.

83. Harrison Wilson of Shawneetown was the son of a member of the first territorial legislature. He was born in Virginia 1788. In 1832, he served as captain of a Gallatin County company in the Black Hawk War, and took part in the battle of Bad Axe, in which he captured, and thereby saved, seven Indian women and children fleeing from the battlefield. Wilson died in 1852, and is buried in Westwood Cemetery near Shawneetown. Whitney, *Black Hawk War*, 1: 258–60; 2: 628 n. 2, and 924; Musgrave, *Handbook*, 393–99; Lawler, *Gallatin County*, 68–69; Miner, *Cemeteries*, 1: 51.

84. Washburne, 86–90.

85. Savage's Ferry was the future site of the short-lived town of Gibraltar. Reynolds, *Pioneer History*, 245; *History of Madison County*, 419.

86. Washburne, *Edwards Papers*, 85.

87. Reynolds, *My Own Times*, 90.

88. Matson, *French and Indians*, 214–22.

89. Ibid.

90. Forsyth to Clark, February 20, 1813, Thomas Forsyth Papers, Missouri History Museum, Saint Louis. ("Capt. Craig's expedition has furnished the Indians with provisions for this winter.")

91. See East, "Lincoln."

92. *TP*, 17: 647, 650, 654.

93. *TP*, 17: 544–45. The exact date of Craig's death remains to be discovered. He last held court on May 21, 1816, and his will was presented in court for probate on August 20 of the same year. *Gallatin County Illinois Court Records*, 47, 52; Estate of Thomas E. Craig, Box 15, Office of the Circuit Clerk, Gallatin County, Shawneetown.

94. Forsyth, "True Account."

95. *Missouri Gazette*, January 30, 1813.

96. Reynolds, *My Own Times*, 90, 150; Reynolds, *Pioneer History*, 350; Stevens, "Illinois," 133.

97. Matson, *French and Indians*, 225.

Chapter 6. Dickson and Forsyth

1. This story is preserved by former Governor John Reynolds, who knew Forsyth well and probably had the story from him. *Pioneer History*, 252. Reynolds is plainly wrong in assigning the meeting to 1815. Dickson could not have visited Saint Louis in that year. The most likely date for the meeting is 1818, when Dickson was brought to Saint Louis under arrest as a suspicious alien.

2. The standard biography of Robert Dickson is still Tohill, "Robert Dickson." See also Helen D. Weaver, "Life of Robert Dickson"; Cruikshank, "Robert Dickson," *WHC* 12: 133–52; *Dictionary of Canadian Biography*, 6: 209–11; Irving, *Officers*, 209, 212 n. 5.

3. Tohill, "Robert Dickson," 3.3: 202–3.

4. Philbrick, *Laws of Indiana*, ccxxxi.

5. Pike, *Account of Expeditions*, 48.

6. Marshall, *Frederick Bates*, 1: 228, 307.

7. *Ibid.*, 2: 16.

8. *Ibid.*

9. *Missouri Gazette*, April 29, 1815.

10. *TP*, 13: 160–62, 203.

11. *TP*, 14: 518–20; Wood, *Select British Documents*, 1: 426–27; *WHC* 9: 178–79; *Missouri Gazette*, June 6, 1812.

12. Robert Forsyth, DM, 22S99–112; Reynolds, *Pioneer History*, 247–52; *TP*, 17: 401–2; Scharf, *History*, 2: 1293–94.

13. Knopf, *Document Transcriptions*, 6: pt. 1, 18–9; pt. 2, 1.

14. Reynolds, *Pioneer History*, 246–47; DM, 22S99–103; *WHC* 6.188 n.

15. Forsyth to Clark, November 1, 1811, Forsyth Papers.

16. Reynolds, *Pioneer History*, 252.

17. Jackson, *Black Hawk*, 61.

18. Quaife, *Chicago and the Old Northwest*, 150–52; Quaife, *Checagou*, 99–101; Indenture of Jeffrey Nash, DM, 1T1; *Forsyth et al. v Nash*, 2 Mart. (o.s.) 305 (La., 1816).

19. *TP*, 16: 310–12.

20. Forsyth to Clark, September 15 and November 11, 1811, Forsyth Papers.

21. Forsyth to Clark, May 27, 1812, Forsyth Papers; Edwards, *History*, 323–25; Washburne, *Edwards Papers*, 80–81; *TP*, 14: 563–69, 591; 16: 250–53; Clark to Forsyth, August 8, 1812, DM, 1T7.

22. Wood, *Select British Documents*, 1: 419–22, 426–27, 431–32; *MPHC*, 15: 91, 180–82, 193–95; *Louisiana Gazette*, June 6, 1812; Kellogg, *British Regime*, 281–82.

23. Edwards, *History*, 332–35; Quaife, "Fort Dearborn Massacre," 567–70; *TP*, 16: 574–75.

24. Wood, *Select British Documents*, 1: 423–24.

25. *Ibid.*, 1: 426–27, 431–32.

26. *Ibid.*, 1: 429, 432–36; Knopf, *Document Transcriptions*, 6: part 2, 104, pt. 3, 6–7, 10–11; Brannan, *Official Letters*, 33–34; *MPHC*, 15: 141–4; Dobbins, "The Dobbins Papers," 8: 303–4; *WHC* 3: 269; Kellogg, "Capture of Mackinac," 60: 124–45.

27. Brannan, *Official Letters*, 44–9; *MPHC*, 15: 180–82; Casselman, *Richardson's War*, 82–83.

28. Jackson, *Black Hawk*, 65–66.

29. As might be expected, the chronology of Black Hawk's autobiography is sometimes confused. It is possible that this meeting took place early the next spring (1813), when Dickson was recruiting the tribes to join in the attack on Fort Meigs, but the fact that Black Hawk places the meeting before the battle on the Raisin, and while Forsyth was still at Peoria, supports a date in the fall of 1812.

30. *TP*, 16: 228–30.

31. *TP*, 16: 255. It is interesting to note that Caldwell, who ended the war as head of the British Indian Department, began it as a spy for the Americans. That may be part of the reason why in later years Caldwell was always very circumspect when discussing the War of 1812. DM, 3YY98–9.

32. Antoine LeClair was a native of Montreal. He had been trained as a blacksmith but only practiced that trade for a few years before his death. He married a Potawatomi woman about 1792. In 1800 LeClair moved to Milwaukee, then an Indian village inhabited by Potawatomi and a few Ottawa. He made a good living trading with the Indians there, but in 1809 he moved with his family to Peoria. In November 1812 LeClair was arrested along with the other inhabitants by Captain Thomas Craig and removed from Peoria. He never returned to Peoria to live, although he did accompany General Howard to Peoria to build Fort Clark in the fall of 1813. LeClair died at Portage des Sioux, Missouri, in 1821, at the age of about 55. *WHC* 11: 238–42; "LeClair's Statement," DM, 24 S 131–41. He must not be confused, as is often done, with his son of the same name, who was one of the founders of Davenport, Iowa.

33. Edwards to Forsyth, January 5, 1812, DM, 1T4; Edwards, *History*, 323; *TP*, 16: 228–30, 250–55.

34. *TP*, 16: 250–53, 261–65; Forsyth to Gibson, July 26, 1812, Chicago History Museum.

35. Burton, "Fort Dearborn Massacre," 15: 89; *TP*, 16.379–82; Drown, *Drown's Record*, 61–62; *TP*, 16.244–47; Forsyth to Clark, November 1, 1811, Forsyth Papers.

36. Much of the whiskey and powder destroyed at Fort Dearborn by order of Captain Heald was the property of Kinzie & Forsyth. *TP*, 16: 261–65; Helm to Forsyth, December 20, 1812, DM, 1T10; Forsyth to Heald, January 2, 1813, DM, 24U6; Quaife, *Chicago and the Old Northwest*, 246, n. 632; Forsyth to Heald, April 10, 1813, DM, 24U10; Heald to Forsyth, July 19, 1813, DM, 24U15; *ASP: Claims*, 424–45; *WHC* 11: 351–55. Congress allowed compensation only for the horses and mules the firm had provided the garrison to assist in the evacuation but reasoned that the powder and whiskey would have been lost anyway.

37. *TP*, 16: 261–65.

38. Knopf, *Document Transcriptions*, 6: pt. 3, 143; *TP*, 16: 261–65, 310–12, 379–82; Forsyth to Clark, July 20, 1813, Forsyth Papers; *Louisiana Gazette*, October 10 and 24, 1812.

39. Apparently Helm had been held by chief Mittitass. Gordon, *Fort Dearborn Massacre*, 23, 76; Forsyth to Heald, January 2, 1813; Burton, "Fort Dearborn Massacre," 15: 89; Forsyth to Clark, July 20, 1813, Forsyth Papers.

40. Thomas Forsyth, "A True Account of the Expedition under Thomas E. Craig of Shawanoe Town to Peoria," DM, 1T11.

41. Edwards to Forsyth, October 14, 1812, DM, 1T8.

42. Forsyth, "A True Account;" "An Account of Losses Sustained by Thomas Forsyth," DM, 1T12; Washburne, *Edwards Papers*, 86–90.

43. Clark to Forsyth, December 15, 1812, DM, 1T9.

44. Edwards to Forsyth, January 28, 1813, DM, 1T13. ("I am surprised at a man of your information asking me to aid and relieve the people of Peoria. . . . No compensation has been asked of me for the injuries sustained at Prairie du Chien; where one man in St. Louis has lost nearly if not quite as much as the whole amount of loss at Peoria.") A year later, however, Edwards softened his attitude. Edwards to Forsyth, January 5, 1814, DM, 1T33: ("I have made representations in favor of the people of Peoria.")

45. *MPHC* 15: 193–95, 202–4; 208–9, 216–22, 263–64; Wood, *Select British Documents*, 1: 426–27.

46. Tohill, "Robert Dickson," 3.2: 97, calls Dickson's accomplishment of his mission "one of the most remarkable journeys in history."

47. *MPHC* 15: 222–23, 250, 258–59, 262, 273–74, 314–18; *TP*, 16: 322.

48. *TP*, 16: 324–27. It is possible that the council at Green Bay described by Black Hawk occurred during Dickson's journey in the spring of 1813, rather than the preceding fall.

49. "Copy of Letter and Council by Blondeau," Edwards Papers, Box 1, Folder 3, Chicago History Museum.

50. *MPHC*, 15: 258–59; *WHC* 12: 108–10; obituary in *Canadian Magazine and*

Literary Repository, vol. 1, no. 2 (August 1823), 192; Quaife (1913), 238–39, 254; *WHC* 3: 280; Casselman, *Richardson's War*, 153–55.

51. *Louisiana Gazette*, June 16 and 20, 1812, January 30, April 17, and May 8, 1813; *Missouri Gazette*, August 28, and September 16, 1813; April 9 and 16, June 18, July 2, 9, and 16, 1814; April 29, 1815; *[Niles] Weekly Register*, 4: 67, 323; 5: 98, 410, 6: 113, 356; 7: 173.

52. *TP*, 14: 637–38; 16: 312–15, 324–27; *Missouri Gazette*, May 8 and August 28, 1813.

53. McAfee, *History*, 297–99, 311.

54. *Ibid.*, 101–2.

55. *WHC* 11: 331–36.

56. Knopf, *Document Transcriptions*, 7: pt. 1, 54; *TP*, 16: 285–89, 305–8, 312–15; *Missouri Gazette*, April 17 and May 29, 1813.

57. Manuel Lisa was born September 8, 1772, at New Orleans, of Spanish ancestry. He entered the western fur trade and in 1802 succeeded in wresting the monopoly on trade with the Osage tribe from Auguste and Pierre Chouteau. From 1809 to 1814, however, he was a partner with the Chouteau brothers, William Clark, and others in the Missouri Fur Company. On August 20, 1814, Governor Clark appointed Lisa subagent for the tribes on the Missouri River. Lisa died at Saint Louis, August 12, 1820. *TP*, 14: 786–87; Christensen et al., *Dictionary of Missouri Biography*, 493–94. Biographies: Oglesby, *Manuel Lisa*; Douglas, *Manuel Lisa*.

58. Robinson, "History of the Dakota," 2: 83–93; French, "Manuel Lisa," 4: 121–36. Lisa enjoyed considerable influence with the tribes along the Missouri River, but during the year 1813 was primarily concerned with his own business interests as a principal in the Missouri Fur Company. He was not appointed a subagent for the United States until the summer of 1814. Of course, even prior to that time keeping the Sioux in good humor furthered both the military interests of the United States and the commercial interests of Lisa's company.

59. *MPHC*, 15: 321–23; Quaife, *Askin Papers*, 2: 760–63.

60. *MPHC*, 15.322–23; McAfee, 297–99, 311; *Missouri Gazette*, October 30, 1813.

61. Forsyth to Clark, February 20, 1813, Forsyth Papers; Edwards to Forsyth, March 5, 1813, DM, 1T15; *TP*, 14: 652–4; 16: 312–5; Edwards to Forsyth, May 11, 1813, DM, 1T23.

62. Edwards to Forsyth, April 7, 1813, DM, 1T17; Edwards to Forsyth, April 8, 1813, DM, 1T18; Edwards to Forsyth, April 11, 1813, DM, 1T19.

63. Forsyth to Clark, July 20, 1813, in Forsyth Papers; Sparr, *Grundy County*, 49; *History of Grundy County*, 290, 294. Kinzie, *Wau-Bun*, 244–45, an untrustworthy source, also places Black Partridge's village on Aux Sable Creek.

64. Edwards to Forsyth, April 7, 1813; Edwards to Forsyth, April 8, 1813; Edwards to

Forsyth, April 11, 1813; *TP*, 14: 667–68; 16: 324–28; Reynolds, *Pioneer History*, 250; Forsyth to Clark, July 20, 1813, Forsyth Papers.

65. *MPHC*, 15: 339–40, 347–50, 357–58; *Weekly Register*, 4 (August 14, 1813): 390; McAfee, *History*, 317–21, 324–28; *WHC* 10: 108–11.

66. Jackson, *Black Hawk*, 68; Robinson, "South Dakota."

67. *WHC* 11: 238–42, 352–55; DM, 24S141.

68. "Claim of Thomas Forsyth," DM, 1T31; Brickey to Lindsay, December 8, 1850, in Drown, 67–70.

69. *MPHC*, 15: 391–92.

70. *MPHC*, 15: 369–69, 371–72, 422–24; *WHC* 12: 111–12. Local tradition asserted that Dickson wintered on Doty Island, but this appears to be incorrect. At least one of his surviving letters is dated "Garlic Island." *WHC* 10: 113–14, n. 1.

71. *WHC* 10: 98–99.

72. John Lawe was born in Montreal December 6, 1779. The fur trade was his primary occupation throughout his life. First settled in Green Bay 1797. Appointed lieutenant in British Indian Department and took part in the successful defense of Mackinac Island, August 4, 1814. After war remained at Green Bay, but was for a time under suspicion for having sided with the British during war. Naturalized as U.S. citizen 1821. Eventually became large landowner and richest man in Green Bay. Served as probate judge of Brown County 1824–32, and as associate judge of Brown County Court 1831. Member of Legislative Council of Wisconsin Territory 1835. Died at Green Bay February 11, 1846. Kay, "John Lawe," 64: 3–27; Irving, *Officers*, 210; *WHC* 3: 249–51, 7: 247–50, 20: 216; Martin, *History of Brown County*, 74–76, 96–98, 103.

73. Louis Grignon was born September 23, 1783. Appointed lieutenant in the British Indian Department. Naturalized U.S. citizen 1819. Resided at Green Bay, where he served as justice of the peace and coroner. Grignon and John Lawe built the first schoolhouse in Green Bay. Ellis, *WHC*: 7: 244, 19: 90; 20: 120, 125; Irving, *Officers*, 210.

74. *WHC* 11: 276, 279–81, 284–85, 292–93; Martin, *History of Brown County*, 1: 74–76.

75. Dickson to Lawe, November 14, 1813, *WHC*, 10: 98–99; December 25, 1813, *ibid.*, 11: 282; January 13, 1814, *ibid.*, 11: 283–84; January 31, 1814, *ibid.*, 11: 288–89; March 9, 1814, *ibid.*, 11: 297–99; March 15, 1814, *ibid.*, 10: 111–12.

76. Two interesting collections of Dickson's letters from Lake Winnebago were published in *WHC*: "The Lawe and Grignon Papers," 10: 90–140, and "The Dickson and Grignon Papers," 11: 271–315.

77. Esarey, *Messages and Letters*, 2: 577–78; Knopf, *Document Transcriptions*, 5: pt. 2, 237; *Missouri Gazette*, December 4, 1813; Edmunds, *Potawatomis*, 198–99.

78. *Niles Weekly Register*, 5: 410, 6: 12; *Missouri Gazette*, January 15, 1814; *TP*, 14: 727–28.

79. *WHC* 10: 101–16, 108–11, 296–97; 11: 289–94, 296–97; Dickson to Lawe, March 20, 1814, *WHC*, 10: 115–16. One plausible conjecture is that Dickson planned for the Winnebago to commit depredations for which the Potawatomi would be blamed. Edmunds, "Illinois River Potawatomi," 360.

80. Forsyth to Clark, March 31, 1814, Forsyth Papers.

81. Forsyth to Clark, May 5, 1814, Forsyth Papers; *Missouri Gazette*, July 16, 1814. Forsyth subsequently entertained friends and family with a more colorful version of the story. Reynolds, *Pioneer History*, 250–51; Robert Forsyth, DM, 22S99–103.

82. *WHC* 11: 352–55.

83. Forsyth to Clark, March 31, 1814, Forsyth Papers; *WHC* 11: 316–18, 327–29, 331–36; *Missouri Gazette*, May 7, 1814.

84. *WHC* 11: 316–24; Howard to Forsyth, July 31, 1814, DM, 1T40; Gomo and Black Partridge to Clark (undated), DM, 2M51; *Niles Weekly Register*, 5: 410, 6: 12.

85. *WHC* 11: 326–36.

86. Edwards to Forsyth, December 4, 1814, DM, 1T41; Clark to Potawatomi (undated), DM, 2M18; Black Partridge and Petchaho to Clark, March 4, 1815, DM, 2M21; LeClair to Clark, March 15, 1815, DM, 2M19; Speech of Thomas Forsyth to Potawatomi, April 7, 1815, DM, 1T45; Forsyth to Clark, April 13, 1815, Forsyth Papers; *Missouri Gazette*, April 15 and 29, 1815.

87. Wood, *Select British Documents*, 3: 273–77; McAfee, *History*, 427–30, 439; *WHC* 3: 271.

88. Wood, *Select British Documents*, 3: 277–82; McAfee, *History*, 439; *Niles Weekly Register*, 7 (November 12, 1814): 156–57, 173.

89. *MPHC*, 15: 41–44, 16: 377–79; *WHC* 11: 100–107, 127–32, 311–12, 347–51; 13: 60–63, 66–78; 84–87, 127, 135; Tohill, "Robert Dickson," 3.3: 186.

90. Tohill, "Robert Dickson," 3.3: 185–202; Weaver, "Life of Robert Dickson," 54–73; *Niles Weekly Register*, 15 (June 10, 1820): 257.

91. *WHC* 11: 347–51; *TP*, 15.262–66; Clark to Puthuff, June 20, 1817, in William Clark Papers, Kansas State Historical Society, Topeka, vol. 2: p. 26.

92. *TP*, 15: 394–96, 407–13; Stephen Hempstead, DM, 22S198.

93. *MPHC*, 23: 524–25; obituary in *Canadian Magazine and Literary Repository*, 1, no. 2 (August 1823): 192; *WHC* 20: 351–53, Dickson was almost certainly buried in the now-vanished British cemetery on the island. Cook, *Drummond Island*, 18–22.

94. *TP*, 17: 196, 253–56, 395–96.

95. Edwards to Forsyth, May 7, 1814, DM, 1T35; *TP*, 17: 121–22, 398–401, 417–18;

15: 379; President Monroe to Forsyth, April 20, 1818, DM, 1T50; Trask, *Black Hawk*, 89.

96. Forsyth, "Original Causes of the Troubles with a Party of Sauk and Fox Indians," in DM, 9T54–59; Reynolds, *Pioneer History*, 252; Wallace, *Prelude to Disaster*, 36.

97. "Genealogy" folder in Forsyth Papers. Forsyth Avenue in Saint Louis perpetuates the family name.

98. Stanley, "Indians in the War of 1812," 153, makes much the same point.

99. *WHC* 10: 213, 215.

Chapter 7. Edwards

1. *TP*, 16: 45, 243, 259–60; Edwards, *History*, 340.

2. Esarey, *Messages and Letters*, 2: 71, 91–92; *TP*, 16: 243, 256–57, 266, and n. 27; Knopf, *Document Transcriptions*, 8: 46; Edwards, *History*, 338–42; Adjutant General to Russell, August 22, 1812, and Adjutant General to Bissell, August 22, 1812 both in NA, RG 94, RAGO, Letters Sent (M 565, Roll 4, 92); Bakalis, "Ninian Edwards," 131–37.

3. *TP*, 16: 324–27; Forsyth to Clark, July 20, 1813, in Forsyth Papers, Missouri History Museum, Saint Louis.

4. *TP*, 14: 652–54, 16: 312–15.

5. Forsyth to Clark, July 20, 1813; Tanner, *Atlas*, 106.

6. Knopf, *Document Transcriptions*, 7: pt. 1, 73; *TP*, 16: 285–89.

7. Esarey, *Messages and Letters*, 2: 696–97; *TP*, 17: 430–37.

8. Knopf, *Document Transcriptions*, 7: pt. 1, 54; *TP*, 16: 285–89, 312–15.

9. *TP*, 16: 218; Edwards, *History*, 536.

10. *TP*, 16: 166–69, 258–59; Hagan, *Sac and Fox*, 43–44.

11. Knopf, *Document Transcriptions*, 6: pt. 2, 107.

12. Jackson, *Black Hawk*, 69–70; Knopf, *Document Transcriptions*, 7: pt. 1, 54, 73, 90; *TP*, 14: 641–42; *Missouri Gazette*, January 23, 1813.

13. Maurice Blondeau was a member of a family who had been early settlers of Mackinac, but who in 1798 had migrated to Missouri, where they received Spanish grants. Meriwether Lewis, who regarded Blondeau as "a very active intelligent man," brought him into American service as subagent to the Sauk and Fox tribes. He was reappointed subagent August 17, 1812, and, despite British efforts to bring him over to their side, served the United States throughout the war. He acted as interpreter at the treaties of 1815. Governor Edwards distrusted him and had a low opinion of his abilities, so after the war Blondeau was superseded as agent by Thomas Forsyth. Blondeau then went to work for the American Fur Company, but by 1821, he had settled on a farm on the

Mississippi, seven miles above Keokuk, Iowa. Blondeau apparently returned to duty as an interpreter, for in 1824 he accompanied an Indian delegation to Washington. He was still living in 1831, a genial old man, but he died before the Black Hawk War of 1832 and was buried near Burlington, Iowa. A street in Keokuk bears his name. *WHC* 20: 356–57, n. 74; Larpenteur, *Forty Years,* 5–6; *TP,* 14: 196–203, 412–15, 17: 398–402; Knopf, *Document Transcriptions,* 8: 63–64.

14. Knopf, *Document Transcriptions,* 7: pt. 1, 53, 199; *TP,* 14: 658–62.

15. Knopf, *Document Transcriptions,* 7: pt. 1, 73; *TP,* 14: 658–62, 16: 306–8, 312–15.

16. Knopf, *Document Transcriptions,* 7: pt. 1, 58–59, 176, 192; *TP,* 8: 227–28, 14: 612–14, 637–38; *Missouri Gazette,* April 3, 1813.

17. Thomas Ramsey was born in Pennsylvania but resided in Ohio when commissioned second lieutenant January 27, 1809. Promoted first lieutenant January 31, 1810, and captain November 30, 1812. Ramsey was honorably discharged June 15, 1815, but reinstated December 2, 1815. He died of wounds received in a duel with Captain Wylie Martin on "Bloody Island," opposite Saint Louis, on August 6, 1818. Ninian Edwards commended Ramsey as "a most industrious and useful officer." Heitman, *Historical Register,* 814; Knopf, *Document Transcriptions,* 7: pt. 1, 47; Steward, *Duels,* 36–37; DM, 22S175. Carter mistakenly gives the captain's name as William H. Ramsey in *TP,* 16: 490.

18. *TP,* 14: 601–2, 646–48; Adjutant General to Anderson, October 9, 1812, in NA, RG 94, RAGO, "Letters Sent" (M 565, Roll 4, 170); Adjutant General to Anderson, October 12, 1812, *ibid.,* (175–76); Adjutant General to Irwin, October 12, 1812, *ibid.,* (176); Adjutant General to Anderson, November 13, 1812, *ibid.,* (236).

19. Philips to [Anderson?], December 22, 1812, in NA, RAGO, "Letters Received" (M 566, Roll 9, 436); Philips: Garrison Order, November 27, 1812, *ibid.,* (437); Anderson to Adjutant General, *ibid.,* (M 566, Roll 6, 146–9); Anderson to Irwin, November 12, 1812, *ibid.,* (151–2); Anderson to Unidentified, November 30, 1812, *ibid.,* (154–7); Anderson to [Adjutant General?], December 24, 1812, *ibid.,* (165); Philips to Secretary of War, December 6, 1812, in NA, RG 107, LRSW (M 221, Roll 55, 9579); Knopf, *Document Transcriptions,* 6: pt. 1, 125, pt. 4, 137, 139, 7: pt. 1, 102; *TP,* 14: 651–54, 657–58; Esarey, *Messages and Letters,* 2: 378–80, 2: 458–60; Adjutant General to Anderson, March 10, 1813, in NA, RG 94, RAGO, "Letters Sent" (M 565, Roll 4, 294); Adjutant General to Anderson, March 13, 1813, *ibid.,* (296); Adjutant General to Bissell, March 25, 1813, *ibid.,* (304); Bissell to Adjutant General, April 7, 1813, "Letters Received" (M 566, Roll 19, 277); Adjutant General to Irwin, April 20, 1813, *ibid.,* "Letters Sent" (M 565, Roll 4, 319); "Returns from U.S. Military Posts," Fort Massac, March 1813, NA, RG 94, RAGO (M 617, Roll 1524); Caldwell, "Fort Massac," 44: 47–60.

20. Philips to Unidentified, May 2, 1813, in NA, RG 94, RAGO, "Letters Received" (M 566, Roll 29, 849–50).

21. Knopf, *Document Transcriptions*, 6: pt. 4, 151–3; *TP*, 14: 614–22, 631, 16: 289–95.

22. Edwards, *History*, 343–45; Edwards to Morrison, December 30, 1812, in Ninian Edwards Papers, SC 447, Letters 1812–33, Folder 1, Abraham Lincoln Presidential Library, Springfield; *TP*, 16: 285–89, 388–89.

23. 2 U.S. Stat. 804; Washburne, *Edwards Papers*, 97; *TP*, 16: 316–18. The services of a company organized by Willis Hargrave were tendered to the governor but had to be declined because only three additional companies of Rangers had been authorized. For the names of Hargrave's volunteers, see *RAGI*, 9: 328; Stevens, "Illinois," 185–86.

24. The present Monroe, Michigan.

25. McAfee, *History*, 200–235; *TP*, 16: 324–27.

26. Knopf, *Document Transcriptions*, 7: pt. 1, 90–91; *TP*, 14: 643–44.

27. *Missouri Gazette*, March 6, 1813; *ASP: Indian Affairs*, 1: 845–6.

28. On the Cache Massacre, see *National Intelligencer*, April 20, 1813, in Knopf, *Document Transcriptions*, 5: pt. 2, 84; 7: pt. 1, 129–30; *Weekly Register*, 4 (April 24, 1813): 135; *Missouri Gazette*, February 20, 1813; Atherton et al., *Pulaski County*, 1: 436–39; Reynolds, *Pioneer History*, 408; Reynolds, *My Own Times*, 92; Perrin, *History of Alexander*, 284, 354, 472, 535–37; Ferguson, "Cache River Massacre," 14–20; Bonnell, *Illinois Ozarks*, 93–94; [Wall], *Moyers' Brief History*, 29–30; Stevens, "Illinois," 144–46; Condon, *Pioneer Sketches*, 6–7, 10. The first names of Mrs. Clark and Mrs. Phillips are not recorded. Shaver's first name is in some accounts given as John and in others as Philip. John Reynolds met him long afterwards and the scars left on his forehead by the tomahawk were still clearly visible. He is said to have died many years later in Alexander County.

29. Ferguson, "Cache River Massacre;" Adams, *History*, 4: 23–31.

30. The muster roll for Fox's detachment is printed in *RAGI*, 9: 337 and Stevens, "Illinois," 188. For Conyers's Fort and the troops stationed there after the Cache River Massacre, see Atherton, *Pulaski County*, 1: 436–39.

31. For Hamlet Ferguson see page 220, note 55.

32. Unfortunately the meager records of Ferguson's expedition are limited to muster rolls and the pension application of Captain Prichard: "Militia Muster Roll" RG 100.013, Records of the Illinois Territory, Illinois State Archives (field officers); Felty, "Territorial Militia," 141–42; NA, RG 94, RAGO, Compiled Military Service Records, "Colonel Ferguson's, subsequently Major Stephenson's, Command," Boxes 299–303, especially envelopes 1, 2, 6, 13, 30, 280, 639, 640, and 866; NA, War of 1812 Pension Application Files, "John Pritchard," OWI

5163. (Although the file is indexed as "Pritchard," the captain himself signed his name without a "t.")

33. Knopf, *Document Transcriptions*, 7: pt. 1, 90–91, 129–30, 148, 157; *TP*, 16: 303–6; *Missouri Gazette*, March 20, 1813.

34. *Western Sun*, February 20, 1813. On Fort Allison, see Lewis, *Fort Allison*; Smith, *History*, 1: 497; White, "Historical Notes," 10: 368–69; Tipton, *Papers*, 1: 245; Buck, *Illinois in 1818*, 66; *Combined History of Edwards, Lawrence, and Wabash Counties*, 70–71, 269–70, 342. The garrison of Fort Allison suffered human casualties as well: On unknown dates a white man named Stockwell was killed while returning from Fort LaMotte and a free black man named Anderson was killed in the neighborhood of Fort Allison itself. On another occasion, a party of thirteen Rangers riding from Fort LaMotte was ambushed within a half-mile of Fort Allison, but none of them was hurt. *Combined History of Edwards, Lawrence, and Wabash Counties*, 71.

35. Thomas Posey to Secretary of War, March 4, 1812, in Esarey, *Messages and Letters*, 2: 377–78; Recollections of Polly Kellogg (1886), printed in *Mattoon Journal-Gazette*, May 17, 1915; Perrin, *History of Crawford*, 34 (preserving recollections of Leonard Cullom). Some thoughtful local historians have questioned whether the skirmish described by Governor Posey is in fact the same event recalled by Kellogg and Cullom. Allowing, however, for the passage of years before the Kellogg and Cullom recollections were recorded, the events described are strikingly similar, are both dated to the spring of 1813, and are both located in the neighborhood of Fort LaMotte. That there were two such events, unremarked by anybody at the time or afterwards, seems unlikely. Posey places the skirmish "six miles above" the fort, Mrs. Kellogg "up Sugar Creek" on a "big pond" and Cullom at a place later called "Africa Point" south and east of the fort along the Wabash. Although local historians have dubbed this event the "Battle of Africa Point," Cullom's description of the location cannot be reconciled with the other two accounts, and the most likely site of the skirmish would be six or so miles above Palestine on Sugar Creek. At the time, much of the area was flooded, making the identity of the "pond" a matter of conjecture.

36. The Grand Rapids were located where Indiana's White River empties into the Wabash, near the present Mt. Carmel, Illinois. *Illinois in 1837*, 33.

37. Esarey, *Messages and Letters*, 2: 381–82; *Western Sun*, March 6, 1813, 3; *Missouri Gazette*, May 1, 1813; Lewis, *Fort Allison*, 3.

38. *Liberty Hall* [Cincinnati], March 30, 1813, transcribed in DM, 20S166–68; *Missouri Gazette*, March 20, 1813; *History of Madison County*, 81; Reynolds, *Pioneer History*, 406; Callary, *Place Names*, 234.

39. *TP*, 16: 303–5; Johnson, *Recollections*, 14–15; Perrin, *History of Jefferson*, 121–23;

Wall, *History of Jefferson*, 199–200, 213–14; *History of Jefferson County, Illinois* (Mount Vernon, Illinois, Continental Historical Bureau, 1962), C-9, D-2, M-17 through M-20, W-8 through W-9; Dearinger, "New Geography," *Outdoor Illinois*, 15.

40. Crest, "Mustering Oak," 162–64; Ferguson, "Battle of the Long Ridge."

41. *Reporter*, May 22, 1813, 3; *TP*, 16: 319–20, 323.

42. *Missouri Gazette*, March 20, 1813; Forsyth to Clark, July 20, 1813, Forsyth Papers; Babcock, *Forty Years*, 141–42; Reynolds, *My Own Times*, 92; Reynolds, *Pioneer History*, 408; Stevens, "Illinois," 144–45; Dearinger, "Sketches," 81–83.

43. *TP*, 16: 303–5; *Missouri Gazette*, March 20, 1813; Reynolds, *My Own Times*, 93; Reynolds, *Pioneer History*, 408; *Combined History*, 59; *Edwards County*, 1: 5, 10; *History of Wayne*, 41–42. The three county histories all make the same mistake of dating the Boultinghouse murder after the war. For another version of the origin of the prairie's name, see Flower, *History*, 63. Boultinghouse Prairie later became better known as the English Prairie. Woods, *Two Years Residence*, 117.

44. Daniel Boultinghouse was born in 1775, probably in Pennsylvania. In 1800 he was living in Scioto County, Ohio, but subsequently moved to what is now White County, Illinois. He was appointed captain in the Fourth Regiment of militia June 21, 1814, and his company has been said, probably incorrectly, to have been the last one called out during the war. He was appointed a justice of the peace for White County, January 11, 1816. Captain Boultinghouse is said to have died in 1823 and to have been buried in the Ralls Cemetery, Phillips Township. Carter, *TP*, 17: 649, 654; *Adjutant General's Report*, 9: 342–43; personal communications from Lecta Hortin, Carmi, Illinois, and Alec Purdy, El Segundo, California.

45. Woolard, "Reminiscences," 42–48; Narrative of Boultinghouse in *Carmi Times*, as "Boy Killed, Stock Stolen, So Pioneers Slew Five Indians," January 2, 1998; *History of Wayne*, 41–42.

46. John Lively was enrolled as a private in Captain William Boon's company of mounted volunteers and an entry on the muster roll states: "killed by Indians, 22 March 1813." The name John Lively also appears on the roll of Captain Jacob Short's company of mounted rangers "called into the actual service of the United States . . . from the 27th day of February, 1813, to the 31st day of May, 1813, inclusive." If this is the same man, and not another of the same name, Lively must have transferred to Boon's company subsequent to his enrollment. Possibly he had moved from the area in which Short's company was raised to the one in which Boon commanded. *RAGI*, 9: 320, 335; Stevens, "Illinois," 178, 191; NA, RG 94, RAGO, Compiled Military Service Records: War of 1812, "Colonel

Ferguson's, subsequently Major Stephenson's, Command, Illinois Militia,"
Envelope 490; Philbrick, *Pope's Digest*, 2: 409–10.

47. *Missouri Gazette*, March 27, 1813; Knopf, *Document Transcriptions*, 7: pt. 1, 194–
95; Edwards, *History*, 346–47; Forsyth to Clark, July 20, 1813; Reynolds, *My Own
Times*, 93; *History of Washington County*, 16–17; Brinkman, *This is Washington
County*, 52–53; *Washington County, Illinois: 1979 History*, 5–6; *History of St. Clair
County*, 327–8.

48. William Boon, a relative of Daniel Boone, first settled near Kaskaskia in 1798,
moved to Degognia in 1806, and the next year to Sand Ridge. Appointed captain
in First Regiment of militia, June 30, 1810, and of a company of mounted
riflemen on March 6, 1813. Justice of the peace, December 21, 1809 (resigned
August 8, 1810), and again March 25, 1816. Represented Jackson County as
senator in the Second and Third General Assemblies (1820–23). Boon died
near Grand Tower, Illinois, in 1836. *TP*, 17: 629, 633, 634 n. 49, 646, 655; Pease,
Election Returns, 188 n. 1, 207; *History of Jackson County*, 32, 33–34; Husband,
Old Brownsville, 13.

49. Boon, "Sketches," 54; *History of Jackson County*, 34.

50. The fort was located in section 26, T7S, R4E, a quarter mile southeast of
Liberty Methodist Church, along Prairie Creek, on the eastern side of the
present railroad embankment. It was a rectangular blockhouse, with portals
on three sides and a heavy barred door on the south. The building collapsed
sometime between 1911 and 1918. Barbrey's grave marker is in the tiny fort
cemetery on the opposite side of the embankment. Sneed, *Ghost Towns*, 18–20;
"Old Timer Recalls Playing in Frank's Fort," *Daily American* [West Frankfort],
September 21, 1955; "Little Is Known about Seven Jordan Brothers," *ibid.*;
personal communication from Max H. Lude.

51. The muster roll of Captain Leonard White's company of militia lists a private
David Barberry who was killed by Indians on May 2, 1813. His official service
record in the National Archives contains an affidavit from his widow "Nancy
Barbre" stating that her husband had been "one of the spies guarding the mail
under Captain Leonard White." In the file are several different spellings of the
surname, while Nancy herself signed with a mark. Jordan brothers' fort was
one of the stops along the mail route between Shawneetown and Kaskaskia,
so it is not unlikely that William and David are the same man, but, if so, the
discrepancies in the date of death and the first name remain to be explained.
James Jordan was enrolled as a corporal in the company of Captain William
McHenry. NA, RG 94, RAGO, Compiled Military Service Records, "Colonel
Ferguson's, Subsequently Major Stephenson's, Command, Illinois Militia,"
envelopes 49 and 425.

52. *Missouri Gazette*, May 15 and 22, 1813; Reynolds, *Pioneer History*, 406; *History of Gallatin*, 339; Hubbs, *Pioneer Folks*, 164–65; Lude, *Historic Shawnee Trails*, p. 4–1–5. According to Lude, the third person who accompanied Jordan and Barbrey outside the fort was Jordan's sister Ester, Barbrey's wife.

53. *Missouri Gazette*, May 22, 1813. The blockhouse was probably Gasaway's, Karnes's, or Brown's, but which one is uncertain. Bonnell, *Saline County*, 228. The reference may also be to a blockhouse rumored to have stood northeast of Raleigh, in NE ¼, Section 6, T8S, R7E. James, *History of Raleigh*, 3; *Land Atlas*, 17.

54. The stockade at New Haven was built by Jonathan Boone, a brother of Daniel Boone. *History of Gallatin*, 114–5.

55. Edwards to Shelby, April 20, 1813, DM, 5X32; Edwards to Forsyth, May 11, 1813, ibid., 1T23; Forsyth to Clark, July 20, 1813, Forsyth Papers; *Missouri Gazette*, May 22, 1813; Woods, *Two Years*, 111; *History of White County*, 451, 452–53; Narrative of Boultinghouse (1938), in *Carmi Times*, as "Man Wounded by Indians Rode 50 Miles to Get Help," January 8, 1998. The latter narrative dates the Davis-Seabolt killings to March 30, but Edwards and Forsyth both say April, which seems more likely if Gomo's party was moving eastward from Jordan Brothers' Fort to the unnamed blockhouse and then on to the house on the Little Wabash.

56. Edwards, *History*, 346–47. Which companies Edwards called out is not completely clear. On March 27 at least ten captains, and perhaps others, were leading militia companies on active duty. Mounted companies: Captains Jacob Short, William Boon, Owen Evans, and William McHenry. Infantry: Captains William Jones, Nathan Chambers, Lewis Barker, Leonard White, and Lieutenant Daniel G. Moore. By water: Captain Nicholas Jarrot. Also in service by April 17 were mounted companies commanded by Captains Samuel Whiteside and James B. Moore. Probably they were already in the field on March 27, but no record of that fact has been found. In addition to the militia companies, Captain William B. Whiteside's company of U.S. Rangers was also in the field. NA, RG 94, RAGO, Compiled Military Service Records: War of 1812, "Colonel Ferguson's, subsequently Major Stephenson's, Command, Illinois Militia," Boxes 299–303; *RAGI*, 9: 334–36, 337.

57. *Missouri Gazette*, May 1, 1813.

58. Knopf, *Document Transcriptions*, 7: pt. 1, 90–91, 100, 129–30, 176; *TP*, 14: 637–38, 657–58, 16: 305–6; Edwards to Shelby, April 3, 1813, DM, 5X28; *TP*, 14: 657–58; *Missouri Gazette*, January 30, April 17, and May 8, 1813; *Weekly Register*, 4 (March 27, 1813): 67.

59. Wood, *Select British Documents*, 2: 3–5, 3: 250–52; *MPHC*, 15: 248–50, 258–59; *TP*, 14: 652–54, 16: 316; Tanner, *Atlas*, 106, 117.

60. *Missouri Gazette*, May 1 and 22, 1813.

61. *Missouri Gazette*, April 24 and May 1, 1813.

62. Edwards to Shelby, April 20, 1813, DM, 5X32; *TP*, 16: 319–20, 428, 17: 230; *Missouri Gazette*, April 24, 1813; *Combined History of Randolph*, 83. According to the *Combined History*, a Mr. Cox resided in sections 17 and 18, T6S, R2W. The original federal plat map drawn in 1826 shows the road between Kaskaskia and Lusk's Ferry crossing Beaucoup Creek on the claim of "Thos. Cox" near the place where the modern Highway 152 crosses the creek today. The discrepancy in the first name makes the identification uncertain, but there is no indication of another Cox family in that area at this early date, so in all probability Thomas was Robert's heir. See original federal plat map in RS 953.012, Illinois State Archives, Springfield.

63. "Extract of a letter ... dated Vincennes, 27th April," in *Reporter*, May 11, 1813, 2: "[T]he Indians are continually hovering around our frontiers. In the course of the last week there were six men killed and three or four wounded, on the lower side of the Wabash a few miles above Vincennes; and they are every week doing mischief of some kind or other, and when pursued, hide in the swamps so it is impracticable to overtake them, altho' we have a number of Rangers on our frontiers."

64. *History of Gallatin*, 23.

65. Musgrave, *Handbook*, 156–57.

66. Edwards to Forsyth, March 5, 1813, DM, 1T15; Edwards to Forsyth, April 7, 1813, DM, 1T17; Edwards to Forsyth, April 8, 1813, DM, 1T18; Edwards to Forsyth, April 11, 1813, DM, 1T9; Edwards to Forsyth, April 11, 1813, DM, 1T20; Edwards to Forsyth, May 6, 1813, DM, 1T21; Edwards to Forsyth, May 6, 1813, DM, 1T22; Edwards to Forsyth, May 11, 1813, DM, 1T23; *TP*, 16: 324–27.

67. The muster rolls of these three companies are printed in *RAGI*, 9: 334–36, 337; Stevens, "Illinois," 190–92.

68. Nicholas Jarrot was born in France but in 1790 fled to the United States to escape the terrors of the revolution. Within a few years of his arrival in the United States Jarrot made his way to Cahokia, where he traded successfully with the Indians and quickly became one of the leading citizens of the village. He served as major in the Saint Clair County militia, and was later appointed aid-de-camp to the governor, October 29, 1810, and captain of a company of volunteer light infantry, March 18, 1813. Jarrot held numerous judicial offices: justice of the peace, justice of quarter sessions, and judge of the county commissioners' court. He died in December, 1820, from exposure suffered while building a mill dam on Cahokia Creek. He was buried in the old cemetery alongside the Church of the Holy Family in Cahokia. The brick house he began to build in 1799 is now

owned by the state and is one of the notable landmarks of Cahokia. *History of St. Clair County*, 50, 64, 70, 80, 131–32, 433–34, 437; *TP*, 17: 622, 634; Corrigan and Temple, "Volunteer Officers," 237; Baldwin, *Echoes*, 57–60, 64, 68.

69. *TP*, 16: 331–35.

70. *RAGI*, 9: 336, 338; Stevens, "Illinois," 193–94. Because Jones and Moore were called into service the day after Stephenson's battalion left Fort Russell, it is unlikely that either company was a part of the expedition.

71. Edwards to Forsyth, May 21, 1813, DM, 1T25; Knopf, *Document Transcriptions*, 7: pt. 2, 130; *TP*, 16: 331–33.

72. Smith, *Grand Village*, 81–89; *History of McLean County*, 192, 211; *TP*, 16: 312–15.

73. *TP*, 16: 331–35; Smith, *Grand Village*, 82–84.

74. *TP*, 16: 333–35.

75. Edwards to Shelby, May 8, 1813, DM, 5X35.

76. *TP*, 14: 656–57; Knopf, *Document Transcriptions*, 8: 142.

77. *TP*, 16: 331–33, 343–44; Edwards to Howard, June 16, 1813, Edwards Papers, Box 1, Folder 3, Chicago History Museum; Edwards to Forsyth, June 22 1813, DM, 1T29; *Missouri Gazette*, June 19, 1813.

78. For an assessment of Edwards as a war leader, see Holden, "Governor Ninian Edwards," 1–8.

Chapter 8. Howard

1. *BDUSC*, 1284; Christensen et al., *Dictionary*, 406–7; *DAB*, vol. 5, pt. 1, 274–75; *Missouri Gazette*, April 3 and April 17, 1813; *Reporter*, March 27, 1813, 3; *TP*, 14: 374, 612–14, 637–39, 656–57; Knopf, *Document Transcriptions*, 7: pt. 1, 176; Howard to Unidentified, May 28, 1813, NA, RG 94, RAGO, "Letters Received" (M 566, Roll 25, 71–2); *ASP: Military Affairs*, 1: 409.

2. Bissell to Howard, July 1, 1813, NA, RG 94, RAGO, "Letters Received" (M 566, Roll 19, 281–83); Howard to Secretary of War, July 4, 1813, *ibid.* (280); Bissell to Secretary of War, March 1, 1813, *ibid.* (M 566, Roll 16, 275).

3. *National Intelligencer*, May 29, 1813, in Knopf, *Document Transcripts*, 5: pt. 2, 122.

4. *MPHC*, 15: 321–23.

5. McAfee, *History*, 291–96; Esarey, *Messages and Letters*, 2: 480–82.

6. *The Western Sun*, July 17, 1813; *TP*, 14: 679–80; Esarey, *Messages and Letters*, 2: 274–84; Dillon, *History*, 524–25; Pence, "Indian History," 23: 217–28; McAfee, *History*, 313–14.

7. Knopf, *Document Transcriptions*, 7: pt. 3, 7, 37–38; Esarey, *Messages and Letters*, 2: 497–99; McAfee, *History*, 314–15; *Western Sun*, July 24, 1813.

8. Esarey, *Messages and Letters*, 2: 450, 484–85; Knopf, *Document Transcriptions*, 7: pt. 3, 7.

9. McAfee, *History*, 308–13, 337–38; *TP*, 16: 321–22; Esarey, *Messages and Letters*, 2: 468, 484–85, 487–92.

10. Richard Mentor Johnson was born in Kentucky, October 17, 1780, served in the Kentucky legislature (1804–6, 1819, and 1850), and in U.S. Congress as a representative (1807–19) and U.S. senator (1819–29). Author of the laws abolishing imprisonment for debt, in Kentucky and the United States. Vice president of the United States (1837–41), to date the only man ever elected to that office by the Senate. Johnson died at Frankfort, Kentucky, on November 19, 1850, and is buried in Frankfort Cemetery. Johnson County, Illinois was named for him. Biography: Meyer, *Life and Times*; Schlesinger, *Age of Jackson*, 140–41; *BDUSC*, 1341. A substantial literature exists on the death of Tecumseh, but Johnson's claim was supported by Shabbona, who was fighting alongside Tecumseh when he died and who later met Johnson in Washington. Matson, *Memories of Shaubena*, 27–28. A competing claim to the honor was made by a man with an Illinois connection: Eli Short, a soldier of Kentucky who in later life settled as a Baptist minister in Steeleville, Illinois. Allen, *Legends and Lore*, 112–14.

11. *Missouri Gazette*, July 10 and July 17, 1813; *TP*, 16: 347–48; Reynolds to Sevier, July 10, 1813, DM 11DD160; Johnson to Clark, July 25, 1813, William Clark Papers, Records of the Superintendency of Indian Affairs, Saint Louis, Kansas Historical Society, vol. 2, p. 7. A somewhat different account of the July 4 fight is given in Houck, *History*, 3: 111.

12. *Missouri Gazette*, July 17, 1813.

13. John Campbell of Virginia, commissioned as ensign in First Infantry Regiment June 13, 1808, promoted second lieutenant, December 31, 1809, first lieutenant January 20, 1813, and captain May 2, 1814, honorably discharged June 15, 1815. Heitman, *Historical Register*, 1: 278; *TP*, 14: 563–69, 614–22.

14. *Missouri Gazette*, July 24, 1813; *Reporter*, August 28, 1813, 2.

15. Reynolds, *My Own Times*, 91–93; Reynolds, "Agricultural Resources" 152–53.

16. *Missouri Gazette*, July 24, 1813; *Reporter*, August 28, 1813; Reynolds, *My Own Times*, 98–99. The *Missouri Gazette*, dates the original encounter to July 17 and Reynolds suggests that the second battle was two days later. O'Neal's military service record shows him as killed on July 18, which is probably correct. NA, RG 94, RAGO, "Compiled Military Service Records," William O'Neal, United States Rangers. Reynolds erroneously dated the fight to August 1814.

17. Brinkerhoff, *History*, 119–20; Geo. A. Ogle & Co., *Plat Book of Marion County*, 67.

18. *TP*, 14: 614–22, 631.

19. *TP*, 16: 347–48, 350, 364; *Missouri Gazette*, August 28, 1813.

20. *Missouri Gazette*, October 9, 1813, Knopf, *Document Transcriptions*, 7: pt. 3, 66–67.

21. Ibid., 7: pt. 3, 3, 65–6; *TP*, 16: 362–63.

22. Howard to Pope, July 24, 1813, and Pope to Judy, August 19, 1813, in Illinois State Archives, Record Series 100.001, "Records of the Illinois Territory: Correspondence," 43, 45; Reynolds, *Pioneer History*, 320; Stevens, "Illinois," 147.

23. Robert Desha, a native of Pennsylvania, was residing in Tennessee when he was commissioned captain in the 24th U.S. Infantry, March 12, 1812. Throughout much of the war his company was on detached service along the Mississippi. Desha was honorably discharged June 15, 1815, and died February 8, 1849. Heitman, *Historical Register*, 1: 369; *Missouri Gazette*, August 7, 1813.

24. Both Boone's crossing place and the location of the skirmish are open to question. Telling the story to Lyman Draper nearly forty years later, Boone said that he had started out from Cap au Gris, and a contemporary issue of the *Missouri Gazette* (August 21, 1813) says that his detachment was attacked between the Mississippi and Illinois Rivers about Fort Mason. That Boone and his men would have crossed the river at Cap au Gris into Calhoun County seems likely. There was a small fort there on the Missouri side, a little east of the present Troy, which took its name from a rock formation on the Illinois side. There Boone and his men could get boats, while crossing higher up would have been more difficult, since Fort Mason had been abandoned. Boone would therefore have crossed into Calhoun County. That a two day's ride took them up the ridge to the latitude of Fort Mason, somewhere in the present Pike County, seems quite probable. For the fort opposite Cap au Gris, see "Missouriana," 285.

25. *Missouri Gazette*, August 7 and 21, 1813; Nathan Boone, DM, 6S256–57; Hurt, *Nathan Boone*, 94–96; Gregg, "War of 1812," 33: 195–96.

26. Howard's expedition is reasonably well documented. There are valuable accounts in the *Missouri Gazette* of September 11 and 18, October 2, 9, 16, and 23, and November 6, 1813. Howard's letters to Secretary of War Armstrong dated September 1 and 3, 1813, discuss his plans for the expedition. Knopf, *Document Transcriptions*, 7: pt. 3, 65–66; *TP*, 16: 364. Howard's letter to Clark, written September 16, 1813, as his army was crossing the Mississippi, appears in the *Missouri Gazette* of October 2, 1813, and is reprinted in Stevens, "Illinois," 149–50. The composition of Howard's "handsom little Army" is discussed in Clark to Secretary of War, September 12, 1813, in *TP*, 14: 697–98. Howard's final report is printed in *TP*, 16: 370–73 and Stevens, "Illinois," 151–53. Long afterwards, John S. Brickey, who rode with the Missouri Volunteers, gave his account of the expedition in a long and interesting letter printed in Drown, *Drown's Record*, 67–70. Lyman Draper's notes of the reminiscences of Major

Nathan Boone are in DM, 6S257–58. The recollections of John Reynolds, who rode as a sergeant in a company of U.S. Rangers, are contained in his books *My Own Times*, 93–97, and *Pioneer History*, 408–9. The brief recollections of Francis LeClair, in DM, 24S141, add a few details. The account of the expedition that Major John Gibson gave Lyman Draper in 1868 was no more than a fanciful tall tale. The old soldier was evidently amusing himself at Draper's expense. DM, 15C96–97, 107. Local historian Nehemiah Matson's account of the expedition relied in part on the reminiscences of Colonel George Davenport, who served as a noncommissioned officer among the regulars. Although as is usually the case with Matson, it can be difficult to tell where Matson's informant breaks off and the historian's own imagination begins, the account is interesting and may have some value. Matson, *French and Indians*, 236–46. John Shaw also claimed to have accompanied Howard's expedition, and his brief account is at *WHC* 2: 212. On Shaw, see page 302, note 30.

27. Alexander McNair was born in Mifflin County, Pennsylvania, May 5, 1775. He moved to Saint Louis in 1804, thereafter holding a number of public offices: judge of the court of common pleas, sheriff, trustee of Saint Louis, and U.S. marshal. During the war, McNair served as adjutant and inspector general of the Missouri territorial militia. Afterwards he served as registrar of the land office and as a member of the convention that drafted the Missouri state constitution. McNair was elected the first governor of the state of Missouri in 1820 and served until 1824. After his term of office, McNair was appointed U.S. agent for the Osage Indians, but he died of influenza on March 18, 1826. He is buried in Calvary Cemetery, Saint Louis. Stevens, "Alexander McNair."

28. William Christy, born January 10, 1764, in Carlisle, Pennsylvania, but moved to Kentucky at the age of fifteen. Served in the Indian wars under Saint Clair and Anthony Wayne. He settled in Saint Louis in 1804, and under the territorial government served as judge, auditor, and registrar of the land office. On April 19, 1813, he was appointed assistant deputy quartermaster general in federal service, with the rank of captain. He was honorably discharged June 15, 1815. Christy later served as the first public auditor of the State of Missouri, 1820–21. He was one of the founders of North Saint Louis, and gave many of its streets names that persist to this day, although when North Saint Louis was absorbed into the larger city in 1841, the street originally named for Christy himself was renamed Lucas to avoid confusion with an existing street. Major Christy died April 3, 1837. Houck, *History*, 3: 49, 266; Heitman, *Historical Register*, 300; Magnan, *Streets*, 50, 195.

29. For the blockhouse, see page 218, note 35. For the Piasa Bird petroglyph, see Voelker, "Piasa"; Temple, "Piasa Bird."

30. Stevens, "Illinois," 147. Stevens gives Journey's rank as captain, but this is an error. Although Journey had served as a captain in the territorial militia, his rank in federal service was first lieutenant in Captain Jacob Short's company of U.S. Rangers. Heitman, *Historical Register*, 585; *ASP: Military Affairs*, 1: 421; *TP*, 16: 300–302. No doubt Short was also part of the expedition.

31. Pierre André was a Frenchman of Vincennes. Although a captain in the territorial militia, he fought at the battle of Tippecanoe as a private in Captain Toussaint Dubois's company of spies. Commissioned captain of Rangers, April 12, 1813. Placed in temporary command of U.S. troops in Indiana and eastern Illinois territories, September 26, 1814. Honorably discharged, June 15, 1815. After André was discharged from federal service, Governor Thomas Posey quickly commissioned him captain of a company of Indiana mounted volunteers. Russell to Gregg, September 26, 1814, in Lasselle Papers, Box 5, Indiana State Library, Indianapolis; Heitman, *Historical Register*, 165; Pirtle, *Tippecanoe*, 112, 133; Woollen et al., *Executive Journal*, 143, 155, 185, 193, 232. Perrin, *History of Crawford*, 32, amusingly anglicizes the captain's name to Pierce Andrew.

32. *Western Sun*, August 14, 1813, 3, and August 21, 1813, 3; *TP*, 16: 370–73. The Indiana Rangers were ordered to Fort Russell, but they may have marched with Howard, as indicated by a letter Lieutenant Hyacinth Lasselle wrote from Portage des Sioux, dated September 10. H. Lasselle to Mme. Lasselle, September 10, 1813, Lasselle Family Papers, Box 4, Indiana State Library.

33. Robert Carter Nicholas, born in Virginia, at an early age moved to Kentucky, where his father served as the state's attorney general. Appointed captain in Seventh Infantry Regiment May 3, 1808, major in Third Infantry Regiment September 3, 1810, lieutenant colonel in First Infantry Regiment, August 15, 1812, and colonel of 19th Infantry Regiment September 4, 1814. Resigned from army April 20, 1819, and died in May 1836. He should not be confused with his cousin of the same name (1793–1857), also an army officer, who was afterwards a U.S. senator from the State of Louisiana. Heitman, *Historical Register*, 746; Van Meter, *Genealogies*, 69–72.

34. Reynolds, *My Own Time*, 94. The Salt Prairie, six miles wide and about a mile long, lay on the Mississippi River side of the peninsula, between the bluffs and Salt Prairie Slough, in the area later known as Coles Grove and now as Gilead. Lammy, *Calhoun County*, 2; Peck, *Gazetteer*, 286.

35. Stevens, "Illinois," 149–50; *TP*, 16: 370–73; *Missouri Gazette*, November 6, 1813; Reynolds, *My Own Times*, 94.

36. During Howard's absence in Kentucky, acting governor Frederick Bates, doubting his ability to defend Missouri with the troops at his disposal, had

sought aid from the Osage of the Upper Missouri. The Osage were allies of the United States, but more important, they were the mortal enemies of the tribes allied with the British, especially the Sioux and the Potawatomi. News that a horde of Indians was moving down the Missouri to "defend" the territory caused an uproar among the citizens, and when Howard returned to Saint Louis almost his first act was to countermand Bates's order. The Osage were already on the move and reacted with resentment. It required the considerable diplomatic skills of the subagent, Pierre Chouteau, to soothe the tribe's wounded feelings. *TP*, 14: 637–40, 671–75.

37. *TP*, 16: 285–89, 305–6.

38. Nicholas Boilvin was a native of France (or, according to another version, of Canada). According to one story, during the American Revolution his father had befriended a wounded American army surgeon held prisoner at Quebec, and many years later the surgeon reciprocated his kindness by procuring the son an appointment as Indian agent. Whatever the truth of that story, in 1806 Boilvin was appointed U.S. subagent to the Sauk on Rock River but in 1811 was commissioned as agent at Prairie du Chien, with jurisdiction over the tribes of the Mississippi. Boilvin served as Indian agent for the rest of his life. He also held appointments under the territories of Illinois and later of Michigan as justice of the peace and after the war continued to reside at Prairie du Chien, administering a rough form of frontier justice. Boilvin died May 18, 1827, at Saint Louis and was buried there. Scanlan, "Boilvin," 27: 145–69; *WHC* 2: 115–16, 122, 126, 150, 11: 247–49, n.; *TP*, 13: 488–89, 14: 401–2, 443–44, 622, 649; *History of Crawford and Richland*, 150 n., 281, 325, 361–62.

39. *Missouri Gazette*, May 29, 1813, October 2, 1813; Knopf, *Document Transcriptions*, 7: pt. 2, 2; *TP*, 14: 697–98, 16: 312–15, 322, 370–73; *MPHC*, 15: 273–74; Stevens, "Illinois," 149–51, 165.

40. Drown, *Drown's Record*, 67–70. Reynolds, *My Own Times*, 94, describes the same scene.

41. Stevens, "Illinois," 149–50; *Missouri Gazette*, October 2, 1813; *TP*, 16: 370–73.

42. Christy's Creek, where Howard's army turned east toward Peoria, has not been identified. Stevens, "Illinois," 62–63, prints a historical map that shows Howard's route turning southeast just north of the present Nauvoo, on what authority he does not explain. Reynolds, *My Own Times*, 95, implies that Howard turned east at a place called "The Two Rivers," possibly near the present Warsaw, Illinois, where the Des Moines then flowed into the Mississippi. Alternatively, what are now the North River and the South River in Marion County, Missouri, which flow into the Mississippi south of the present Quincy, Illinois, were once known as Two Rivers. H. S. Tanner, "Illinois and Missouri" (map, c. 1823), D.H. Vance,

"Map of the State of Missouri and Territory of Arkansas, Compiled from the Latest Authorities" (A. Finley, Philadelphia, c. 1826).

43. This encounter is mentioned only by Howard and Reynolds. Howard says that at Christy's Creek his army was "opposite" the Sauk. Possibly he meant that the Indians were already camped on the west side of the Mississippi; Reynolds gives no hint of any such separation. *TP*, 16: 370–73; Reynolds, *My Own Times*, 95.

44. Across from the present Havana, Illinois.

45. Keokuk was born at Saukenuk (now Rock Island, Illinois), about 1790. Despite the manner in which he rose to prominence, Keokuk became leader of the peace party among the Sauk and was opposed to Black Hawk. In the 1820s, he led the portion of the tribe that consented to move into Iowa in accordance with the 1804 treaty of Saint Louis, although he initially resisted U.S. pressure to cede the tribe's lands west of the Mississippi. Keokuk kept his followers neutral during the Black Hawk War of 1832. U.S. officials proclaimed Keokuk "civil chief" of the Sauk and Fox, and dealt with him in negotiations in 1836, 1837, and 1842 that ended in the tribes' sale of their remaining 12,000,000 acres of land in Iowa. In 1845, Keokuk led the migration to the new home of the Sauk in east-central Kansas, but the land was suitable for neither agriculture nor hunting and the tribe did not flourish. Keokuk died in Kansas in 1848. In 1883 his remains were reinterred in the city park of Keokuk, Iowa. Hodge, *Handbook*, 1: 673–74; *ANB*, 12: 613.

46. Jackson, *Black Hawk*, 72–73. One modern retelling of the story attributes the alarm that resulted in Keokuk's elevation to the approach of a scouting detachment led by Nathan Boone while Howard's army was building the fort at Peoria. Hagan, *Sac and Fox*, 56–58. Such an account is not implausible, but it seems to be contradicted by Black Hawk's own statement that the council was called when the American force was seen "going towards Peoria." Jackson, *Black Hawk*, 72.

47. *TP*, 16: 370–73; *Missouri Gazette*, November 6, 1813.

48. DM, 1T31.

49. Matson, *French and Indians*, 241–43.

50. *Missouri Gazette*, October 16, 1813; *TP*, 16: 370–73; Nathan Boone, DM, 6 S 258; Matson, *French and Indians*, 241–44. Matson's vividly written accounts must always be read with caution, but he received this story from Davenport, an eyewitness, and it contains nothing that is inherently improbable or flatly contradicted by other information.

51. Reynolds, *My Own Times*, 95; Drown, *Drown's Record*, 67–70.

52. Reynolds, *My Own Times*, 95–96; *TP*, 16: 370–73; *Missouri Gazette*, November 6, 1813; Reynolds, *My Own Times*, 95–96; Drown, *Drown's Record*, 67–70; Nathan Boone, DM, 6S257.

53. Ballance, *History of Peoria*, 40–42. Ballance's estimate of the fort's overall dimensions has been criticized as too small. McCulloch, *History of Peoria*, 1: 51.

54. *TP*, 16: 370–73. Despite Howard's opinion, a military engineer who viewed Fort Clark three years later was very critical of both its location and its design. "Stephen H. Long's Plan" 47: 417–21.

55. *TP*, 16: 370–73; Reynolds, *My Own Times*, 96.

56. On the rapids, see *Illinois in 1837*, 34.

57. Matson, *French and Indians*, 237–39, says that this was the village of a chief named Comas, but no contemporary mention of such a chief has been found.

58. *Ibid.*, 237–41; Bradsby, *History of Bureau County*, 226, 243; *ASP: Military Affairs*, 1: 421.

59. *TP*, 16: 370–73; *Missouri Gazette*, November 6, 1813; Nathan Boone, DM 6S257; Shaw, "Shaw's Narrative," *WHC* 2: 212. The Sauk had informed the British that Howard intended to march on Prairie du Chien by way of the Rock River. *WHC* 11: 283.

60. This village was five miles above (south) the mouth of the Iroquois River. Forsyth to Clark, July 20, 1813, Thomas Forsyth Papers, Missouri History Museum, Saint Louis; Tanner, *Atlas*, 106.

61. *Missouri Gazette*, October 23, 1813; *TP*, 16: 370–73. What appears to be a fragment of General Howard's written order to André's company has survived in the Lasselle Family Papers, Box 4, dated by the archivist to "1813–1814."

62. Frederick Shoults of Franklin County, Indiana, before the war an officer of the territorial militia, was appointed captain of Rangers May 20, 1813. He was honorably discharged on June 15, 1815. In May 1816 Shoults was commissioned a justice of the peace for Knox County. Heitman, *Historical Register*, 1: 884; *ASP: Military Affairs*, 1: 421; Esarey, *Messages and Letters*, 570–72; Woollen et al., *Executive Journal*, 180, 185, 245.

63. *Western Sun*, October 9, 1813, 3; *Missouri Gazette*, October 23, 1813; *Combined History of Edwards*, 71.

64. Knopf, *Document Transcriptions*, 7: pt. 3, 23–24; *Missouri Gazette*, November 20, 1813; Gregg, "War of 1812," 33: 200–202; Jackson, "Old Fort Madison," 57–62. The date on which Fort Madison was evacuated is unknown. War Department records of the event have not been found, although an early author who claimed to have seen them gave the date as September 3. That date seems unlikely to be correct. If Hamilton had left Fort Madison on that date, his boats would certainly have met Howard on his march up the Mississippi, but Howard does not mention any such meeting. Moreover, the *Missouri Gazette* did not report the evacuation until its issue of November 10, 1813, when it described Saint Louis as being agitated by news of the abandonment of Fort Madison eight or ten days earlier.

65. Stevens, "Illinois," 150–51, 165; Gregg, "War of 1812," 33: 198–200; Temple, *Indian Villages*, 106; Hagan, *Sac and Fox*, 58.

66. McAfee, *History*, 386–96; Cleaves, *Old Tippecanoe*, 197–205; Edmunds, *Potawatomis*, 197–99.

67. Knopf, *Document Transcriptions*, 5: pt. 2, 237; Esarey, *Messages and Letters*, 2: 573–81; Edmunds, *Potawatomis*, 198–99; McAfee, *History*, 400.

68. *Missouri Gazette*, January 15, 1814; *Niles Weekly Register*, 6 (March 6, 1814): 12; *TP*, 14: 727–28; *Reporter*, March 5, 1814, 2; "Minutes of a Council," January 2, 1814, NA, LRSW (M 221, Roll 51, 5932–34); Jackson, *Black Hawk*, 75–77; Edmunds, *Potawatomis*, 201.

Chapter 9. Clark

1. *ASP: Military Affairs*, 1: 387; Knopf, *Document Transcriptions*, 8: 142–43.

2. Knopf, *Document Transcriptions*, 8: 160, 169.

3. Cleaves, *Old Tippecanoe*, 214.

4. Esarey, *Messages and Letters*, 2: 610–15; *TP*, 14: 724.

5. Two recent biographies of Clark are Jones, *William Clark*, and Foley, *Wilderness Journey*.

6. *TP*, 14: 108–10, 443.

7. Gregg, "War of 1812," 33: 326–28.

8. *TP*, 14: 738–40, 744–48; Adjutant General to Harrison, April 3, 1814, NA, RG 94, RAGO, "Letters Sent" (M 565, Roll 4, 452); Washburne, *Edwards Papers*, 108; The Western Sun [Vincennes], February 9, 1814.

9. 3 U.S. Stat. 98; Washburne, *Edwards Papers*, 110–11.

10. John Rector had served in the Revolution under George Rogers Clark. He was killed by Indians in 1805 while surveying land north of the present city of Eldorado. *History of Gallatin*, 243; Bonnell, *Saline County*, 32, 293; Hamm, *Soldiers*, 197. The slain surveyor has sometimes been assumed to have been one of the nine Rector brothers who played a prominent part in Illinois and Missouri Territories during and immediately after the War of 1812, but this cannot be correct. As a soldier of the Revolution, this John Rector belonged to an older generation, and there was besides among the brothers another "John Rector" who began practicing law in Cahokia and Kaskaskia after John the surveyor had been killed. Francis S. Philbrick, *Laws of Indiana Territory*, cclxxxi, n. 91; Reynolds, *Pioneer History*, 360.

11. *Missouri Gazette*, March 12, 1814; *TP*, 16: 397–99, 401–2, 17: 192–94; Hall, *Letters*, 205–9. Whether Rector Creek and Rector Township in Saline County take their name from John Rector or Nelson Rector is disputed: Hall, 208, says that this is the stream along which Nelson was ambushed and that it takes its

name from him; *History of Gallatin*, 243, attributes the name to John's earlier
death nearby. Callary, *Place Names*, 292–93, accepts the latter explanation.

12. Little is recorded about the early life of Leonard White, although from the fact
of his owning real estate in Berkeley County, Virginia [now West Virginia], a
connection with that county may be presumed. He had reached what is now
Gallatin County, Illinois, by 1808. He served as government agent at the Salines
from about 1812 until about 1834. Under the territorial government White was
appointed justice of the peace, February 2, 1810; captain in Third Regiment
of militia, August 3, 1810; captain in Fourth Regiment, January 10, 1812; judge
of court of common pleas for Gallatin County, February 8, 1813; paymaster of
Fourth Regiment, February 12, 1814; major, March 12, 1814; judge of county
court of Gallatin County, December 24, 1814, and January 10, 1816; colonel
of Fourth Regiment, September 25, 1816; brigadier general of state militia,
December 16, 1817. In 1818 he represented Gallatin County in the convention
that drafted the first state constitution. After statehood, White served as clerk
of both the Gallatin County Court and the Circuit Court. In 1833 he was elected
a trustee of the Village of Equality, and from 1838 to 1841 served as president of
the board of trustees. General White died in January 1843. His burial place is
unknown, but was probably near the marked grave of his wife in the Equality
village cemetery. Whether White County was named for General Leonard
White or for Colonel Isaac White, killed at the battle of Tippecanoe, is an
unresolved question. Gallatin County, Illinois, Court Records, 49 (120–21);
Smith, "Salines," 249; *TP*, 16: 434; 17: 512, 522, 552 n., 631, 634, 638, 646, 648, 650,
654, 657 n.; *History of Gallatin*, 43–44, 123; Musgrave, *Handbook*, 24, 108–9;
Estate of Leonard White, Gallatin County Probate Records, Office of Circuit
Clerk, Shawneetown, Box 100, File 43; Miner, Cemeteries, 12; Callary, Place
Name, 373–74.

13. *Missouri Gazette*, March 12, 1814; *TP*, 16: 401–2; *WHC* 11: 320–24.

14. *TP*, 17: 648.

15. *Niles Weekly Register*, 6: 113–14 (April 16, 1814).

16. Washburne, *Edwards Papers*, 111–12, 113–14.

17. *TP*, 14: 737 n., 746–48, 759–60, 16: 406.

18. *TP*, 14: 750. There is nothing in the surviving papers of President Madison to
prove directly that the order originated with the president, but the inference is
suggested by (1) the language of Armstrong's letter to Howard, (2) Armstrong's
abrupt change of course, and (3) the fact that Bond was now taking his concerns
directly to the president.

19. Washburne, *Edwards Papers*, 111–12.

20. Howard seems to have been used as a pawn in Secretary Armstrong's campaign

to oust Harrison from command. Unable to fire such a popular and successful general, who still had the confidence of the president, Armstrong sought to provoke Harrison into resigning by communicating directly with the general's subordinates. Although Harrison refrained from resigning on this occasion, he would resign soon afterwards over an order Armstrong issued directly to Major A. H. Holmes in connection with the Mackinac expedition. Cleaves, *Old Tippecanoe*, 221–24.

21. *TP*, 14: 762, 16: 413–14.

22. *TP*, 14: 746–48, 16: 350, 364, 422–24; Clark to Howard, May 5, 1814, in NA, RG 107, LRSW (M 221, Roll 62, 5544).

23. See, for example, *TP*, 13: 172–74.

24. Joseph Perkins of Louisiana, commissioned ensign in the 24th Infantry Regiment, July 2, 1812, promoted second lieutenant, January 22, 1813, and promoted to first lieutenant August 15, 1813. Honorably discharged, June 15, 1815. According to early settler Stephen Hempstead, Perkins joined the Missouri Fur Company after the war, but when the company failed, he went to Kentucky, where he died. Hempstead described Perkins as "a worthy, amiable man." Heitman, *Historical Register*, 1: 784; DM, 22S197.

25. Clark to Howard, May 5, 1814; *TP*, 14: 784–86; "Autobiography, 1826," Zachary Taylor Papers, Series 1, Library of Congress; Taylor to Perkins, District Orders, April 29, 1814, NA, RG 94, RAGO, "Letters Received" (M 566, Roll 35, 538); Anderson to Secretary of War, May 19, 1814, *ibid.* 535–36; Anderson to Secretary of War, September 10, 1814, *ibid.* 551–53; Hamilton, *Zachary Taylor: Soldier*, 54–56.

26. Clark to Howard, May 5 and May 8, 1814, NA, RG 107, LRSW (M 221, Roll 62, 5546); *Missouri Gazette*, May 7, 1814; *Reporter*, July 2, 1814, 2.

27. *TP*, 16: 154–57, 316; *Louisiana Gazette*, April 25, 1812; *Missouri Gazette*, August 21, 1813; *WHC* 2: 119–20; Scanlan, *Prairie du Chien*, 166–80.

28. Louis Bibeau traded for many years at Peoria and elsewhere along the Illinois River. After the war he was employed by the American Fur Company. He died at his trading house opposite the mouth of Bureau Creek about 1822. Hubbard, *Autobiography*, 29, 47, 52, 59, 117–18, 136–37; Franke, *French Peoria*, 105.

29. Scanlan, *Boilvin Letters*, Letters 29 and 31; *WHC* 11: 289–92; Forsyth to Clark, March 31 and May 5, 1814, in Thomas Forsyth Papers.

30. Francis Dease was born at Niagara, August 10, 1786, and spent most of his life in the Indian trade. During the War of 1812 he served as captain of "Dease's Mississippi Volunteers" (Prairie du Chien militia) and took part in the capture of Fort Shelby, for which he was mentioned in dispatches. Appointed captain in the Indian Department September 2, 1814. Dease died on the Red River, not far from Winnipeg, in what is now Manitoba, on August 15, 1865. He never

married. A nephew left this description of Captain Dease: "He was about five feet ten inches in height, strongly built, with broad shoulders, remarkably strong, and possessing a kind and pleasing countenance." *WHC* 9: 297–98 and n., 467, 13: 89–90; Irving, *Officers*, 97–98, 211.

31. MPHC, 15: 496–97, 564–65; *TP*, 14: 768–69; *Missouri Gazette*, June 18, 1814; McAfee, *History*, 439; Bulger, "Events at Prairie du Chien," *WHC* 13: 1–9.

32. *TP*, 14: 768–9, 784–86; "Indian Speech," July 21, 1814, NA, RG 107, LRSW (M 221, Roll 60, 3871); *Missouri Gazette*, June 18, 1814, and July 2, 1814; McAfee, *History*, 440; Scanlan, *Prairie du Chien*, 117, 120.

33. *WHC* 11: 260–63, 324–25, 12: 117.

34. *TP*, 14: 725–27.

35. *TP*, 14: 768–69, 775–77; *Missouri Gazette*, July 16, 1814.

36. It seems highly probable that this man was John C. Sullivan, a native of Kentucky who in 1814 was serving as collector of U.S. Revenue for Missouri Territory. He subsequently served in the last territorial legislature and the convention that drafted the first Missouri state constitution. As principal deputy surveyor to William Rector, Sullivan was credited with establishing the northern boundary of Missouri. Billon, *Annals*, 52, 128; Houck, *History of Missouri*, 3: 8, 249, 255; *TP*, 15: 170.

37. Frederick Yeizer was a Saint Louis merchant. Billon, *Annals*, 122.

38. George Rogers Clark to William Clark, July 30, 1814, in William Clark Papers, Box 12, Folder 6, Missouri History Museum; *Missouri Gazette*, June 18, 1814, and July 2, 1814; Foley, *Wilderness Journey*, 199–200.

39. *TP*, 14:786–87; Foley, *Wilderness Journey*, 200. Stevens, "Illinois," 158, 162, unfairly blames Governor Edwards. In fact, Edwards had nothing to do with the expedition to Prairie du Chien, aside from having, like all western statesmen, frequently expressed his opinion that the place should be seized and fortified.

40. *TP*, 14: 772–73, 16: 422–24.

41. Fort Cap au Gris, also known as Fort Independence, was built in the summer of 1813, on the west bank of the river, about three miles east of the future site of Winfield, Missouri. At one time there was a small French settlement in the vicinity, but the settlers were run off by the Indians during the war. Some of these families found shelter within the walls of the fort, where Captain David Musick of the Missouri Rangers commanded. Because of its exposed position, frequent clashes took place in the vicinity of Fort Cap au Gris, which was finally burned by Indians on June 8, 1815, after it had been evacuated to escape high water. "Missouriana," 285; *Missouri Gazette*, July 16, 1814, May 20, 1815, and June 10, 1815; Peck, *Gazetteer*, 172. On the Cap au Gris rock formation, see Underwood, "New Geography," 14, 22.

42. Caldwell, "Fort Massac," 59; *TP*, 16: 422–24.

43. Simon Owens of Virginia was commissioned ensign in Eighth Infantry, January 14, 1799, and honorably discharged as first lieutenant June 15, 1800. Recommissioned as second lieutenant, February 16, 1801, promoted to first lieutenant December 15, 1803, captain August 18, 1808, and major January 31, 1814. Convicted by court-martial for conduct unbecoming an officer and a gentleman while commanding Fort Clark and dismissed from the service, October 2, 1814. Heitman, *Historical Register*, 1: 764; NA, RG 153, Records of the Judge Advocate General (Army), Court Martial Case Files, N 14.

44. *Missouri Gazette*, April 30, 1814; *TP*, 14: 446–49.

45. David Musick (1763–1837) was born in Albemarle County, Virginia, in 1763. During the Revolution he fought as a teenaged soldier in the Battle of Guilford Courthouse. The family reached what is now Missouri in 1794. Musick served in the territorial legislature, but in June 1813 he resigned to accept appointment as a captain of U.S. Rangers. He died in 1837 and was buried in Fee Fee Cemetery, Bridgton, Missouri. *Missouri Gazette*, June 12, 1813; *ASP: Military Affairs*, vol. 1, p. 421; Heitman, *Historical Register*, 1: 739; Billon, *Annals*, 44, 47, 51, 71; Musick, *Genealogy*, 12, 231–32.

46. *TP*, 14: 764–68, 16: 422–24; *Missouri Gazette*, May 21, 1814; James Long, DM, 24S153; Uel Musick, DM, 24S185.

47. Forsyth to Clark, May 5, 1814, in Forsyth Papers; *Missouri Gazette*, May 7, 1814.

48. On Clark's letter, Armstrong wrote a note: "I cannot believe in the wisdom of establishing a post 600 miles in the enemy's Country. Once established it must be supported & at an enormous expence." *TP*, 14: 763. The decision was not left to Armstrong, however. On Armstrong's note President Madison wrote a note of his own: "The apparent objections to the proposed establishment of a post so distant are very strong. Much weight however is due to the concurring opinions of Govr. Clarke and Genl. Howard, both men of judgment, and possessed of many advantages for a correct exercise of it in such a case." "Note on a note of the Secretary of War," June 19, 1814, in James Madison Papers, Series 3, p. 91, Library of Congress.

49. *TP*, 14: 763, 16: 422–24, 444.

50. *TP*, 14: 772–73, 16: 422–24; *Missouri Gazette*, May 21, 1814; *Reporter*, June 4, 1814, 3.

51. Joseph Philips, born October 6, 1784, in what is now Kentucky, practiced law in Tennessee before enlisting in the 2d artillery as a captain, March 12, 1812. During his service, Philips commanded both Fort Massac and Fort Clark. Honorably discharged June 15, 1815, because of a reduction in forces, but remained in service to command Fort Clark until May 31, 1816. Commissioned secretary of Illinois

Territory, December 17, 1816 and served until November 1818, part of the time as acting governor. Chosen by the Illinois General Assembly as first chief justice of the Supreme Court of Illinois, October 9, 1818. Resigned July 4, 1822, in order to run as proslavery candidate for governor. After defeat for that office by Edward Coles, Philips returned to Tennessee, where he was afterwards president of People's Bank, Nashville, and a successful farmer in Rutherford County. Died July 25, 1857, in Rutherford County, Tennessee, and buried in the Old Murfreesboro Cemetery. Heitman, *Historical Register*, 1: 788; *TP*, 17: 453–54; Pease, *Illinois Election Returns*, 14–18; Alvord, *Governor Edward Coles*, 50, 318, 321–22; Speer, *Sketches*, 27; widow's pension file for Dorothy Philips, War of 1812 Pension Applications, NA, RG 15; 1850 U.S. Census, Rutherford County, Tennessee, Fort Camp District, 340. On Philips's desire for a transfer, see Anderson to Adjutant General, March 25, and April 25, 1814, NA, RG 94, RAGO, "Letters Received" (M 566, Roll 35, 518 and 526–28); Philips to Unidentified, April 26, 1814, *ibid.*, Roll 54, 729.

52. *TP*, 16: 444–46.

53. For Indian depredations in Missouri, see Gregg, "War of 1812," 33: 328–29.

54. *Western Sun*, April 23, 1814, 3; and April 30, 1814, 3.

55. *Ibid.*, April 30, 1814, 3, May 7, 1814, 3, and May 21, 1814, 3.

56. The blockhouse stood on the east fork of Wood River, NW ¼ Section 10, T5N, R9W, at or near the present Moore Park. Wilson and Kaegy, *Forts*, 160–61; U.S. General Land Office, "Receiver's General and Individual Ledgers (Credit System), RS 952.036, 23: 150, Illinois State Archives, Springfield.

57. For contemporary references to the Wood River Massacre, see *Missouri Gazette*, July 16 and 23, 1814; *TP*, 16: 444–46. Although they differ in some details, a number of later accounts trace directly or indirectly to members of the Moore family: Lippincott, "Wood River Massacre"; Richmond, "Wood River Massacre"; Norton, *Centennial History*, 1: 38–40. A different version, purporting to derive from Mrs. Reagan's brother, one Samuel Thomas, in which Mrs. Reagan's maiden name is given as Thomas, rather than Moore, and in which Mr. Thomas plays the part played in other accounts by William Moore, is found in *Madison County School Journal* 1, no. 2 (October 1908), 5–6. Other accounts of varying degrees of trustworthiness are in *History of Madison County*, 81–82, 418; Reynolds, *My Own Times*, 97–98; "Madison County in the Days of the Indians and Pioneers," *Greenville Advocate*, July 4, 1889. The location of the massacre was in the SW 1/4, Section 5, T5N, R9W, now part of Alton.

58. *WHC* 9: 320–25; *TP*, 16: 446–48.

59. The creek is identified as the Sangamon in *Missouri Gazette*, July 23, 1814; Norton, *Centennial History*, 1: 40; *History of Madison County*, 82; and Reynolds,

My Own Times, 98. The sources that identify the stream as Indian Creek, (which is said to have taken its name from the incident), are Lippincott, "Wood River Massacre," 509; Richmond, "Wood River Massacre," 94; *History of Morgan County*, 283; and Vogel, *Indian Place Names*, 41. The *Missouri Gazette* account is the earliest and was based on information received from Major William B. Whiteside, very soon after the Rangers' return.

60. See page 000, above.

61. Vaughn Cemetery is in section 24, T5N, R9W, just off Route 111, in Wood River Township.

Chapter 10. Headwinds

1. *MPHC*, 15: 396–97, 424–25, 496–97; Wood, *Select British Documents*, 3: 266–67; Tanner, *Atlas*, 119.

2. Wood, *Select British Documents*, 1: 444–47; *WHC* 12: 108–10, 13: 271–73; *MPHC*, 15: 616–19.

3. Robert McDouall was born in March 1774, at Stranraer, Scotland. Purchased commissions as ensign and lieutenant, 1797. Took part in British expedition to Egypt, 1801, and promoted to captain 1804. Saw active service at Copenhagen, 1807, and Martinique, 1809. Transferred to Canada with his battalion in 1810. Appointed aide-de-camp to Sir George Prevost, 1812. Present at battles of Sackets Harbor and Stoney Creek, 1813. Promoted to major and brevet lieutenant colonel, same year. Appointed to command at Mackinac, late 1813. After war, conducted British evacuation of Mackinac and established new base at Drummond's Island. Commanded there until June 1816, when he returned to Scotland. Companion to Order of Bath, 1817. Never again called to active duty, but promoted to colonel, 1830, and major general, 1841. Died Stranraer, November 15, 1848. *Dictionary of Canadian Biography*, 7: 556–57.

4. Thomas Gummersall Anderson was born at Sorel, Quebec, November 12, 1779. Engaged in the fur trade at Mackinac, Prairie du Chien, and along the upper Mississippi between 1800 and 1814. Appointed captain of Mississippi volunteers, July 1814. Mentioned in dispatches for his part in capture of Fort Shelby, July 19, 1814. Appointed captain in Indian Department, September 1, 1814. Acting commander of Fort McKay, Prairie du Chien, August 10 to November 30, 1814. After war, served as Indian agent and superintendent at Drummond Island and elsewhere, and as chief superintendent, 1845–58. Died at Port Hope, Ontario, February 10, 1875. *Dictionary of Canadian Biography*, 10: 11–13; Irving, *Officers*, 96–97, 210; Anderson, "Personal Narrative.": Anderson's long life enabled him to rewrite the history of his military service without fear of contradiction, and

his "Personal Narrative" seduced both Lyman Draper and the author of the biographical notice in *Dictionary of Canadian Biography*.

5. Jean Joseph Rolette was born in Canada about 1787. Although originally educated for the church, by 1804 he had settled at Prairie du Chien, where he began trading successfully with the Indians. Rolette was at Mackinac when the Americans captured Prairie du Chien and led a company of volunteers in the expedition to reclaim it. He was mentioned in dispatches for his part in the capture of Fort Shelby. Immediately after capture of the fort, Rolette resigned his commission and undertook the contract to supply the new British post with provisions. After the war, Rolette continued to live at Prairie du Chien, where his wartime support for the British caused him some initial difficulties. From 1820 to 1836 Rolette was in charge of the northwestern operations of John Jacob Astor's American Fur Company. He died at Prairie du Chien December 1, 1842, and was buried in the Catholic cemetery. Irving, *Officers*, 97; *WHC* 2: 173–75, 5: 275, 9: 293–94, 465–67.

6. James Keating was born in Templeshort Parish, County Wexford, Ireland, in 1786. Enlisted in Royal Artillery, 1804. Awarded silver medal with clasp for service at Martinique. As sergeant of the Royal Artillery, mentioned in dispatches for service at Fort Shelby and Credit Island. Promoted to lieutenant March 1, 1815. Fort adjutant at Saint Joseph, Drummond's Island, Amherstburg, and Penetanguishene, at which place he was promoted to captain and adjutant in charge of garrison. Died there in November 1849. Quaife, "Forgotten Hero," 23: 652–63; Irving, *Officers*, 96–97; *WHC* 9: 206, n., 13: 19–20.

7. Michel Brisbois Jr., son of a French trader and a Winnebago woman, was born about 1790, probably at Prairie du Chien. Commissioned lieutenant in British Indian Department, June 5, 1814, and took part in capture of Fort Shelby and battle of Credit Island. After the war, his extensive knowledge of Indian languages led Governor William Clark to employ him as an interpreter. Brisbois was shot and killed by an unknown hand while hunting near Saint Louis in 1820. *WHC* 9: 284; Irving, *Officers*, 210. Irving gives the date of his death as 1839, evidently confusing the lieutenant with his father, who bore the same name.

8. On the British capture of Prairie du Chien, see *WHC* 2: 124, 3: 270–79, 9: 262–81, 9: 295–99, 11: 254–70; *TP*, 14: 784–86; Yeizer to Clark, July 26, 1814, NA, RG 107, LRSW (M 221, Roll 60, 3939); Scanlan, *Boilvin Letters*, Letter 32; *Missouri Gazette*, August 6 and 13, 1814; Draper, "Traditions and Recollections," 295–96. Sadly disappointing is Anderson, "Personal Narrative." Anderson played an important supporting role in the capture of Fort Shelby. He deserved part of the credit for the victory, but telling the story in his old age, Anderson was

inclined to award himself *all* of it, rewriting history to place himself in overall command of the expedition and reducing McKay to a mere drunken figurehead. His account is contrary to others and must be read with skepticism. Useful secondary accounts of the campaign are in McAfee, *History*, 439–43; *History of Crawford and Richland Counties*, 147–54; Kellogg, *British Regime*, 316–20.

9. William McKay, born 1772, probably in the Mohawk Valley of New York. Entered service of Northwest Company, 1790. Carried secret dispatches for General Isaac Brock, 1812. Appointed captain, October 2, 1812. Brevetted major of Michigan Fencibles, April 15, 1814. Temporary rank of lieutenant colonel, July 1814. Deputy superintendent and agent of Indian Department, December 25, 1814. Superintendent of Indian Affairs, Drummond Island, 1820–28, and superintendent of Indian Department for District of Montreal, 1830–32. Died of cholera at Montreal, August 18, 1832, and buried in Mount Royal Cemetery. *Dictionary of Canadian Biography*, 6: 464–66; Irving, *Officers*, 96, 114, 209.

10. *WHC* 3: 271, 11: 260–63.

11. Irving, *Officers*, 97, 99; *WHC* 3: 271–72.

12. *WHC* 11: 260–70.

13. *Missouri Gazette*, July 2, 1814.

14. *WHC* 11: 256; *Missouri Gazette*, July 2, 1814.

15. *Missouri Gazette*, August 6, 1814; *WHC* 11: 263–70.

16. Although Perkins was the only regular officer present, he was assisted by Missouri militia officers Captain George Kennerly and Lieutenant James Kennerly, who remained behind when their companies departed downriver. The two were brothers, cousins of Governor William Clark's wife.

17. *TP*, 14: 784–85; Anderson to Secretary of War, September 21, 1814, in NA, RG 94, RAGO, LRSW (M 566, Roll 54, 542–45); Perkins to Anderson, December 21, 1814, *ibid.* (56–57); *WHC* 3: 276, 278–79, 11: 263–70. The names of the men surrendered by Lieutenant Perkins are printed in Scanlan, *Prairie du Chien*, 226, n. 8.

18. *WHC* 11: 257, 263–70; *TP*, 14: 784–86; *Missouri Gazette*, August 6, 1814.

19. McAfee, *History*, 442: "However incredible it may appear to our readers, we can assure them that these terms were honorably fulfilled on the part of colonel M'Kay!!! Though a *British* officer, and acting in concert *as usual* with a great body of Indians, yet he would not suffer them, however anxious they might be, to murder a single prisoner, nor to maltreat them in any manner!! With a degree of firmness and humanity, which would have been honorable to a Kentuckian, he restrained the savages and fulfilled his engagements! With pleasure we record the solitary instance." Kellogg, *British Regime*, 320: "McKay's conduct at the capture of Fort Shelby greatly redounds to his credit, as a soldier and a Briton." Stevens,

"Illinois," 162, praised the "magnanimous" conduct of the British commander, under the misimpression that the British commander had been Robert Dickson.

20. McKay to McDouall, July 27, 1814. In his self-aggrandizing memoir written about 1870, Thomas Anderson claimed that McKay was drunk throughout the expedition and siege, and that real management of the British force fell on the captains. "Personal Narrative," 194–96. There is no indication of this in contemporary records, and indeed at the time Anderson praised "our undaunted and able commander, Lieut. Col. McKay, to whose judicious management the inhabitants of this place, and the Indian tribes on the Mississippi, acknowledge a happy and easy deliverance from an enemy that absolute necessity compelled them for a moment to countenance": (Anderson, "Journal at Fort McKay," 230–32). Fifty-six years later, Anderson concluded that McKay had in fact been a drunken fool. Nevertheless, about 1882 Rolette's daughter related a similar story to Lyman Draper (*WHC* 9: 465–66), and the one thing B. W. Brisbois, a boy in Prairie du Chien at the time of the siege, remembered hearing about McKay was that he was "fond of brandy." *WHC* 9: 296. All contemporary references to McKay are positive. *WHC* 13: 118–23.

21. All told, including troops, contractors, boatmen, women, and children, Campbell's party probably numbered a little over 130 souls.

22. Jonathan Riggs of Missouri served as cornet in Captain James Callaway's company of Missouri militia. He was commissioned ensign, U.S. Rangers, March 26, 1814, and brevetted second lieutenant as of July 13, 1814. Honorably discharged June 15, 1815. Died February 20, 1834. Heitman, *Historical Register*, 1: 831; Wesley, "James Callaway," 5: 77–78, 81.

23. Stephen Rector was born April 4, 1771, in Fauquier County, Virginia. Moved to Kaskaskia with the family, 1806. Commissioned third lieutenant of U.S. Rangers, August 1, 1813, serving in Captain Moore's company. Brevetted second lieutenant as of July 13, 1814. Honorably discharged, June 15, 1815. After the war, he moved to Saint Louis, where he was appointed deputy surveyor under his brother William in 1818. Third lieutenant, Saint Louis Guards, 1819. Unsuccessful candidate for Missouri legislature, July 1822. Died July 15, 1826. Heitman, *Historical Register*, 1: 820; *ASP: Military Affairs*, 1: 421; King, *Rector Records*, 8; Shinn, *Pioneers*, 389, 391; Billon, *Annals*, 99; Reynolds, *Pioneer History*, 353.

24. On the battle of Campbell's Island, see *TP*, 16: 444–46, 17: 3–8, 10–11; *WHC* 11: 263–70, 12: 114–15; *Missouri Gazette*, July 30, 1814; Jackson, *Black Hawk*, 77–80; Reynolds, *My Own Times*, 99–101. Useful secondary accounts are McAfee, *History*, 442–43; *The Past and Present of Rock Island*, 114–15; Meese, *Campbell's Island*; *Historic Rock Island*, 17–21; Hauberg, "Rock Island," 7: 287–90.

25. *Missouri Gazette*, May 14, 1814; *WHC* 11: 331–36; Stevens, "Illinois," 165.

26. *WHC* 10: 115–16, 11: 279–82, 300–302.

27. *WHC* 11: 318–19; *Missouri Gazette*, June 4, 1814; Temple, *Indian Villages*, 106–7.

28. *TP*, 17: 5–7; Forsyth to Secretary of War, November 15, 1814, in NA, RG 107, LRSW (M 221, Roll 61, 5018).

29. *TP*, 17: 5–7; Jackson, *Black Hawk*, 77–78; *Missouri Gazette*, May 28, 1814; Reynolds, *My Own Times*, 99.

30. The date of the battle of Campbell's Island has been disputed. The official reports of both Campbell and Riggs give the date as July 21, 1814. The 21st is also the date given for the battle in Dr. Stewart's letter of resignation as surgeon's mate and in Campbell's application for an invalid pension. Stewart to Russell, February 9, 1815, in NA, RG 94, RAGO, LRSW (M 566, Roll 81, 683–84); Stewart to Secretary of War, April 14, 1815, *ibid.*, (685–87). Nevertheless, historian William A. Meese argued forcefully that Campbell and Riggs, and by implication Stewart, were all mistaken, and that the battle had actually been fought on July 19. That date is also given by Reynolds's editor and has been accepted by some secondary sources influenced by Meese. See Meese, *Campbell's Island*, 20–23; Reynolds, *Pioneer History*, 409; *Historic Rock Island*, 18; Hauberg, "Rock Island," 287. Campbell's report says that the little fleet was twenty miles from Rock River on July 18, and Meese argues that Campbell would not have tarried near Rock Island for three days, and would have noted it in his report had he done so. Campbell, however, was moving against the current and his report indicates that he was averaging about twelve miles a day. To have covered the twenty-four miles from his first encounter with the Sauk on July 18 to Four Mile Camp could easily have consumed two days, and Campbell also spent a day in council with Black Hawk. As for the supposed omission from the report, Campbell's phrase "We lay at four mile camp above Rock River until the morning of the 21st" is nothing if not elastic. Meese also seems to have been unaware of a never-completed report of Major Campbell, captured by the Sauk, given by them to the British, and preserved in the Canadian archives. That report, written at Four Mile Camp, is dated July 20, 1814, the day *after* Meese believed the battle to have been fought. *WHC* 12: 115. Finally, Yeizer's report says that a skiff he sent out witnessed the battle in progress on the afternoon of July 21. Yeizer to Clark, July 26, 1814. In short, Meese's objections to the date of July 21 must be overruled. Nevertheless, the incorrect date remains inscribed on the monument.

31. *WHC* 11: 263–70; Jackson, *Black Hawk*, 77–78; Forsyth to Secretary of War, November 15, 1814.

32. *WHC* 13: 54–60.

33. *TP*, 17: 5–7; *Historic Rock Island County*, 19–21. Campbell's gunboat was beached very near to the present monument.

34. Abraham (also Abram) Stewart of Massachusetts, appointed garrison surgeon's mate, March 6, 1806. Wounded in action, July 21, 1814. Resigned, March 20, 1816. On July 27, 1816, Dr. Stewart married Emily Ayres and they afterwards lived in Saint Louis, Saint Charles, Pike, and Marion counties, Missouri. Dr. Stewart died at Hannibal, Missouri, on October 11, 1834. Heitman, *Historical Register*, 1: 924; Meese, "Campbell's Island," 26; NA, War of 1812 Pension Application Files, "Abram Stewart," OWI 24827, Widow's Certificate 18173.

35. *TP*, 5–8; *WHC* 11: 263–70; Jackson, *Black Hawk*, 78.

36. At what point in the battle Campbell received his wounds is unclear. In his report, Campbell does not mention his own wounds, and Howard, who was not there, reported that Campbell was shot through the body and then in the arm immediately after he went aboard Rector's boat. *TP*, 17: 3–5. Reynolds, who also was not present, but who met the boats as they returned to Saint Louis, describes Campbell lying wounded on the bottom of his own boat during the first phase of the battle. Reynolds, *My Own Times*, 100.

37. John Weaver of Kentucky, commissioned ensign in Seventh Infantry, February 10, 1812, promoted third lieutenant March 12, 1813, second lieutenant October 11, 1813, and first lieutenant May 15, 1814. Honorably discharged June 15, 1815. Died August 29, 1821. Heitman, *Historical Register*, 1: 1011.

38. *TP*, 17: 5–8; Reynolds, *My Own Times*, 100.

39. *TP*, 17: 7–8; Jackson, *Black Hawk*, 78–79; *Missouri Gazette*, July 30, 1814.

40. *TP*, 17: 5–8; *WHC* 11: 263–70; Jackson, *Black Hawk*, 79.

41. Yeizer to Clark, July 26, 1814; Scanlan, *Boilvin Letters*, 32; *Missouri Gazette*, July 30 and August 6, 1814.

42. *Missouri Gazette*, July 30, 1814; *TP*, 14: 804–5; Clark to Secretary of War, December 5, 1814, in NA, RG 94, RAGO, LRSW (M 566, Roll 55, 690–91).

43. Campbell afterwards settled at Saint Louis, making a living by trading with the Indians. Arrested in 1818 for illegal trading, he escaped prosecution by jumping bail. In 1837 Campbell moved to the District of Columbia and faded from history, having bequeathed his name to the island where he had fought so unsuccessfully. *TP*, 15:380–82, 416–17; 17: 3–5; Campbell to Secretary of War, October 24, 1814, NA, RG 94, RAGO, LRSW (M 566, Roll 39, 233); Campbell to Secretary of War, January 22, 1815, *ibid.*, (M 566, Roll 67, 228–29); Russell to Secretary of War, March 18, 1815, *ibid.*, (231); Clark to Secretary of War, March 20, 1815, *ibid.*, (230); NA, War of 1812 Pension Applications, "John Campbell," OWI20672; Callary, *Place Names*, 56. Much of the criticism afterwards directed at Campbell came from people who either had not been present at the battle

or whose own character for trustworthiness was not high. See John Gibson, DM, 15C98, 107(9); Stephen Hempstead, DM, 22S195; John Shaw, "Shaw's Narrative," *WHC* 2: 220.

44. *WHC* 11: 325–26.

45. *WHC* 13: 273–77; McAfee, 427–32; Dunnigan, "Battle of Mackinac," 59: 239–54.

46. Ormsby to Secretary of War, October 21, 1814, in NA, RG 94, RAGO, "Letters Received" (M 566, Roll 59, 101–3); Stuart to Unidentified, December 3, 1814, *ibid.*, (105–9).

47. *JISHS*, 34: 88–89; Hamilton, *Zachary Taylor*, 47–50.

48. Taylor, *Autobiography* (c. 1826), Zachary Taylor Papers, Series 1, Library of Congress. The text is printed in *JISHS*, 34: 86–91.

49. Secretary of War to Howard, July 14, 1814, NA, RG 107, "Letters Sent" (M 6, Roll 7, 136).

50. *Louisiana Gazette*, July 18, 1811; *TP*, 17: 8–9. In May 1814, not long after he was wounded, Nelson Rector wrote Governor Edwards a letter from Shawneetown resigning his commission as the governor's aide de camp, for the reason that he intended to move out of the territory. Apparently the letter miscarried, and in a later meeting Rector learned that the governor was unaware of it. On July 15, 1814, he wrote a second letter of resignation. The following month Rector would actively recruit a company of Illinois volunteers to go upriver with Clark. Nelson Rector to Edwards, July 15, 1814, in "Miscellaneous Executive Records, 1809–1818," Folder 16, Record Series 100.002, Illinois State Archives, Springfield.

51. American sources for the Battle of Credit Island include Taylor to Howard, September 6, 1814 (printed in *Missouri Gazette*, September 17, 1814, and *Niles Weekly Register (Supplement)* 7: 137–38; Zachary Taylor, *Autobiography* (c. 1826); Hamilton, "Zachary Taylor in Illinois"; Wesley, "James Callaway." Relevant articles appear in the *Missouri Gazette* of August 20 and September 3, 17, and 24, 1814. Also notable is the vivid account of the battle in Reynolds, *My Own Times*, 101–3. Reynolds was not present, but his two brothers fought at Credit Island and he probably had the benefit of their descriptions. There is also an account of the battle in John Shaw, "Shaw's Narrative," *WHC* 2: 220–22. Shaw claimed to have accompanied Taylor, and perhaps he did, but Shaw was prone to exaggeration or worse, and whether any part of his story is true is unknown. It contains some obvious errors. (On Shaw, see page 302, note 30.) For the British and Indian perspectives, see the reports and correspondence of Lieutenant Duncan Graham and Captain Thomas G. Anderson in Anderson, "Journal," 207–61; miscellaneous documents in *WHC* 9: 262–81; and Jackson, *Black Hawk*, 80–82. Secondary accounts are *Historic Rock Island*, 21–23; Meese,

"Credit Island," 7: 349–73; Quaife, "Forgotten Hero," 23: 652–63; Hamilton, *Zachary Taylor*, 49–54.

52. *Missouri Gazette*, August 20 and September 24, 1814. On Dodge's expedition see p. 200.

53. Anderson, "Journal," 207, 216; *WHC* 12: 115–17, 263–70.

54. Duncan Graham was born in Scotland about 1772. He was engaged in the fur trade at Prairie du Chien by 1802. Commissioned lieutenant in the British Indian Department 1813 and promoted to captain as of September 6, 1814. Was in action at Fort Meigs, Fort Stephenson, Prairie du Chien (mentioned in dispatches), and Credit Island. Although viewed with suspicion by American authorities, Graham continued in the fur trade with the Sioux after the war. There is an unconfirmed report that he eventually became an American citizen. In his later years, Graham resided at Wabasha, Minnesota, a town which he named. He died December 5, 1847, at Mendota, Minnesota, and is said to have been buried in Saint Felix Cemetery, Wabasha. One who knew Graham recalled: "He was a small sized man, quite unassuming, upright in his intercourse with his fellow-men, and highly respected." Graham's Island in Devil's Lake, North Dakota, was named for him. *WHC* 9: 298–99 and n., 467, 13: 19–20; *History of Wabasha County*, 435–36; Irving, *Officers*, 211.

55. *TP*, 263–70.

56. *WHC* 9: 214–20, 223.

57. *Missouri Gazette*, September 17, 1814; Wesley, "James Callaway," 74–77; *WHC* 9: 224–28.

58. *JISHS*, 34: 88–89; Taylor to Howard, September 6, 1814.

59. Taylor and Callaway both date the next day's battle to September 5. Graham's report, however, says September 6 (*WHC* 9: 226–28).

60. Taylor to Howard, September 6, 1814; Wesley, "James Callaway," 69–71; *WHC* 9: 225–28, 230–32.

61. Taylor to Howard, September 6, 1814; *WHC* 9: 225–28; Reynolds, *My Own Times*, 101–2.

62. Reynolds, *My Own Times*, 101–2; Taylor to Howard, September 6, 1814; Wesley, "James Callaway," 74–77. Because of Nelson Rector's heroism at Credit Island, a number of politically influential men tried to procure for him a commission as major in the regular army, but the treaty of peace intervened and the drastic reduction of the wartime army that followed almost immediately afterward made the effort moot. Illinois Legislature to Secretary of War, November 26, 1814, in NA, RG 94, RAGO, "Letters Received" (M 566, Roll 55, 687–88); Edwards to Secretary of War, November 29, 1814, *ibid*. (680–81); Jones to Secretary of War, November 29, 1814, *ibid*. (679); Thomas to Secretary of War,

November 29, 1814, *ibid.* (682–83); Clark to Secretary of War, December 5, 1814, *ibid.* (690–91); Easton and Stephenson to Secretary of War, December 16, 1814, *ibid.* (684–85).

63. Taylor to Howard, September 6, 1814; Taylor, *Autobiography* (c. 1826), Reynolds, *My Own Times*, 102.

64. Hamilton, "Zachary Taylor in Illinois," 85; *WHC* 9: 330–31.

65. *WHC* 9: 225–28, 269–72; Quaife, "Forgotten Hero," 662–63; Irving, *Officers*, 97.

66. *Missouri Gazette*, October 8, 1814; Taylor, *Autobiography* (c. 1826); Wesley, "James Callaway," 71–73 (with sketch of Fort Johnson); *WHC* 9: 243–45: Jackson, *Black Hawk*, 81–82; Talbot, "Fort Edwards," 136–40; David J. Nolan, "Fort Johnson," 85–94; "Vestiges of Conflict, Frontier Converge at Warsaw Site," *Quincy Herald-Whig*, October 11, 2009. Fort Johnson has often been confused with Fort Edwards, built not by Zachary Taylor, but in the spring of 1815 by U.S. troops commanded first by Major White Young and then by Captain Thomas Ramsey. Fort Edwards stood about a half-mile from the site of Fort Johnson, on the site now marked by a monument. Typical of confusion between the two forts are Dallam, "Dedication"; Aleshire, "Warsaw and Fort Edwards," 200–201, and Davis, *Frontier Illinois*, 149. Long ago, Gregg, *History of Hancock County*, 379–81, tried to distinguish the two forts but added errors of his own. Talbot's careful review of the sources, cited above, should forever dispel the confusion.

67. *JISHS*, 34: 90–91; Wesley, "James Callaway," 71–73; *Missouri Gazette*, October 8 and 22, 1814; *WHC* 9: 250.

68. See the obituary in *Missouri Gazette*, October 1, 1814, and the brief notice in *Western Sun*, September 24, 1814. Howard left no descendants and, aside from correspondence contained in the records of the War Department, no significant collection of his papers has been preserved. After the general's death, his public papers fell into the hands of his adjutant, Captain John Campbell. Campbell asked the War Department for instructions about disposition of the papers, but no record has been found to indicate that he received a response. Campbell to Secretary of War, January 22, 1815.

69. Russell to Gregg, c. September 26, 1814, in Lasselle Family Papers, Folder 9, Indiana State Library, Indianapolis; Russell to Secretary of War, September 28, 1814, in NA, RG 107, LRSW (M 221, Roll 65, 8702); *Missouri Gazette*, October 15, 1814; *TP*, 17: 35–36.

70. See Gregg, "War of 1812," 33: 328–29.

71. *Missouri Gazette*, July 16, 1814 (Bowles), and October 8, 1814 (McNair and Piew).

72. There is no record that Echols ever received a formal appointment as captain, so the title must have been conferred by the men he led. Jesse Echols was appointed

justice of the peace for Johnson County, July 4, 1814, and for Union County, January 13, 1818. He also served as deputy registrar for the Kaskaskia Land Office. In 1818 Echols was elected from Union County as a representative in the First General Assembly. In 1832 he ran unsuccessfully to represent Alexander County in the Eighth General Assembly. Carter, *TP*, 17: 446, 649, 667; Pease, *Illinois Election Returns*, 185, 256.

73. Echols to Blount, August 1, 1814, in NA, RG 107, LRSW (M 221, Roll 59, 3154); Blount to Echols, September 14, 1814, *ibid.* (3153). A certain mystery lingers about this shooting. According to Captain Echols, his company of militia "found the body of a certain John Humphreys who had been shot thro' the body on the banks of the Ohio River by the Indians." A man named Humphreys was the first settler on the site of what later became Caledonia in Pulaski County, and according to a later account "Mr. Humphrey was afterwards shot through the shoulder, but succeeded in getting to the fort, where he recovered." Atherton, *Pulaski County*, 1: 437–39; Perrin, *History of Alexander*, 268, 535. Whether these accounts refer to the same or different incidents is uncertain. In December 1816, a John Humphreys purchased land along the river in what is now the southwest corner of Massac County. Volkel, *Shawneetown Land District*, 31.

74. *Missouri Gazette*, August 20, 1814; "Old Settlers' Reports," *Greenville Advocate*, September 27, 1860; Perrin, *History of Bond*, 20–21, 146–47; *Bond County History*, 12; Reynolds, *My Own Times*, 98; Reynolds, *Pioneer History*, 409; Wilson and Kaegy, *Tales of Hill's Fort*, 85–87; Wilson and Kaegy, *Tales Continue*, 52, 67; *RAGI*, 9: 336; "Madison County Records & Indentures, 1812–1815," 27, 40, Illinois State Archives, Springfield. The location of Henry Cox's cabin presents a problem. All the accounts just cited, except Reynolds, place the cabin on Beaver Creek, about a mile southwest of what would later be Dudleyville, presumably in section 3 of Mills Township (T4N, R3W). This location is accepted by Wilson and Kaegy, *Tales Continue*, 85. In April 1815, however, the heirs of Henry Cox filed a preemption claim to the land Cox had cultivated and improved prior to February 5, 1813, and on which he had continued to reside "until he was killed by the Indians in Aug 1814." This land is identified as the north ½ of section 6, T4N, R3W, which is in fact about three miles *west* of Dudleyville. Hammes, "Squatters," 353. So nearly contemporary a record would ordinarily be dispositive, were it not that this places the cabin less than half a mile from Hill's Fort, a location which makes a poor fit with the traditional account. Reynolds, however, says that Cox was killed on Shoal Creek, near Hill's Fort. There is no creek in the north half of section 6, but a branch of Shoal Creek runs nearby. As the events of the next month proved, it was by no means impossible for a war party to be operating so close to Hill's Fort in early August 1814.

75. *Western Sun*, September 3, 1814, 3.

76. John Journey (Jurney, Jerney) Jr. was born in Virginia about 1780. Married to Nancy McMullen in Lincoln County, Kentucky, October 2, 1798. The family moved to Illinois, where, with father and brother Nathaniel, he built Journey's Fort near Aviston. He settled in what is now Clinton County, about a half mile east of Sugar Creek, on the NE ¼, section 11, T2N, R5W. Commissioned ensign in Captain Jacob Short's company of U.S. Rangers, August 1, 1813. Killed in action near Hill's Fort, September 9, 1814. Wilson, *Tales of Hill's Fort*, 36, 51–52; *ASP: Military Affairs*, 1: 421; *TP*, 16: 301; Hammes, "Squatters," 362; *History of Marion*, 199. There has been a persistent erroneous tradition in Bond County that the officer who led the Rangers from Hill's Fort and died in the ambush was not John Journey but his brother Nathaniel. See, "Report on Hill's Fort," *Greenville Advocate*, March 29, 1988; John H. Nowlan, "Bond County's Records and Traditions: Battle of Hill's Fort," *Greenville Advocate*, January 7, 1935. Nathaniel was indeed an officer in the war, but the service record of John Journey reproduced in Wilson and Kaegy, *Tales of Hill's Fort*, 36, should settle the issue.

77. Three of the Rangers who died in the ambush can be identified with certainty: Ensign John Journey Jr., Private Robert Lynn, and Private William Grotts. About the fourth, William Pruitt, there has been some doubt, because of confusion between him and a cousin of the same name. See two careful studies by Wilson and Kaegy: *Tales of Hill's Fort*, 29–31, 35–36, 54–55, 67, and *Tales Continue*, 34–36, 47–49.

78. *WHC* 11: 330–31; Hall, "Adventure of a Ranger," 1: 76–81; Reynolds, *Pioneer History*, 378–81; Perrin, *History of Bond*, 21–23; *History of Fayette County*, 30–31, 67; Power, *History of the Early Settlers*, 459; *History of Sangamon County*, 191, 457–58; Johnson, "National Road," 59–65; "Daughters of 1812 Honor Memory of Thomas Higgins," 17: 740–45; John H. Nowlan, "Bond County's Records and Traditions: Battle of Hill's Fort, August, 1814," *Greenville Advocate*, January 7, 1935, 3; "Battle of Hill's Fort," *Greenville Advocate*, September 18, 1944, 3; Wilson and Kaegy, *Tales of Hill's Fort*, 11–67, and *Tales Continue*, 37–46.

79. Judge Joseph Gillespie, January 25, 1883, quoted in Stevens, "Illinois," 167, and Reynolds, *Pioneer History*, 381, n.

80. The location was about 150 yards southwest of the now destroyed Brown cemetery, in SW ¼, Section 6, T4N, R3W. Monuments to the dead have been erected along Hill's Fort Avenue, nearer the site of the fort. See the map in Wilson and Kaegy, *Tales of Hill's Fort*, 4B; Wilson and Kaegy, *Tales Continue*, 50–51; "Some Hill's Fort History," *Greenville Advocate*, June 20, 1947.

81. Reynolds, *My Own Times*, 98, gives the location of the ambush as "on Sugar

Creek, a few miles above the crossing of that creek by the railroad." *History of Marion and Clinton Counties*, 199, says the ambush was "in the Sugar Creek timber, a short distance north of the state road, east of the creek."

82. Reynolds, *My Own Times*, 98; Reynolds, *Pioneer History*, 409; Stevens, "Illinois," 168; Hammes, "Squatters," 342; *History of Marion*, 50, 199.

83. Kinzie to Cass, September 22, 1814, NA, RG 107, LRSW (M 221, Roll 60, 4001–2); Esarey, *Messages and Letters*, 2: 666–67; Edmunds, "Main Poc," 9: 268; Tanner, *Atlas*, 106, 119.

84. Esarey, *Messages and Letters*, 2: 665, 667–69.

85. John G. Lofton was an early settler of Madison County, which he served in various judicial roles and represented in the Territorial Assembly. Moved about 1819 to the present Jersey County, where he served as first probate judge of Greene County. Unsuccessful antislavery candidate for lieutenant governor, 1822. Died 1837 and buried in Newbern Cemetery, NE ¼ Section 32, T7N, R11W. *TP*, 17: 626, 644, 650, 670; *History of Madison County*, 40, 41, 73–74, 81, 116–17, 120, 122–23, 218, 333, 502; *History of Greene and Jersey Counties*, 74, 84, 433, 453.

86. *RAGI*, 9: 342–43; *History of Madison County*, 218; *Missouri Gazette*, November 12, 1814; Pope to Judy, August 19, 1813, RS 100.001, "Correspondence," Illinois State Archives, Springfield; *TP*, 14: 796–97.

87. Philbrick, *Laws of Illinois Territory*, 177–78.

88. *WHC* 11: 330–31; Tanner, *Atlas*, 105–7.

89. *Missouri Gazette*, August 13, 1814; Loos, *Walk through Marine*, 1.

90. *TP*, 16: 312–15, 17: 33–36, 126; Edwards to Howard, June 1, 1814, and June 15, 1814, in Edwards Papers, Box 1, Folder 4, Chicago History Museum; Washburne, *Edwards Papers*, 119; Kappler, *Indian Affairs*, 2: 67–68.

91. Forsyth to Secretary of War, November 15, 1814.

92. The most important sources for this massacre are Captain Moore's report, Moore to Russell, December 3, 1814, printed in *Missouri Gazette*, December 3, 1814, and the record of the Court of Enquiry held by order of Colonel Russell the following March. "Court of Enquiry into the Conduct of Captain James B. Moore," NA, RG 153, Records of the Office of the Judge Advocate General (Army), Court Martial Case Files, AA 13. An early report can be found in *Missouri Gazette*, November 26, 1814. The traditional story, which has Moredock indirectly causing the death of Hewitt by trying to shoot Matatah after his surrender, is not found in any contemporary account, and first saw print in *History of St. Clair County*, 126. It is contradicted by the testimony at the Court of Enquiry, which placed Moredock up to 300 yards from the place where Matatah and Hewitt were shot. The story may have been inspired by

John Reynolds's similar account of Samuel Judy killing an Indian who tried to surrender during Edwards's march to Peoria. (See page 83, above.) For an Indian perspective, see Black Hawk's narrative of Gomo's account, in Jackson, *Black Hawk*, 84–86. See also *TP*, 14: 800–801 and Edwards to Forsyth, December 4, 1814, in DM, 1T41; "Indian Losses," DM, 1T32. None of the surviving accounts of the massacre preserves the date, but Hewitt's military service record states that he was "Killed by the Indians Nov. 16, 1814." NA, RG 94, Compiled Military Service Records, War of 1812. Because Hewitt died during the night after he was wounded, it is uncertain whether the massacre took place on the 15th or the 16th.

93. Moore to Russell, December 3, 1814. Hewitt's body was said to have been buried on Lick Creek in Loami Township, Sangamon County, the first burial in what afterwards became Sulphur Spring Cemetery. *History of Sangamon County*, 191, 458.

94. *TP*, 14: 800–801; *Missouri Gazette*, November 19 and December 8, 1814.

95. *TP*, 14: 800–801, 804–5; Edwards to Forsyth, December 4, 1814.

96. Jackson, *Black Hawk*, 85–86.

Chapter 11. Peace?

1. On the Treaty of Ghent, see *ASP: Foreign Affairs*, 3: 695–726, 730–48; Perkins, *Castlereagh and Adams*, chapters 5–7; Updyke, *Diplomacy*, chapters 5 and 6.

2. *ASP: Foreign Affairs*, 3: 745–48.

3. Jackson, *Black Hawk*, 82.

4. See, e.g., Esarey, *Messages and Letters*, 2: 673; Hagan, *Sac and Fox*, 9–12.

5. Adjutant General to Russell, December 14, 1814, NA, RG 94, Records of the Adjutant General's Office (RAGO), "Letters Sent" (M 565, Roll 5, 156); Desha, Johnson, and others to the President, October 12, 1814, NA, RG 94, RAGO, LRSW (M 566, Roll 56, 537–39); Russell to Adjutant General, January 15, 1815, *ibid*. (Roll 79, 1032–34).

6. *TP*, 14: 796–97, 800–801, 15: 15–16; see also Rufus Easton to Secretary of War, December 17, 1814, NA, RG 107, LRSW (M 221, Roll 61, 4822–25) (arguing the ineffectiveness of defensive measures and calling for 3,000 mounted troops to ride against the Indians by April 20).

7. *MPHC*, 16: 41 ("Should the operation of the war allow an Expedition to go & attack St. Louis, it would be attended with the best consequences—it would annoy and distress the enemy, it would place this country in a state of security, and it would impress the Indians with the highest ideas of the energy & courage of British Soldiers—Five hundred regular Troops accompanied by two thousand good Indian warriors would fully effect the business.")

8. *WHC* 13: 25–34.

9. *WHC* 13: 60–62.

10. *WHC* 10: 122–3, 12: 132, 13: 38–43, 54–60.

11. *WHC* 13: 52–60.

12. *WHC* 13: 19, 85–87, 100–101.

13. *MPHC*, 15: 219–21, 16: 41–44; *WHC* 10: 127–32, 11: 311–12, 13: 20–22, 60–62, 66–85.

14. *TP*, 17: 137–39. In forwarding the names of the volunteers to the War Department, Edwards described Judy as "equally distinguished by his bravery & prudence as a soldier, & his respectability as a citizen." It is not clear whether these volunteers were ever called into service.

15. *TP*, 17: 137.

16. Strictly speaking, the division of Gallatin County on November 28, 1814, placed the Cannon family in Edwards County, but the new county had only recently been organized. *Origin and Evolution of Illinois Counties*, 26–29.

17. *Combined History of Edwards*, 78, 291; Harvey, "Historical Sketch," 11: 17; Lindley, "Cannon-Stark Massacre"; *History of White County*, 452. The identification of the Cannon massacre with the murders mentioned by Edwards, while highly probable, is nevertheless speculative. Sources written long after the event place the murders in 1814 or 1815. The location and the governor's reference to the taking of prisoners by the Indians, very rare during the War of 1812, support the identification. The Painter Cemetery is located in section 26, T2S, R14W.

18. *History of Wayne*, 46.

19. *Combined History of Edwards*, 334. The location is in the NE ¼, section 14, T2S, R13W.

20. *Ibid.*, 75, 332; Harvey, "Historical Sketch," 17–18; *Western Sun*, March 18, 1815, 3; *Missouri Gazette*, March 25, 1815. The bodies were found in the southeast ¼ of section 15, T2S, R13W. The date is supplied by the *Western Sun*, although the later article in the *Missouri Gazette* dates the killings to March 13. The victims are not named in the newspapers, but the identification is tolerably certain, both from the location and from the date soon after the Cannon-Stark massacre.

21. Forsyth to Clark, April 13, 1815, in Forsyth Papers.

22. *Missouri Gazette*, March 25, 1815.

23. *Western Sun*, April 8, 1815, 3; *Combined History of Edwards*, 72, 82, 99, 270, 334; Perrin, *History of Crawford*, 34. Baird was killed on his farm in the northwest ¼, Section 18, T4N, R10W, in Russell Township.

24. *Combined History of Edwards*, 70.

25. *History of Coles*, 242; "Crawford County Fort May Have Links to Coles," *Journal Gazette/Times-Courier* [Mattoon], April 19, 2010.

26. *TP*, 17: 143.

27. Volumes 184–89, "Federal Land Surveyors' Field Notes," RS 953.005, Illinois State Archives, Springfield.

28. *Western Sun*, March 25, 1815; *TP*, 15: 15–16; Gregg, "War of 1812," 33: 342–43; Wesley, "James Callaway," 5: 50–52, 73; *Missouri Gazette*, March 11, March 25, and April 1, 1815.

29. John McNair was the nephew of Colonel Alexander McNair, afterward first governor of the state of Missouri. After service as a private in the companies of Captain Nathan Boone and others, John McNair was commissioned ensign in the U.S. Rangers, July 19, 1813. Promoted 2d lieutenant July 13, 1814. Killed by Indians, April 1815. *ASP: Military Affairs*, 1: 421; Williams, *Soldiers*, 1: 949; Heitman, *Historical Register*, 1: 678. Heitman erroneously shows McNair as having been discharged in June 1815, after he was already dead.

30. *TP*, 15: 23; *Missouri Gazette*, April 8 and 15, 1815; *History of Lincoln County*, 224. John Shaw left a vivid and inaccurate account of this affair in *WHC*, 2: 209–11. The account is highly embellished and the number of dead inflated. As usual, Shaw made himself the hero of the affair, but there is no reason to assume that he was even present. Certainly he was not a member of McNair's command, as he represents. Unfortunately Shaw's seductively colorful narrative has led some historians to accept it as fact, including Houck, 3: 108–9. Shaw, however, was a picturesque scoundrel, at one time the virtual ruler of Calhoun County, Illinois, where he was known as "The Black Prince." He even served briefly in the Illinois legislature, but after disappearing with a steamboat filled with goods sent to market by the unlucky citizens of Calhoun County, Shaw resettled in Wisconsin, where he lived to a good old age. In September 1855 Shaw dictated his memoirs to Lyman Draper, dwelling in detail on his own exploits in the War of 1812. Let it suffice to say that Shaw greatly magnified the role he had played in the war and that not all his information can be corroborated. For Shaw's colorful career, see *History of Pike*, 197; Carpenter, *Calhoun*, 22–4; Alvord, *Governor Edward Coles*, 63–72; Underwood, "Passing," 15–16; Underwood, "New Geography," 16–18.

31. Blasdell to Sholts [December 5, 1814], and Sholts to André, December 5, 1814, both in Lasselle Papers; Esarey, *Messages and Letters*, 2: 679–83; *Western Sun*, December 10 and 24, 1814. The chief is not named.

32. *Missouri Gazette*, January 7, 1815; "To the Potawatomies of Illinois River," DM, 2M18; LeClair to Clark, March 15, 1815, DM, 2M19; Speech of Black Partridge and Petchaho, DM, 2M21; Clark to Secretary of War, March 20, 1815, NA, RG 107, LRSW (M 221, Roll 60, 4223).

33. Forsyth to Potawatomies, April 7, 1815, DM, 1T45; *Missouri Gazette*, April 15 and April 29, 1815; Gregg, "War of 1812," 339–40.

34. Forsyth to Clark, April 13, 1815, in Forsyth Papers; *TP*, 15: 25–26.

35. *TP*, 17: 116–17, 170–72; Clark to Secretary of War, March 20, 1815; Court of Enquiry into Conduct of Captain James B. Moore, NA, RG 153, Records of the Office of the Judge Advocate General (Army), "Court Martial Case Files, 1809–1894," AA 13. Major William B. Whiteside was president of the Court of Enquiry, and captains Jacob Short and Peter Craig members.

36. *JISHS*, 39: 392 (September 1946).

37. Senachwine lived at or near what had been Gomo's village until about 1830 or 1831, when he died and was buried on the SE ¼, section 18, T1N, R1E, in Putnam County, Illinois. Francis LeClair, DM, 24S140; Hamlin to Draper, August 17, 1874, DM, 9YY45; Fulton to Draper, September 6, 1874, DM, 9YY48; Matson to Draper, August 6, 1874, DM, 9YY30; Armstrong to Draper, July 2, 1874, DM, 9YY44; Durley to Draper, November 28, 1875, DM, 9YY20; Taliaferro to Draper, August 20, 1874, DM, 9YY49; Gurnea to Draper, November 16, 1874, DM, 9YY51.

38. Hamlin to Draper, August 17, 1874. The places that bear Senachwine's name are discussed in Vogel, *Indian Place Names*, 130–31.

39. *MPHC* 16: 51.

40. *TP*, 17: 145; Clark to Secretary of War, March 13 (or 10th), 1815, NA, RG 107, LRSW (M 221, Roll 60, 4221); *WHC* 13: 148–49; *MPHC* 16: 290–302.

41. Clark to Secretary of War, March 13, 1815; *TP*, 15: 15–16, 23, 47–49. The later claim of John Shaw to have led a regiment of Missouri volunteers to hunt Indians along the Rock, Spoon, and Illinois rivers during April 1815, has no apparent basis in fact. *WHC* 2: 222–23.

42. Taylor Berry was a native of Kentucky. There is a story that Berry acted as paymaster to General William Hull and that after the surrender of Detroit he saved the payroll money by concealing it in his clothing and in that of other officers. Commissioned ensign in the 17th U. S. Infantry March 30, 1813, and promoted to 3d lieutenant the same day. On March 31, 1813, Berry was promoted to major and appointed assistant deputy quartermaster general for Missouri. Honorably discharged June 15, 1815. After the war, Berry engaged in land speculation and practiced law in Howard County, Missouri. He was appointed postmaster of Franklin, Missouri, October 20, 1823. In June 1824, he was indicted for forgery. Berry was acquitted, but after the trial he took a horsewhip to the unarmed prosecutor, Abiel Leonard, later a justice of the supreme court of Missouri. Leonard challenged Berry, and in the duel Berry was fatally wounded. He died of his wounds at New Madrid, September 22, 1824. Houck, 3: 27–29; Heitman, *Historical Register*, 1: 215; *History of Howard*, 171, 247–9; Culmer, "Abiel Leonard," 27: 119; *Missouri Historical Review* 8: 115.

43. *TP*, 15: 47–49; Russell to [Secretary of War], May 15, 1815, and enclosures, NA, RG 107, LRSW (M 221, Roll 65, 8796–8810; *WHC* 13: 130; *Missouri Gazette*, April 29, 1815.

44. *WHC* 9: 133, 13: 129–33.

45. *WHC* 13: 135, 140–42, 149–51.

46. Secretary of War to Edwards, March 13, 1815, NA, RG 107, "Letters Sent" (M 6, Roll 8, 59).

47. Auguste Chouteau was born in New Orleans, probably on September 26, 1750, although that date has been doubted. Took part in the founding of Saint Louis in 1764. Although he held appointments as lieutenant colonel of territorial militia, justice of the court of common pleas, and member of the Legislative Council, his primary occupation was always commerce, with the result that he was considered the richest man in Saint Louis at the time of his death, February 24, 1829. Originally buried in downtown Saint Louis, but remains subsequently moved to Calvary Cemetery. Christensen et al., *Dictionary*, 167–70; *Missouri Historical Review* 8: 117 (January 1914); biographies: Foley and Rice, *First Chouteaus*; Christian, *Before Lewis and Clark*.

48. *TP*, 15: 14–15; 17: 143, 149; Chouteau to Secretary of War, May 27, 1815, in NA, RG 107, LRSW (M 221, Roll 60, 4272).

49. John Miller was born in Berkeley County, Virginia (now West Virginia), November 25, 1781. Moved to Steubenville, Ohio, about 1803. Commissioned lieutenant colonel, 17th U.S. Infantry, March 12, 1812. Promoted colonel of 19th Infantry, July 16, 1812. Commanded Fort Meigs during successful defense, 1813. Transferred to 3d Infantry, May 17, 1815. Retained in army after war and commanded troops during peace conference at Portage des Sioux. Resigned from army, February 10, 1818, to accept appointment as register of land office at Franklin, Missouri. Governor of Missouri, 1825–1832. Congressman, 1837–1843. Died at Florissant, Missouri, March 18, 1846. Reinterment in Bellefontaine Cemetery, Saint Louis. Miller County, Missouri, is named for him. *BDUSC*, 1586; Christensen et al., *Dictionary*, 546–47; Heitman, *Historical Register*, I: 711; *DAB*, vol. 6, pt. 2, 628–29.

50. *TP* 15: 13.

51. *WHC* 11: 336–38.

52. *ASP: Indian Affairs*, 2: 9–11.

53. Oglesby, *Manuel Lisa*; French, "Manuel Lisa."

54. *WHC* 11: 338–41. Forsyth's letters to the Menominee, Kickapoo, Potawatomi, and Sauk and Fox of Rock River are at DM, 2M26–29.

55. *WHC* 11: 338–41.

56. *Western Sun*, May 20, 1815, 3; Dillon, 538–39; Esarey, *Messages and Letters*, 2:

691–92. This event, serious enough in reality, was probably the basis of the report that reached Saint Louis that thirty-six Rangers from Fort Harrison had been surprised, all but three being killed, and that the fort itself was in jeopardy. *Missouri Gazette*, June 3, 1815.

57. *Missouri Gazette*, May 27, 1815; *Niles Weekly Register*, 8: 271 (June 17, 1815); Russell to Secretary of War, May 22, 1815, NA, RG 107, LRSW (M 221, Roll 65, 8811); Commissioners to Secretary of War, May 22, 1815, *ibid.* (Roll 60, 4262).

58. *WHC* 13: 148–51; *MPHC* 16: 290–302.

59. On Fort Howard, see "Missouriana," 26: 285–86; *History of Lincoln County*, 218–19.

60. Peter Craig of Cape Girardeau, Missouri, was commissioned 2d lieutenant of U.S. Rangers July 19, 1813, and promoted to captain July 13, 1814. Craig was killed in action near Fort Howard, Missouri, May 24, 1815. Heitman, *Historical Register*, 1: 333; Williams, *Soldiers*, 1: 355. Craig has sometimes been confused with Captain Thomas Craig of Shawneetown, Illinois, a different person. See, e.g., *TP* 15: 763.

61. On the Battle of the Sinkhole, see *TP* 15: 57–58; *Niles Weekly Register* 8: 311–12 (July 1, 1815); *Missouri Gazette*, May 27 and June 3, 1815; *Charleston [S.C.] City Gazette,* June 28 and July 6, 1815, transcribed in DM, 15C91–92; Jackson, *Black Hawk*, 74–75; *History of Lincoln County*, 221–23; Gregg, "War of 1812," 33: 343–44. As usual, John Shaw left a vivid account of the battle that places himself in the thick of it. For once, his account does not appear to be grossly inaccurate. *WHC* 2: 213–18.

62. *WHC* 13: 149–51; Alfred Edward Bulger, "Last Days."

63. *WHC* 13: 149–51.

64. *WHC* 13: 143–47, 149–51.

65. *TP* 15: 62–63.

66. *TP* 14: 593–94.

67. Russell to Secretary of War, June 18, 1815, NA, RG 107, LRSW (M 221, Roll 65, 8850); "Russell's Valedictory Address," June 15, 1815, in *Missouri Gazette*, June 17, 1815; Bissell to Jackson, July 2, 1815, Bissell Papers (photostat).

68. 3 U.S. Stat. 224; Graham to Secretary of War, July 15, 1815, NA, RG 107, LRSW (M 221, Roll 61, 5414). ("The sudden reduction of the army is, I believe, almost universally condemned.—In all my travels I have not met with a single individual who has approved of it"—Graham to Secretary of War, July 15, 1815.)

69. Wash to Bissell, June 24, 1815, in Bissell Papers (photostat); Bissell to Jackson, July 2, 1815; *TP,* 15: 68–70; "Monthly Return of a Company of Mounted Militia Commanded by Captain Hyacinthe Lasselle," Lasselle Family Papers, Box 4; Woollen et al., *Executive Journal*, 232.

70. *ASP: Indian Affairs*, 2: 6–7.

71. *Missouri Gazette*, July 8, 1815.

72. Bissell to Secretary of War, July 2, 1815; *Niles Weekly Register* 8: 362 (July 22, 1815); *Missouri Gazette*, July 8, 1815; Commissioners to Bissell, July 11, 1815, NA, RG 107, LRSW (M 221, Roll 59, 3045–46); *ASP: Indian Affairs*, 2: 8–9.

73. For the treaties of Portage des Sioux, see Fisher, "Treaties"; Brown, "Pacification of the Indians"; Gregg, "War of 1812," 33: 346–48.

74. *Missouri Gazette*, July 15, 1815; *Reporter*, August 9, 1815; *MPHC* 16: 193–95.

75. Isaac Piggott, DM, Z37; NA, RG 94, RAGO, Compiled Military Service Records, Illinois Militia, Box 294, Envelope 89.

76. Kappler, *Indian Affairs*, 2: 110–11; *WHC* 11: 345–47.

77. *TP*, 17: 226–29, 237–38; *ASP: Indian Affairs*, 2: 11–12; *TP*, 17: 259–60, 430–37; Kappler, *Indian Affairs*, 2: 132–33; Edmunds, *Potawatomis*, 215–19; Wheeler-Voegelin, "Anthropological Report," 251–70.

78. Kappler, *Indian Affairs*, 2: 111–12; Cleaves, *Old Tippecanoe*, 70; *ASP: Indian Affairs*, 2: 9; Esarey, *Messages and Letters*, 2: 696–97; *TP*, 17: 430–37; Henry Dodge, DM 15C99–100; Houck, 3: 120–23; *Missouri Gazette*, September 24, 1814; Flower, 357–58; Libby, "Anthropological Report," 213–30, 252–54.

79. Kappler, *Indian Affairs*, 2: 112–16.

80. *Missouri Gazette*, July 22, 1815.

81. Clark to Jackson, July 20, 1815, Series 1, Volume 37, Roll 19; Jackson to Graham, August 29, 1815, Series 3, Volume G, Roll 62; Jackson to Bissell, September 4, 1815 Series 3, Volume G, Roll 62—all in Andrew Jackson Papers.

82. Clark to Jackson, August 6, 1815; Wash to Bissell, August 26, 1815; Bissell to Jackson, August 27, 1815—both in Andrew Jackson Papers, Series 1, Volume 37, Roll 19.

83. Edwards to Jackson, August 9, 1815, in Andrew Jackson Papers, Series 5, Volume 8, Roll 68.

84. *MPHC*, 16: 192–97, 203–4, 245–46, 283–85.

85. *MPHC*, 16: 283–85.

86. *MPHC*, 16: 196–97.

87. Little Deer's village was on the Vermilion River in 1810, but by 1812 it might have been moved to the Illinois River. He attended Edwards's peace conference at Cahokia in April 1812 and assured the governor that he was "a peaceable Indian" from a small village who had never listened to the Prophet. Within a year, however, Little Deer was leading Kickapoo war parties in raids on the Illinois frontier. Where he was living at this time is not clear, but the Kankakee and Vermilion rivers are the most likely possibilities. Thomas Forsyth regarded

Little Deer's band as separate from that of Pemwatome. *WHC* 11: 329–30; Tanner, *Atlas*, 98, 106; Edwards, *History*, 56, 60; *TP*, 16: 312–15.

88. Forsyth to Clark, August 3, 1815, in Forsyth Papers; *WHC* 11: 342–45; Clark to Jackson, August 6, 1815; Philips to Bissell, August 7, 1815—both in Andrew Jackson Papers, Series 1, Volume 37, Roll 19. The three white captives taken to Fort Clark may have been the prisoners from the Cannon-Stark massacre (p. 000).

89. *ASP: Indian Affairs*, 2: 9; Scanlan, *Boilvin Letters*, Letter 35.

90. *Missouri Gazette*, September 16, 1815. Thomas Forsyth reported that fifty Menominee had come downriver almost to Fort Clark but had become afraid to go any farther and returned home. Whether this was a war party that lost its nerve or a peace delegation that feared a trap he did not indicate. Forsyth to Clark, August 3, 1815.

91. Kappler, *Indian Affairs*, 2: 116–17.

92. *Ibid.*, 2: 120–21.

93. *Ibid.*, 2: 121–22.

94. *Ibid.*, 2: 119–20, 122–23; Commissioners to Secretary of War, September 18, 1815, NA, LRSW, RG 107 (M221, Roll 60, 4455); *ASP: Indian Affairs*, 2: 9.

95. *Missouri Gazette*, September 16, 1815.

96. *Missouri Gazette*, October 14, 1815; Jackson, *Black Hawk*, 82–83. The commissioners had recently been notified that the funds appropriated for the Indian Department had been nearly exhausted, which might partly explain their unwillingness to reopen the conference for the benefit of the Sauk. Graham to Clark, August 28, 1815, NA, RG 107, "Letters Sent," (M 6, Roll 8, 168).

97. *TP*, 17: 328–29, 352–56; *Missouri Gazette*, May 18, 1816.

98. Flint, *Recollections*, 112.

99. Yarborough, *Reminiscences*, 16–19.

100. Flint, *Recollections*, 112–13. Black Hawk afterwards gave a different version of this incident. Jackson, *Black Hawk*, 86–87.

101. On Cantonment Davis, see Nolan, "Fort Johnson," 87.

102. Kappler, *Indian Affairs*, 2: 126–28; *Missouri Gazette*, May 18, 1816; Jackson, *Black Hawk*, 87.

103. Kappler, *Indian Affairs*, 2: 138; *WHC* 19: 455–56; *TP*, 17: 352–56.

104. Wood, *Select British Documents*, 532–36.

105. *TP*, 17: 398–401.

106. Masters, *Spoon River Anthology* (Toronto: Macmillan, 1969), 212.

BIBLIOGRAPHY

Abbreviations

The following abbreviations have been used in the notes and bibliography:

ASP—*American State Papers*

BDUSC—*Biographical Directory of the United States Congress*

DM—Draper Manuscripts, Wisconsin Historical Society

JISHS—Journal of the Illinois State Historical Society

LRSW—Letters Received by the Secretary of War

MPHC—Michigan Pioneer and Historical Collections

NA—National Archives

RAGI—Report of the Adjutant General of Illinois

RAGO—Records of the Adjutant General's Office

RG—Record Group

RS—Record Series

TP—Carter, *Territorial Papers of the United States*

WHC—*Wisconsin Historical Collections*, also known as *Collections of the State Historical Society of Wisconsin*

Manuscripts and Archival Collections

ABRAHAM LINCOLN PRESIDENTIAL LIBRARY, SPRINGFIELD
Ninian Edwards Papers

BRADLEY UNIVERSITY, DAVIS-CULLUM LIBRARY, PEORIA
Peoria Historical Society Collection

CHICAGO HISTORY MUSEUM, CHICAGO
Fort Dearborn Manuscript Collection
John Kinzie Collection
Ninian Edwards Papers
William R. Head Papers
Wilson, James G., "Chicago from 1803 to 1812"

ILLINOIS STATE ARCHIVES, SPRINGFIELD
Federal Land Office Records

Madison County Records and Indentures, 1813–1815
Perrin Collection
Records of the Illinois Territory

INDIANA STATE LIBRARY, INDIANAPOLIS
Lasselle Family Papers

KANSAS HISTORICAL SOCIETY, TOPEKA
William Clark Papers

KENTUCKY DEPARTMENT OF ARCHIVES AND LIBRARIES, FRANKFORT
Governor Charles Scott, Correspondence 1809–1812
Governor Isaac Shelby (Second Term), Letter Book A
Governor Isaac Shelby (Second Term), Military Correspondence

LIBRARY OF CONGRESS, WASHINGTON
Andrew Jackson Papers
James Madison Papers
Zachary Taylor Papers

MISSOURI HISTORY MUSEUM, SAINT LOUIS
Daniel Bissell Papers
Thomas Forsyth Papers
William Clark Papers

NATIONAL ARCHIVES AND RECORDS ADMINISTRATION, WASHINGTON
Compiled Military Service Records, War of 1812, Record Group 94
Court Martial Case Files, Judge Advocate General, Record Group 153
Letters Received by the Adjutant General, Record Group 94
Letters Sent by the Office of the Adjutant General, Record Group 94
Letters Received by the Secretary of War, Record Group 107
Letters Sent by the Secretary of War, Record Group 107
Returns from U.S. Military Posts, Record Group 94
War of 1812, Pension Application Files

WISCONSIN HISTORICAL SOCIETY, MADISON
Draper Manuscripts

Period Newspapers and Magazines

Crawford Weekly Messenger, Meadville, Pennsylvania
Canadian Magazine and Literary Repository, Montreal, Québec
Louisiana Gazette (from July 18, 1812 called *Missouri Gazette*), Saint Louis
Missouri Intelligencer, Franklin, Missouri
Niles Weekly Register, Washington, D.C.
The Reporter (often called the *Kentucky Reporter*), Lexington, Kentucky
Western Sun, Vincennes, Indiana

Books and Articles

Adams, Henry. *History of the United States of America during the Administration of James Madison.* New York: Albert and Charles Boni, 1930.

Aleshire, Ruth Cory. "Warsaw and Fort Edwards on the Mississippi." Pp. 200–209 in *Transactions of the Illinois State Historical Society for the Year 1930.* Publications of the Illinois State Historical Library, vol. 37. Springfield: Journal Printing, 1930.

Allen, John W. *Legends and Lore of Southern Illinois.* Carbondale: Southern Illinois University Press, 1963.

———. *Pope County Notes.* Carbondale: Southern Illinois University, Museum of Natural and Social Sciences, 1949.

———. *Randolph County Notes.* Carbondale: Southern Illinois Normal University, 1944.

Allen, William B. *A History of Kentucky.* Louisville, Ky.: Bradley & Gilbert, 1872.

Allers, Wanda Warkins, Margaret Sager Hohimer, and Eileen Lynch. *Menard County Cemetery Inscriptions.* Springfield, 1983.

Alvord, Clarence Walworth. *Governor Edward Coles.* Collections of the Illinois State Historical Library, vol. 15. Springfield: Illinois State Historical Library, 1920.

———. *The Illinois Country, 1673–1818.* Chicago: A. C. McClurg, 1922; repr. Chicago: Loyola University Press, 1965.

American State Papers: Claims. Washington, D.C.: Gales and Seaton, 1834.

American State Papers: Foreign Affairs. Washington, D.C.: Gales and Seaton, 1832.

American State Papers: Indian Affairs. Washington, D.C.: Gales and Seaton, 1832.

American State Papers: Military Affairs. Washington, D.C.: Gales and Seaton, 1832.

American State Papers: Public Lands. Washington, D.C.: Duff Green, 1834.

Anderson, Thomas G. "Journal at Fort McKay, August 10–November 23, 1814." *WHC* 9 (1882): 207–61.

———. "Military Orders at Fort McKay, August 10—November 28, 1814." *WHC* 9 (1882): 25–61.

———. "Personal Narrative of Captain Thomas G. Anderson," ed. Lyman C. Draper. *WHC* 9 (1882): 137–206.

Andreas, A. T. *History of Chicago.* 3 vols. Chicago: A.T. Andreas, 1884.

Andrews, Edward Deming. *The People Called Shakers.* New York: Oxford University Press, 1953.

Angle, Paul M. "Fort Dearborn, 1802–1812." *Chicago History* 4 (1949): 97–102.

———. "Nathaniel Pope, 1784–1850: A Memoir." Pp. 111–81 in *Transactions of the Illinois State Historical Society for the Year 1936.* Publications of the Illinois State Historical Library, vol. 43. Springfield: Journal Printing, 1936.

Anson, Bert. *The Miami Indians.* Norman: University of Oklahoma Press, 1970.

Atherton, Wanda L., Glenna Conant Badgley, and Martha W. McMunn, comp.

Pulaski County Genealogy Notes. Carterville, Ill.: Genealogy Society of Southern Illinois, 1988.

Audubon, John James. *Writings and Drawings.* New York: Library of America 113, 1999.

Babcock, Rufus, ed. *Forty Years of Pioneer Life: A Memoir of John Mason Peck.* Philadelphia: American Baptist Publications Society, 1864.

Babson, Jane F. "The Architecture of Early Illinois Forts." *JISHS* 61 (Spring 1968): 9–40.

Bakalis, Michael John. "Ninian Edwards and Territorial Politics in Illinois, 1775–1818." Ph.D. diss., Northwestern University, 1966.

Baldwin, Carl R. *Echoes of Their Voices.* Saint Louis: Hawthorn, 1978.

Ballance, Charles. *History of Peoria, Illinois.* Peoria, Ill.: N. C. Nason, 1870.

Barce, Elmore. "Topenebee and the Decline of the Potawatomie Nation." *Indiana Magazine of History* 14 (March 1918): 3–12.

Barge, William D. "Rejected Illinois County Names." *Transactions of the Illinois State Historical Society for the Year 1906.* Publications of the Illinois State Historical Library, vol. 11 (1906): 122–37.

Barnhart, John D. "A New Letter about the Massacre at Fort Dearborn." *Indiana Magazine of History* 41 (June 1945):187–99.

Baskett, Katheryn Howe. "General Samuel Hopkins: Soldier, Statesman, 'Father' of Henderson, Kentucky." Henderson, Kentucky, *Gleaner Journal*, April 8, 1973.

Bateman, Newton, and Paul Selby. *Historical Encyclopedia of Illinois.* Chicago: Munsell, 1907.

———. *Illinois Historical, Crawford County Biographical.* Chicago: Munsell, 1909.

Beard, Reed. *The Battle of Tippecanoe,* 4th ed. Chicago: Conkey, 1911.

Beckwith, Hiram W. *History of Vermilion County, Illinois.* Chicago: H. H. Hill, 1879; repr. Evansville, Ind.: Unigraphic, 1975.

———. *The Illinois and Indiana Indians.* Fergus Historical Series 27. Chicago: Fergus, 1884; repr. New York: Arno Press, 1975.

Bent, Charles. *History of Whiteside County, Illinois.* Morrison, Ill.: n.p.

Berkson, Alice. "Cultural Resistance of the Prairie Kickapoo at the Grand Village, McLean County, Illinois." *Illinois Archaeology* 4 (1992): 107–205.

Billon, Frederick L. *Annals of St. Louis in Its Territorial Days from 1804 to 1821.* Saint Louis: privately printed, 1888.

Blackburn, Glen A., Nellie Armstrong Robertson, and Dorothy Riker, comp. and ed. *The John Tipton Papers.* Indiana Historical Collections, no. 24. Indianapolis: Indiana Historical Bureau, 1942.

Blanchard, John. *The Roar of God's Thunder,* ed. Ronald L. Nelson. Elizabethtown, Ill.: Nelson's, 1978.

Blanchard, Rufus. *Discovery and Conquests of the Northwest, with History of Chicago.* Chicago: R. Blanchard, 1898.

Blasingham, Emily J. "The Depopulation of the Illinois Indians." *Ethnohistory* 3 (1956): 193–224, 361–412.

Blevins, Henry R. "Historical Sketch of Cahokia Township, Macoupin County, Illinois." *JISHS* 8 (January 1916): 581–87.

Boice, Martha, Dale Covington, and Richard Spence. *Maps of the Shaker West.* Dayton, Ohio: Knot Garden Press, 1997.

Boilvin, Nicholas. "Prairie du Chien in 1811." *WHC* 11 (1888): 247–53.

Bond County History: A History of Bond County, Illinois. Greenville, Ill.: Bond County Historical Society, 1979.

Bonnell, Clarence. *The Illinois Ozarks.* Harrisburg, Ill.: Register Publishing, 1946.

Bonnell, Clarence, et al. *Saline County: A Century of History.* Harrisburg, Ill.: Register Publishing, 1947.

Boon, Benningsen. "Sketches of the Early History of Jackson County, Ill." Pp. 25–75 in Edmund Newsome, ed., *Historical Sketches of Jackson County, Illinois,* Carbondale: E. Newsome, 1894; repr. Murphysboro, Ill.: Jackson County Historical Society, 1987.

Boultinghouse, John Sherman. *Carmi Times,* January 2, 1998, 3; January 8, 1998, 3; and January 15, 1998, 3.

Bradsby, H. C. *History of Bureau County, Illinois.* Chicago: World, 1885.

———. *History of Vigo County, Indiana.* Chicago: S. B. Nelson, 1891.

Brady, David M. "Religion, Murder, and Politics: John Moredock and the American Conscience." *Springhouse* 24, no. 3 (2007): 6–19.

Brannan, John, ed. *Official Letters of the Military and Naval Officers of the United States during the War with Great Britain in the Years 1812, 13, 14, & 15.* Washington, D.C.: Way & Gideon, 1823.

Brice, Wallace. *History of Fort Wayne.* Fort Wayne, Ind.: D. W. Jones and Sons, 1868.

Brinkerhoff, J. H. G. *Brinkerhoff's History of Marion County, Illinois.* Indianapolis: B. F. Bowen, 1909.

Brinkman, Grover, ed. *This Is Washington County.* Nashville, Ill.: Historical Society of Washington County, 1968.

Brown, Henry. *History of Illinois.* New York: J. Winchester, New World Press, 1844.

Brown, Lizzie M. "The Pacification of the Indians of Illinois after the War of 1812." *JISHS* 8 (January 1916): 550–58.

Brymner, Douglas. "Capture of Fort McKay, Prairie du Chien, in 1814." *WHC* 11 (1888): 254–70.

Buck, Solon J. *Illinois in 1818.* Springfield: Illinois Centennial Commission, 1917; repr. Urbana: University of Illinois Press, 1967.

Buley, R. Carlyle. *The Old Northwest: Pioneer Period, 1815–1840*. 2 vols. Bloomington: Indiana University Press, 1950.

Bulger, Alfred Edward. "Events at Prairie du Chien Previous to the American Occupation, 1814." *WHC* 13 (1895): 1–9.

———. "Last Days of the British at Prairie du Chien." *WHC* 13 (1895): 154–62.

Burton, Clarence M. "The Fort Dearborn Massacre." *Magazine of History, with Notes and Queries* 15 (February 1912): 74–96.

Butler, Mann. *A History of the Commonwealth of Kentucky*. Louisville: Wilcox, Dickerman, 1834; repr. Berea, Ky.: Oscar Rucker Jr., 1968.

Caldwell, Norman W. "Fort Massac in the French and Indian War." *JISHS* 43 (Summer 1950): 100–19.

———. "Fort Massac: The American Frontier Post." *JISHS* 43 (Winter 1950): 265–81.

———. "Fort Massac since 1805." *JISHS* 44 (Spring 1951): 47–60.

Caldwell, Norman W. "Shawneetown: A Chapter in the Indian History of Illinois." *JISHS* 32 (January 1939): 193–205.

Callary, Edward. *Place Names of Illinois*. Urbana: University of Illinois Press, 2009.

Carpenter, George W. *Calhoun Is My Kingdom*. n.p.: Dan Merkle, 1967.

Carpenter, Richard V. "The Illinois Constitutional Convention of 1818." *JISHS* 6 (October 1913): 327–424.

Carrière, J. M. "Life and Customs in the French Villages of the Old Illinois Country." *Report of the Annual Meeting of the Canadian Historical Association* 18 (1939): 34–47.

Carter, Clarence E. *The Territorial Papers of the United States*. 26 vols. Washington, D.C.: Government Printing Office, 1934–62. [Abbreviated as *TP* in the Notes.]

Casselman, Alexander Clark, ed. *Richardson's War of 1812*. Toronto: Historical Publishing, 1902.

Christensen, Lawrence O., William E. Foley, Gary R. Kremer, and Kenneth H. Winn, eds. *Dictionary of Missouri Biography*. Columbia: University of Missouri Press, 1999.

Christian, Shirley. *Before Lewis and Clark: The Story of the Chouteaus, the French Dynasty That Ruled America's Frontier*. New York: Farrar, Straus and Giroux, 2004.

Clayton, John. *The Illinois Fact Book and Historical Almanac, 1673–1968*. Carbondale: Southern Illinois University Press, 1970.

Cleaves, Freeman. *Old Tippecanoe: William Henry Harrison and His Time*. New York: Charles Scribner's Sons, 1939.

Clifton, James A. "Chicago Was Theirs." *Chicago History*, n.s. 1, no. 1 (Spring 1970): 5–17.

———. "Merchant, Soldier, Broker, Chief: A Corrected Obituary of Captain Billy Caldwell." *JISHS* 71 (August 1978): 185–210.

———. *The Prairie People: Continuity and Change in Potawatomi Indian Culture 1665–1965*. Lawrence: Regents Press of Kansas, 1977.

"Collections and Researches Made by the Michigan Pioneer and Historical Society." Lansing, Mich. MPHC, 1876–1929.

Collins, Lewis. *History of Kentucky*. 2 vols. Covington, Ky.: Collins, 1874.

Combined History of Edwards, Lawrence, and Wabash Counties, Illinois. Philadelphia: J. L. McDonough, 1883.

Combined History of Randolph, Monroe, and Perry Counties, Illinois. Philadelphia: J. L. McDonough, 1883.

Condon, Sidney S. *Pioneer Sketches of Union County*. Anna, Ill.: Gazette-Democrat, 1987.

Conway, Thomas G. "Potawatomi Politics." *JISHS* 65 (Winter 1972): 395–418.

Cook, Samuel F. *Drummond Island: The Story of the British Occupation, 1815–1828*. Lansing, Mich.: privately printed, 1896.

Cornelius, James M. "John Hart Crenshaw and Hickory Hill: Final Report." Unpublished paper. Springfield, Ill.: Historic Preservation Agency, 2002.

Corrigan, Mary Lynn, and Wayne C. Temple. "Illinois Volunteer Officers in the War of 1812." *Illinois Libraries* 57 (March 1975): 235–41.

Crest, Vernon H. "The Mustering Oak." Pp. 162–64 in Jon Musgrave, ed., *Handbook of Old Gallatin County and Southeastern Illinois*. Marion, Ill.: IllinoisHistory. com, 2002.

Croghan, George. "Croghan's Journal." Pp. 47–173 in Reuben Gold Thwaites, ed., *Early Western Travels, 1748–1846*, vol. 1. Cleveland, Ohio: Arthur H. Clark, 1904–7.

Cruikshank, Ernest A. "Robert Dickson, the Indian Trader," *WHC* 12 (1891): 133–52.

Cullum, George W. *Biographical Register of Officers and Graduates of the United States Military Academy, West Point, N.Y.*, 3d ed. Boston: Houghton, Mifflin, 1891.

Culmer, Frederic A. "Abiel Leonard: Part I." *Missouri Historical Review* 27 (January 1933): 113–31.

Cuming, Fortescue. "Sketches of a Tour to the Western Country." Pp. 19–353 in Reuben Gold Thwaites, *Early Western Travels, 1748–1846*, vol. 4. Cleveland, Ohio: Arthur H. Clark, 1904–7.

Cunningham, J. O. *History of Champaign County*. Urbana, Ill.: Champaign County Herald, 1876; repr. Urbana, Ill.: Champaign County Historical Archives, 1984.

Currey, J. Seymour. *The Story of Old Fort Dearborn*. Chicago: A. C. McClurg, 1912.

Dallam, Philip. "Dedication of Fort Edwards Monument, Warsaw, Illinois." *JISHS* 8 (April 1915): 139–42.

Danckers, Ilrich, and Jane Meredith. *A Compendium of the Early History of Chicago to the Year 1835 When the Indians Left*. River Forest, Ill.: Early Chicago, 2000.

Darby, William. *Emigrant's Guide to the Western and Southwestern States and Territories*. New York: Kirk & Mercein, 1812.

"Daughters of 1812 Honor Memory of Thomas Higgins, Famous Indian Fighter." *JISHS* 17 (January 1925): 740–45.

Davis, James E. *Frontier Illinois*. Bloomington: Indiana University Press, 1998.

Dearinger, Lowell A. "A New Geography of Jefferson County." *Outdoor Illinois* 13, no. 8 (October 1974): 15–38.

———. "Sketches from Carlyle." *Clinton County Historical Society Quarterly* 5, no. 4 (1982): 81–83.

Des Cognets, Anna Russell. *William Russell and His Descendants*. Samuel F. Wilson: Lexington, Ky.: privately printed by Samuel F. Wilson, 1884.

Detmer, Kristen. "The Goshen Settlement and Samuel Judy." *Illinois History* 53, no. 1 (December 1999): 2.

Dillon, John B. *History of Indiana*. Indianapolis: Bingham & Doughty, 1859.

Dobbins, William W. "The Dobbins Papers: Early Days on the Lakes, and Episodes of the War of 1812." *Publications of the Buffalo Historical Society* 8 (1905): 283–379.

Douglas, Walter B. *Manuel Lisa*. Ed. Abraham Nasatir. New York: Argosy-Antiquarian, 1964.

Dowd, James. *Built like a Bear*. Fairfield, Wash.: Ye Galleon Press, 1979.

Drake, Benjamin. *Life of Tecumseh and of His Brother the Prophet*. Cincinnati, Ohio: E. Morgan, 1841.

Drake, Francis S. *Dictionary of American Biography*. Boston: James R. Osgood, 1872.

Draper, Lyman C. *King's Mountain and Its Heroes*. Cincinnati, Peter G. Thomson, 1881; repr. Marietta, Ga.: Continental, 1954.

———, ed. "Antoine LeClair's Statement." *WHC* 11 (1888): 238–42.

———, ed. "Traditions and Recollections of Prairie du Chien, Related by Hon. B. W. Brisbois." *WHC* 9 (1882): 282–302.

Drown, Simeon DeWitt. *Drown's Record and Historical View of Peoria*. Peoria, Ill.: E. O. Woodcock, 1850.

Duddleston, A. C. "Fort Harrison in History." *Magazine of American History with Notes and Queries* 28, no. 1 (July 1892): 20–26.

Dunnigan, Brian Leigh. "The Battle of Mackinac Island." *Michigan History* 59 (Winter 1975): 239–54.

East, Ernest R. "Lincoln and the Peoria Land Claims." *JISHS* 42 (March 1949): 41–56.

Edmunds, R. David. "The Illinois River Potawatomi in the War of 1812." *JISHS* 62 (Winter 1969): 341–62.

———. "Main Poc: Potawatomi Wabeno." *American Indian Quarterly* 9 (Summer 1985): 259–72.

————. *The Potawatomis: Keepers of the Fire.* Norman: University of Oklahoma Press, 1978.

————. *The Shawnee Prophet.* Lincoln: University of Nebraska Press, 1983.

Edwards, Ninian Wirt. *History of Illinois from 1778 to 1833, and Life and Times of Ninian Edwards.* Springfield: Illinois State Journal, 1870; repr. New York: Arno Press, 1975.

Ellis, Albert G. "Fifty-Four Years' Recollections of Men and Events in Wisconsin." *WHC* 7 (1876): 207–68.

Ellsworth, Spencer. *Records of the Olden Time; or, Fifty Years on the Prairies.* Lacon, Ill.:Home Journal, 1880.

Esarey, Logan. *Messages and Letters of William Henry Harrison.* 2 vols. Indianapolis: Indiana Historical Commission, 1922.

Felty, Harold G. "Illinois Territory Militia—War of 1812." *Illinois State Genealogical Society Quarterly* 5, no. 2 (Summer 1973): 137–44.

Ferguson, Gillum. "The Battle of the Long Ridge." *Springhouse* 28, no. 3 (2011): 12–14.

————. "The Cache River Massacre in Context." *Springhouse* 21, nos. 1, 2, 3 (2004): 14–20.

————. "'He Acted Well His Part': Hamlet Ferguson and Southern Illinois." *Journal of Illinois History* 6 (Winter 2003): 271–96.

————. "The Perilous Infancy of Saline County." *Journal of Illinois History* 10 (Spring 2007): 49–74.

Ferguson, Richard G. "Central Themes in Shaker Thought." *Register of the Kentucky Historical Society* 74 (July 1976): 216–29.

Fisher, Robert L. "The Treaties of Portage des Sioux." *Mississippi Valley Historical Review* 19 (March 1933): 495–508.

————. "The Western Prologue to the War of 1812." *Missouri Historical Review* 30 (1936): 267–81.

Flint, Timothy. *Recollections of the Last Ten Years.* Boston: Boston, Cumming, Hilliard, 1826; repr. New York: Da Capo Press, 1968.

Flower, George. *History of the English Settlement in Edwards County.* Chicago Historical Society Collection I. Chicago: Fergus, 1882; repr. Ann Arbor, Mich.: University Microfilms, 1968.

Foley, William E. *Wilderness Journey: The Life of William Clark.* Columbia: University of Missouri Press, 2004.

Foley, William E., and C. David Rice. *The First Chouteaus: River Barons of Early St. Louis.* Urbana: University of Illinois Press, 1983.

Fonda, John H. "Historical Reminiscences of Times and Events in Wisconsin." *WHC* 5 (1868): 205–84.

Ford, Thomas. *History of Illinois, from its Commencement as a State in 1818 to 1847*. Chicago: S. C. Griggs; New York: Ivison & Phinney, 1854.

Fordham, Elias Pym. *Personal Narrative of Travels in Virginia, Maryland, Pennsylvania, Ohio, Indiana, Kentucky, and of a Residence in the Illinois Territory, 1817–1818*. Cleveland, Ohio: Arthur H. Clark, 1906.

"Fort Dearborn Massacre from an Indian's Point of View." *Chicago Tribune*, February 7, 1897, 37.

Franke, Judith. *French Peoria and the Illinois Country, 1673–1846*. Springfield: Illinois State Museum Society, 1995.

Franz, William. "'To Live by Depredations': Main Poc's Strategic Use of Violence." *JISHS* 102, nos. 3 & 4 (Fall–Winter 2009): 238–47.

Frazier, Arthur H. "The Military Frontier: Fort Dearborn." *Chicago History* n.s. 9, no. 2 (Summer 1985): 81–85.

French, Kathryn M. "Manuel Lisa." *South Dakota Historical Collections* 4 (1908): 121–36.

Gallatin County, Illinois, Court Records, 1813–1820. Harrisburg, Ill.: Saline County Genealogical Society, 1988.

Geo. A. Ogle. *Plat Book of Marion County, Illinois*. Chicago: Occidental, 1892.

Gibson, Arrell Morgan. *The Kickapoos: Lords of the Middle Border*. Norman: University of Oklahoma Press, 1963.

Gilpin, Alec R. *The War of 1812 in the Old Northwest*. East Lansing: Michigan State University Press, 1958.

Gordon, Eleanor Lytle Kinzie. *The Fort Dearborn Massacre, Written in 1814 by Lieutenant Helm, One of the Survivors*. Chicago: Rand, McNally, 1912.

———. "John Kinzie: A Sketch." Pp. 55–69 in *Fergus Historical Series—Number 30: The Massacre at Chicago*. Chicago: Fergus, 1914.

Gregg, Kate L. "The War of 1812 on the Missouri Frontier." *Missouri Historical Review* 33 (1938): 3–22; 33 (1939): 184–202, 326–48.

Gregg, Thomas. *History of Hancock County, Illinois*. Chicago: Chas. C. Chapman, 1880.

Grignon, Augustin. "Seventy-Two Years Recollections of Wisconsin," ed. Lyman C. Draper. *WHC* 3 (1857): 195–295.

Gussow, Zachary. "An Anthropological Report on Indian Use and Occupancy of Royce Areas 69 and 120, which were Ceded to the United States by the Sac, Fox, and Iowa Indians under the Treaty of August 4, 1824." Pp. 29–120 in *Sac, Fox, and Iowa Indians*, vol. 1. New York: Garland, 1974.

———. "An Ethnological Report on the Historic Habitat of the Sauk, Fox, and Iowa Indians." Pp. 121–84 in *Sac, Fox, and Iowa Indians*, vol. 1. New York: Garland, 1974.

Hagan, William T. *The Sac and Fox Indians*. Norman: University of Oklahoma Press, 1958.

Hair, James T. *A Gazetteer of Madison County*. Alton, Ill.: James T. Hair, 1866.

Hale, Stan J. *Williamson County Illinois Sesquicentennial History*. Paducah, Ky.: Turner, 1993.

Hall, James. "Adventure of a Ranger." *Illinois Monthly Magazine*, 1 (November 1830): 76–81.

———. *Letters from the West*. London: Henry Colburn, 1828; repr. Gainesville, Fla.: Scholars' Facsimiles & Reprints, 1967.

———. *The Romance of Western History; or, Sketches of History, Life, and Manners in the West*. Cincinnati: R. Clarke, 1885.

Hamilton, Henry Raymond. *The Epic of Chicago*. Chicago: Willett, Clark, 1932.

Hamilton, Holman. "Zachary Taylor in Illinois." *JISHS* 34 (March 1941): 84–91.

———. *Zachary Taylor: Soldier of the Republic*. Indianapolis: Bobbs-Merrill, 1941.

Hamm, Ruth Bitting, ed. *Soldiers of the American Revolution Buried in Illinois*. Springfield: Illinois State Genealogical Society, 1976.

Hammes, Raymond. "Squatters in Territorial Illinois." *Illinois Libraries* 59 (May 1977): 319–82.

Hammon, Neal O., ed. *My Father, Daniel Boone: The Draper Interviews with Nathan Boone*. Lexington: University Press of Kentucky, 1999.

Harper, Josephine Louise. "John Reynolds, 'The Old Ranger,' of Illinois, 1788–1865." Ph.D. diss., University of Illinois—Champaign-Urbana, 1949.

Harris, Norman Dwight. *The History of Negro Servitude in Illinois*. Chicago: A. C. McClurg, 1904; repr. Ann Arbor, Mich.: University Microfilms, 1968.

Harvey, B. A. "Historical Sketch of Wabash County, State of Illinois." *JISHS* 11 (April 1918): 14–27.

Hatch, Luther Augustus. *The Indian Chief Shabbona*. DeKalb, Ill.: privately printed, 1915.

Hauberg, John H. "The Rock Island Historical Society Celebration of the 100th Anniversary of the Battle of Campbell's Island." *JISHS* 7 (October 1914): 287–90.

Haydon, James Ryan. "John Kinzie's Place in History." *Transactions of the Illinois State Historical Society for the Year 1932*. Publications of the Illinois State Historical Library, vol. 39 (1932): 183–99.

Heitman, Francis B. *Historical Register and Dictionary of the United States Army*. 2 vols. Washington, D.C.: Government Printing Office, 1903.

Hickey, Donald R. *The War of 1812: A Forgotten Conflict*. Urbana: University of Illinois Press, 1990.

Hicks, E. W. *History of Kendall County*. Aurora, Ill.: Knickerbocker & Hodder, 1877.

Historic Rock Island County. Rock Island, Ill.: Kramer, 1908.

"Historic Sites of Alton." *The Stalker* 12, no. 2 (Spring 1992): 72.

"Historical Notes: The Life and Death of Shabbona." *JISHS* 31 (September 1938): 344–48.

History of Clay and Wayne Counties, Illinois. Chicago: Globe, 1884.

History of Coles County, Illinois. Chicago: Wm. Le Baron, 1879.

History of Crawford and Richland Counties, Wisconsin. Springfield, Ill.: Union, 1881.

History of DeWitt County, Illinois. Philadelphia: W. R. Brink, 1882.

History of Fayette County, Illinois. Philadelphia: Brink, McDonough, 1878.

History of Gallatin, Saline, Hamilton, Franklin, and Williamson Counties, Illinois. Chicago: Goodspeed, 1887.

History of Greene County, Illinois. Chicago: Donnelley, Gassette, & Loyd, 1879.

History of Greene and Jersey Counties, Illinois. Springfield, Ill.: Continental Historical, 1885.

History of Grundy County, Illinois. Chicago: O. L. Baskin, 1882.

History of Howard and Cooper Counties, Missouri. Saint Louis: National Historical, 1883.

History of Jackson County, Illinois. Philadelphia: Brink, McDonough, 1878.

History of Jefferson County, Illinois. Mount Vernon, Ill.: Continental Historical Bureau, 1962.

History of Jo Daviess County, Illinois. Chicago: H. F. Kett, 1878.

History of Lincoln County, Missouri. Chicago: Goodspeed, 1888.

History of Madison County, Illinois. Edwardsville, Ill.: W. R. Brink, 1882.

History of Marion and Clinton Counties, Illinois. Philadelphia: Brink, McDonough, 1881.

History of McLean County, Illinois. Chicago: William LeBaron Jr., 1879.

History of Morgan County, Illinois: Its Past and Present. Chicago: Donnelley, Loyd, 1878.

History of Pike County, Illinois. Chicago: Charles C. Chapman, 1880.

History of Sangamon County, Illinois. Chicago: Inter-State, 1881.

History of St. Clair County, Illinois. Philadelphia: Brink, McDonough, 1881.

History of Tazewell County, Illinois. Chicago: Chas. C. Chapman, 1879.

History of Wabasha County [Minnesota]. Chicago: H. H. Hill, 1884.

History of Washington County, Illinois. Philadelphia: Brink, McDonough, 1879.

History of Wayne and Clay Counties, Illinois. Chicago: Globe, 1884.

History of White County, Illinois. Chicago: Inter-State, 1883; repr. Carmi, Ill.: White County Historical Society, 1973.

Hodge, Frederick Webb. *Handbook of American Indians North of Mexico.* 2 vols. Washington, D.C.: Government Printing Office, 1907–10; repr. (1 vol.) Totowa, N.J.: Rowman and Littlefield, 1975.

Hoffmeister, Donald F. *Mammals of Illinois.* Urbana: University of Illinois Press, 1999.

Holden, Robert J. "Governor Ninian Edwards and the War of 1812." Pp. 1–8 in *Selected Papers in Illinois History, 1980.* Springfield: Illinois State Historical Society, 1982.

Houck, Louis. *History of Missouri*. 3 vols. Chicago: R. R. Donnelley, 1908.

Howard, Robert P. *Illinois: A History of the Prairie State*. Grand Rapids, Mich.: William B. Eerdmans, 1972.

———. *The Illinois Governors: Mostly Good and Competent Men*. Springfield: Illinois Issues, Sangamon State University, and Illinois State Historical Society, 1988; rev. ed., Springfield: University of Illinois at Springfield, 2007.

Hubbard, Gurdon Saltonstall. *The Autobiography of Gurdon Saltonstall Hubbard*. Chicago: R. R. Donnelley, 1911.

Hubbs, Barbara Burr. *Pioneer Folks and Places*. Herrin, Ill.: Press of the Herrin Daily Journal, 1939.

Hull, William. *Defense of Brigadier General W. Hull*. Boston: Wells & Lilly, 1814.

Hulme, Thomas. "Journal Made during a Tour in the Western Countries of America." Pp. 19–48 in Reuben Gold Thwaites, *Early Western Travels, 1748–1846*, vol. 10. Cleveland: Arthur H. Clark, 1904–7.

Hurlbut, Henry H. *Chicago Antiquities*. Chicago: Fergus, 1881.

Hurt, R. Douglas. *Nathan Boone and the American Frontier*. Columbia: University of Missouri Press, 1998.

Husband, Will W. *Old Brownsville Days*. Ava, Ill.?: n.p., 1935; repr. Murphysboro, Ill.: Jackson County Historical Society, 1973.

Hutson, Austin. "Killed by the Indians." *JISHS* 5, no. 1 (April 1912): 96–103.

Hutton, Paul A. "The Two Worlds of William Wells." *American History Illustrated* 18, no. 2 (April 1983): 33–41.

Irving, L. Homfray. *Officers of the British Forces in Canada during the War of 1812–15*. Toronto: Royal Canadian Military Institute, 1908.

Jablow, Joseph. "A Study of Indian Tribes in Royce Areas 48, 96-A, 110, 117, and 98, Indiana and Illinois, 1640–1832." Pp. 37–436 in *Indians of Illinois and Indiana: Illinois, Kickapoo, and Potawatomi Indians*. New York: Garland, 1974.

Jackson, Donald L. "Old Fort Madison, 1808–1813." *Palimpsest* 47 (January 1966): 1–62.

———, ed. *Black Hawk: An autobiography*. Urbana: University of Illinois Press, 1964.

James, Edwin. *Account of an Expedition from Pittsburgh to the Rocky Mountains*, vol. 14 of *Early Western Travels, 1748–1846*, edited by Reuben Gold Thwaites. Cleveland: Arthur H. Clark, 1904–7.

James, Georgia. *History of Raleigh, Illinois, 1847–1879*. Hartford, Ky., McDowell, 1979.

Jensen, George Peter. *Historic Chicago*. Excella Press for Creative Enterprises, 1953.

Johnson, Adam Clark. *Recollections of Jefferson County and Its People*. Mount Vernon, Ill.: Jefferson County Historical Society, 2000.

Johnson, Charles B. "On and about the National Road in the Early Fifties." Pp. 59–65 in *Transactions of the Illinois State Historical Society for the Year 1922*.

Publications of the Illinois State Historical Library, vol. 29. Springfield: Schnepp & Barnes, 1923.

Jones, Landon Y. *William Clark and the Shaping of the West*. New York: Hill and Wang, 2004.

Kappler, Charles J. *Indian Affairs: Laws and Treaties*. 7 vols. Washington, D.C.: Government Printing Office, 1904.

Kay, Jeanne. "John Lawe, Green Bay Trader." *Wisconsin Magazine of History* 64 (Autumn 1980): 3–27.

Keesing, Felix M. *The Menomini Indians of Wisconsin*. Memoirs of the American Philosophical Society 10. Philadelphia: American Philosophical Society, 1939.

Kellogg, Louise Phelps. *The British Regime in Wisconsin and the Northwest*. Madison: n.p., 1935; repr. New York: Da Capo Press, 1971.

———. "The Capture of Mackinac in 1812." *Proceedings of the State Historical Society of Wisconsin at Its Sixtieth Annual Meeting*. Madison: State Historical Society of Wisconsin, 1913.

King, Larry. *Rector Records*. Hendersonville, Tenn.: privately printed, 1986.

Kingston, John T. "Early Western Days." *WHC* 7 (1879): 297–344.

Kinzie, Juliette A. *Wau-Bun, the Early Day in the Northwest*. New York: Derby & Jackson; Cincinnati: H. W. Derby, 1856.

Kirkland, Joseph. "The Chicago Massacre in 1812." *Magazine of American History* 28, no. 2 (August 1892): 111–22.

Kirkland, Joseph. *The Chicago Massacre of 1812, with Illustrations and Historical Documents*. Chicago: Dibble, 1893.

Kirkland, Joseph. *The Story of Chicago*. 2 vols. Chicago: Dibble, 1892.

Klein, Helen Ragland, ed. *Arrowheads to Aerojets*. Valmeyer, Ill.: Myron Roever, 1967.

Knopf, Richard C., transcriber. *Document Transcriptions of the War of 1812 in the Northwest*. 9 vols. Columbus: Ohio State Museum, 1954–62.

Koeper, Frederick. *Illinois Architecture*. Chicago: University of Chicago Press, 1968.

Lammy, John. *Calhoun County: Its Early History and First Settlers*. n.p.: c. 1876; repr. Hardin, Ill.: Republican, 1904.

Land Atlas and Plat Book—Saline County, Illinois.; Harrisburg, Ill.: Saline County Farm Bureau, 1983.

Larpenteur, Charles. *Forty Years a Fur Trader on the Upper Missouri*. New York: Francis P. Harper, 1898.

"Lawe and Grignon Papers." *WHC* 10 (1888): 90–140.

Lawler, Lucille. *Gallatin County: Gateway to Illinois*. Crossville, Ill.: Gregg Offset Printing, 1968.

"Letter Book of Thomas Forsyth, 1814–1818." *WHC* 11 (1888): 316–55.

"Letters of Captain Robert Hamilton." *Indiana Magazine of History* 43 (December 1947): 393–402.

Levering, John. *The Levering Family, History and Genealogy.* n.p.: Levering Historical Association, 1897.

Lewis, Byron R. *Fort Allison.* Lawrenceville, Ill., Lawrenceville Publishing, 1962.

Libby, Dorothy. "An Anthropological Report on the Piankashaw Indians." Pages 21–341 in *Piankashaw and Kaskaskia Indians.* New York: Garland, 1974.

Lippincott, Thomas. "The Wood River Massacre." *JISHS* 4, no. 4 (January 1912): 504–9.

List of State Officers [The "Blue Book"], 2d ed. Springfield, Ill.: Secretary of State, 1900.

Lockwood, James H. "Early Times and Events in Wisconsin." *WHC* 2 (1856): 98–196.

Loos, Ronald W. *A Walk through Marine, from the Past to the Present: A History of Marine Township, Madison County, Illinois 1813–1988.* n.p.: privately printed, 1988.

Lossing, Benson J. "The Kinzie House, Chicago." *Potter's American Monthly* 6 (May 1876): 322–27.

Lude, Max H. *The Historic Shawnee Trails: Franklin County.* West Frankfort, Ill.: Frankfort Area Genealogical Society, 2006.

"Madison County in the Days of the Indians and Pioneers." *Greenville* [Ill.] *Advocate,* July 4, 1889.

Magnan, William B., and Marcella C. Magnan. *The Streets of St. Louis.* Saint Louis: Virginia Publishing, 1996.

Mahon, John K. *The War of 1812.* Gainesville: University Press of Florida, 1972.

Marshall, Thomas M. *The Life and Papers of Frederick Bates.* 2 vols. Saint Louis: Missouri Historical Society, 1926.

Martin, Deborah B. *History of Brown County, Wisconsin: Past and Present.* Chicago: S. J. Clarke, 1913.

Mason, Richard Lee. *Narrative of Richard Lee Mason in the Pioneer West, 1819.* Heartman's Historical Series, no. 6. New York: Chas. Fred. Heartman, 1915.

Matson, Nehemiah. *French and Indians of Illinois River.* Princeton, Ill.: Republican Job Printing Establishment, 1874; repr. Carbondale: Southern Illinois University Press, 2001.

———. *Memories of Shaubena.* Chicago: D. B. Cooke, 1878.

———. *Reminiscences of Bureau County.* Princeton, Ill.: Republican Book and Job Office, 1872.

Mazrim, Robert. *The Sangamo Frontier.* Chicago: University of Chicago Press, 2007.

McAfee, Robert Breckinridge. *History of the Late War in the Western Country.* Lexington, Ky.: Worsley & Smith, 1816; repr. Ann Arbor, Mich.: University Microfilms 1966.

McClelland, Samuel Swan. "Memorandum of Remarkable Events." Pp. 281–346 in J. P. MacLean, *Shakers of Ohio*. Columbus, Ohio, F. J. Heer, 1907; repr. Philadelphia: Porcupine Press, 1975.

McClure, James B. *Stories and Sketches of Chicago*. Chicago: Rhodes & McClure, 1880.

McCormick, Mildred B. "Ferguson and O'Melveny, Pope County Signers of the Constitution of the State of Illinois." *Springhouse* 9, no. 6 (1992): 18–20.

McCulloch, David. *History of Peoria County, Illinois*. Chicago: Munsell, 1902.

McDonald, John. *Biographical Sketches of General Nathaniel Massie, General Duncan McArthur, Captain William Wells, and General Simon Kenton*. Cincinnati: E. Morgan and Son, 1838.

McVicker, George G., ed. "A Chapter in the Warfare against the Indians in Illinois during the Year 1812." *JISHS* 24, no. 2 (July 1931): 342–43.

Meese, William A. *The Battle of Campbell's Island*. Moline, Ill.: Desaulniers, 1904.

———. "Credit Island, 1814–1914." *JISHS* 7 (January 1915): 349–73.

———. "Nathaniel Pope." *JISHS* 3 (January 1911): 7–21.

Meyer, Leland Winfield. *The Life and Times of Colonel Richard M. Johnson of Kentucky*. New York: Columbia University Press, 1932.

Michigan Pioneer and Historical Collections. 40 vols. Lansing, Mich.: Author, 1876–1929. [Abbreviated in Notes as *MPHC*.]

Miller, R. D. *Past and Present of Menard County, Illinois*. Chicago: S. J. Clarke, 1903.

Miner, Glen A., comp. *Gallatin County, Illinois, Cemeteries*. 2 vols. Thomson, Ill.: Heritage House, 1973.

"Missouriana: Missouri Forts in the War of 1812." *Missouri Historical Review* 26, no. 3 (April 1932): 281–93.

Mitchell, S. Augustus. *Illinois in 1837*. Philadelphia: Grigg & Elliot, 1837.

Montague, E. J. *A Directory Business, Mirror, and Historical Sketches of Randolph County*. Alton, Ill.: Courier Steam Book and Job Printing House, 1859.

Musgrave, Jon. *Handbook of Old Gallatin County and Southeastern Illinois*. Marion, Ill.: IllinoisHistory.com, 2002.

Musham, H. A. "Where Did the Battle of Chicago Take Place?" *JISHS* 36 (March 1943): 21–40.

Musick, Egbert S. *Genealogy of the Musick Family and Some Kindred Lines*. Wytheville, Va.: privately printed, 1978.

Musselman, T. E. "A History of the Birds of Illinois." *JISHS* 14 (April 1921): 1–73.

Myers, Jacob W. "History of the Gallatin County Salines." *JISHS* 14 (October 1921–January 1922): 337–50.

"News and Comment." *JISHS* 39 (September 1946): 393.

Nolan, David J. "Fort Johnson, Cantonment Davis, and Fort Edwards, 1814–1824." Pp.

85–94 in William E. Whittaker, ed., *Frontier Forts of Iowa*. Iowa City: University of Iowa Press, 2009.

Norton, W. T., ed. *Centennial History of Madison County and Its People*. 2 vols. Chicago: Lewis, 1912.

Nowlan, John H. "Bond County's Records and Traditions: Battle of Hill's Fort, August, 1814." *Greenville* [Ill.] *Advocate*, January 7, 1935.

Oglesby, Edward. *Manuel Lisa and the Opening of the Missouri Fur Trade*. Norman: University of Oklahoma Press, 1963.

Origin and Evolution of Illinois Counties. Springfield: Illinois Secretary of State, 2003.

Ourada, Patricia K. *The Menominee Indians*. Norman: University of Oklahoma Press, 1979.

Owens, Robert M. "Jean Baptiste Ducoigne, the Kaskaskias, and the Limits of Thomas Jefferson's Friendship." *Journal of Illinois History* 5 (Summer 2002): 109–36.

———. *Mr. Jefferson's Hammer: William Henry Harrison and the Origins of American Indian Policy*. Norman: University of Oklahoma Press, 2007.

Palmer, Friend. *Early Days in Detroit*. Detroit, Mich.: Hunt & June, 1906.

"Papers from the Canadian Archives, 1767–1814." *WHC* 12 (1892): 23–132.

"Papers of Thomas G. Anderson, British Indian Agent, 1814–1821." *WHC* 10 (1888): 142–49.

Past and Present of Kane County, Illinois. Chicago: Wm. LeBaron Jr., 1878.

Past and Present of Rock Island County, Ill. Chicago: H. F. Kett, 1877.

Pease, Theodore Calvin, ed. *Illinois Election Returns, 1818–1848*. Collections of the Illinois State Historical Library, vol. 18. Springfield: Illinois State Historical Library, 1923.

Peck, John Mason. *A Gazetteer of Illinois in Three Parts*. Philadelphia: Griggs & Elliott, 1837.

———. *A New Guide for Emigrants to the West*. Boston: Gould Kendall & Lincoln, 1836.

Pence, George. "Indian History of Bartholomew County." *Indiana Magazine of History* 23, No. 2 (June 1927): 217–28.

Perkins, Bradford. *Castlereagh and Adams*. Berkeley: University of California Press, 1964.

Perrin, William Henry, ed. *History of Alexander, Union, and Pulaski Counties, Illinois*. Chicago: O. L. Baskin, 1883.

———. *History of Bond and Montgomery Counties, Illinois*. Chicago: O. L. Baskin, 1882.

———. *History of Crawford and Clark Counties, Illinois*. Chicago: O. L. Baskin, 1883.

————. *History of Jefferson County, Illinois*. Chicago: Globe, 1883.

Philbrick, Francis S. ed., *The Laws of Illinois Territory 1809–1818*. Collections of the Illinois State Historical Library, vol. 25. Springfield: Illinois State Historical library, 1950.

————, ed. *The Laws of Indiana Territory*. Collections of the Illinois State Historical Library, vol. 21. Springfield: Illinois State Historical Library, 1930.

————, ed. *Pope's Digest*. 2 vols. Collections of the Illinois State Historical Library, vols. 28 and 30. Springfield: Illinois State Historical Library, 1938 and 1940.

Pike, Zebulon. *An Account of Expeditions to the Sources of the Mississippi and through the Western Parts of Louisiana*. Philadelphia: C. & A. Conrad, 1810.

Pirtle, Alfred. *The Battle of Tippecanoe*. Louisville, Ky.: John P. Morton, 1900.

Pokagon, Simon. "The Massacre at Fort Dearborn at Chicago, gathered from the traditions of the Indian tribes engaged in the massacre and from the published accounts." *Harper's New Monthly Magazine* 98 (March 1899): 649–56.

Postlewait, Ruby. *History of Jersey County, Illinois: Sesquicentennial Edition*. Dallas,Tex.: Curtis Media, 1991.

Power, John Carroll, and S. A. Power. *History of the Early Settlers: Sangamon County, Illinois*. Springfield: E. A. Wilson, 1876; repr. Mount Vernon, Ind.: Windmill, 1970.

"Prairie du Chien Documents." *WHC* 9 (1882): 262–81.

Quaife, Milo M. *Checagou*. Chicago: University of Chicago Press, 1933.

————. *Chicago and the Old Northwest*. Chicago: University of Chicago Press, 1913.

————. "A Forgotten Hero of Rock Island." *JISHS* 23 (January 1931): 652–63.

————. "The Fort Dearborn Massacre." *Mississippi Valley Historical Review* 1, no. 4 (March 1915): 561–73.

————. "Some Notes on the Fort Dearborn Massacre." Pp. 112–28 in *Proceedings of the Mississippi Valley Historical Association for the Year 1910–11*, vol. 4. Cedar Rapids, Iowa: Torch Press, 1912.

————. "The Story of James Corbin, a Soldier of Fort Dearborn." *Mississippi Valley Historical Review* 3 (September 1916): 219–28.

————, ed. *The Askin Papers*. Detroit, Mich.: Detroit Library Commission, 1931.

Railey, William Edward. *History of Woodford County, Kentucky*. Frankfort, Ky.: 1938.

Reece, Jasper N., and Isaac H. Elliott. *Report of the Adjutant General of the State of Illinois*. 9 vols. Springfield, Ill.: Phillips Bros., 1900–1902.

Report of the Adjutant General of the State of Kentucky: Soldiers of the War of 1812. Frankfort, Ky.: E. Polk Johnson, public printer, 1891.

Reynolds, John. "The Agricultural Resources of Southern Illinois." Pp. 141–60 in Transactions of *the Illinois State Historical Society for the Year 1917*. Publications of the Illinois State Historical Library, vol. 23. Springfield: Illinois State Historical

Library, 1917. [Reprinted from *Transactions of the Illinois State Agricultural Society* 2 (1856–57): 346–71.]

———. *My Own Times*. Chicago: Fergus, 1879; repr. Ann Arbor, Mich.: University Microfilms, 1968.

———. *The Pioneer History of Illinois*, 2d ed. Chicago: Fergus, 1887.

Richmond, Volney P. "The Wood River Massacre." Pp. 93–95 in *Transactions of the Illinois State Historical Society for the Year 1901*. Publications of the Illinois State Historical Library, vol. 6. Springfield: Illinois State Historical Library, 1901.

Robinson, Doane. "A History of the Dakota or Sioux Indians—Chapter VII." *South Dakota Historical Collections* 2 (1904): 83–93.

———. "South Dakota and the War of 1812." *South Dakota Historical Collections* 12 (1924): 85–98.

Russell, Herbert. "The Indian Hater." *Springhouse* 21, nos. 1, 2, 3 (2004): 13.

Salmans, Levi Brimner. *History of the Descendants of John Jacob Rector*. Guanajuato, Mexico, n.p., 1936.

Sandham, William R. "Colonel Isaac White." *JISHS* 10 (July 1917): 260–62.

Scanlan, Marian, ed. and trans. *Nicholas Boilvin Letters: 1811–1823*. Madison: State Historical Society of Wisconsin, 1942.

Scanlan, Peter Lawrence. "Nicholas Boilvin, Indian Agent." *Wisconsin Magazine of History* 27, no. 2 (1943): 145–69.

———. *Prairie du Chien: French, British, American*. Menasha, Wisc.: George Banta, 1937.

Scharf, J. Thomas. *History of St. Louis City and County*. Philadelphia: Louis H. Everts, 1883.

Schlesinger, Arthur M. Jr. *The Age of Jackson*. Boston: Little, Brown, 1953.

Schoolcraft, Henry Rowe. *Schoolcraft's Narrative Journal of Travels through the Northwestern Regions of the United States Extending from Detroit through the Great Chain of American Lakes to the Sources of the Mississippi River in the Year 1820*, ed. Mentor L. Williams. East Lansing: Michigan State University Press, 1992.

Selected Monroe County, Illinois Cemetery Inscriptions. Millstadt, Ill.: n.p., n.d.

Shaw, John. "Shaw's Narrative," ed. Lyman C. Draper. *WHC* 2 (1856): 197–236.

———. "Sketches of Indian Chiefs and Pioneers of the Northwest." Ed. Lyman C. Draper, *WHC* 10 (1888): 213–22.

Shinn, Josiah H. *Pioneers and Makers of Arkansas*. Washington, D.C.: Genealogical and Historical Publishing, 1908.

Simeone, James. "Ninian Edwards's Republican Dilemma." *Illinois Historical Journal* 90 (Winter 1997): 245–64.

Simmons, N[oah]. *Heroes and Heroines of the Fort Dearborn Massacre*. Lawrence, Kans.: Journal Publishing, 1896.

Smelser, Marshall. "Material Customs in the Territory of Illinois." *JISHS* 29 (April 1936): 5–41.

Smith, C. Henry. *Metamora*. Bluffton, Ohio: College Bookstore, 1947.

Smith, Charles Raymond. "The Grand Village of the Kickapoo: An Historic Site." Master's thesis, Illinois State University, 1978.

Smith, George Washington. *History of Southern Illinois*. 3 vols. Chicago: Lewis, 1912.

———. "The Salines of Southern Illinois." Pp. 245–58 in *Transactions of the Illinois State Historical Society for the Year 1904*. Publication No. 9 of the Illinois State Historical Library. Springfield: Phillips Bros. State Printers, 1904.

Sneed, Glenn J. *Ghost Towns of Southern Illinois*. Royalton, Ill.: self-published, 1977.

Sparr, Virginia. *Grundy County Landmarks*. Morris, Ill.: Grundy County Historical Society, 1997.

"Speck of Indian Warfare on the Frontier of Illinois in 1811, A." *JISHS* 5 (April 1912): 119–20.

Speer, William S. *Sketches of Prominent Tennesseeans*. Nashville, Tenn.: Alfred B. Tavel, 1888.

Spooner, Harry L. "The Historic Indian Villages of the Peoria Lake Area." *Journal of the Illinois State Archaeological Society* 1 (January 1944): 15–18.

Stanley, George F. G. "The Indians in the War of 1812." *Canadian Historical Review* 31 (June 1950): 145–65.

Starling, Edmund L. *History of Henderson County, Kentucky*. Henderson, Ky.: 1887.

Stein, Stephen J. *The Shaker Experience in America*. New Haven, Conn.: Yale University Press, 1992.

"Stephen H. Long's Plan for a New Fort at Peoria." *JISHS* 47 (Winter 1954): 217–21.

Stevens, Frank E. "Illinois in the War of 1812." Pp. 62–197 in *Transactions of the Illinois State Historical Society for the Year 1904*. Publication No. 9 of the Illinois State Historical Library, vol. 9. Springfield, Ill.: Phillips Bros., 1904.

Stevens, Walter B. "Alexander McNair." *Missouri Historical Review* 17 (October 1922): 2–21.

Steward, Dick. *Duels and the Roots of Violence in Missouri*. Columbia: University of Missouri Press, 2000.

Stout, David B. "Report on the Kickapoo, Illinois, and Potawatomi Indians." Pp. 279–414 in *Indians of Illinois and Northwestern Indiana*. New York: Garland, 1974.

Stout, David B., Erminie Wheeler-Voegelin, and Emily J. Blasingham. "An Anthropological Report on the Indian Occupancy of Royce Area 50." Pp. 234–93 in *Sac, Fox, and Iowa Indians*, vol. 2. New York: Garland, 1974.

Strange, Alexander Taylor, ed. *History of Montgomery County*. Chicago: Munsell, 1918.

Stringer, Lawrence W. *History of Logan County, Illinois*. Chicago: Pioneer, 1911.

Sugden, John. *Tecumseh: A Life*. New York: Henry Holt, 1997.

———. "Tecumseh's Travels Revisited." *Indiana Magazine of History* 96 (June 2000): 151–68.

Talbot, William L. "Fort Edwards: Military Post and Fur Trade Center." Pp. 133–61 in *History of Hancock County, Illinois: Illinois Sesquicentennial Edition*. Carthage, Ill.: Board of Supervisors of Hancock County, 1968.

Tanner, Helen Hornbeck. *Atlas of Great Lakes Indian History*. Norman: University of Oklahoma Press, 1987.

Tanner, John W. *Cemetery Inscriptions of Clay County, Illinois*. Olney, Ill.: Richland County Genealogical and Historical Society, n.d.

Temple, Wayne C. *Indian Villages of the Illinois Country*. Illinois State Museum Scientific Papers, vol. 2, pt. 2. Springfield, Ill.: Illinois State Museum, 1977.

———. "The Piasa Bird: Fact or Fiction?" *JISHS* 49 (Autumn 1956): 307–27.

Throop, Addison J. *The Last Village of the Kaskaskia Indians*. East Saint Louis, Ill.: Call, 1953.

Thwaites, Reuben Gold, ed. "Bulger Papers." *WHC* 13 (1895): 10–153.

———, ed. "The Fur Trade in Wisconsin, 1812–1825." *WHC* 20 (1911).

———, ed. "Dickson and Grignon Papers, 1812–1815." *WHC* 11 (1888): 271–315.

Tohill, Louis A. "Robert Dickson, British Fur Trader on the Upper Mississippi." *North Dakota Historical Quarterly* 3, no. 1 (1928): 4–49; vol. 3, no. 2 (1929): 83–129; vol. 3, no. 3 (1929): 182–203.

Tolle, Christy. "Hutsonville Historical Society and Memorial Village." *Illinois History* 52, no. 2 (April 1999): 60.

Trask, Kerry A. *Black Hawk: The Battle for the Heart of America*. New York: Henry Holt, 2006.

Underwood, Larry. "A New Geography of Calhoun County." *Outdoor Illinois* 14, no. 6 (June–July 1975): 13–42.

———. "The Passing of an Era." *Outdoor Illinois* 14, no. 2 (February 1975): 8–17.

Updyke, Frank A. *The Diplomacy of the War of 1812*. Baltimore: Johns Hopkins University Press, 1915.

[Van Horne, James]. *Narrative of the Captivity & Sufferings of James Van Horne, Who Was Nine Months a Prisoner by the Indians on the Plains of Michigan*. Middlebury, Vt.: n.p., 1817; repr. Middleboro, Mass., L. B. Romaine, 1957.

Van Meter, Benjamin F. *Genealogies and Sketches of Some Old Families*. Louisville, Ky.: John P. Morton, 1901.

Van Voorhis, Elias W. *Notes on the Ancestry on Major Wm. Roe Van Voorhis*. New York: privately printed, 1881.

Vierling, Philip E. "The Fur Trade at Chicago, 1816–1836." *Chicago Portage Ledger* 7, no. 1 (January–April 2006): 1–33.

———. "The Fur Trade at Chicago, 1775–1816." *Chicago Portage Ledger* 7, no. 2 (May–August 2006): 1–33.

———. "The Kankakee and Iroquois Rivers." *Chicago Portage Ledger* 8, No. 2 (May–August 2007): 1–23.

Voelker, Frederick E. "The Piasa." *JISHS* 7, no. 1 (April 1914): 82–91.

Vogel, Virgil J. *Indian Place Names in Illinois*. Pamphlet Series of the Illinois State Historical Society, no. 4. Springfield: Illinois State Historical Society, 1963.

Volkel, Lowell W., ed. *Shawneetown Land District Records, 1814–1820*. Indianapolis: Ye Olde Genealogie Shoppe, 1978.

[Wall, J. L.]. *Moyers' Brief History of Pulaski County, 1843–1943*. Mound City, Ill.: Pulaski Enterprise, 1943.

Wall, John A. *Wall's History of Jefferson County, Illinois*. Indianapolis: B. F. Bowen, 1909.

Wallace, Anthony F. C. *Prelude to Disaster: The Course of Indian-White Relations Which Led to the Black Hawk War of 1832*. Springfield: Illinois State Historical Society, 1970.

Wallace, Joseph. *Past and Present of the City of Springfield and Sangamon County, Illinois*. Chicago: S. J. Clarke, 1904.

Walters, Alta P. "Shabonee." *JISHS* 17 (October 1924): 381–97.

Washburne, E. B., ed. *The Edwards Papers*. Collection of the Chicago Historical Society, no. 3. Chicago: Fergus, 1884.

Washington County, Illinois: 1979 History. Nashville, Ill.: Historical Society of Washington County, 1980.

Weaver, Helen D. "The Life of Robert Dickson." Master's thesis, University of Iowa, 1924.

Wentworth, John. *Early Chicago: Fort Dearborn*. Fergus Historical Series, no. 16. Chicago: Fergus, 1881.

Wesley, Edgar Bruce. "James Callaway in the War of 1812." *Missouri Historical Society Collections* 5 (October 1927): 38–81.

Wheeler-Voegelin, Erminie. "Anthropological Report on the Indian Occupancy of Royce Areas 77 and 78." Pp. 51–299 in *Indians of Western Illinois and Southern Wisconsin*. New York: Garland, 1974.

White, George Fauntleroy. *Sketch of the Life of Colonel Isaac White of Vincennes, Indiana*. Washington, D.C.: Gibson Bros., 1889.

White, Mary Tracy. "Historical Notes on Lawrence County, Illinois." *JISHS* 10 (October 1917): 367–93.

Whitney, Helen M., ed. *The Black Hawk War*. 2 vols. in 4, Collections of the Illinois State Historical Library, vols. 35–38. Springfield: Illinois State Historical Library, 1970–78.

Williams, Betty Harvey. *Soldiers of the War of 1812 with a Missouri Connection*. 2 vols. Independence, Mo.: Two Trails, 2002.

Williams, Mentor L. "John Kinzie's Narrative of the Fort Dearborn Massacre." *JISHS* 46 (Autumn 1953): 343–62.

Wilson, James Grant. "Chicago from 1803 to 1812: Mainly Drawn from the Verbal Account of Dr. John Cooper, Surgeon of Fort Dearborn." *Chicago Portage Ledger* 8, no. 3 (September–December 2007): 1–6.

Wilson, William, and Kevin Kaegy. *Forts and Blockhouses of Illinois*. Victoria, B.C., Canada: Trafford, 2006.

———. *Hill's Fort, The Tales Continue*. Greenville, Ill.: Hill's Fort Society, 2010.

———. *The Tales of Hill's Fort*. Greenville, Ill.: Hill's Fort Society, 2003.

Wisconsin Historical Collections, also known as *Collections of the State Historical Society of Wisconsin*. 20 vols. Madison: State Historical Society of Wisconsin, 1855–. [Abbreviated in Notes and Bibliography as *WHC*.]

Wixon, Richard L. "Ninian Edwards: A Founding Father of Illinois." Ph.D. diss., Southern Illinois University, 1983.

Woehrmann, Paul. *At the Headwaters of the Maumee: A History of the Forts of Fort Wayne*. Indiana Historical Society Publications, no. 24. Indianapolis: Indiana Historical Society, 1971.

Wood, William, ed. *Select British Documents of the Canadian War of 1812*. 3 vols. Publications of the Champlain Society, nos. 13–15. Toronto, Canada: 1920–26.

Woollen, William Wesley, Daniel Wait Howe, and Jacob Piatt Dunn, eds. *Executive Journal of Indiana Territory 1800–1816*, Indiana Historical Society Publications, vol. 3, no. 3, Indianapolis: Indiana Historical Society, 1900.

Woods, John. *Two Years Residence on the English Prairie of Illinois*, ed. Paul M. Angle. Chicago: Lakeside Press, 1968.

Woolard, F. M. "Reminiscences of a Tragedy in Pioneer Life." *JISHS* 2, no. 3 (October 1909): 42–48.

Yarborough, Minnie Clare, ed. *The Reminiscences of William C. Preston*. Chapel Hill: University of North Carolina Press, 1933.

Zeman, Alice Fitch. *Wabansi: Fiend or Friend?* n.p., 1991.

INDEX

GILLUM FERGUSON is an attorney practicing in Naperville, Illinois. His articles have appeared in *The Journal of Illinois History*, *The Journal of the Illinois State Historical Society*, *Illinois Bar Journal*, and other journals.

The University of Illinois Press
is a founding member of the
Association of American University Presses.

———————————————————

Designed by Kelly Gray
Composed in 10.25/14 Adobe Jensen Pro
by Jim Proefrock
at the University of Illinois Press
Manufactured by Thomson-Shore, Inc.

University of Illinois Press
1325 South Oak Street
Champaign, IL 61820-6903
www.press.uillinois.edu